LARS K. CHRISTENSEN

BETWEEN DENMARK AND DETROIT

Ford Motor Company A/S and the Transformation of Fordism 1919–1966

Aarhus University Press

Between Denmark and Detroit

Cover illustration: Showroom in Copenhagen established by Ford in 1934.
Unknown photographer. Thalbitzer: *Ford Motor Company A/S gennem 25 Aar*

Layout, typesetting, and cover: Carl-H.K. Zakrisson and Tod Alan Spoerl
Publishing editors: Søren Hein Rasmussen and Karina Bell Ottosen
This book is typeset in Kabel and DTL Documenta
and printed on Munken Lynx, 120 g
Printed by Narayana Press, Denmark
Printed in Denmark 2021

ISBN 978 87 7184 835 9

Aarhus University Press
aarhusuniversitypress.dk

Published with the financial support of Farumgaard-Fonden, The Foundation for the benefit of the National Museum of Denmark's Danish collections after 1660, the Hielmstierne-Rosencroneske Foundation, Konsul George Jorck og Hustru Emma Jorck's Fond, and the Otto Moensted Foundation

International distributors:
Oxbow Books Ltd., oxbowbooks.com
ISD, isdistribution.com

PEER REVIEWED

FSC
www.fsc.org
MIX
Paper from responsible sources
FSC® C010651

Content

Acknowledgements

During my research for this book, I have spent countless hours in the reading rooms of archives and libraries. Without the help I have had from the knowledgeable staff of those institutions, my work would never had been finished. They are all listed in the Appendix, but I would especially like to thank the present and former staff of the Library and Archive of the Workers Museum. Not only is this a formidable collection of material related to labour history, but it is also being managed with great dedication and professionalism.

Another indispensable repository of source material has been the historical archive of Ford Motor Company A/S. I am very grateful to the company for showing me the confidence of letting me use their archive. And I would like to thank Lene Dahlquist, Head of Communication and Public Affairs, for always finding the time to be helpful and hospitable during my many visits. My thanks also go to the other members of the staff and management of Ford Motor Company A/S, whom I have had the chance to meet along the way.

During my research I came into contact with Ben Larsen, son of Orla Larsen who was employed at Ford Motor Company A/S almost from its start, and for more than forty years thereafter, as part of the management. Ben granted me access to his father's private collection of notes, clippings, and photographs, for which I am very grateful.

After working on the research for this book for almost ten years, the list of people with whom I have had the chance to discuss aspects of it has grown very long. It is impossible for me to list them all. But at least two deserve special mentioning: Kenn Tarbensen, Senior Researcher at the Danish National Archives, with whom I have had several fruitful discussions along the way; and Per Boje, professor emeritus at the University of Southern Denmark, who has provided me with very useful comments on the manuscript. Others, who have been kind enough to provide me with specific bits of information, have been mentioned in the notes where appropriate.

I have also had the privilege of being part of several forums, in which I have had the chance to present my research and get feedback and ideas for further work. These include my former colleagues at the National Museum, the Danish Society for Labour History (SFAH) and, last but not least, the Working Group on Factory History within the European Labour History Network. Without inspiration from so many people, not only would my work have been tedious, but the result would have suffered in quality. But in the end, the responsibility for any errors and omissions in the following text is of course mine alone.

The staff at Aarhus University press have been of great help in bringing this project from the stage of a manuscript to a finished book.

During the long period of time I have been working on this project, my family and friends have had to endure my lengthy talks about the peculiarities of Fordism ever so often. I am thankful that they are still here and still my friends. I especially want to express my gratitude to the one who has endured more than anyone in this respect, my wife Jytte Christensen, for her patience and support.

Finally, the publication of this book would not have been possible without generous financial support from a number of foundations. I am very grateful for the contributions received from Farumgaard-Fonden, the Otto Moensted Foundation, Konsul George Jorck og Hustru Emma Jorck's Fond, the Hielmstierne-Rosencroneske Foundation and The Foundation for the benefit of the National Museum of Denmark's Danish collections after 1660. The Farumgaard Foundation has furthermore supported my research trip to the Benson Ford Research Centre in Dearborn, Detroit.

When I grew up, my father worked as an industrial spray painter. He had done his apprenticeship as a house painter in the 1950s, but since there were no jobs to be found as such, he started spray painting at a local producer of farm equipment. On one occasion, he took me to see his workplace. I still have a vivid memory of him and his colleagues, standing in the paint both in their space suits, which were meant to protect them from inhaling paint fumes. It probably did so—to an extent. But I also remember my mother complaining about how the bedsheets always had a slightly pink hue to them, due to my father sweating out residues of the red paint from the factory at night. This book is dedicated to the memory of my father, Knud Erik Christensen (1930–2016), and to all the industrial workers around the world, who are still producing the goods the rest of us use or consume every day.

Introduction

This is the story about one of the first ever factories in Europe, making cars by modern methods of mass production, including the assembly line. The factory was located in Copenhagen, Denmark, and its name was Ford Motor Company A/S.

Not many foreign observers in general, or historians of business, labour, or technology in particular, would associate Denmark with any type of car industry. To Danes of the present generation, cars are something that we import from Asia or from much larger European countries, not least neighbouring Germany—or even from our close cousins in Sweden. But there was in fact a time, when a rudimentary German auto industry looked with envy upon the state of affairs in Denmark, and when Sweden was flooded with cars from Copenhagen.

To be honest, the golden age of our car industry cannot entirely be attributed to Danish ingenuity and resourcefulness. On the contrary, as the name Ford Motor Company suggests, it was brought to the country from outside, as the then-largest manufacturer of cars in the world decided to establish an assembly plant in Denmark in 1919. The immediate success of Ford attracted other foreign operators, most notably General Motors and Citroën, and for a period in the interwar years, Copenhagen was a Detroit in miniature.

Having passed through the Copenhagen South port area several times, noticing the iconic building that once housed the Ford assembly plant, I became interested in knowing more about its history. I was also vaguely aware that it had been the site of conflict between Fordist principles of management and Danish trade unions.

Then I became involved in setting up an exhibition on industrial culture at the National Museum of Denmark. I suggested that we should exhibit a Ford Model T, assembled in Copenhagen, to represent this almost forgotten history. After some research I was able to obtain a car for the museum, which had papers to prove beyond reasonable doubt that it had been assembled in Denmark in 1924.

This was what prompted me to dig more deeply into the history of Ford Motor Company A/S. As I found more and more source material, the story unfolded, expanded, and became increasingly fascinating. Sadly, the remains of the Copenhagen Ford plant have since been demolished, despite attempts to have it listed as an industrial landmark. The National Museum has abandoned its commitment to industrial heritage and removed the Danish Ford T from its exhibitions. But at least the history of the company, which brought mass-produced automobiles to Denmark, the people who assembled them, and the impact it made may now be read on the following pages.

As the subtitle implies, this is a book not just about the Danish Ford factory, but also about the transformation of Fordism from Detroit to Denmark. It has the ambition of bringing the Danish experience into the international history of Fordism, and of using it as a case for better understanding that history. For that, and in order to be able to see the changes that took place over time and space, it starts out with a chapter on the historical creation of Fordism, starting with Detroit in the early 20th century. In this chapter, I also present my understanding of Fordism as made up of three aspects: as a form of production, as a regime of industrial relations between workers and management, and finally as a social vision.

The following five chapters, which form the main part of the book, present the history of Ford Motor Company A/S. To help the reader getting an overview of the narrative, it has been broken up into five chronological periods. Within each period, it is structured under five recurring themes: Production, Markets and models, Management, Industrial relations, and Presence. The reasons for choosing these themes and what they imply will be explained in more detail at the end of the first chapter.

Fordism may be seen as a special case of Americanism and its transfer to Europe as a form of Americanisation. In public debate, Americanism has often been understood as a one-way process, in which

American cultural, political, or economic power has simply been conquering other nations. But this simplistic picture has been challenged by research. Today, according to the prevailing notion, it is an active process, in which the nations, cultures, and economies being Americanised play an active role themselves, ranging from resistance to embrace—and that which is transferred from America to the receiving nations is also transformed, as part of this active process.[1]

It is this process I refer to as the transformation of Fordism. Through the empirical narrative of the history of Ford Motor Company A/S, this process may be traced through time. Consequently, a prevailing theme throughout the narrative is how the orders, expectations, and impulses coming from Detroit were implemented, adapted, or ignored in Copenhagen.

The last part of the book ties together a theoretical understanding of Fordism with the previous narrative of the history of Ford in Denmark and tries to point out what we might learn from this narrative about the actual transformation of Fordism from its origin in Detroit in the early 20th century to post-war Europe.

When discussing this last topic, special attention will be given to the Social Democratic Party and the labour movement. The reason for this is that the social democrats became the leading political party and rose to power during the period in which Ford established itself in Denmark. At the same time, the party started on the political path which would lead to the welfare state. During the post-war years, when Denmark became firmly included in the "western camp", the social democrats were also a leading political force. The Social Democratic Party was heading the government in roughly 35 out of the 47 years covered in this book. It is therefore of interest, if any influence or inspiration from Fordism can be identified in relation to this party.

My own academic background is in labour history, especially that of labour unions in industry, which has gradually expanded over the years, into the social and cultural history of industrial society in general. To write the story of Ford Motor Company A/S, I have had to reach out into disciplines with which I am not totally unfamiliar but in no way an expert, most notably business history and economic history. Grazing beyond one's usual academic pastures may enhance the risk of misstatement, but compared to the safe but tedious results of confining oneself to the same, small plot, it is a risk worth taking.

In a study like this, many topics arise, and many questions pose themselves, which may not always be answered. Just one example: a systematic comparison between Ford Motor Company A/S and one or more of Ford's other European assembly plants, especially in regard to management and industrial relations, would have been beneficial to our understanding of what was specific and what was general to the history of Ford in Denmark. Unfortunately, this would require work beyond the resources available. I have tried to strike a balance, which includes both relevant theoretical discussion of Fordism as well as parts of its European context, where it is needed most—but still allows for a detailed and vivid presentation of the actual history of Ford Motor Company A/S.

The text is generally British English. But several terms related to cars, such as specific parts and types are different in American English. And since the American terms of course are used by Ford, the same will be the case in this book to avoid confusion. For example, the cover of the engine is called the hood (not the bonnet), while conversely the part that can be raised to cover an open body is called the top (not the hood). Chassis can refer to the frame on which a car is built, as well as a complete car just without a body mounted. Similarly, a load-carrying motor vehicle is called a truck. If necessary, the meaning is specified in the text.

Inside the auto-industry, cars that are delivered for sales as pre-assembled, as opposed to being assembled locally, are known as built-ups. Pre-assembled and built-up are used interchangeably in the following.

Ford Motor Company A/S is always a reference to the Danish company. When only the name Ford or Ford Motor Company is used, it might be a reference to the global enterprise or to a specific, national subsidiary. If the meaning is not clear from the context, national subsidiaries will be identified with the name or abbreviation of the country in question, for instance Ford UK.

In colloquial Danish, the term for union might be used for both local branches as well as national associations. To avoid misunderstandings, the term association is used in the following, when referring specifically to the national level of union organisations. An agreement is to be understood as the written result of collective bargaining between unions and employers, roughly similar to what is sometimes called a union contract in English. A shop steward is a union representative, elected by and among workers at shop floor level. A leading shop steward is the elected spokesperson of all workers at an enterprise. Further details about concepts and institutions in the Danish system of industrial relations are given at relevant points in the text.

The distinction between skilled and unskilled labour is important for understanding the conflicts caused by the transformation of Fordist industrial relations into a Danish context. In the following, a craftsman means a skilled worker, who has completed an apprenticeship, while a workman is a worker with no formal training.

Dates are generally given in the order of day, month, and year, except in quotations where the original format is retained. Danish quotations have been translated by the author, unless otherwise noted.

Henry Ford had no ideas on mass production

Charles Sorensen

The Creation of Fordism

What is Fordism? Unfortunately, there is no simple answer to that. In contemporary public debate, Fordism is often used to label a certain period in the history of the western economy, a period characterised by mass production, high productivity, and a social compromise between organised labour and capital, as well as a period of rising consumption and the establishment of some variation of welfare state in large parts of Western Europe. Fordism in this sense is an era of the post-war period, reaching its apex in the 1950s and 1960s, before it was challenged and maybe even defeated by other regimes of accumulation by the end of the 20th century.

But we may trace the historic roots of Fordism to a time long before that: the very beginning of the 20th century. It was then that Henry Ford entered onto a path towards a novel form of industrial mass production, based on the assembly line, taking place in a factory regime where intensive labour and strict discipline are remunerated by high wages. Fordism in this sense reached its apex around 1920, when Ford Motor Company had become the world's largest manufacturer of mass-produced automobiles. This was also the Fordism that was popularised, envied, but also criticised by many in Europe during the period between the two world wars.

Not only does the conceptual understanding of Fordism, prevalent today, focuses on a period several decades later than that in which Fordism came into being as an empirical reality. In fact, a strict interpretation of contemporary concepts will also lead to the paradoxical conclusion that what Henry Ford practised in Detroit in the 1920s was not really Fordism, the most obvious out of several reasons being that there was no welfare state in the USA in the 1920s and certainly no organised labour at Ford Motor Company in Detroit.

Fordism Made in Detroit

The historical development of Fordism is inseparably bound to the creation and success of the Ford Model T. Charles Sorensen was a Danish immigrant who started working for Ford in Detroit as a pattern maker and ended up being vice president of the company. Sorensen was deeply involved in the design and development of the Model T, and he would later claim that:

> Henry Ford had no ideas on mass production. He wanted to build a lot of autos. He was determined but, like everyone else at that time, he didn't know how. In later years he was glorified as the originator of the mass production idea. Far from it; he just grew into it, like the rest of us.[1]

While it might not be quite fair to say about a man who worked with Fords determination that he "just grew into it", Sorensen's claim is to the point in the sense that the development of the Fordist Model of production did not follow a previously thought-out masterplan. It was a step-by-step process, based to a great extent on trial and error.[2]

Since the marketing of the first commercially available petrol-driven automobile by Carl Benz in 1886, most cars had been produced in limited quantities at high prices. Around the turn of the century serial production had gradually been introduced, especially in the USA, but the car was still considered a luxury product. It was Henry Ford's vision to make "a motor car for the great multitude", built by "the simplest designs that modern engineering can devise" and, consequently, "so low in price that no man making a good salary will be unable to own one".[3]

Ford Motor Company had already introduced serial production with the Model N, the predecessor to the Model T. For the Model N, Ford had applied the use of special purpose machines, jigs, and fixtures, making it possible to produce completely interchangeable parts, and thereby eliminating the time-consuming process of fitting by hand during final assembly. Already in the period of the Model N, Ford Motor Company proudly declared: "We are making 40,000 cylinders, 10,000 engines, 40,000 wheels, 20,000 axles, 10,000 bodies, 10,000 of every part that goes into the car ... all *exactly alike*".[4]

With the Model T, Ford added to this a number of novel design ideas, resulting in a car that was at the same time lighter than most, but strong and durable—ideal for use on the bumpy, unpaved roads of rural America. But the design choices were also made to cut down on production costs, meaning it could be sold at a lower price than any competing model at the time.

The Model T was introduced in 1908, and within a year Ford decided to stop the simultaneous production of Model N and concentrate all the company's efforts on this new model only. It was to be produced in a handful of different body-variants, but all based on the same engine, chassis, and drivetrain.[5] The use of colours was also gradually limited, and from early 1915 the Model T was available to customers in one colour only: black.[6] By such radical standardisation, Ford Motor Company now committed itself fully to a strategy of producing and selling by volume.[7]

Development of the Model T had taken place at Ford's original Piquette Avenue plant in Detroit, but in 1910 a completely new factory was opened in Highland Park, also in Detroit. Following the decision to concentrate on the Model T only, this new facility had been planned in detail for the most optimal production of this specific model. Machines were installed in a sequence determined by when they were needed in the production process. Several new special-purpose machines were designed for mass production, such as a drill that would simultaneously drill forty-five holes in four sides of an engine block or a milling machine that would accurately machine fifteen engine blocks at a time.[8]

In 1909, the first full year of Model T production at the Piquette Plant, 13,840 cars had been produced. In 1912, the year before the assembly line was even introduced, 82,388 units were produced at Highland Park. Even more importantly, however, the sales price of each car had dropped from US$950 to 600, testament to a substantial decrease in unit production cost.[9]

The assembly line

Despite all the advancements in production, the final assembly of the Ford Model T at Highland Park in 1912 was done in basically the same way as the Model N had been assembled at the Piquette Plant, and as cars were generally assembled throughout the industry: each car was built up from the ground at a fixed place, by teams of assembly workers moving from car to car, with the parts and tools necessary to do their job.

In 1913, the first assembly line was introduced in Highland Park. The first line was manual, and the chassis had to be pushed forward on its own wheels from station to station along the line. Then in early 1914, the assembly line was motorised.[10]

With the introduction of the line, the whole logic of assembly was changed: instead of workers coming to the job, the job was coming to the workers. And regulation of the speed of work was now—at least in principle – a simple matter of adjusting the speed at which the line was moving forward[11]. Specialised tools could be installed, and parts could be stored along the line, at the exact places and in the quantities needed. Furthermore, the assembly line was combined with a system of conveyors and slides for moving parts and partly assembled cars around.

The line became the proverbial backbone in the production system developed at the Ford Motor Company. Before the assembly line, it would take an average of 12 hours 28 minutes to assemble one Model T chassis. In early 1914, when the assembly line had been developed into its mature form, this took just 1 hour 33 minutes.[12] The assembly line became the apex of the gradual development of the original Fordist productive model, a model characterised by the manufacturing of one single, standard model, in a highly centralised and rationalised production process.[13]

Fordism is sometimes conflated with the "scientific management" of F.W. Taylor. Both were part of a general effort in the USA in the early 20th century to increase industrial output by applying rational, so-called scientific methods. But they are also different in a fundamental sense. Broadly speaking, Taylor's aim was to teach workers how to use the existing production apparatus as rationally and efficiently as possible. Ford's approach was to change the whole production process.[14]

In this sense, Fordism was a radical new step in the history of division of labour. It was made possible only by a rigorous separation of design and execution in the work process.[15] The result was a strict hierarchy among workers. At the top was a small group of highly qualified skilled workers and engineers, with their ability to construct specialised tools and to plan the optimal production process.[16] The rest of the workforce, on the other hand, those who operated the machines or manned the assembly line, only needed minimal training.

In the words of Henry Ford himself:

> While [...] we have skilled mechanics in plenty, they do not produce automobiles—they make it easy for others to produce them. Our skilled men are the tool makers, the experimental workmen, the machinists, and the pattern makers. They are as good as any men in the world—so good, indeed, that they should not be wasted in doing that which the machines they contrive can do better. The rank and file of men come to us unskilled; they learn their jobs within a few hours or a few days.[17]

This was also reflected in how the workers were looked upon from above. When explaining how moulding-machines in the foundry made it possible to reduce skilled moulders to only five percent of the workforce, while the remaining 95 percent of the workers could be unskilled, Henry Ford adds: "Or to put it more accurately, must be skilled in exactly one operation which the most stupid man can learn within two days."[18]

Industrial relations

Substitution of skilled labour with unskilled was a general development in the industrial labour market in USA in the early 20th century. The rapidly growing mass-producing industries found themselves unable to satisfy the need for labour power from the limited number of skilled workers alone, and therefore had to find ways to tap into the much larger resource of unskilled labour power. Ford Motor Company may have been at the forefront, but they were not alone. In 1923, a survey of the auto industry found that only nine percent of the workers were skilled craftsmen, such as machinists, while another nine percent were unskilled, common labourers. The great majority consisted of unskilled workers, trained either for work at the assembly line (18 percent) or as machine tenders (47 percent).[19]

For the skilled worker, this might have been a negative development. But for the unskilled worker, things looked different; it was a step up from being a common labourer outside the industry and would often lead to a higher paycheck.[20] But from a perspective above that of the individual worker, the "dilution of skills" was part and parcel of the transfer of control over the labour process, away from the workers and into the hands of supervisors and management. Apart from making a much larger potential workforce available to industry, it also had the effect of undermining labour unions, as these were traditionally craft based.

Instead of certain skills, what was demanded more than anything else from the Fordist worker was, in the words of a contemporary observer:

> The ability to meet ('to hit') and maintain a constant pace, to be able to eliminate all waste and false motions; to follow without wavering printed instructions emanating from an unseen lodge in some far off planning department—these constitute the requirements of a successful machine tender.[21]

The constant pace was secured by the assembly line, and the workers were now in principle no longer in control of the labour process but controlled by it.[22]

But the human spirit is, after all, not that easily broken. Workers at Ford Motor Company reacted in increasing numbers to what they saw as a boring, repetitive, and fast-paced job by simply quitting, often from day to day and without notice. During 1913, the first year of the assembly line at Highland Park, the rate of people leaving the factory reached a staggering 370 percent of the total workforce.[23] Furthermore, there were massive problems with absenteeism and lack of work discipline.

High wages and strict discipline

Henry Ford's solution to this was the sudden rise of the daily wage to $5—roughly two times the payment for comparable jobs in other industries—in January 1914, and the simultaneous reduction of the daily working hours from 9 to 8. In line with Ford's ideological message of employer and employees being united by a common interest in production, this was presented as a profit-sharing program: the $5 was made up by a basic wage plus an extra bonus, supposed to be the workers' share of company profit.[24]

To receive the bonus, a worker initially had to live up to certain social and moral standards. A special department, the Ford Sociological Department, was set up to manage the program. Files were kept on each worker, and company investigators visited workers at home, checked their personal economy and even interviewed neighbours to learn about their "habits", to decide if they were eligible. However, after a few years these paternalistic elements were removed, and the bonus wage made dependent on seniority only.[25]

But the initiative had paid off: following the introduction of the $5 day, labour turnover at Highland Park was reduced to 16 percent in 1915, and there had been an overall rise in productivity.[26] Moreover, this widely published initiative gave Henry Ford an image as "the people's tycoon" and his company as a workplace where high wages were paid.

Henry Ford might have enjoyed this acclaim, but he nevertheless made it very clear that the $5 wage was not an act of philanthropy. There was:

> ... no charity in any way involved [...] We wanted to pay these wages, so that the business would be on a lasting foundation. We were building for the future. A low wage business is always insecure [...] The payment of five dollars a day for an eight hour day was one of the finest cost cutting moves we ever made.[27]

As a side note, an inspiration for Henry Ford in this matter was Percival Perry, who was then manager of Ford's British operations in Manchester, but who would later come to play an important role in the history of the Danish Ford company too. In Manchester, Perry had gained a substantial productivity benefit from raising wages.[28]

It has been suggested that Henry Ford was an early proponent of what came later to be known as efficiency wages. According to the theory of efficiency wages, employers might benefit from paying wages higher than those determined purely by supply and demand of labour. The reason would be that a higher wage will diminish shirking and labour turnover and strengthen the workers' commitment and loyalty to the company, thereby leading to a higher productivity. If the result is an increase in revenue above the increased cost of higher wages, paying these higher wages is effective in relation to profitability.

Leaving the details of this discussion aside, the important point to make is that paying high wages was a rational choice in the eyes of Henry Ford. Not only that: the wage level could be discussed and determined, based on objective parameters, such as the cost of wages versus the costs of absenteeism and labour turnover. In this sense, Henry Ford was firmly seated within the broad spectrum of believers in scientific management.[29] He believed that wages were to be determined by management by rational calculation, not arbitrarily through negotiations with unions. He also believed that any sensible worker would accept such scientifically established wage levels.

In return for the high wages paid, Henry Ford expected loyalty to his company and to his ideas about industrial relations. These ideas were based on his conviction that the relationship between the employer and the worker was a purely personal one, and that both parties had a common interest in high productivity. Labour unions, according to this view, were a hindrance to achieving the highest productivity possible, and thereby working against this common interest.[30]

Henry Ford himself described his ideal of labour management as a "friendly autocracy".[31] His attitude towards workers' self-representation was aptly characterised by his own words:

> We expect the men to do what they are told. The organization is so highly specialized and one part is so dependent upon another that we could not for a moment consider allowing

> men to have their own way. Without the most rigid discipline we would have the utmost confusion. [...] The men are there to get the greatest possible amount of work done and to receive the highest possible pay.[32]

In Henry Ford's own narrative, the production process at Highland Park and River Rouge is presented as a gradual but constant process towards technological and organisational perfection. But this picture of one great machine, in which every part ran smoothly and in total sync, is not necessarily true.

Deprived of organisation or other means of representation, workers at the assembly line devised their own ways of individual or collective regulation. One method was to "go into the hole", meaning gradually, almost imperceptibly, exceeding the time assigned for their task, thereby being forced to move slowly up the line, ultimately forcing collapse in production—and thereby a break. "The biggest trouble was the men," said one of Ford's foremen. "Everybody would get in everybody's way and they would all be in a bunch. Then they would have to stop the line whether they wanted to or not."[33]

It was the job of the foremen to enforce work discipline and factory rules, such as a complete ban on singing, whistling, and even talking during work hours. Interestingly, the ratio of foremen to workers grew steadily as the production process evolved; from one foreman per 60 workers in 1909, to one per 30 workers in 1913–1914, to one per 15 workers after the assembly line was fully introduced: a testament to the fact that technology alone was not enough to keep up work speed and discipline.[34]

A social vision

From being in the interest of the enterprise, Henry Ford would go on to argue that high wages were in the interest not only of industry as such, but of society in general. He was well aware that to secure a market for the mass-producing industry, its consumer base had to be widened. From a social point of view:

> ...the owner, the employees and the buying public are all one and the same, and unless an industry can so manage itself as to keep wages high and prices low, it destroys itself, for otherwise it limits the number of its customers.[35]

Henry Ford presented a vision, according to which a constant striving to lower the cost of production would make it possible for industry to mass-produce consumer goods for sale at low prices, and at the same time pay high wages. The high wages would ensure a mass-market for the goods produced. The result would be a positive spiral of growing production, cheaper prices, more consumption and so forth:

> Poverty can be done away with only by plenty, and we have now gone far enough along in the science of production to be able to see, as a natural development, the day when production and distribution will be so scientific that all may have according to ability and industry.[36]

Henry Ford's social vision falls under the broad term of productivism.[37] To him, there were no other agents for progress than industry. He made no secret of his distrust in anything or anyone not immediately associated with the production of material goods, including politicians and the political system. In fact, government in his view was "essentially negative": the best government could do was to facilitate industry by removing any obstacles to its progress and, apart from that, stay out of the way as much as possible. The only human agents capable of creating progress are those in command of industrial enterprise, who are moved by "intelligent individual leadership".[38]

Ford explicitly offered his own vision as an alternative to socialism. To him, society was divided not by class, but between productive and unproductive people. Employers and workers both belonged to the productive people, and therefore they had mutual interests. Politicians, academics, and even bankers and the whole financial sector were unproductive. This might also have been a cause for his fierce and well-known anti-Semitism, drawing upon common stereotypes of associating Jews with those groups he despised as not being productive.[39]

Figure 1 Advertisement illustrating Henry Ford's social vision of an affluent consumer society, based on industrial mass production. Published in 1925 as part of a series in *The Saturday Evening Post,* one of the most widely read magazines by the American middle class. Painting by John Jay Baumgarten / BFRC, The Henry Ford

Henry Ford's ideas about the need for paying high wages did not, however, resonate well with his fellow American employers in the early 1920s. Without any resourceful agents with the power to push for higher wages across industries, individual employers had no incentive to raise wages. Labour unions would of course have been such an agent, but union organisation was very low in American industry in the 1920s, and employers were generally successful in keeping so-called "open shops", without any union agreements. And Henry Ford was among the employers who fought hardest against any union presence. The result was that the average real wages of industrial workers increased only marginally—and much less than the increase in productivity—meaning that Ford's vision of a generalised consumer society remained just a vision.[40]

Volume versus flexibility

Initially, the sales curve for the Model T had pointed only upwards, but from around 1923 it started to drop. Ford's difficulties were products of structural changes in the car market. It was the middle class who had bought the Model T in large quantities, but this market was now starting to become saturated. The industrial working class on the other hand, whom Henry Ford had hoped would become his customers, were not yet able to become mass consumers on the car market, even at its low end. At the other end of the market, part of the middle class had become more affluent and would start to demand more from a car than just four wheels at a low price.[41]

But Ford Motor Company had nothing to offer to this diversifying market. It kept churning out Model Ts, despite the fact that the once-revolutionary car appeared increasingly outdated.[42] In 1926 a "new" Model T was introduced, with a redesigned all-steel body, a choice of colour—between black, dark red and dark blue—and several smaller enhancements. But these changes were too late and too small to convince the public, and sales continued to drop.[43]

At the same time, General Motors (GM) was developing a productive model based on a combination of volume and diversity. It would offer separate brands and models for each market segment, distinguishable by differences in body, trimming and other visible parts. But different cars would at the same time share less visible parts, including engines and drivetrains, which could therefore be manufactured through centralised, high volume production.

For the lower end of the market, and in direct competition with the Ford Model T, GM was offering the Chevrolet. It was assembled on a line, just like the Model T. But for producing the parts, GM would use less single-purpose machinery, and more standard equipment. This approach offered a greater degree of flexibility in production, which allowed GM to introduce something that would become commonplace in the automobile industry: the regular product upgrade.[44]

The combination of diversity and volume allowed General Motors to expand its sales at the expense of Ford Motor Company, whose share of the market dropped from 55 percent in 1921 to only 30 percent in 1926, despite price reductions.[45]

Among the reasons Ford came to lag behind General Motors were the stubbornness and idiosyncrasies of Henry Ford himself. Several top managers either were sacked or chose to leave of their own accord. One of them was William S. Knudsen, who—as we shall see later—had been instrumental in setting up Ford in Denmark. In 1921 he felt so alienated by Henry Ford that he left the company to work for General Motors instead. At GM, Knudsen was a driving force behind the successful development of more flexible methods of mass production, and ended his career as president of the company.[46]

There was, however, also a more rational reason for clinging to the Model T, which had to do with the Fordist production model in itself: the highly specialised production apparatus, with its extensive use of purpose-built machines, made the changeover from one model to another very difficult and time-consuming. So, when Henry Ford finally gave in to the development of a new model, an erratic process began, in which a new car was developed and the production facilities were completely retooled, almost in parallel.[47] In May 1927, the last Model T rolled off the assembly line, but it was not before 1 December 1927 that a new Model A could be presented to the public. It took several more months before full production of the new model could be reached.

Ford Motor Company had learned a hard lesson. The Ford A was not to live nearly as long as the Model T. As soon as 1931, planning started for another new model, which would eventually take its name from its most distinguishing feature: a V8 engine. This time the changeover was not without difficulties either, but it took much less time and effort than the change for Model A.[48] Ford had now entered the path to what Henry Ford himself would call "flexible mass production",[49] and beginning with the Model A but further elaborated with the V8, regular upgrades now became the norm for Ford cars, just like those of GM.

Just as General Motors had originally copied elements of the Fordist model, not only Ford but all major car manufacturers copied back elements of GM's model of combining volume and diversity during the 1930s. Indeed, it was this model that spread from America to Western Europe with increasing strength in the aftermath of World War II. It has therefore been suggested that we should talk about a Sloanist rather than a Fordist production model, in reference to Alfred P. Sloan, president and CEO of GM from 1923.[50]

However, I would rather suggest that we see this process as an example of the dynamic character of Fordism, and part of the transformations it underwent from its birth in Detroit at the beginning of the 20th century, until it achieved its hegemonic character in western economies about half a century later.

The changing role of labour

During the 1920s, Ford's reputation for paying high wages became increasingly challenged by reality. The real value of the $5 daily wage introduced in 1914 had been cut almost in half by inflation as early as 1918. In 1919 the basic wage was raised from $5 to $6, but by the mid-1920s, wages at Ford in Detroit were no longer significantly higher than in other auto companies; in fact there were some areas where they were lower.[51]

Industrial relations at Ford Motor Company had always been based on a combination of the carrot and the stick. But during the 1920s, the carrot was shrinking, and the stick became longer. Henry Ford continued to maintain his ideological conviction of a common interest between employers and employees both vocally and in print. But his self-proclaimed "friendly autocracy" would turn more and more unfriendly. Under the leadership of the notorious Harry Bennet, the so-called Service Department would expand into a vast organisation for controlling and disciplining the workers, with methods ranging from a sophisticated system of surveillance to simple violence. Agents of the department patrolled the factory, both openly and undercover. Their job was not only to come down hard on any breach of discipline by the workers, but also to expose any foreman who was not severe enough in "pushing" the workers.[52]

Another important duty of the Service Department was of course to repress any attempt to "talk union" at the Ford Motor Company, even by means of physical violence. This was successful for a period, but soon pressure would amount on Ford from both below and above.

During the 1930s, workers in the American auto industry began to question the authority of their employers and demand the right to organize. The creation of the Congress for Industrial Organization (CIO) and its breakaway from the American Federation of Labor (AFL) to form a new federation for unions in mass production industries marked an upswing in labour militancy. In 1935 the United Auto Workers (UAW) had been formed inside the AFL, but it soon became a leading member of the CIO.

At the same time, the political climate in the USA had changed drastically with Roosevelt's election and the New Deal. The National Industrial Recovery Act of 1933 specifically gave workers the right to join a union of their own choice and bargain collectively. This right was pursued by the UAW with great vigour and growing support, and in 1937 the union had a breakthrough, when both General Motors and Chrysler accepted collective bargaining after several sit-down strikes.[53]

Ford Motor Company, however, continued its resistance against trade unions. Despite several investigations by the National Labor Relations Board, all concluding that Ford's practices were in violation of workers' rights, the repression continued until 1941, when Ford finally gave in and accepted collective bargaining with the UAW. For the first time ever, workers at Ford now had the right to collective representation.

The Second World War was a time of profound change in industrial relations in the USA. Generally, concessions were given to those workers still left in the factories, to keep up production. On the other hand, even the more militant unions, such as the UAW, committed themselves to a national class-compromise, to support the war effort. A result of this extraordinary situation was a new political hegemony, based on forward-thinking industrialists, liberal politicians, and moderate union leaders.[54]

It was only under pressure that Ford Motor Company had accepted collective bargaining in 1941. But in 1945 a new leadership took over, headed by Henry Ford II, grandson of Henry Ford.[55] This new leadership was committed to collective bargaining to a much higher degree, and the following period has been described as a "social compact", based on cooperation between management and unions for mutual benefit.[56] Harry Bennet was ousted from the company, and with him the old practice of foremen constantly "driving" or "pushing" by means of threats. But that did not mean that Ford gave up the goal of high productivity. Instead, this had to be achieved by rational and "scientific" means, such as time studies.[57]

The UAW gained influence through collective agreements, while the same agreements were seen by management as a way to curb wildcat strikes and involve the unions in maintaining high productivity. The last was partly obtained by what were known as "speedups" among the autoworkers: the process of increasing the speed of the assembly line. The UAW was not against rationalisation as such. But they generally feared that the company would push too hard in their efforts, thereby putting too much strain on the workers. A wave of strikes against speedups swept through Ford plants in Detroit and elsewhere in the USA during 1949. The outcome of these strikes was a higher degree of union influence on assembly line speed. Nevertheless, spontaneous, unauthorised strikes against work pressure kept occurring throughout the 1950s.[58]

In this way, the "social compact" did not in any way imply that antagonism between workers and management disappeared altogether. But the day-to-day conflicts became subsumed under a consensus that both parties had a mutual interest in rising productivity. This was increasingly the case as the economic boom from the late 1950s onwards led to a general rise in living standards and a rapid increase in the demand for automobiles. It was in this period that the workers at Ford Motor Company, together with other autoworkers, became part of the most affluent and socially secure stratum of the American working class.

In summary, then, Fordism was in constant development from the beginning of the 20th century and well into the post-war period. This should be kept in mind, as we now turn away from empirical history towards Fordism as a concept.

Conceptualising Fordism

Henry Ford himself never used and much less defined the term Fordism. It was his admirers and critics, mostly in Europe, who coined the phrase and brought it into use from the 1920s. The first appearance of the word Fordism in print seems to have been in a German booklet titled *Fordismus? Paraphrasen über das Verhältnis von Wirtschaft und Technischer Vernunft bei Henry Ford und Frederick W. Taylor,* published in 1924 by the economist Friedrich von Gottl-Ottlilienfeld.[59]

This was no coincidence, since Germany in the 1920s was the scene of what historian Mary Nolan has described as "an infatuation with Fordism".[60] There was an immense interest in Henry Ford, his thoughts, and the accomplishments of his company, not only among economists and managers of industry, but also among politicians, ranging from left-wing social democrats to the far right, and even among labour unionists. This interest was reflected in books and pamphlets and study trips to the USA. Fordism—or at least what passed for Fordism in the German debate—was considered a possible remedy for the economic and social instability that haunted the Weimar Republic.

But while much was said and written about Fordism in Germany, especially during the 1920s, the practical effects were of a limited and indirect nature. Fordism was never implemented as a complete model. And gradually the concept of Fordism gave way to that of "Rationalisierung", a term which allowed for combining selected elements of Fordism with other sources of inspiration, into a much more German-sounding package.[61]

In other parts of Europe, the interest in Henry Ford and Fordism was less pronounced than in Germany. Ford Motor Company was a practical inspiration for some, such as André Citroën in France, who employed an assembly line at his Quai de Javel auto-plant in Paris from 1919. In Italy, Fiat also embarked on mass production of cars at the massive Lingotto plant in Turin, built between 1916 and 1923 and partly inspired by Ford's Highland Park.[62]

But even if both André Citroën and Fiat's Giovanni Agnelli saw themselves as proponents of industrial modernism in Europe, neither of their companies was a simple copy of Ford in Detroit. The European market for cars was generally more diversified than in the USA, and both Citroën and Fiat produced several different models for different buyers. Furthermore, the industrial labour force was of another composition and generally better organised in Europa than in the USA, thereby putting a limit on the transfer of Fordist work organisation. It is telling that even after Mussolini had outlawed autonomous labour unions and banned strikes, workers at Fiat were still willing and able to resist the company's attempt to rationalize and intensify work.[63]

Workers' militancy had reached its peak in Turin by the summer of 1920, when thousands of labourers at Fiat occupied the factories, and for a brief period ran them under the leadership of workers' councils. This had been a crucial experience for Antonio Gramsci, Italian Marxist and later co-founder of the Italian Communist Party. In 1934, when incarcerated by the fascist regime, Gramsci devoted a chapter of his *Prison Notebooks* to the subject of "Americanism and Fordism".

While Gottl-Ottlilienfeld and many others sought to promote Fordism as an alternative to socialism, Gramsci on the contrary was analysing it from the perspective of the left. To Gramsci, Fordism was born out of an imminent need in modern, industrial capitalism for planning and rationalisation.[64] He saw Fordism, fascism, and bolshevism as three different answers to this need—the last one of course entailing a break away from capitalism, while the other two were a transformation inside the existing mode of production.

But to Gramsci, Fordism was more than just a form of industrial production. It also had an important cultural and even moral element. The monitoring of the lifestyle and personal morals of the workers, carried out by Ford's Sociological Department, could not be written off as only an expression of Henry Ford's own puritanism. It was an example of how a rationalised production needed workers with a rational mindset and a rational lifestyle. A truly Fordist society therefore entails new forms of social life, in which human relations and lifestyle reflect the need of mass production on all levels. As such, Fordism is a type of "passive revolution", a transformation of society brought about by an elite—*in casu* American industrialists—with the passive consent of the masses.

While not noticeably clear on the subject, it seems like Gramsci was hoping for a potential for a progressive renewal in Europe to be found in Fordism, while at the same time expressing his scepticism as to if and how American methods and culture could be transferred back to the old continent.[65]

On the issues of Fordism and Americanism, the importance of Antonio Gramsci lies not as much in the answers he gives—or refrains from giving—as in the issues he raises and the questions he inspires. But Gramsci's analysis did not become known to the public at the time of writing, due to his personal fate. He died in 1937, and his notebooks were only published long afterwards and not generally known in academic circles outside Italy, before the renewed interest in Marxist theory from the late 1960s.[66]

Ironically, Fordism as a concept was out of vogue for several decades of the post-WWII period, when a transformed Fordism made a greater impact on western industry and economy than ever before. But the concept was reintroduced during the 1970s. The reason for this was the empirical observation that the long-term trend of economic expansion since the 1950s was coming to an end, and that the prevailing model of mass production seemed to lose ground to alternative models, such as those emanating from Japan or elsewhere. Added to this was a renewed interest in Marxist analysis within academia.

This was the starting point for so-called regulation theory, a school of economists and sociologists united by an interest in how specific systems of capital accumulation were produced and reproduced or "regulated".[67] According to regulation theory, a specific regime of accumulation could be identified as dominating Western Europe and the USA during the 1950s and 1960s, a regime they named Fordism.

Fordism according to regulation theory is based on mass production. However, it is further characterised by wages being raised in parallel with productivity growth, the recognition of unions and collective bargaining by management, and a state that plays an active role in managing demand and securing mass consumption—the Fordist state, according to sociologist Bob Jessop, is "a Keynesian welfare state".[68]

Regulation theory offered a comprehensive description of the hegemonic economic regime of post-war Western Europe. Furthermore, it had the merit of at least attempting to include both the system of production and the state in the analysis. But it was also mainly preoccupied with political economy and social formation on a rather abstract level. This has led to the not unfounded criticism that, in regulation theory, people at work tend to disappear out of sight as subjects in history and to be reduced to passive objects, moved around by the inescapable logic of capital accumulation.[69]

Furthermore, regulation theory is firmly focused on the post-war period. This is reflected in the claim that the Fordist state plays an active role in securing mass consumption, and that industrial relations are based on collective bargaining between unions and management. But as we have already seen, this is in sharp contrast with the historical realities of Detroit in the 1920s. On the contrary: the American state during this period was far from any type of welfare state, and Henry Ford himself was clearly opposed to any form of state intervention in the economy. Also, there was no recognition of labour unions and no collective bargaining at Ford Motor Company in Detroit.

Taking the concept of Fordism offered by regulation theory at face value would therefore lead to the paradox that neither the actual praxis of Ford Motor Company in Detroit during the interwar period nor the normative declarations of Henry Ford himself qualifies as Fordism. Regulation theory in its original form does not pay any attention to this paradox and is therefore inadequate for historical analysis.

Productive models—and more

However, the understanding of Fordism has evolved, as regulation theory has been applied to empirical studies of the car industry, at various times and places. One of the outcomes has been the concept of productive models, developed by Boyer, Freyssenet, and others.[70]

A productive model may be perceived as the combination of three core elements: a specific organisation of production, a product policy, and a certain employment relationship. These elements must be fitted together coherently by management, in pursuit of a certain profit strategy. Productive models exist within various growth modes, made up by the specific combination of investments, domestic consumption, and export, that drives the economic growth of a national economy. The relative success of any productive model is therefore dependent on, how well its profit strategy fits into the growth mode of the countries in which the company is active.[71]

Fordism, according to this approach, is a productive model characterised by a strategy of producing in high volumes (as opposed to a strategy of quality production or product diversification). Its productive organisation is highly centralised and mechanised, with workflow split into standardised operations. The product policy is to offer a standard model to the largest part of the market for the lowest price. And its employment relationship is based on offering unskilled workers a fixed and potentially increasing wage for a fixed day's work. These elements are fitted together within a company governance compromise, in which workers accept the productive organisation in exchange for access to mass consumption.[72]

Fordism, in this perspective, is just one possible productive model, among others. Different productive models will be put to use at different times, sometimes in parallel by different enterprises, and their success will depend on how well they fit into market conditions, national growth modes, etc. Productive models do not come into being as fully developed master plans, but "[materialise] at the conclusion of a largely unintentional process".[73]

Most writers still seem to associate Fordism as a productive model with the post-war period only, for instance by stressing that its governance compromise is based on an agreement between management and unions, thereby effectively leaving the model followed by Ford until 1941 out of sight.[74] But if we see the relationship between high wages and high productivity as the core element of the employment relationship, not the question of how this relationship is organised, the model could be stretched backwards to include the original praxis of Fordism in Detroit as well.

In that sense, this model may offer a greater sensibility towards history than that found in the original regulation theory. Furthermore, it has also been developed further into a theory of hybridisation, aimed at understanding how productive models change as they are diffused and transformed into different national contexts.[75]

The concept of productive models may be useful, at least as a heuristic tool, when trying to sort out and make sense of the different components of Fordism and their interaction. But it still has its limits. One of them is a lack of interest in the cultural aspects of Fordism, in the sense that Gramsci wrote about in his prison cell back in the 1930s. Gramsci was concerned about Fordism as the "rationalisation" of not only production, but also daily life and human relations. He was reflecting on the cultural differences between the USA and Europe, and how they would affect the spread of Fordism.

The revival of the concept of Fordism from the 1970s did not pay much interest to such issues. This is not to say, of course, that there has been no interest in culture at all. On the contrary: there has been a wealth of public debate as well as scholarly inquiries into the influence of the USA on Europe—and other parts of the world—in the realm of culture and everyday life.[76] But this has largely been separated as a discourse from that of the American productive system and of Fordism.[77]

There are of course exceptions to this, such as the analysis of the reception of Fordism in Weimar Germany by Mary Nolan, already mentioned above.[78] Another example is David Nye, who has told the story of the assembly line as a combination of history of technology and cultural history. According to Nye, Fordist mass production was rooted in the specific context of a "highly accelerated society", based on standardisation of time and space and the rapid transportation of people, goods, and communication.[79] As mass production based on the assembly line spread from the USA to Europe and the rest of the world, it did so in cycles of contraction and expansion, based on political and cultural context but at the same time changing politics and culture itself. During the depression of the 1930s, as an example, the assembly line came increasingly under scrutiny, not just for contributing to unemployment, but also as a source of alienation, in both Europe and the USA. But this changed fundamentally during World War II, when the assembly line became the symbol of a highly effective system of production, essential to ensuring allied victory. After the victory, the same notion was carried on into the Cold War.[80]

The relationship between Fordism and the Cold War is a reminder that we also need to include the realms of politics and ideology in our analysis. This has been done by Mark Rupert, in a Gramsci-inspired study of Fordism and international politics. Rupert takes as his starting point the crisis of Ford Motor Company in the late 1920s. He convincingly argues that the failure of Ford's volume strategy is a symptom of general instability within the American mass-producing industry, an instability caused by a mismatch between production capabilities and the consumption power of the masses. This mismatch was addressed by the New Deal and during World War II, by the aforementioned hegemonic bloc. This explains how the class compromise based on high wages for high productivity, which became typical for Fordism in the post-war period, came into being, and how it became the productive basis for the expansion of American political and cultural power throughout Western Europe during the era of the Cold War.[81]

Thus, the social aim of Fordism is an affluent society, based on mass production and mass consumption. This aim is to be reached by technical means, through a highly mechanised and rationalised serial production, and by an organisation of work, in which wages are a function of productivity. This is the most general definition of Fordism, in its technical, organisational, and social aspects.

However, it is a main point of this book that there are great differences in how these overall principles were realised in practice over time and place. The Fordism of Detroit in the 1920s and that of Western Europe in the 1960s are quite dissimilar in several key aspects. It is therefore also the aim of the book to trace the real, historical transformation of Fordism from the first to the last.

The narrative

Two approaches to Fordism have been outlined above. The first one could be considered diachronic, looking at Fordism in its historical specificity, and from below or within. It is mainly concerned with Fordism as a production and labour process. The second one is synchronic, especially in the case of regulation theory, and other perspectives concerned with Fordism at a macro-economic level or from above.

But of course, the synchronic and diachronic perspectives on Fordism are not mutually exclusive. On the contrary, I would argue, they are both relevant, as two different perspectives on the same theme. The challenge is to bring them coherently together. Ford Motor Company A/S is an obvious case for doing so, due to its timespan: it was established in 1919, when Fordism was still primarily just a way of mass-producing cars. When it ceased production in 1966, Fordism had been transformed into a hegemonic model for the western economy.

But more than being a case of the transformation of Fordism, the history of Ford Motor Company A/S is important and fascinating in its own right, as part of the history of business, industry, and labour in Denmark in the first half of the 20th century. It is the empirical history of the company that will form the backbone of the following narrative. The narrative is structured chronologically into five time periods. The breaks between periods represent moments in time when external and internal conditions came together in such a way that the overall developments of the company took on a new direction.

To unravel the complexities of the Danish Ford company during its almost fifty years of existence, a wide variety of empirical sources must be employed. These sources include material produced by the company itself, such as minutes of board meetings, sales accounts, photographs, correspondence, and company magazines and advertisements, but also minutes of meetings, correspondence, and other material produced by labour unions active at the Ford plant. To this should be added such material that elucidates the relations between the company and its cultural and political environment, such as correspondence with authorities, newspaper articles and even political debates and comments. A full overview of the source material used and a complete list of references may be found in the Appendix.

In order to incorporate a synchronic perspective into the chronological narrative, each time period is divided into five main themes. The first theme is the production process, which forms a necessary condition for any industrial company that wants to bring a commodity to the market. The product also needs to be adapted for the market, and the second theme is therefore about markets and models. A third theme, which follows logically after the two others, is that of management, its challenges, and its decisions. Then follows the theme of industrial relations, and finally a theme called presence, dealing with the activities through which Ford Motor Company A/S made itself culturally, politically, and ideologically present in Denmark and the other countries in which it operated.

There is of course some overlap between these themes. Consequently, issues that appear under one theme in one period will in a few instances appear under another in the next period. This has been done for the sake of a coherent narrative. Unfortunately, the remnants of history do not always fall neatly into our analytical boxes. Nevertheless, structuring the empirical parts of the book around these themes will hopefully make the theoretical approaches presented above useful.

The first four themes are closely related to the main elements of the productive model, thereby allowing for the use of this model as a heuristic tool for probing into the complex empirical realities of the narrative. The last theme is there to make sure that cultural and political perspectives are included.

The findings presented throughout the chronological narrative are summed up in a chapter on the transformation of Fordism. Based on a summary of the five themes, and the historical developments within them, the Danish Ford company is presented as an example of what is termed a hybrid within the theory of productive models. Finally, Ford Motor Company A/S is discussed as an example of Fordism and of Americanism in general.

Something has been created, which never existed here before

Politiken, 25 November 1919

1919–1928
Pioneering Years

PRODUCTION

Making Cars in Copenhagen

Tuesday 13 May 1919 was a nice spring day in Detroit, Michigan. At that day, a board meeting was held at the Ford Motor Company, the world's largest car company. On the agenda was the expansion of Ford's activities in Europe. This was no minor issue but judging from the brevity of the minutes, decisions were made without much ado: two new assembly plants were to be established. One in Copenhagen, the capital of Denmark, and one in Cadiz, a port town in Southern Spain.[1]

Ford had already been assembling cars in Europe since 1911, when a plant had been set up in Manchester, England. Like the assembly plants that the company had established around the United States, the one in Manchester received complete engine and chassis kits from Detroit and added locally made bodies. In fact, Manchester was more advanced than many of the American plants, which were still based on stationary assembly. An assembly line was installed in Manchester only months after the completion of the first one in Detroit.[2]

The car produced was of course the Model T, which was hitting a sweet spot in the British market at the time, being larger than many domestic cars, but cheaper than most cars of the same size. As a result, just before the outbreak of the World War, the Ford Model T had become the best-selling car in Britain, and Manchester the largest producer of cars in Europe with more than 6,000 units per year. Not everything went smoothly, though, as there had been difficulties in combining an American and a British work culture, and Henry Ford had had to send his number one trouble-shooter, Charles Sorensen, to Manchester to fight the British labour unions.[3]

Nevertheless, the British sales figures were inspiring, and expansion to the continent was planned. Warehouse facilities were acquired in Paris, France and Hamburg, Germany. Then war was declared. During the following years of death, destruction, and economic turmoil, buying a car was the last thing that most Europeans would be thinking about.

Finally, the war came to an end, and just six months later, in March 1919, William S. Knudsen was sent over from Detroit to evaluate the present situation. Knudsen was a Danish-born immigrant to America, and had been with Ford since 1911. Based on his practical experience and training as an engineer, he had been involved in setting up no fewer than fourteen local assembly plants throughout the United States in just a couple of years, before being appointed production manager of the Highland Park plant in Detroit in 1915.[4] In the field of production setup and factory management, Ford could not have chosen a more experienced person.

Reporting back to Detroit, Knudsen proposed Denmark and Spain, two countries on the periphery of Europe, as candidates for assembly plants. Why not follow the steps already taken towards France and Germany before the war? In Germany, the political situation was extremely volatile, the economy in ruins, and import of cars and car parts severely restricted in favour of the domestic industry. In France, the situation was somewhat better, and rudimentary assembly had in fact taken place there before and especially during the war, as fenders, wheels and so on had been mounted on otherwise finished cars in a purely manual process. But Knudsen found French politicians inclined to protect the nation's own industry too, and his experience with the local Ford management so far had not been positive.[5]

Denmark had been neutral during the war, its infrastructure was intact, and it was politically stable. Copenhagen was also well placed for importing parts from Detroit by ship and re-exporting finished cars to the Nordic and Baltic countries.[6] But what about Knudsen's personal roots in Denmark? It is sometimes suggested that the real reason he chose Copenhagen was out of nostalgia for his old country. It might have been a factor, but Knudsen was seriously considering other options, such as the city of Gothenburg in Sweden. However, the Swedes were unwilling to offer tax exemption for imported car parts. Danish government officials, on the other hand, promised Knudsen that the duty on parts would be as low as 10 percent of that levied on complete cars.[7]

The Danish authorities also offered the company a licence to establish its own warehouse under customs control on the premises of the factory, and a duty officer was to be assigned there.[8] This would mean not only that duty on items that would later be re-exported could be waived, but also less paperwork. That finally tipped the scale in favour of Copenhagen.

According to Knudsen's elaborate plans for Europe, Copenhagen would become the headquarters of the "North European Division", comprising the Nordic Countries, the Baltic Countries, Poland, Germany, and the Netherlands. The goal was to produce and sell 6,000 Ford Model T's a year, equal to pre-war Manchester and double what was expected in Spain, making Denmark the primary bridgehead for Ford into continental Europe.[9]

Setting up the plant

After his trip to Europe in March, Knudsen returned to Detroit, but he hurried back as soon as the decision to establish new plants was taken in May. At first, he went to Manchester and London, where he took care of several issues at the British Ford company, including the nomination of a new manager. On 9 June 1919, Knudsen arrived in Copenhagen and only two weeks later, on 25 June, he had managed to put together a board and arrange the founding of Ford Motor Company, Dansk Monteringsfabrik, Aktieselskab (Ford Motor Company, Danish Assembly Plant, Limited).[10]

Parallel to this, Knudsen was looking for a suitable place to set up the actual plant. Finally premises on Heimdalsgade in the northern part of Copenhagen were rented. The place was not exactly glamorous. Among its previous uses was the collecting and sorting of old rags and, in the words of George "Geo" Carlson, who arrived a few months later to become assistant manager, the whole area was "dilapidated" and "not very nice".[11]

On the ground there was an office building and a one-story factory building. It had an engine room, but it lacked a boiler. Neither was there any supply of electricity, heating, or toilets. Writing to Detroit, Knudsen had to admit that "the premises [...] are not by any means what we would like to have secured, but they will be ample and adequate for our present needs".[12] It seems like an odd place to choose for a state-of-the-art car manufacture, but Knudsen was in a hurry and had to accept what was available to him. At least the place in Heimdalsgade had one crucial advantage: it was very close to the Nørrebro train station, with a railway line going directly to the Copenhagen Free Port. Finally, it is possible that Knudsen was aware, right from the start, that this would only be a temporary solution.

In any case, Knudsen did not waste time: the premises were cleaned out, a 75 KW electrical plant was commissioned, as well as other technical installations, and production equipment soon came in from the USA. Production began on 26 October, when the first of a batch of 700 Model TT's, the slightly longer and sturdier version of the Model T chassis meant for trucks, rolled off the assembly line and was shipped to distributors in Norway, Sweden, and Denmark.[13] For the first time ever, cars were now produced in Copenhagen on a large scale. Knudsen himself had no time to wait for this. He had already left Denmark for Spain in order to get things going there. In Copenhagen he was replaced by James J. Harrington, an American who brought with him experience as branch manager from Boston and Cincinatti.[14]

The workforce at the new factory was not very large, even by Danish standards, but it was growing: from 104 blue-collar and 19 white-collar workers by the end of 1919, to 245 and 52 respectively by the end of 1922.[15] The original premises in Heimdalsgade no. 42 soon proved to be too small for the burgeoning activity. In the beginning of 1920, a large steel building was brought in from the USA and erected in the yard behind the factory. While assembly, trim, and painting were done in the original factory building, the new building was used for storage and some sub-assembly, presumably bodies for the Ford T Touring model. Not long after that, the neighbouring building no. 44 was added for storing service stock, while another building further down the street, no. 28, was rented. This was a former carpentry shop, consisting of a one-storey brick building at the front and a yard behind with several sheds. The yard and the sheds were used for receiving and storing parts, while the front building was used for offices—including one for the customs officer assigned to the factory—as well as dining and washing facilities for workers.[16] Irrespective of these incremental expansions, production was still limited by lack of space, and at a board meeting in January 1920 it was decided to start searching for larger premises.[17]

Modernity in a confined space

In just a few months, William S. Knudsen and his employees had managed to set up a production line in Copenhagen, which emulated the Detroit way of doing things to a remarkable degree—even if on a rather diminutive scale.

One thing that helped speed up the board's decision to set up a new European facility, that day in May 1919, was the fact that sending car parts from Detroit to another plant for assembly had already become commonplace for Ford. The company had built its first branch assembly plant in the USA in 1910, and by 1915 the number had already reached 28, assembling a total of 2,500 Model T's per day compared to 1,200 in Highland Park, Detroit.[18] From a purely production point of view, shipping car parts to Copenhagen instead of Kansas City was basically a matter of travelling a bit further.

Cars destined for final assembly at an assembly plant were referred to as "knocked down units", but the state of disassembly would vary. In the case of American branches, the cars might actually have been almost finished in Highland Park before being transported as major parts—chassis, body, wheels—to be assembled locally.[19] But the Model T's for Copenhagen arrived for the most part in a much more disassembled state. Some major parts were pre-assembled, while bodies arrived totally in parts. The storage space in Heimdalsgade no. 28 was crammed with wheels, axles, gas tanks, and other kinds of spare parts—including a box filled with horns.[20]

The different parts were brought together in no. 42 for assembly, literally from the ground up. First the frame for the chassis was assembled with rivets at a stationary workstation. Front and rear axles, which came pre-assembled, were partly disassembled to be re-greased, and then the complete drivetrain was put together at another stationary workstation.[21] Wheels and gasoline tank arrived in a complete state. So did the engines, which had to be run on testbeds before mounting, thereby filling the factory with noise and smell.

Then, finally, as the drivetrain, engine, wheels and so on were mounted to the chassis, the assembly line was put to use. Compared to Highland Park, the line in Copenhagen was a short and simple one: it would hold only a few units in different stages of assembly at one time, and it might not even have been motorised. Nevertheless, it was the first ever assembly line in Denmark.[22]

While there was only one Ford Model T, it came in several different versions.[23] Yet all these versions were built on the same chassis, with the same engine and transmission. What made them different were different body versions. The only exception to this was the TT, with its reinforced and extended chassis. The TT was for trucks, and this and some regular Model T's sold for the same purpose were delivered to customers as chassis only, since they were to be fitted with custom-made bodies. Passenger cars, on the other hand, were fitted with bodies at the assembly plant. Bodies for the smaller versions, such as the runabout, were delivered pre-assembled.[24] However, for the touring version, a 5-person open car with a foldable top, and probably also the closed-body sedan, bodies were delivered as parts and had to be assembled and painted at the factory.[25]

Painting of the bodies was the most time-consuming part of the assembly. It was done with four layers: a primer, two layers of coloured paint and a final coat of uncoloured varnish. Even if certain components had been added to make it dry faster, the paint was still based on traditional linseed oil, and between each of the four layers of paint the body had to dry for 24 hours.

To speed up the process, Ford had introduced new ways of applying the paint. The primer was sprayed on.[26] The three other layers were applied by a method called "flow-painting": paint was flowing from an elevated tank through a hose to a handheld device, looking somewhat similar to the nozzle of a vacuum cleaner. By moving this device along the upper edge of the body, paint was applied and allowed to flow down the side panels. Any excess paint would drip into a catch tray and be pumped back into the tank above.[27] The exact same technology was used for painting bodies in Heimdalsgade, only here it was done at a stationary workstation, not on a moving line.

Figure 2 Assembly line in Heimdalsgade. Photo: Holger Damgaard / Ritzau Scanpix

The bodies were placed on small, wheeled carriages, so that they could easily be moved in and out of the drying hall between paintings. In the drying hall, some of the bodies had to be tipped and stored vertically to save space—a testament to drying being a bottleneck in the assembly process.[28]

Upholstery for the bodies was prepared in a special workshop. The bodies were then completed on another assembly line, where upholstery was put in together with elements such as the dashboard, and finally the folding tops were mounted.[29]

Figure 3 Flow-painting in Heimdalsgade. Photo: Holger Damgaard / Ritzau Scanpix

Body assembly, painting, and trimming is an interesting aspect of the assembly in Heimdalsgade, since this was in fact a relatively new activity for Ford Motor Company even in Detroit. Until early 1914, Ford had received 95 percent of its bodies in a finished state from subcontractors. But later that year, a large expansion of Highland Park created room for producing 40 percent of the bodies in-house. In his classic 1915 account of "Ford Methods", Horace Arnold remarks how body finishing "has been but recently introduced".[30] Nevertheless it was implemented in Heimdalsgade from the start in 1919.

While several manual tools were still used in assembly, the number of power tools was a striking feature of the factory. For example, electric cutters were used in the trimming workshop for cutting several layers of fabric at a time, and pneumatic tools were used for riveting the chassis parts together, as well as in body assembly. Such

Figure 4 Cutting layers of fabric for body trim at Heimdalsgade. Notice the use of electric cutters. Photo: Peter Elfelt / Museum of Copenhagen

tools were just about to be put to common use in other parts of industry at the time.[31]

The plant in Heimdalsgade might have been limited in size and established in a haphazard process, but the production principles and technologies applied were state of the art: it was modernity in a confined space.

In the beginning, production was a bit erratic, following the rhythm of the arrival of parts, which were almost all delivered by ship from Detroit. But sometimes bits and pieces were missing in the shipments, and had to be manufactured or procured locally, if possible.[32] Since there was a great demand for the product, creative solutions sometimes had to be found. In February 1920, the newspaper *Politiken* showed a picture on its front page of partly knocked down Model T's being unloaded from a cargo ship in the Copenhagen Free Port and being assembled directly on the quay area beside the ship. The paper claimed that this had become a "daily occurrence", which is most likely an exaggeration.[33]

Despite all the initial problems production was rising steadily, from 6013 units in 1920 to 17,387 in 1923, the last full year of production in the Heimdalsgade plant.[34]

South Port plant

The seemingly endless demand for cars continued to put heavy strain on the plant in Heimdalsgade. During 1922 the factory was often running with 3 hours of daily overtime, but nevertheless production could not keep up with demand, and pre-assembled, so-called built-up cars still had to be imported to supplement those assembled at the plant.[35]

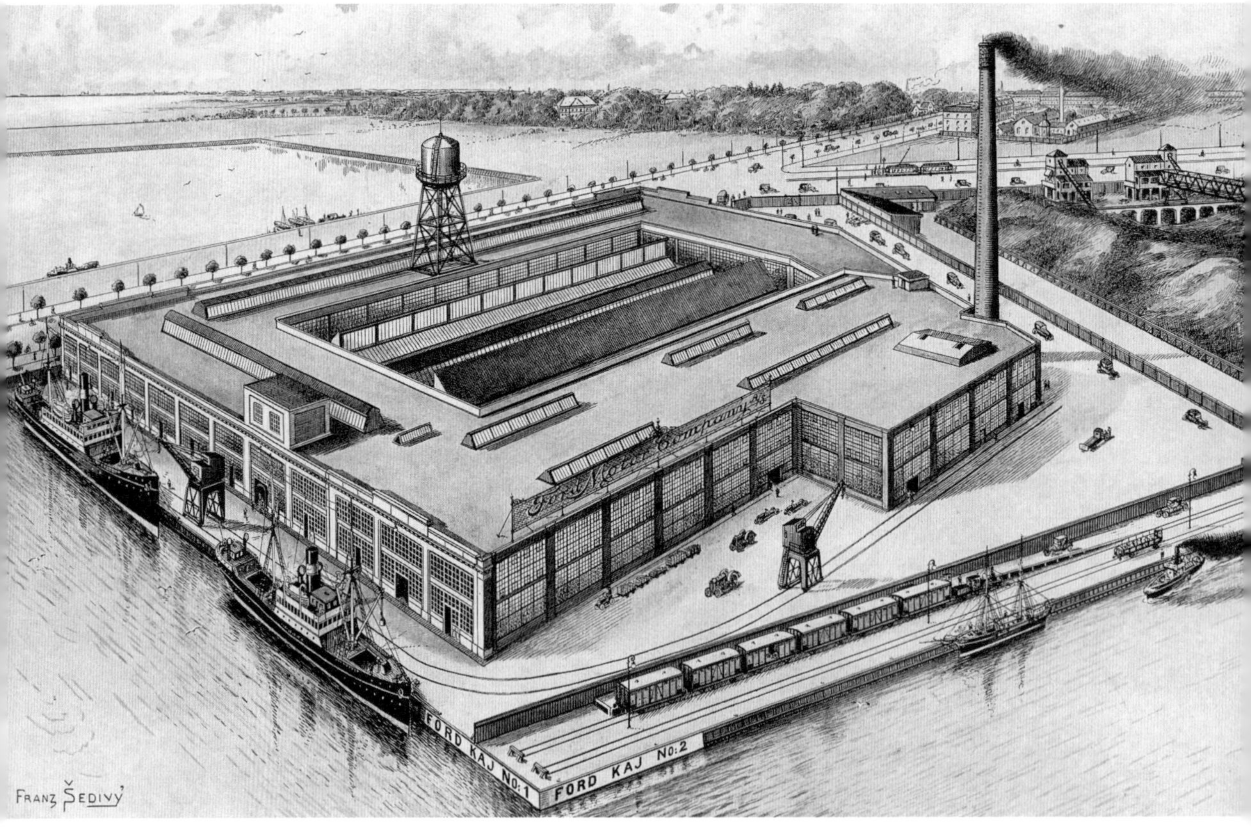

Figure 5 Aerial view of the South Port plant, seen from the port side. Drawing: Franz Šedivý / The Royal Danish Library

In September 1920 J.J. Harrington left Copenhagen and his post as manager when he went to London to become European general manager.[36] His former assistant manager, George Carlson, was promoted to manager. It now became Carlson's job to find a suitable place for a new factory and larger production facility.

After some time, Carlson located two adjacent building sites in the newly developed South Port area, near to both water and road, and suggested these to Charles Sorensen in Detroit. Sorensen was at that time running Ford's River Rouge complex and was the *de facto* chief of production of the company. After conferring with Edsel Ford, son of Henry Ford and president of the Ford Company, Sorensen approved the purchase of land, but also enlarged the project, asking for an option to be placed on a third site. Things now began to move quite fast: during the next few months, drawings were exchanged between Copenhagen and Detroit, and by May 1922 Sorensen was sending plans for the new factory to Copenhagen.[37]

When local negotiations started with the Copenhagen building authorities, however, these would not act with the same speed and vigour as Sorensen in Detroit. In October 1922, Carlson was asked by cable why nothing had happened and was in return asking Detroit for more detailed drawings and computations to present to the authorities. Despite the overall positive attitudes towards Ford, the building authorities were keen to make sure that the project would fit in with the overall plans for development of the South Port area.[38]

Finally the green light was given, and construction started. The plant was built by Monberg & Thorsen, a major Danish construction company, but it was designed by Albert Kahn Associates. Together with his brother Julius, Albert Kahn had pioneered the use of steel-reinforced concrete for factory buildings in the USA. The use of concrete allowed Kahn to use a larger portion of the facade for windows, creating what he called a "daylight factory".[39] He was first commissioned by Henry Ford to design the Highland Park factory, which became known in Detroit as the "Crystal Palace", due to its large window areas. Later he designed the River Rouge Complex and several other Ford buildings and plants.

The use of reinforced concrete was not unknown for Danish factory buildings at the time.[40] However, the new Ford factory had a very distinctive appearance, with the large window areas and the rational layout of its facade, supplemented by the emblematic feature of American urban architecture: a roof-based water tank. From the outside, the Danish plant looked exactly like a scaled down version of Highland Park—as if a small part of Detroit had simply been pulled up by its roots and re-planted in Copenhagen.

Kahn was also known for his functional approach, in which the optimal layout of machines and the flow of production were to determine the structure of the plant. Likewise, in Copenhagen: the factory was planned so that car parts could be loaded from ships directly into the plant. Assembly took place in a straight-line production process, and finally the finished cars could be loaded back on ships for export from the quay alongside the factory.

The plant was built around a central one-storey assembly hall. The hall was surrounded on three sides by two-storey buildings, used for different sub-assemblies, as well as offices etc. Along the north side of the assembly hall ran a storage hall, the same height as the two-storey buildings but one storey inside, to make room for two overhead cranes. Further north was the powerhouse. The total floor area covered was 18,300 m^2.[41]

The South Port plant commenced production in November 1924. Not only was it much larger than the one in Heimdalsgade, but even more importantly it was designed and built from the ground up for its purpose. Basically, it was one great machine, optimised to assemble Ford Model T's in the most rational way possible.

The rational design was apparent even from the outside: around the perimeter of the factory building to the south-east and north-east was a large crane running on tracks. The crane was used for unloading boxes with car parts from transport ships docking alongside the plant, and moving them into the storage building, which made up the north-eastern part of the factory. The storage, with its double height, was 2,900 m^2 in floor space. From there car parts would be unboxed and transported into the production halls.[42]

Assembly was divided horizontally, so that chassis, engines, and drivetrains were assembled on the ground floor, while all the bodywork, including trim and painting, took part on the first floor. On both levels, emphasis had been on planning for straight production

Figure 6 Engine sub-assembly line. Notice the pneumatic hand-tool hanging above the work-place. This and the following photos, up to and including Figure 9, are not dated, but must be from ca. 1925. Unknown photographer. The National Museum of Denmark

lines and a significant number of conveyers—many in the form of rails hanging from the ceiling—were used to rationalise the flow of production.

On the ground floor, chassis frames were riveted at stationary workstations, and then placed at the beginning of the assembly line.[43] Apart from more space and the use of small cranes running on rails from the ceiling, this was principally similar to how it was done in

Heimdalsgade. But the rest of the process was significantly different, since several parts that had previously been delivered in a finished state were now assembled at the factory. Most prominently this was the case with engines, but dashboards, wheels, and gasoline tanks were now also to be assembled locally.[44]

These sub-assemblies were placed in the main assembly hall on the ground floor, between the storage hall and the final assembly line, so that they could be conveniently supplied from the former and would feed into the latter at the right point. At the beginning of the line, just after the chassis frame sub-assembly, was the sub-assembly for engines, gas tanks, and dashboards, and later followed axles, fenders, and wheels. The main assembly line thus became the literal backbone of the production facility. It ran 80 meters, from one end to the other of the 3,000 m^2 large central assembly hall.[45]

While some parts had previously been received in a painted state, they were now all painted at the factory. Some of them were "baked". This was the internal slang for a process whereby parts were painted by simply dipping them in black enamel at semi-automatic workstations. The enamel would contain up to 35 percent asphalt, and the painted part would be transported by a conveyor directly into an oven, where it would dry in about an hour at a temperature of 200°C. This process had been introduced by Ford for two reasons: partly to produce a durable, glossy surface, partly to overcome the time-consuming drying of parts, painted with traditional linseed oil-based paint.[46]

This procedure was unsuitable for the original Model T bodies, since they consisted of metal plates attached to a wooden frame, but fenders, hoods, chassis frames, and other all metal parts were dip-painted and "baked" at workstations on the ground floor, from where they would be delivered directly to the main assembly line.

All body work, painting included, was done on the first floor. The workshop for body assembly could also be supplied directly from the storage hall. The first stage of body assembly was done at stationary workstations, but from there the partly finished bodies were moved to a conveyor.[47] Both at the workstations on the ground floor, as well as in the body shop on the second floor, pneumatic tools were used in great numbers, and apparently to an even wider extent than in Heimdalsgade. Ford was definitely an early adapter of such tools.[48]

Figure 7 Rear axles hanging from a conveyor, ready to be "baked" in the oven.
Photo: Pacht & Crones Eftf. / The National Museum of Denmark

Unfortunately, no photos of the actual painting of bodies exist from the time of the opening of the plant. But since the varnish was still oil-based, it must have been applied by flow-painting like in Heimdalsgade, or some similar method, after spraying on the primer. However, the bodies were now moved around different parts of the paint shop hanging from overhead chain conveyors, and the actual painting could have been done while they were moving, instead of at stationary workstations, similar to the methods used in Detroit at the time. Photos from the paint shops also confirm the use of ovens for forced drying of the painted bodies.[49]

Figure 8 Stationary assembly of open bodies. Photo: Pacht & Crones Eftf. / The National Museum of Denmark

Upholstering, trimming, and—for the open-body versions—mounting of the top, were done in between different stages of the painting, on an assembly line running parallel to the paint shops. The finished bodies were then transported from the second floor to the ground floor by an inclined conveyor and lifted onto the chassis at the appropriate section of the main assembly line. After mounting the body to the chassis and assembling the final details, the engine was started by a starting device (as the electric self-starter was not standard on the Model T). The car would drive off the line by its own force, and out into a yard to the north-west of the factory, used for storage of finished units

Figure 9 Open bodies hanging from a conveyer in one of the paint shops. The bodies are probably coming out of the force drying oven at the back, and the workers are finishing them up before the next layer of paint. To the left are bodies stored vertically. Photo: Pacht & Crones Eftf. / The National Museum of Denmark

A state-of-the-art factory

Ford introduced several changes to the Model T during the mid-1920s. In an effort to counteract the rapidly declining sales in England, a special "English body" was introduced in 1924. Its most striking characteristic was a new colour scheme: a grey finish of the body, known as Empire grey, with a matching interior trim. Furthermore, the chassis was lowered, and the body altered slightly.[50]

Back home in Detroit, other changes were made to renew the appeal of the Model T, which was increasingly seen as outdated by critics and customers in America too. Aside from some minor improvements, the "new" Model T was characterised by two things: it had an all-steel body, with the slightly lower silhouette known from the English model; and it was available in two colours, a dark red and a dark blue, in addition to the traditional black.

The move away from constructing the Model T body over a wooden frame—a technology dating back to the horse carriage—in favour of an all-steel body offered advantages in both production and design and had been pioneered already by other car makers. But Henry Ford's reluctance to accept changes to the Model T had made him cling to the old method. Nevertheless, the amount of wood used had gradually diminished for some years, and Ford was now finally entering the future of car body construction.[51]

The all-steel body also had an effect on painting, since the removal of wooden parts made it possible to force-dry painted bodies at high temperatures, thereby reducing drying time. The paint used was still a revised version of the traditional oil- and resin-based varnish, though, and the fact that the two new colours were rather dark suggests that they might have contained asphalt too.[52]

Both the "English" and the "new" models were offered by the Danish Ford company. While not revolutionary, the changes made must have had at least some consequences for the production process. Unfortunately, they are not described in any direct sources. What is remarkable, though, is the time of introduction of the two revised models. The English body was available from Copenhagen almost parallel to its introduction in Britain. But more surprisingly: the "new" Model T was offered to customers in Denmark in the spring of 1925, at least a year before it was available to the American market.[53]

In March 1925, the company magazine wrote that the introduction of the "new" Model T to the Danish market had been made possible because the new South Port plant had "at its disposal the most modern technical Equipment of the Automobile Industry".[54] It follows from the introduction of the all-steel body models in January 1925 that the plant must have been equipped to make such bodies, as well as using the revised paint methods, some time before that—maybe since its opening in November 1924. These same methods were not introduced at Ford's main production facility, the River Rouge plant in Dearborn, until around August 1925.[55] For a short period in 1924–1925, the Copenhagen assembly plant was actually technologically ahead of Ford's American plants.

In terms of production capacity, 24,579 cars and trucks were assembled in Copenhagen during 1925, the first full year of production at the new South Port plant. This was a number never since surpassed in the history of Ford Motor Company A/S. On 12 May that year, a record-breaking 253 cars were assembled in one-10 hour working day. Employment was also peaking during that month, with 820 blue-collar and 132 white-collar workers.[56]

These were impressive figures, but still quite far away from the 600 cars per day that was advertised by Ford as the maximum capacity of the new factory.[57] Nevertheless, back home in Detroit, Ford was proud of its new Danish offspring. The South Port plan was featured in several articles in *Ford News* and described as "the second largest foreign factory of the company" and "the most modern manufacturing establishment in the Scandinavian countries, if not in Continental Europe".[58]

These claims were not unsubstantiated. During the record year 1925, more cars were assembled in Copenhagen than in Manchester, thereby for a short time making Denmark the home of Ford's largest industrial operation outside North America. Manchester would be back in the lead the following year but trailed quite closely by Copenhagen: from 1925 to 1930 the average yearly production would be 19,500 units in England and 15,800 in Denmark.[59]

With the lack of significant native car producers, the South Port plant was of course unrivalled in Scandinavia. But how about the rest of Continental Europe? In France, Citroën had successfully mass-produced affordable cars at its Quai de Javel plant in Paris, utilising an assembly line and other techniques inspired by Ford, since 1919. In 1923 Fiat opened its modernist masterpiece, the Lingotto factory in Turin. It certainly dwarfed Ford's Copenhagen plant in size, but not necessarily in technology. More than a handful of plants the size of that in Copenhagen could easily have fitted into the Lingotto complex. Nevertheless, the production capacity of the Italian factory was only 300 cars per day. But there is of course the important difference that the Lingotto figures were not just for assembly, but for the production of complete cars.[60]

In short: the Danish Ford factory was not the largest of its kind in Europe, but it was certainly among the most modern and potentially most productive in the 1920s.

Up to speed?

150 percent of the time used in Detroit. That was the initial benchmark set for the assembly of Ford Model T's in Heimdalsgade. Ford was aware that due to lack of experience and the less-than-optimal facilities, assembly could be expected to take place at a somewhat slower pace in Copenhagen than in Detroit. This benchmark was reached within half a year.[61]

At first glance, productivity actually suffered due to the move from Heimdalsgade to the South Port plant: in 1923 each blue-collar worker was assembling 53 cars per year on average, while the number was only 46 in 1925.[62] But it should be taken into consideration that the production process had become much more elaborate and complicated at the South Port plant, since a number of parts like engines, transmissions, wheels, etc. which were previously received as complete units were now assembled locally too. Therefore, a direct comparison of labour productivity between Heimdalsgade and the South Port is not possible.

For the same reason, a direct comparison of productivity between Ford's American plants and the South Port one would not make much sense, even if the relevant numbers could be obtained. But if we turn away from labour productivity as such, to the more subjective issue of how work speed was perceived by the workers, we might at least get some indirect indications. Since the introduction of the assembly line, so-called speedups had been a constant source of complaints and conflicts at Ford in the USA. In the times before unions, it was met mostly with tacit forms of resistance, such as workers quitting or deliberately slowing down the production process.[63]

In Denmark, however, we would expect any protest against speedups to be voiced through the unions. As we shall see below, the unions were not slow to react against whatever grievances they should have with the management at the Copenhagen Ford plants. But it would take more than 6 years before criticism of work speed at Ford was raised for the first time.

It happened in *Clarté*, a non-partisan socialist journal, which wrote critically about the work environment at the South Port plant in 1926. The source was not a worker on the assembly line, though, but a "former white-collar worker".[64] Nevertheless, that same year there was a short strike in June, as workers in the paint shop found the heat and foul air intolerable during hot summer days. The strike was ended, as management agreed to bring in the Working Environment Authority and let them decide if anything had to be done. What the Authority decided is not known, but it seems to have settled the case.[65]

One year later, the union magazine of the Metalworkers' Association wrote about how workers at Ford Motor Company were "overheated and dirty from Monday morning to Friday night", due to the exaggerated speed of work. Characteristically, the article was not based on evidence from Ford Motor Company A/S, but on a Detroit worker quoted in *Forbes Magazine*.[66] But again the claim was to some extent substantiated by the actions of Danish Ford workers. At a union meeting in March 1927, workers complained that "the speed of work had been forced much too much".[67] This was the first time ever that work speed had been raised as a specific issue. It is not clear, though, if the meeting resulted in any changes, but the issue was never on the agenda again during the inter-war period.

On the one hand, Danish Ford workers started to raise concerns about work speed during the late 1920s. On the other hand, compared to Detroit the level of complaints regarding work speed were low at the Danish plant. Apparently, productivity and work speed were not pushed to as high a level in Denmark as it was in Ford's American plants.

On 19 August 1927, production at the South Port plant came to a complete stop.[68] It was a planned stop, though, as the plant had to be completely re-tooled in order to be able to assemble the new Ford Model A. The stop lasted for almost a year. This was an effect of the Fordist productive model: because of the many purpose-built machines, tools, and fixtures, a very large part of the means of production had to be changed or reorganised for the manufacture of a new product. But the need for retooling was probably not the only reason why the Danish plant stood idle for so long. The new Model A was officially launched in the USA in December 1927, but Ford would experience a number of problems in the production process, meaning that it would take several months of 1928 before the Model A could be produced in sufficient numbers to supply even the American domestic market.[69] It is therefore likely that the long standstill in Copenhagen also had to do with Detroit not being able to supply parts for assembly. Finally, on 17 July 1928 the assembly line started rolling again, and the first Model A's came out of the South Port plant.

Emulation of a success

Ford's success in assembling cars in Copenhagen did not go unnoticed by some of its major competitors. In 1923 General Motors decided to establish itself in Denmark, and production was started in January 1924 in rented premises on Vasbygade in the South Port area, close to where Ford was building its new plant. In the beginning, only Chevrolets were produced, the car which had proven to be GM's best weapon in the battle with Ford over market share.[70]

This was actually GM's first assembly plant in Europe, and again William S. Knudsen is part of the story. In 1921 he had left the Ford Motor Company for General Motors, and was in charge of developing Chevrolet's production methods with the title of vice-president.[71] It is hard to imagine that Knudsen was not somehow involved in the decision to go for Copenhagen as GM's bridgehead to Europe. In Copenhagen, General Motors employed 300 blue- and white-collar workers, and production in the first year amounted to 4,905 passenger cars and 2,187 trucks. Between 60 and 85 percent of the cars were exported to countries in North and Central Europe.[72]

A third carmaker to establish itself in Copenhagen was French Citroën. Citroën was a European pioneer in mass production, and its Model A from 1919 had proven quite successful in the market for relatively affordable cars. In 1924 a Danish subsidiary was established, and in 1927 an assembly plant began operating. This plant too was placed in the South Port area, on Sydhavnsgade just a few hundred metres away from the Ford plant. In 1929 Automobiles Citroën A/S employed around 450 workers.[73]

With two of the "big three" American automakers and one of the largest European manufacturers all based only a few hundred metres apart, the Copenhagen South Port had truly become a North European centre for car assembly during the 1920s.

MARKETS AND MODELS

Model T for Export

It was the ambition right from the start that the cars assembled in Copenhagen should be sold not only in Denmark, but in the whole Nordic and Baltic area. This ambition was clearly fulfilled. Unfortunately, complete sales and export figures for this period do not exist, but enough figures have been compiled to allow the estimation that at least half, but perhaps as many as two-thirds, of the sales in this period were for export. The largest export market was Sweden, followed by Poland. After the import restrictions on foreign cars in Germany were lifted in 1925, export to that country boomed, with more than 10,000 cars exported that year. That was a one-time event, however, as Ford soon established an assembly plant in Berlin to take care of this new market. Norway and Finland were smaller but significant markets, while export to Iceland, Danzig, and the Baltic States was fairly limited.[74]

Marketed as "the universal car", the Ford Model T was offered in several variations to suit different purposes. But except for the so-called TT version, with its extended and reinforced chassis used for trucks only (known in Denmark as the 1-ton Truck), these variations were all based on the same technical platform, in terms of chassis, engine, and drivetrain; only the bodies were different. Another thing that all variants initially had in common was colour: until 1924 they were all black. Additionally, most of them were sold without an electric starter, though it was available as an option.

In the 1923 product portfolio of Ford Motor Company A/S, all major variants are present, except for some versions of the Sedan. The Sedan was available in the USA as a Tudor and a Fordor model. Rumour had it that Tudor was meant to evoke connotations of English nobility, but in reality, Tudor and Fordor were just Ford's way of shortening the words two-door and four-door. It is possible that only the Tudor was offered in Denmark initially, but at least from early 1924 both the Tudor and the Fordor were available.[75] Finally, there was also a Center-Door Model, which was quite uncommon in Denmark.

Apart from variations of the Ford Model T, Ford Motor Company A/S was offering two additional products. One was the Fordson tractor, which was not assembled in Copenhagen but imported as built-up units only, in this period mainly from Ford's tractor plant in Cork, Ireland. Another one was the Lincoln passenger car. Lincoln was an American luxury car brand, acquired by Ford in 1922 and continued as a separate division. Lincoln cars were imported as built-up by Ford Motor Company A/S from 1923 and sold by Ford dealers but marketed as a separate brand.[76]

The distribution of sales across variations and models confirms that the initial strength of Ford Motor Company A/S was its appeal to the most cost-conscious part of the market. By far the most popular variation of the Ford Model T was the one offering most value for money, the open Touring which had room for 4–5 people at a significantly lower price than the closed Sedan. At the other end of the scale, the Lincoln, which was priced at about ten times that of a Ford Model T, sold in negligible quantities. Trucks, in the form of T and TT chassis, sold between a quarter and one-third of the passenger cars, making them an important part of the business too (the chassis, while counted as passenger cars, were almost certainly used for utility vehicles or trucks). Finally, the sale of tractors was limited, but not insignificant.

Yet there were also telling differences between markets. While Model T passenger cars made up almost 75 percent of the vehicles sold in Denmark in 1927, it was less than 50 percent in the small Lithuanian market and slightly above 60 percent in the larger Polish market. The lower sales of passenger cars in relation to trucks and tractors in these latter markets is a reflection of the fact that the car-buying middle class was not yet as well established as in the former.

It is also noteworthy that the relatively more expensive Sedan version of the Model T had gained in popularity from 1922 to 1927. But again, this was especially the case in Denmark—where the Sedan sold more than double the number of the cheaper Touring in 1927—and

Model	Ford T						Lincoln	Tractor
	Passenger cars					Trucks		
	Touring	Sedan	Coupe	Runabout	Chassis			
1920	4699	195	75	237	50	1351	n/a	438
1927	1934	1335	83	80	320	1147	17	680

Table 1 Number of different variations and models sold in 1920 and 1927, in total for all markets. Source: FMC: Balance sheet, 1920 & Deliveries, 1927

to some degree in Sweden, but not in Poland, where the Sedan was still by far outsold by cheaper versions.[77] Just as in the USA, car buyers in Scandinavia were raising their expectations for comfort and style, as they became more affluent.

Dealerships and departure

Ford cars had in fact been available in Denmark since 1906, when the company F. Bülow, later F. Bülow & Co., had been appointed local sales agent. The start was modest, with only 12 cars sold in 1907, but the company worked hard on recruiting dealers, and in 1916 sales reached 220 units, supplied from Manchester.[78] A role similar to Bülow in Denmark was played by Amerikanska Motor Importen A/B in Sweden and E.C. Gjestvangs Automobilforretning AS in Norway.

It was Carl A. Bülow, son of Frederik Bülow, with a reputation of knowing the Ford Model T inside out, who did most of the travelling sales work. From around 1918, C.A. Bülow also became deeply involved in selling tractors produced by Henry Ford & Son, a company that had been set up parallel to Ford Motor Company for this purpose. Even though the two companies were formally separate, it was customary for Ford dealers also to sell tractors, later known under the brand name Fordson.[79]

The dealerships that had been established by Frederik and Carl A. Bülow were not very formal: sometimes a general mechanical workshop or a bicycle dealer would expand its business by selling a few cars, and there was no such thing as districts and exclusivity.[80] In Norway and Sweden, it was probably similar. As Ford Motor

Figure 10 Full-page advertisement from Ford, *Politiken*, 6 January 1923

Company A/S took over, it was decided initially to honour the existing contracts with the three Scandinavian sales agents, but as these would come to an end during 1920, dealerships would be rearranged according to the lines laid out from Detroit.[81]

It was Georg Carlson who had the responsibility of setting up new dealerships from April 1920. There were initial difficulties, such as overcoming suspicion from potential dealers when they were asked to sign a contract in English. But the number of dealers rose quickly, as selling Ford cars was a profitable business in the early twenties. In late 1921 there were 76 dealers, of which about 22 were in Denmark, 17 in Sweden, 14 in Norway, and the rest in Finland, Estonia, and even one in Soviet Russia—judging from sales figures, the latter did not have much business.[82]

As newly appointed head of the Foreign Department of Ford Motor Company, R.I. Roberge made a survey of the state of the European plants in late 1921, with an emphasis on sales. For Denmark he concluded:

> Altogether, the Copenhagen plant seems to be in excellent shape from a sales standpoint, and the dealers are apparently developed to a higher point of efficiency than dealers under any other Continental Branch.[83]

Sometimes during the 1920s, Copenhagen was asked to further implement the Detroit system of subdividing dealers into three formal categories: main-, sub-, and limited, with different levels of rebate. It was the strict implementation of this system in England that made two-thirds of the existing dealers quit in anger, and Ford's share of the English market plummet.[84] The Danish Ford Company adopted the same system on paper, but not in practice, where most dealers were still treated to the same discount.[85]

In contrast with England, no dealer upheavals took place in Denmark, with one prominent exception: that of F. Bülow & Co. As compensation for stepping down as general sales agent, Bülow was given the dealership rights in the three major cities of Copenhagen, Odense, and Aarhus. However, these rights were not exclusive, and Ford Motor Company A/S soon appointed another two dealers in Copenhagen.

Frederik Bülow was concerned about the rising number of competitors, but maybe even more so about the way he and his company were being treated by Ford in general. One of the new Detroit principles that had been implemented was an obligation on the dealers to receive a fixed number of cars annually—in the case of F. Bülow & Co. 1,000 units—evenly distributed through the year. From the point of view of Ford this was a rational way of securing an even and continuous flow in production. But to Bülow it was incomprehensible why they should receive the same number of open touring cars for sale in the winter as in the summer. In September 1920, F. Bülow asked to be freed from this obligation and declared his frustration in no uncertain terms in a letter to the local Ford management:

> We all too often have been treated by Ford Motor Company [...], without taking into consideration the present conditions, our interests and our suggestions, which must be considered as an offence to a company that is doing its utmost to represent the Ford brand ...[86]

Georg Carlson not only denied the request but did so in a rather sarcastic tone of voice, doing little to cool down Bülow's simmering anger.

A few months later, a meeting had to be called for all three Copenhagen dealers, including Bülow, as they had mutually accused each other of unfair competition by undercutting prices. In a report from the meeting, Georg Carlson concluded that the meeting brought out some good points for further discussion, but he also scolded the participants, claiming that they had "acted as children and not as businessmen". This triggered another letter from F. Bülow, in which he wrote:

> It will probably be of no surprise to you—upon proper consideration—that I, who have been conducting my own company for 42 years, cannot acknowledge your judgement as competent, in regard to my behaviour as a businessman or, as you claim, a child at said meeting.[87]

In 1922 Ford Motor Company A/S signed up with yet another dealer in Copenhagen. Parallel to this, disagreements had been building up between C.A. Bülow and Charles Sorensen in Detroit over the trac-

Figure 11 The organising committee of the joint exhibition by Copenhagen dealers and Ford Motor Company A/S in January 1924. Seated are Ford manager G. Carlson (left) and dealer F. Bülow, head of the committee. Unknown photographer. *Motor*, no. 2, 12 January 1924

tor business, as Bülow was denied the right to sell tractors outside Denmark, despite his efforts to investigate new markets. These differences had been handled by Sorensen in his usual way: blunt and with no time for diplomacy.[88]

On 5-14 January 1924, an exhibition of Ford cars took place in central Copenhagen, organised jointly by four dealers and the Ford Motor Company A/S. Chairman of the organising committee was Frederik Bülow. A photo of the committee shows Bülow sitting at the front, beside manager Georg Carlson, with the rest of the committee standing behind them. Carlson is staring straight into the camera with a rather sullen expression, while Bülow is looking at him with an attitude that does little to hide his unfriendly emotions.

About three weeks after this photo was taken, F. Bülow & Co. cancelled their contract with Ford Motor Company A/S, in favour of a new contract with General Motors. Ford had lost one of its largest and most experienced dealers to its main competitor. The break, however, did not seem to have had any significant effect on the company's total sales.

Selling the T

In the spring of 1923, a correspondent of *Der Motorwagen*, a journal published by the German auto- and aviation industry, was sent to Denmark on a reconnaissance mission. Germany had been the technological birthplace of the automobile, but in the 1920s the country was far from leading the industry. Under the heading "The flooding of the Danish car market by Ford", the correspondent informed his German readers how Copenhagen had become "a focal point for selling cars from the whole wide world". Several German Adler cars were roaming the streets of the city as taxi cabs, but unfortunately the private customers seemed to prefer cars that were practical and economical—not the large, expensive German cars. The correspondent noticed cars such as French Citroën, Peugeot, and Renault, Italian Fiat, and English Humber; but one car was seen more often that all the others: the Ford Model T. The journal quoted "one of the largest car dealers in Denmark" for estimating that about 80 percent of all cars sold at the time were Fords.[89]

This might be only a slight exaggeration. Evidence of the total number of cars in Denmark is somewhat scanty for the early 1920s, but according to the Department of Statistics the total number of registered cars rose by 4,603 from September 1920 to October 1921.[90] The total number of cars sold by Ford in the same period can be roughly calculated as around 6,000, and it is reasonable to assume that at least one-third of these, or 2,000, were sold in Denmark.[91] This is consistent with a detailed local study from the provincial town of Vordingborg, which shows that 44 out of 83 cars registered in the period 1914–1932 were Fords.[92] In other words: very roughly, every other car sold in Denmark during the 1920s was a Ford.

The sales figures of the Model T did not only climb rapidly from 1919, but they stayed at a relatively high level until the end of its production. This is even more remarkable compared to England, where the company's share of the market diminished catastrophically, from around 24 percent in 1913 to 4 percent in 1929. There were several reasons for this, including bad management, but foremost among them was the lack of adaptation to the local market, combined with Ford's hesitation to replace the aging Model T.[93]

In the markets to which Copenhagen catered, the Model T was easy to sell in the 1920s, according to Arthur Beck, who worked as a "road man" in the early 1920s, travelling to Sweden and Finland to set up dealerships.[94] We can only make some educated guesses about the reasons why Ford Denmark fared so much better than in England. First of all, Ford Motor Company A/S does not seem to have been hampered by bad management in the way the English company was in those years. On the contrary, Georg Carlson and his executives were quite effective not only in managing production, but also in building up a sales network. Furthermore, a great deal of effort was invested in promoting Ford via events, advertising, and other forms of PR.

Of no less importance was the fact that some of the obstacles that Ford faced in the British market did not exist in the Nordic and Baltic countries. In England, domestic manufacturers such as Austin and Morris succeeded in bringing a range of smaller, but at the same time better equipped cars to the market. Furthermore, the British government had no interest in promoting manufacture of "foreign" cars in England, and the taxation of cars introduced in 1910 benefitted domestic producers, even if this might have been an incidental side effect.[95]

In Denmark, a yearly tax on cars had been introduced the same year as in England. But contrary to in England, the Danish tax did not affect Ford more than other brands. Originally, it was based on the horsepower of the engine on a progressive scale with three levels. The Ford Model T would be taxed according to the highest level (above 12HP), but so would most of its competitors. From 1927 onwards, the yearly tax would be based on weight, instead of horsepower. In 1924 the yearly tax was supplemented by a sales tax on private cars, based on the value of the car.[96] The tax was 15 percent for the cheapest cars, but increased gradually to 40 percent for the most expensive models.[97] Even though this was a quite high level of taxation for its time, it did not seem to have affected the general sales of cars much, as they kept their upward momentum.

The fact that it was easier to sell the Ford Model T in Denmark than in England did not make the Danes blind to its shortcomings, though. Hans Christian Møller, sales manager from 1920, was not completely satisfied with his product: "I do not think that Ford changed its body or its engineering sufficiently", he said in retrospect. And when it came to adaptation to local markets, Møller found that "Dearborn never listened"—they were simply too focused on their much larger American market. Arthur Beck points to the planetary gear of the Model T as a sales handicap. This was of course more than just a matter of local adaptation; it was a fundamental part of the Model T's design. On the positive side there were few mechanical problems with the relatively simple car. But when it came to updating his beloved Model T, "everyone felt that Henry Ford was slow and too orthodox".[98]

Even to its loyal customers, the low-cost but simple solutions offered by the Model T must have seemed increasingly outdated. This is apparent from the flourishing market for third-party add-ons and modifications, ranging from cosmetic improvements, such as flower vases, through rear-view mirrors and windshield-wipers to carburettors and shock-absorbers. Even a complete change of the body was marketed.[99] Some of the add-ons that were offered were actually standard equipment on slightly more expensive models from other

Figure 12 Model T touring cars lined up in front of the Heimdalsgade plant, sporting the new grey colour introduced in Denmark in 1924. They also have the new nickel-plated radiator casing. The updated Model T's were introduced very early on the Danish market. Photo: Peter Elfelt / Museum of Copenhagen

brands, such as the Chevrolet, which made the low-priced Ford T relatively less appealing.

In 1922 the magazine *Motor* wrote favourably about a rather radical modification, in which the chassis frame was cut apart and re-welded, to lower the car. This was in the period when no modifications for adapting to local markets by Ford dealers were allowed, according to Detroit rules. Nevertheless, this operation was offered by F. Bülow, at that time still an official Ford dealer. No advertising of this modification has been found, though—maybe a reflection of its "semi-legal" character?[100]

But in the spring of 1924, the Model T was modified in a fully official way, as the new "English body" was introduced, with a slightly altered body on a lowered chassis, and in a new Empire grey colour, with a matching interior trim. For the first time since 1915, a Ford car was now available in another colour than black.[101] A year later, more colours were introduced with the new Model T, which was offered in Orriford Lake, a dark red, and Cobalt Blue. Beside the new colours, it sported an all-steel body, and a windshield wiper and balloon tyres as standard.[102] While the "English body" was only available in a touring version, the new model was sedan only.

Despite these efforts to revive the appeal of the Model T and make it look more modern, the most importing selling point was still its low price: and the pricing was very competitive. In his October 1919 report, William Knudsen had estimated a possible sales price of 3,800 Danish kroner (DKK). But the rather volatile economic situation of 1919–1920, including a sharp increase in the exchange rate between Danish kroner and US dollars, undermined Knudsen's calculations, and the first advertised sales price, from November 1920, was considerably higher, at DKK 5,625. But from then on, the price of a Ford Model T went practically one way only: downwards. In the spring of 1927, just before the Model T was discontinued, the price of the cheapest version was DKK 2,175—less than half of the initial price.[103] The 1920s were generally a period of deflation, but even taking that into account, the Model T was roughly 45 percent cheaper in 1927 than in 1920. The price drop was even greater if we take into account that an electric self-starter and balloon tyres, previously optional, had become standard by the end of the period.

Compared to other cars in the same class, the Model T was definitely cheaper. In 1924, when the slightly updated Model T sold for DKK 2,750, the price of a Chevrolet Superior Touring, one of its closest competitors, was DKK 3,975 and the cheapest comparable Citroën model was sold for DKK 5,300.[104] However, these latter cars were also rather more modern than the Model T.

Together with the incremental updates in design, the still lower prices helped keep up the sales of the Model T. With 25,276 Model T's of different versions sold, 1925 was a record year, not surpassed in company history until the 1960s. The rest of the period until the end

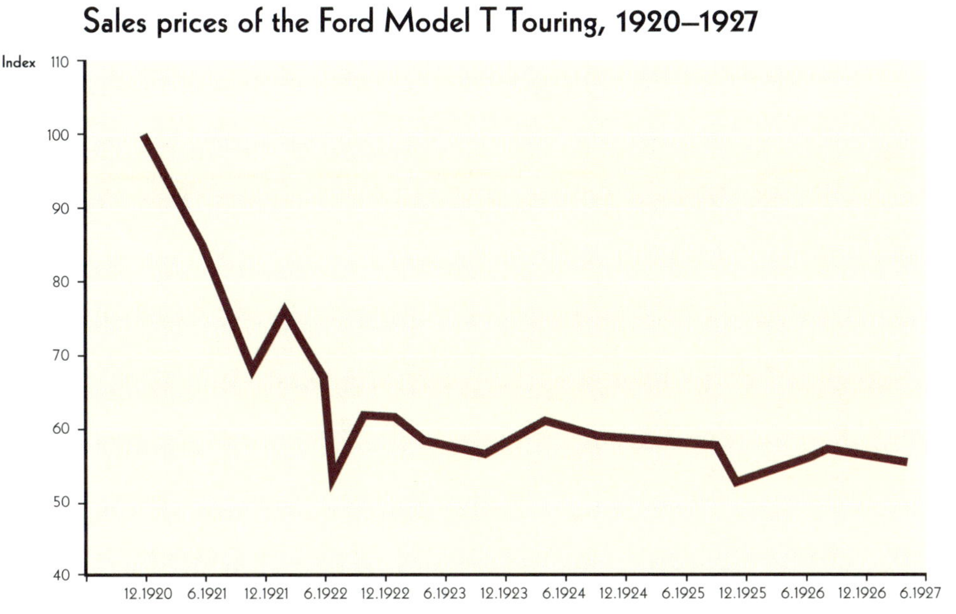

Figure 13 Index of sales prices of the Ford Model T Touring, 1920–1927, relative to general cost of living. Source: Prices from FMC: Balance sheets or as advertised in *Politiken*. Index of cost of living for the nearest previous month, in *Statistisk Aabog*, 1928, table 100

of Model T production in August 1927 saw gradually, but not radically, diminishing figures. In 1926, the last full year of production, a respectable 19,059 Model T's were sold.[105] But these sales figures literally came at a price which, as we shall see later, threatened to make the whole business economically unsustainable in terms of revenue.

MANAGEMENT

By Proxy from Detroit

When Knudsen was faced with the task of setting up a Danish Ford company in the summer of 1919, he asked the Royal Danish Automobile Club (KDAK),for a recommendation for a legal advisor. The KDAK suggested Viggo Falbe-Hansen, who had handled several cases for the club. In his later report to Detroit, Knudsen described Falbe-Hansen as being in "a very good standing in Copenhagen as a conservative attorney".[106]

Knudsen discovered that setting up the company as a formal branch of Ford Motor Company in Detroit would require a special licence from the Ministry of Commerce to the individual in whose name the branch was to be registered. This procedure would take quite a long time, and Knudsen was in a hurry to get started. Consequently, he asked Falbe-Hansen to draft the articles for a formally independent company: Ford Motor Company A/S. The company was founded on 25 June 1919.[107] Of the 500 shares issued at a nominal value of DKK 1,000 each, 276 were owned by Henry Ford personally, 202 by his son Edsel, and 16 by his wife Clara. The remaining six shares were divided between the other board members and the manager, with one each.[108]

Knudsen's job had been to establish the company and set up a plant, which he did with tremendous energy during the summer of 1919. But as soon as the assembly line was ready to roll, he continued to Cadiz to establish the Spanish company. Instead, James J. Harrington arrived from the USA in August to take up his position as managing director of the new plant in Copenhagen. Harrington was only 30 at the time but brought with him experience as former manager of two different assembly plants in the United States. However, he stayed only briefly: in September 1920 he was transferred to London as European Manager and thereby left his position as both managing director and chairman of the board in Copenhagen. He was replaced by assistant manager George "Geo" Carlson, who became the new manager and chairman of the company.[109]

While Harrington was an interim person, George Carlson would be the manager that made his mark in the formative years of the company. Carlson was also an American but, as the name suggests, had Swedish ancestry. He had worked for Ford in the United States, mainly in sales, but was chosen for a job as assistant manager in Copenhagen partly because he understood Swedish and thereby was also able to communicate in Danish, as the two languages are very similar. He arrived in Copenhagen in late 1919, and was only 29 years old when he was promoted to manager less than a year later. Becoming a plant manager at a relatively early age was not uncommon in the Ford organisation at that time.[110]

Having successfully overseen the expansion of the Danish company and the opening of the new South Harbour plant in 1924, Carlson was sent on a tour to Germany to investigate the possibilities of establishing a company there. The conclusion was that there was basis for a German subsidiary, and Carlson was chosen to create it: in early 1926 he moved permanently to Berlin, and his position in Denmark was taken over by Hans Christian Møller in March that year.[111]

Møller was a Dane, with a degree from the Technical University of Copenhagen. As a young man he emigrated to Canada, but ended up in Detroit, working for Ford as an engineer. In 1920 he returned to Copenhagen to work for the Danish Ford company, being responsible for setting up a network of dealers. During Carlson's leadership, Møller was promoted to assistant manager. He was 40 when he succeeded Carlson as manager.[112]

While Carlson had thrived in building up, Møller was focused on keeping the business running, without too many disruptions. He steered the company through the restructuring of the late 1920s, the economic recession of the 1930s, and the German occupation 1940–1945, before finally retiring in 1949. That made him by far the longest-reigning managing director in the period of Ford's car plant operations in Denmark. What made both Carlson and especially Møller different from most other Ford managers outside the USA was their familiarity with the local context in which they had to work. Almost all other managers of Ford Motor Company's early overseas operations were Americans who did not necessarily have any prior knowledge of the culture and habits of enterprise at the destination they were sent to.[113]

The managers had to answer to a board of directors. According to law, the majority of the board of a limited Danish company had to be naturalised Danes and living in the country. That was of course the case for Ford Motor Company A/S too, but in 1919 Knudsen assured the American owners that they would be in full control: board meetings would be a mere formality, he wrote, "with decisions made by proxy from Detroit".[114]

During the first year or two, the board was in a state of fluctuation. Initially, it was made up of Knudsen as chairman, Falbe-Hansen, and two businessmen already well known to the Ford Company: Frederik L. Bülow and his son Carl A. Bülow of the sales company F. Bülow, which had represented the Ford brand in Denmark since 1906. These directors were further authorised to incorporate Edsel B. Ford, president of the American Ford Motor Company, and Frank L. Klingensmith, treasurer of the American company into the board.[115] However, that might never have been formally realised, as nothing is mentioned about the latter two in connection with the board before 1921.

When Harrington was appointed manager of the new plant in August 1919, he was also elected to the board where he replaced Knudsen as chairman. But even though Knudsen left for Cadiz, and would have no more business in Copenhagen, for some reason he stayed on as a board member.[116] When Harrington left again in September 1920, George Carlson became member and chairman of the board.[117]

With the animosity between George Carlson and the Bülows reaching breaking point, however, the board soon had to be changed again.[118] At a general meeting held in March 1921, both Frederik and Carl Bülow resigned, and at a following board meeting the same day it was decided to buy back their personal shares in the company. As a replacement for the Bülows, two executives of the company, office manager K.L. Swenson and bookkeeper Otto L. Brøndum, were elected. Falbe-Hansen also left the board but kept his close connection with the company as its principal legal adviser.[119]

The 1921 general meeting was not only marked by the internal grievances in the Danish company. Back in Detroit, 1920 had been a difficult year for Ford, with an economic recession impeding sales and forcing the company to cut costs. Henry Ford's ways of countering the crisis had brought simmering dissatisfaction with his autocratic leadership to a point where some of his senior executives decided to part with him and his company: most notably William S. Knudsen, who left Ford Motor Company in favour of General Motors 1921.[120] He was now finally formally dismissed from the board of the Danish company he had himself created, but in which he had not taken active part since 1919. Another senior executive who left Ford in 1921 was Frank L. Klingensmith. Apparently, he was considered a member of the Danish board, even if he had never been properly elected or taken part in its activities. Nonetheless he was officially ousted at the 1921 general

Figure 14 Management and white-collar staff in front of the modest first headquarters of Ford Motor Company A/S in Heimdalsgade. The third person from left is Georg Carlson, general manager 1920–1926. Unknown photographer. OEL private collection

meeting. Finally, the president of Ford Motor Company, Edsel B. Ford, was now formally elected to the board per request from Detroit.[121]

From now on, the board found a more stable form. It would be chaired by the managing director of the company: Georg Carlson until March 1926, and from then on H.C. Møller. The other Danish members would be a couple of other executives, such as the above-mentioned Swenson and Brøndum or from 1926 the new assistant manager Hjalmar Mortensen. Detroit would be represented by Edsel B. Ford, who would continue to be a member of the board until his death in 1943. He would take personal part in only three board meetings during that time, but there was no doubt that he had the final say in any important decisions.[122] In 1926, B.J. Craig, financial controller of Ford Motor Company with whom Edsel B. Ford was working closely, was made an additional representative of Detroit in the Danish board.

American years?

From a desk in Ford headquarters in Dearborn, Detroit, any assembly plant, foreign or domestic, was regarded the same, and in principle subjected to the same kind of management. That is why the history of Ford in Europe until 1928, when the organisation was thoroughly changed, has been characterised as the "years of Americanisation".[123]

The workings of the board of directors of Ford Motor Company A/S do in some ways corroborate that Detroit was in control. Not just by calling for the occasional meeting in the USA, when something important was on the agenda, which after all happened very rarely; but more so by sending instructions by letter to the board and the general meeting, stipulating for instance how much dividend should be paid or who should be elected to the board. This happened quite frequently and was never contested from Copenhagen.

But not only did the board act little on its own during these years; it acted very little at all. Between the 1921 general meeting and the one in 1929, which confirmed the restructuring under British leadership, a total of 28 board meetings were held—roughly 4 per year. However, with the November 1923 meeting mentioned above as the major exception, most of these meetings dealt with only very trivial matters. 19 of them had either nothing at all on the agenda, or only one issue: confirmation of the semi-annual payment of interest to those employees having bought investment certificates in the company. The board was, in this period, never a forum for any substantial discussion of company matters. And while there might have been a bit more discussion at the yearly General Meetings, no real initiatives emanated from this forum either.[124]

The board-meetings were simply not the nexus of management between Detroit and Copenhagen. Of course, this is not all that surprising: the Danish board was a formal necessity, no American Ford branch had one, and the natural thing for Detroit would be to go directly to the Danish management. Therefore, the real relations between Detroit and Denmark are to be found in the practical routines of management, such as how audits from Detroit were carried out and specific issues and conflicts were dealt with.

In the early 1920s, Ford's managerial hierarchy in Europe was still under construction. In 1919 Knudsen had taken with him the so-called "Foreign Department" from England to Copenhagen. It is not clear precisely how long the department was active in Copenhagen, and neither is its authority, but it seems to have taken care of those markets in which there was no Ford subsidiary yet. Since Harrington moved to London, no more was heard of it in Copenhagen, so the "Foreign Department" either ceased to exist or moved with him. Likewise, Harrington's authority as European Manager, working first out of London and later Paris, is also not clear. In 1921 he escorted two of Henry Ford's senior executives, Sorensen and Brubaker, when they made a round trip of several European countries, evaluating the prospect of setting up new subsidiaries.[125] But except for a short period between March 1924 and August 1925, when he for unknown reasons was granted power of attorney over the funds of the Danish company, there is no evidence that he had any managerial power, indicating that his authority might have been over markets, but not over production. In 1925 he went back to Detroit, and his position disappeared.[126]

Back in the United States, a programme of branch plant expansion was carried out under the auspices of Ernest Kanzler in cooperation with Edsel Ford. Between 1921 and 1925, the number of American branches was expanded to more than thirty. In 1923, Kanzler was promoted to second vice president of the Ford Motor Company, and as such he resumed responsibility for the foreign branches too.[127]

As Kanzler took control, the European subsidiaries were directed from Detroit along the same line and methods as Ford's local branches in the United States.[128] In the early 1920s, it was the English, Danish, Spanish, and French Ford companies, with assembly plants in the first mentioned three. They all received the same instructions concerning production, sales, and accounting as the American branches. These instructions were kept in binders at each factory and referred to internally as "The Ford Bible". Dealerships also had to be restructured along the principles used in the USA, and marketing had to be approved by Detroit. We have already seen above how Ford maintained the Model T as a "universal car", suitable for any market, and how any attempts to do local modifications or adaptations were strictly prohibited.[129] To ensure conformity in procedures, European subsidiaries were regularly visited by auditors from Detroit. Copenhagen was visited by such auditors almost every year between 1919 and 1929.

There can be no doubt as to the intentions: Detroit wanted to be in control. But intention is not necessarily the same as reality. In principle, the auditors had extensive decision-making power, but as one of them, the later head of the Auditing Department H.L. Moekle, recalls:

> I don't believe the auditors assumed certain controls. Actually auditors never were really effective managers of the operations over there. [...] If I remember correctly, Mr. Harrington and later Mr. Carlson acted as sort of general representatives and exercised a sort of general control, working always under the advice of the Detroit offices.[130]

Another auditor, L. E. Briggs, describes his responsibilities mainly as the application and control of accounting procedures, etc. He did not intervene in questions regarding production.[131]

On certain occasions, however, Detroit made it very clear who had the power to decide. During Ford Motor Company's recession in 1920–1921, an urge to cut costs swept through all of the company, Europe included. However, Copenhagen was the only place more or less excluded, as sales were going well there, contrary to most other subsidiaries.[132]

The most dramatic intervention was in late 1926, when production plummeted due to low sales of the Model T and preparations for the upcoming Model A. In November that year, a group of three—George Brubaker, Fred Hoffman, and J.J. Harrington—was sent to Europe to thoroughly evaluate every subsidiary. They were empowered to check the quality of operations and the functioning of the plant, and to eliminate useless paperwork, but most importantly they were supposed to cut down the number of employees. They did that with such rigour that they were dubbed "The three horsemen" by European employees, as a reference to the biblical tale of the four horsemen of the apocalypse.[133] When they left Copenhagen in January 1927, 23 clerks, 50 blue-collar workers, and 4 territory representatives had been dismissed. The number of clerks fired was second only to the 29 fired in Manchester. The auditors also remarked that "superficially [the] plant presents good appearance", but there were room for improvement, such as taking care of too much "junk" stored around the plant, including unidentified tools and machinery.[134]

But even this demonstration of power was not without ambiguity. One of the regular auditors, the aforementioned Briggs, later commented on the work of the "three horsemen". He was not impressed by Brubaker who, according to Briggs, calculated the number of clerks that had to go "by some method known only to himself", making the whole exercise "unscientific". Consequently, the local managers complied with Brubaker's instructions, but "reverted to a normal basis" again as soon as he and his colleagues had left.[135] If this was also the case in Copenhagen is unknown. But Detroit was clearly satisfied with how the horsemen had decimated both people and expenses, while in Europe they received a Christmas greeting by cable from Charles Sorensen, complimenting them on their good work.[136]

Managers of the European subsidiaries were also sometimes called to Detroit for conferences and meetings. One important conference was held in June 1920, when all foreign branch managers were gathered under the presidency of Edsel Ford. Harrington was there as the Danish manager and as we shall explore further below, matters relating to the Copenhagen plant were specifically on the agenda.[137] There were, however, rather long periods between these visits. Carlson visited Detroit at least once during his years in Copenhagen, for a board meeting in November 1923.[138] H.C. Møller attended a managers' conference in 1927, and all in all visited Detroit four times during his 23 years as manager.[139]

Buildings and banquets

Two slightly connected instances may be seen as examples of how Detroit exercised its power of determination, and how it was dealt with from Copenhagen. The first one is the planning and building of the new South Port plant.

It comes as no surprise that Detroit followed this project closely, considering its size, cost, and importance. Correspondence reveals that the actual overall responsibility for the project was in the hands of Charles Sorensen. Sorensen had already proven his capability in the field of factory design and production management, not least by his role in managing production at the enormous River Rouge complex in Dearborn.[140] Compared to this the Copenhagen plant was, after all, a small undertaking. Nevertheless, it was monitored by Sorensen with great attention. It was Sorensen who approved the acquisition of the building site that Carlson had found and suggested. It was also Sorensen who—in his usual blunt way—was asking the Copenhagen management to speed up, when negotiations with local building authorities dragged on. And finally, it was Sorensen with the assistance of B.R. Brown, superintendent in charge of plant construction, who followed the final planning and building process in minute detail. Apart from sending drawings, computations, etc. by regular mail, cables regarding technical details and decisions were in some periods exchanged on a daily basis.[141]

The specific issues discussed in these telegrams ranged from small details, such as if the planned wooden sliding doors could be swapped for steel (suggested by Copenhagen and approved by Detroit), to much larger issues, such as adding extra space to the building or the choice of power sources.

On most issues, Detroit insisted on the practical solution: a suggestion from Copenhagen for a more elaborate ornamentation of parts of the facade, undoubtedly initiated by the building authorities, was brushed aside without further argument. Electric cabling had to be run in exposed conduits, for easier maintenance and repair. But cost cutting was not necessarily first priority: sometimes Detroit would insist on more costly solutions if they were believed to be advantageous in the long run. A suggestion from Copenhagen to construct the water tower for the sprinklers in reinforced concrete was turned down, in favour of a more expensive steel construction, with the argument that a steel tower could be easily relocated, should the need arise. In hindsight though, not all decisions were farsighted. Most notably, it was suggested by Copenhagen to install a forced air ventilation system. This was rejected from Detroit, since such a system would require all sashes to be kept permanently closed and thereby making window cleaning much more impractical. Considering the issues of heated and polluted working environment that would arise later, this would prove not to be a wise decision.

Even though many of the proposed alterations from Copenhagen were rejected, Detroit was not just flat-out refusing everything. On the contrary: some rather expensive proposals such as a second floor on the north-west wing of the plant and an additional crane way in the storage hall were in fact accepted by Sorensen.

The largest issue discussed was that of the power system. These discussions also included William B. Mayo, chief power engineer of the Ford Motor Company. After investigating several solutions, including building a power station equipped with either diesel or steam engines, local management recommended getting electricity from the municipal power grid. According to their computations, this would be marginally more expensive per KWh than a private power station, but considerably cheaper if the need for power should fall below the level planned for, since the fixed costs were much lower.

Detroit on the contrary preferred a power station at the factory, with coal-fired boilers. The last part reflected Henry Ford's personal obsession with eliminating waste and reusing excess material, as such boilers would also permit the burning of scrap for heating, as was done at River Rouge.[142] Counter to this, Copenhagen claimed that it would be more profitable simply to sell the packing boxes and other scrap timber than to burn it.

In the meantime, the Danish company Atlas had presented itself with a solution based on steam turbines, from which the excess steam could be used for heating and thereby making separate boilers for this purpose unnecessary. Furthermore, such a solution would permit the burning of scrap in the boilers. Eventually Detroit decided on the steam turbines. Shortly after its completion, the power station and its turbines were the object of a detailed report, featured prominently in the Danish journal of building professionals, *Tidsskrift for Ingeniør- og Bygningsvæsen*.[143] The steam turbines were a novel solution in a Danish context, which explains why the Copenhagen management hesitated. But to Detroit, this was a well-known technology since steam turbines was already powering parts of the River Rouge.

There is no denying that as the South Port plant stood ready for production in November 1924, not only the power station but the complete facility was a remarkable and advanced construction. As described below, it was honoured with a grand opening, attended by a great number of prominent guests, and attracting public interest. This opening was also the direct cause of the other issue which we shall examine, as an example of interaction between Copenhagen management and Detroit.

The grand opening provoked a reaction from Detroit, as auditors had found the expenses too excessive and the liberal serving of alcohol and tobacco inappropriate. In March 1925, a letter was sent to Carlson, listing the expenses in detail, and requiring an explanation in a rather patronising voice:

> You have been connected with the organization long enough to know that it is not our custom to have dinners, picnics, etc, and pay for them out of the Company's funds. [...] you at least should have written to Detroit outlining your plans [concerning the opening] and secured permission before going ahead and spending approximately $8,000 for a banquet, a large portion of which was for drinks and cigars.[144]

At first, the letter was ignored, and Detroit had to send a new request before they finally received an answer from Carlson in June 1925. And if they had expected a humble excuse, they must have been surprised. In seven closely written pages Carlson not only defended his decisions in polite but no uncertain terms; he also requested that he be given more authority to act on his own in similar and other matters of management in the future.

Regarding the opening of the factory, Carlson notes that the participants at the banquet were

> Leading businessmen, bankers, politicians and Press representatives of Denmark, Norway, Sweden, Finland, Estonia, Latvia, Lithuania, Free State of Danzig, Poland and Germany, [representing] 113 mill. people, and which are under the control of the Danish and Swedish Company.[145]

He argues that the opening was part of the company's effort to establish its prestige and gain "ready access to any State, Municipal, Legislative, and other Government department", the alleged results of which are detailed in a list of 10 examples.

Apart from the political and public relations effect of the opening in general, Carlson also argues with reference to local customs. The food and drinks served were not excessive in view of the guests present, "and to practically all it would have been an insult had we served non-intoxicating beverages". He also defends other decisions picked up on by the auditors, such as having a Christmas tree and contributing to a yearly picnic for employees, as a reflection of Danish customs and traditions.

Carlson finishes his letter with a list of no less than 22 points for which he seeks Detroit's approval. The first points on the list will basically authorize him to do in the future what has just been questioned, such as giving picnics, entertaining the press, etc. From small issues, such as an annual dinner for board members and management, the list goes on to larger ones, such as a permission to offer cars at reduced prices to any government department in any country that the Danish branch was exporting to. Some issues are specific, while others are very general, such as a mandate to lease property, establish bank accounts, cut or increase prices, etc.

One of the activities that had delayed Carlson in his response to the complaint from Detroit was the fact that he was deeply involved in setting up a Ford company in Germany. In late 1924, he had been sent to Berlin to investigate the possibilities there, with an authorisation from Edsel B. Ford to plan for investments up to 10 million Marks.[146] This was in the period after the banquet, but before the critical letter from Detroit. Even though the precise reaction to Carlson's answer is not known, it is clear that his bold defence and suggestions did not make him fall from grace: in early 1926, he was officially appointed administrating director of Ford Motor Company A/G in Berlin. Consequently, he resigned from his assignment in Copenhagen, which was taken over by H.C. Møller on 31 March that year.[147]

In an interview, given some 36 years later, Carlson does not mention this episode. But he does make a point of how he was able to act as a manager on his own, not following detailed instructions from

Detroit and being independent "in all the business".[148] Carlson's reminiscence could have been coloured by his considerable self-esteem. But the examples above—and even more so examples related to industrial relations at the Copenhagen plant, which shall be presented in the following—indicate that, even though Detroit tried to keep control, the Danish business and its management were not simply a puppet on a string.

Detroit wanted, and was able, to follow crucial developments, most notably the planning and construction of the new plant, in even minute detail. They were also willing and able to interfere in specific issues, such as collective bargaining with the unions, as described below. But at the same time, Carlson—and later H.C. Møller—would still have quite some leeway, even if informally, to act in accordance with what they, from a local point of view, thought was in the best interest of the business.

In the interest of the company

Henry Ford believed in individualism as a principle. This made him alien to organisations, not only of labour but also of employers. During his reign, Ford in America never joined the Automobile Manufacturers Association. And he even demonstratively staged his very own show of Ford cars at the Waldorf Hotel in New York each year, parallel to the show by the Manufacturers Association at the Madison Square Garden.[149]

In Denmark, Ford started out by following the same line: not taking part in any trade or employers' organisation but working to promote its economic and political interests on its own. The company had good experiences doing so since the time of its establishment. During his original reconnaissance trip, William Knudsen had focused on two potential places for establishing a new assembly plant in Northern Europe: Copenhagen, Denmark and Gothenburg, Sweden. Both were equally well placed from a geographical point of view, but as already noted above, Knudsen was able to play the Danish and Swedish authorities against each other, ending up with a favourable offer from Denmark, including tax reduction on imported parts and a smooth administration, with a public customs officer posted at the factory.[150] The deal was struck just before a meeting of the ministers of finance of the three Scandinavian countries in October 1919, which was aimed at finding a common policy regarding foreign investments and taxation.[151]

When Knudsen chose Falbe–Hansen as the company's attorney and had him elected to the first board of Ford Motor Company A/S in 1919, it was not least because of his many personal and political connections. Besides having represented the Royal Danish Automobile Club, (KDAK), as an attorney, he was well connected with other groups, which would be of interest to a car manufacturing company. First of all, he was on the board of several companies, including Falck rescue service, a pioneer in motorised firefighting. He was also on the leadership of the Board of Tourism and had been the initiator of the Danish Society for Nature Conservation, where he would mingle with those well-off members of local society to whom a car was the new leisure vehicle.[152]

Apart from a break of seven years during the mid-1920s, Falbe-Hansen would remain on the board until 1957 and become central in representing Ford Motor Company A/S in relation to politicians, authorities, and other business circles. His first job in this regard was in 1921, when rumours escalated in the press that import duty on car parts was to be increased substantially. Falbe-Hansen took up the matter directly and personally with the Ministry of Justice and was able to report back to the board that "we need have no fear of any adverse legislation in this respect".[153]

But Denmark was not America. As automobilism developed, it became apparent that some type of regulation was needed. In the beginning, such issues as putting up road signs were dealt with as a private initiative, by the Royal Danish Automobile Club, and the Federation of Danish Motorists, (FDM).[154] But soon, public authorities took over. And when it came to issues regarding the industry as such, they found it irrational to deal with one company at a time.

An illuminating example, even if of limited importance by itself, is that of the single rear light. According to Danish law, a car was required to have a rear light. In the early 20s, this was interpreted by the authorities as one, and only one light. Since all Ford cars were originally equipped with two rear lights, the practical effect was that one of these had to be removed. When H.C. Møller approached the Ministry of Justice about this matter on behalf of Ford, the rules were changed, allowing for two rear lights. But the Ministry also used the opportunity to encouraged Ford to join a trade organisation: "When we had to apply to the Government, the minister would say we can't do that for you alone, can you get an organisation to ask for it [...] I can send these regulations to the association for approval."[155]

An unsustainable model

From the start, the Danish plant had been a hugely successful investment for Ford Motor Company. During the first years of activity, profits were rising steeply—from 5.8 million DKK before tax in 1920 to a record high 13.8 million DKK in 1923. For the rest of the period, profits drifted up and down—but mostly down. In 1925 the accounts even ended in red, which happened only twice in the period 1919–1966. The 1925 deficit was of a technical nature, however. Both sales and revenues that year were actually better than the year before, but the balance sheets include an extraordinary disbursement of 8.7 million DKK for "exchange adjustments". In 1926–1927, profits were on the level of 1.0-1.2 million DKK—not a small amount, but well below the huge earnings of the early 1920s.[156]

Despite a profit amounting to an average of 5.4 million DKK per year in 1920–1927, very little dividend was paid. At the 1921 General Meeting, the majority shareholders, i.e. the Ford family, made a request that the profit of the previous year should be "placed in reserve for expansion and betterment". The same decision was made in 1922 and 1923.[157] Instead of sending the profit to the USA—and taxation—it was to be kept as investment capital in the Danish company.

On 5 November 1923, an extraordinary General Meeting of Ford Motor Company A/S was called for. It was held not in Copenhagen, but in Detroit, with Edsel Ford, president of the international Ford Motor Company, and Danish manager Georg Carlson as the only two board members attending in person. The other shareholders, including Henry Ford, were represented by proxy. The meeting had one principal decision to make: the share capital was increased from the original 500,000 DKK to 30 million DKK. This was made effective from 1 January 1924, in the form of a stock dividend paid for by the previously accumulated profit.[158] For a Danish company, this was an enormous sum of money. For comparison, it was three times the share capital of Burmeister & Wain shipyard, the largest industrial company in Denmark at the time.[159]

The transformation of the accumulated profit into share capital was done to prepare for the vast expansion planned, in the form of the new South Port plant. In the end, however, the total amount spent on the new plant was roughly 5 million DKK.[160] The net result was not only that Ford Motor Company's new state-of-the-art assembly plant in Copenhagen had been paid for completely out of the revenue of the preceding four years, but on top of that there was still a very substantial capital reserve left.

In 1925 a dividend was paid to the shareholders for the year of 1924. The dividend was set to 19 percent, equal to a total amount of 5.7 million DKK, and since Henry, Edsel, and Clara Ford were the owners of almost all the shares in Ford Motor Company A/S, the vast majority of this sum must have been transferred to Detroit.

This was the first and only time dividends were paid during this period, and nothing is mentioned in the minutes of the board about the reasons why. But given how the board was working around this time, the actual decision was most certainly made in Detroit, and passed on to the board as an imperative. In 1924–1925, the sales of the Model T were going downwards in the USA and the American Ford Company was aggressively lowering prices, in an attempt to fight back against competition. It is likely that Detroit needed funding for its domestic price war and found the time right to cash in on some of the profit earned in Denmark.

However, the declining profit of the Danish company from 1925 onwards was a sign that Ford's profit model was starting to experience problems in Denmark too. As mentioned above, Ford Motor Company A/S had used the same method as Ford in America to keep up sales of the aging Model T: by lowering the price.

To accomplish that, Ford in Denmark had been indirectly supported by Ford's effort to lower the US price, as this meant a continuous effort to bring down production cost, which was again reflected in lower prices on the parts and material that was imported from Detroit by Ford Motor Company A/S. Payment for these parts was settled in US dollars, and it was therefore an additional help in keeping down cost, when the exchange rate between US dollars and Danish kroner gradually dropped from around DKK 600 to the dollar in 1920–1921 to a much more favourable 375 in 1927.

By 1927, not all material for the Ford Model T was delivered from Detroit anymore. A limited number of parts came from Manchester, and some material, such as fabric for trimming, was bought locally from Danish suppliers, but the bulk was still American. All in all, the combined result of cost-cutting in Detroit and better exchange rates had contributed to the total cost of material for one Model T assembled in Copenhagen now being less than half of what it had been in 1921.[161]

But even this rather substantial reduction in material cost was not enough to keep up with the steep price drop. In January 1927 Ford Motor Company A/S had to deliver cars to its dealers at a price well below that which was calculated based on cost and a standard profit of 12 percent, in order to meet the desired price point to the end customer of DKK 2,275. The calculated profit of DKK 225 per car was thereby turned into a net loss of DKK 455: every car delivered to dealers in January 1927 was costing the company money.

Such cost-based price calculations could differ quite a lot during relatively short periods, and 1927 ended with positive revenue per car sold, after all. But it was the lowest since the start of manufacture. Calculations of the revenue per car sold for each year since 1919 display a very distinct decline, from over DKK 1,200 in the beginning to DKK 75 in 1927.

Such a decline in revenue for a product that made up more than 95 percent of the sales would be detrimental to the profit of any company in the long run. Nevertheless, it did not prompt any discussion about the matter by the board. At no time during the period 1924–1927 were the diminishing revenues on its agenda. But this is not very surprising, despite the importance of the issue. Firstly because, as

	May 1921			January 1927		
Detroit material & freight		2469			861	
Manchester material & freight					98	
Local material					231	
Total material cost			2469			1190
Duty		79			117	
Handling etc.		18			11	
Assembly expenses		332			417	
Assembly labour		83			136	
Total assembly cost			512			682
Commercial expenses			176			404
Profit calculated	15.0 %:		447	12.0 %:		225
Calculated sales price to dealer			3603			2500
Actual sales price to dealer			3603			1820
Loss						-680
Profit realised (calculated minus loss)			**447**			**-455**
Calculated sales price to customers			4367			2955
Actual sales price to customers			4825			2275

Table 2 Calculated sales price to dealers for Ford Model T Touring in Danish kroner, 1921 and 1927. These calculations represent the first and the last found for the Model T. Source: FMC: Balance sheets, appended calculations

already described above, the board was mostly a formal device, without much real work to do during this period. Secondly because, even if the board had turned its attention to the problem, there was not much it could have done about it.

The centre of the problem was Ford's profit model: offering one basic car, sold in large quantities at low prices. This model was becoming unsustainable in Denmark, as it had become unsustainable in America. But this was a problem which could be remedied only in Detroit.

Revenue per Car

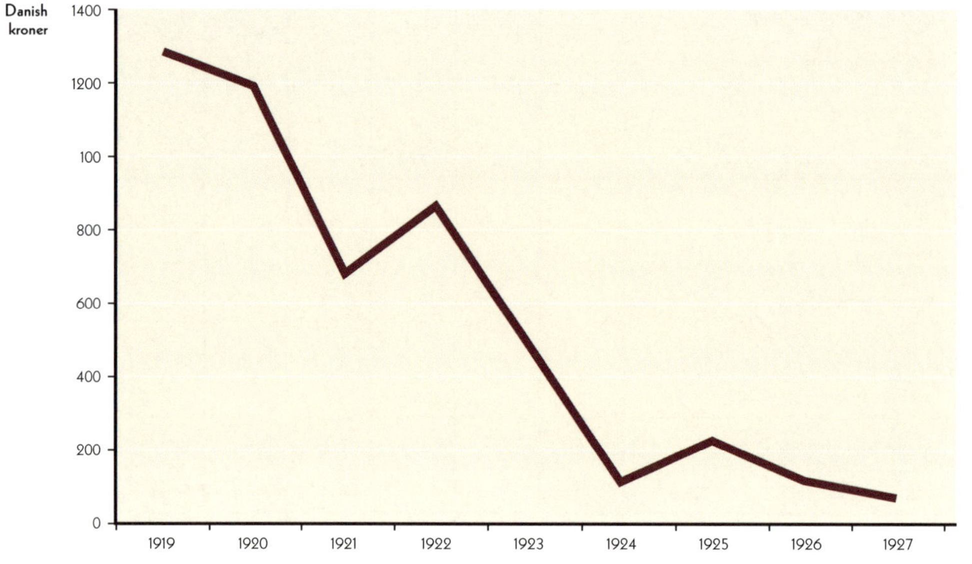

Figure 15 Revenue earned per car sold on average for each year 1919–1927.
Source: FMC: Balance sheets

INDUSTRIAL RELATIONS

Defying Henry's Plans

> We have no crafts in our industries, and although we are not opposed to unions, we have no dealings with them, because there is nothing that they can furnish to aid us in our management [...]. In Copenhagen, where we established a plant in 1919, we met for the first time a labour government which regulated hours, wages, and conditions of work, and practically made union regulations a part of the law of the land. We hired barbers, preachers, blacksmiths, plumbers, unskilled labourers, and whoever applied, and put them to work, side by side, on the machines—as has been our custom everywhere. [...] Our plant was put there to serve and does serve, but it could not have served had it been forced into an academic classification.[162]

These are Henry Ford's recollections of his company's first encounter with the Danish labour market, published in 1926 in his book *Today and Tomorrow*. It is, however, closer to imagination than to a description of real developments. It reflects how things were supposed to have happened, according to Henry Ford's ideals. And Ford might even have felt assured by the reports he received from his managers, that this was also what really happened; but it was not.

When Ford decided to start up production in Denmark, the product, the methods, and the technology could be transferred from Detroit. What could not immediately be transferred were the industrial relations that Ford had established in the USA. The Danish labour market was simply too different from Detroit's. Two issues would prove to be of special importance: the role of skill among workers and the strength of the labour movement.

The evolution of mass-producing industry in the USA had led to a "dilution of skill", exemplified by the fact that only nine percent of the workers in the American auto-industry were considered skilled in 1923.[163] In Denmark, industrialisation had eroded skill to a certain degree too, but to a much lesser extent. In 1925, two-thirds of all workers in Danish metal industries were still skilled craftsmen.[164] But the difference was not just about numbers; the reduction of the relative number of skilled workers in American industry correlated with a dilution of the very concept of skill.

While Ford, in his own words, had "no crafts in our industries", the concept of skill is nevertheless used in Fordist industrial relations. But it is in a quite different sense than how it was perceived in a labour market, in which traditional concepts of skill still played an important role, as in Denmark around 1919.

A major example is the list of different job categories that was used inside Ford Motor Company to establish the pay rate for each job. This list originated in Detroit, but a version of it was translated into Danish and became a centrepiece of industrial relations at the Danish Ford company, albeit in a different form and context, as we shall see. All the main functions that had to be performed when assembling cars are on the list, and for each function it was noted if it was considered skilled, semi-skilled, or unskilled, since each category was paid differently. For instance, gas tank assembly, fender building, and body painting were marked as skilled, while painting of other parts as well as loading and unloading were semi-skilled. Only a few functions, not directly related to assembly, such as cleaning and sweeping, were designated as unskilled.[165]

This, however, resonates poorly with the fact that Henry Ford, according to his own account, had managed to bring the number of skilled workers down to a very small number in Detroit—as low as five percent in some departments.[166] The simple explanation is that skill in this sense has nothing to do with that which had been acquired through an apprenticeship. Skill, in this specific sense, was something acquired at the job, regardless of formal background: as you became adept in assembling gas tanks, you became a skilled gas tank assembler. Skill, in the Fordist sense, was something acquired on the job, not something the worker brought to the job. On the contrary, an all-round training as a mechanic or engineer would be superfluous for mastering these specific tasks.

Opposite to that, the concept of being a skilled worker was quite well defined in Danish industry. It was a continuation of the tradition of craftsmanship, and a worker would have to go through 4–5 years of apprenticeship, including courses at a vocational school, and pass a formal test before he would become what was still sometimes called a journeyman, but in industry mostly referred to as craftsman or just simply "skilled".

Craftsmanship played a great role in industry, both formally and informally: formally, because most industrial workplaces were covered by union agreements that would specify which formal skills were required to perform which jobs; informally, because craftsmanship was an important part of the workplace culture of the skilled, male workers. It would emphasize values such as masculinity, self-esteem, and ingenuity, and it would lead to an expectation of being treated with a certain respect by foremen and managers in the workplace.[167]

The Danish model

Henry Ford had no dealings with labour unions in Detroit in 1919, mostly because they were practically non-existent until the emergence of the United Auto Workers during the 1930s. In contrast, 98 percent of the workers in the Danish metal industries were union members in 1919.[168]

Craftsmanship also came into play in relation to labour unions. Most of the important unions within industry had initially been formed by skilled workers according to trades, even if a union for unskilled workers had been established too. A worker without documentation of formal skills, in the form of an apprenticeship, would not be allowed into the relevant union, and would therefore also be prevented from taking on any job considered skilled.

Since unions were organised along trades, there would be several unions organising workers at any larger workplace, depending on the types of jobs and thereby the trades represented. This was also the case at Ford Motor Company A/S. No exact numbers for union membership have been recorded, but there is nothing to suggest that it was different from similar industries in Copenhagen at the time: close to 100 percent.[169] Based on the production process, as well as the general level of activity reflected in the sources, the Danish Metalworkers' Association (DSMF), and the unskilled Danish Workmen's Association (DAF) must have been those with the largest membership at the Copenhagen Ford plant.[170]

The Metalworkers' Association, one of the largest and most influential in the labour movement, was represented at Ford through its Copenhagen local branch no. 14: The Union of Automobile and Bicycle Mechanics. This local branch had only been established in August 1919 but experienced a rapid growth in the 1920s, from 460 members in 1919 to 1199 in 1927[171]. Relative to the unions of skilled workers, the unskilled Workmen's Association came from a weak starting point but grew considerably in the early decades of the 1900s and became a rival to the Metalworkers' Association as the most influential national union association. Like the DSMF, it had several branches in Copenhagen and was represented at Ford through its local Union of Workmen in the Metal Industries.

The Painters' Association in Denmark and the Scandinavian Upholsterers' Association were both smaller than the two aforementioned on the national level.[172] But at times they played an important role at Ford. The Painters, represented through its Copenhagen branch the Coach Painters' Union, because painting was in the middle of some of the tensions created by new production technologies. The Upholsterers, because its local branch, the Union of Upholsterers, had a politically more militant leadership than the others.

Finally, there were the Joiners' Association, represented through its local Union of Joiners and Chair-makers, and the Plumbers' Association, represented through its local Plumbers' Union of 1873. These two unions were either less active or smaller in membership than the others at Ford.

The above-mentioned names of the unions are the official ones. Colloquially speaking, unions were often just named by the trade of their members, for example the metal workers' union or the workmen's union, instead of the more cumbersome Union of Automobile and Bicycle Mechanics or Union of Workmen in the Metal Industries.

While the local union branch was the nucleus of union activity, each branch normally spanned a number of workplaces, and therefore union clubs were often formed at each workplace. Union clubs also existed at the Copenhagen Ford plant, but with changing levels of activity, the most enduring being those of the metalworkers and the workmen. Often all the union clubs at a workplace would form a combined club, which would be where any matters of interest to the workers in general would be discussed and decided upon. A combined union club was first formed at Ford Motor Company A/S in 1924.[173]

Workers would also elect local shop stewards, typically one for each union represented. At Ford Motor Company A/S, the shop stewards elected a so-called leading shop steward amongst themselves. The leading shop steward, who would for most of the time also carry the title of chairman of the combined union club, would be the "first among equals" and the principal spokesperson of the workers vis-à-vis the management.

Contrary to Detroit, where the absence of labour unions logically also meant the absence of any form of collective bargaining about wages and working conditions, collective bargaining had been the established basis of industrial relations in Denmark since 1899. In that year, a general agreement had been reached between the Danish Confederation of Trade Unions (DSF), representing practically all union associations, and the national Confederation of Danish Employers (DA). The agreement stipulated that the workers had the right to organize and to bargain collectively. Each association would negotiate its own national and local agreements, typically every second or third year. In return, unions agreed to confine strikes to situations where an agreement was either not in place or had expired, and a new one could not be reached by negotiation. For the employers, the primary benefit of signing an agreement would be that it would contribute to peace and predictability in the workplace.[174]

To solve disputes arising from the implementation or interpretation of an agreement, a system of arbitration was established on different levels, including a Permanent Board of Arbitration. The board had equal representation from unions and employers under a neutral chairman.

Thus, the leading principle of what would later become known as the Danish model for industrial relations was that not only wages but also most of the conditions of work in general, such as working hours, right to representation, etc. would be regulated through bargaining directly between strong unions and organised employers, as opposed to, for instance, through legislation.[175]

While this was generally regarded as beneficial by both unions and employers, the flip side was of course that recognition of unions and collective bargaining was only compulsory for those companies that were members of the Confederation of Danish Employers. That was mainly an issue in rural areas, while in the larger cities most employers either were members of the confederation or, at least, chose to obey the relevant national agreements. Only very few did not, and one of them was Ford Motor Company A/S.

In other words: it was not "the law of the land" in a judicial sense, but rather the presence of strong labour unions and the established practice and institutions of the labour market, that constituted the major challenges to Fordist industrial relations in Copenhagen. But of course, the political and parliamentary situation was not without significance. The great majority of unions, at Ford Motor Company A/S and elsewhere, were ideologically oriented towards and closely allied with the Social Democratic Party, which rose to political power during the 1920s. As the labour movement grew politically stronger, it would use the parliament to fill the gaps in industrial relations not already covered by collective bargaining. One such gap was the right to paid vacation, which was introduced by law in 1938. Probably just as importantly, though, the feeling of having a government that was sympathetic towards the unions and their cause gave a general morale boost to organised labour.

While the labour movement was generally oriented towards social democracy, syndicalism gained a foothold for a short period around 1919, leading to a split among social democrats and the forming of what would become the Communist Party. During the 1920s and 1930s, the communists were a small but active minority in the labour movement. In relation to Ford, only the upholsterers' union was under communist leadership for a while during these years. During the post-war period, the Communist Party attracted a wider following, as detailed later.[176] But generally, the whole period 1919–1966 was characterised not only by a hegemony for social democracy within the labour movement, but also, as already mentioned, by the social democrats being in government for most of the time.

The American plan

Not only did the Danish model represent a challenge for Ford Motor Company A/S and the transfer of Fordist industrial relations—the opposite was also the case.

Whether or not any barbers and preachers actually were assembling cars for Ford is unknown, but it is true that those initially employed were a diverse group, hired rather indiscriminately in regard to formal training.[177] Only in one aspect were the blue-collar Ford workers very homogenous: they were all men. In Detroit, some women were employed in production, for instance in the upholstering shop.[178] In principle, this could have been the case in Copenhagen too as female industrial workers were not uncommon, even though mostly in areas other than the metal industries.[179] Yet the photos from the upholstery shop in Heimdalsgade show only men. A group photo of management and white-collar workers, taken outside the office in Heimdalsgade in 1920, displays 20 people, of whom just two are women.[180] We can safely assume, then, that the blue-collars workers were exclusively male and the white-collars predominantly so as well.

As Ford began hiring, the unions also had to consider their positions. The majority of the first group of workers hired were unskilled, and therefore were or became members of the Union of Workmen in the Metal Industries. And while a few of the workers might have been craftsmen, the workmen's union found that the jobs they were doing could rightly be considered unskilled. Consequently, they made an effort to gather all the workers in Heimdalsgade under their wings, beginning in October 1919.[181]

As the number of employees expanded, the initially small number of craftsmen working at Ford expanded too—especially skilled machinists, but also upholsterers, painters, and others. Soon the unions traditionally organising such crafts started demanding that certain job functions should be considered skilled—not only in a Ford sense, but in a Danish sense, meaning that they should be reserved for their members. The metalworkers Union of Automobile and Bicycle Mechanics demanded that the job of testing the engines as well as all positions along the assembly line should be manned by skilled mechanics. The Union of Upholsterers demanded that all new jobs becoming available at the upholstery shop should be reserved for their members.

In January 1920, the metal workers succeed in convincing the management that some unskilled workers on the assembly line should be replaced by skilled machinists, being members of that union. This enraged the workmen's union, which interpreted this move from the management as a stand in favour of the craftsmen.[182]

Meetings were held between the unions, at which proposals for an agreement were exchanged, but no compromise was reached. On 10 February, the metalworkers Union of Automobile and Bicycle Mechanics as well as the Union of Upholsterers declared a strike, with the purpose of having their right to specific jobs formally recognised by management. The workmen's union, on the other hand, issued a statement that its members would be free to take over any job in the factory, as long as there was no agreement between the unions, and threatened to set up a blockade of the factory if the management accepted the demands put forward by the metalworkers' union.[183]

The management was baffled by these developments. There was no relevant experience from Detroit on how to handle such a situation. At first, the company announced that which union organised which workers was of no concern to them. Consequently, the unions would have to work out an agreement among themselves.[184] But this position soon became unsustainable, as the quarrels among the workforce became a threat to continued production.

The production manager then tried to negotiate directly with different groups of workers on the shop floor, to find a pragmatic solution. But he soon found himself in a minefield, where giving in to one group could provoke the anger of another. When the strike broke out, management was practically sidelined, as the unions negotiated between themselves.

Finally, negotiations led to an understanding between the workmen's union and the metalworkers' union. In a signed statement, they agreed that the assembly of rear axles as well as work at the first part of the assembly line, up to the point of mounting bodies and fenders, were to be considered skilled jobs and reserved for members of the metalworkers' Union of Automobile and Bicycle Mechanics.[185] The workmen, on the other hand, were free to take up positions at the final part of the line, as well as in other parts of the assembly.

The upholsterers, for their part, could not come to terms with the workmen, and continued their strike. Finally, the management lost its patience, and on 12 March 1920 all workers were given an ultimatum either to return to work or to consider themselves fired. Effective from 17 March, a wage scheme, based on the Detroit principles of job classifications mentioned above, was presented by management.[186] As the upholsterers were promised a status quo on the ratio of jobs between them and the workmen, they reluctantly went back to work.[187] As a result of these events, there were now two different and partly inconsistent classifications based on skill at play in Heimdalsgade. The one agreed upon among the labour unions, based on traditional Danish concepts of trade and craftmanship, and the Detroit plan, reflecting official management policy.

The management came under further pressure to stick to the Fordist plan, as news of the situation in Copenhagen reached Detroit. In June 1920, a conference was held there, assembling all managers of Ford's assembly plants—domestic as well as those few that had been established outside the USA. Ford Motor Company A/S was represented by J.J. Harrington. Among other issues, labour relations at the Danish Ford Company were on the agenda. A section of the concluding memorandum, under the headline "Copenhagen", reads:

> Will continue running as at present, but in case of labor troubles, they should be met strictly on our American Plan regardless of whether the Plant keeps operating or not.[188]

Of course, Detroit could and would not let the workers at its Copenhagen plant draw up their own classifications of skilled and unskilled work, reserving certain jobs for members of certain unions only. That would go directly against the Fordist principle of putting workers "to work, side by side, on the machines", regardless of formal skills.

But while the Danish management undoubtedly had to follow such direct orders from Detroit, they also had another major concern: to keep production running. Having experienced first-hand the willingness of the Danish unions to defend what they saw as their customary rights, J.J. Harrington and his successor had a much better understanding of the need to find a compromise than the top management in Detroit.

Given the readiness already displayed by both unions and rank-and-file workers to go to conflict over these issues, a strict implementation of the American plan would most certainly have led to renewed tension. But little if any conflict related to the distribution of jobs between skilled and unskilled is registered in the following years. In principle, this could be because the workers simply succumbed to the American plan, without further resistance. But that is most unlikely, not just because of their initial resistance, but also because they showed a continued readiness to fight against attempts by management to replace skilled workers with unskilled, as the issue became hot again at a later point in time.

The relative peace can only be explained by pragmatism from the local management: implementing the American plan in principle, but at the same time tacitly respecting the demarcation lines between skilled and unskilled jobs, drawn up by the workers themselves. In that case, the only practical result for the workers of implementing the American plan would be that most of them would fall into the highest wage class. The unions therefore had no reason for further conflict. Even so, Fordist industrial relations had been contested and made subject to transformation right from the inauguration of the Danish plant

Transferring the 6-dollar day

When Henry Ford had introduced the 5-dollar day in Detroit in 1914, it gave him a reputation for paying high wages that reached far beyond the borders of the USA.[189] Right from the start, there was an expectation among Copenhagen workers that there would be good money to be earned at the Ford plant. Shortly after the opening in Heimdalsgade, the newspaper *Politiken* referred to a rumour that Ford had "bought" almost every tailor in the country by offering them "princely" wages; a rumour that the paper was happy to falsify.[190] But wages paid at Ford Motor Company A/S were actually, if not exactly "princely", then at least more than decent compared to the average. Knudsen started out by paying DKK 2 per hour in October 1919, including DKK 0.40 in "profit-sharing". For comparison, a machinist in Copenhagen would be paid DKK 1.66 an hour on average in 1919, and an unskilled worker in the metal industries DKK 1.25.[191]

The wages paid from early 1920 were even higher. There would be a hiring-in wage for all groups of DKK 17.60 per day for 30 days. After that, daily wages for unskilled workers would be DKK 22.40. Semi-skilled workers would have a minimum of DKK 22.40 with the possibility of rising to DKK 24.00, while skilled workers would earn DKK 24.00 rising to DKK 25.20.[192]

These wages were a result of Ford's determination to follow a standard wage policy in all its subsidiaries, even across national borders. Shortly after the 5-dollar day had been introduced in Detroit, efforts had been made to transfer it into equivalent wages in Ford Motor Company's Canadian and English assembly plants.[193] It is therefore no surprise that the same effort was made in Copenhagen, with the only difference being that the pay rate in Detroit had now been raised to six dollars per day. What is surprising, though, is the way it was done.

In a notice to the workers dated 17 March 1920, the wages scheme is presented in print for the first time. It is introduced with a text stating that it had been

> ... decided and determined that, from that same date, payment will be made according to the same wage scale that is now used in the American factories, as it will be translated into Danish Kroner, calculated at par value.[194]

Par value usually refers to a situation when currencies are exchanged according to their gold value. However, like several other countries, Denmark had detached its currency from the gold standard in 1914. In 1920, exchange rates were determined by market value, and therefore no par value as such existed.[195]

Backward calculation from DKK to US dollars of the wages stipulated in 1920 nevertheless reveals that they must have been based on the early 1914 exchange rate, just before the time when the gold value was abandoned. Because if this rate is used, the Danish minimum wage of DKK 22.40 per day will equal US $ 6, which was the minimum wage in Detroit at the time. In the same manner, backwards calculations of the wages stipulated two years later, in the 1922 agreement, result in amounts almost exactly equal to what was paid in Detroit that same year, as minimum as well as maximum, when the 1914 exchange rate based on gold standard is used.[196] It is a true conundrum as to why Ford Motor Company A/S insisted on using a six-year-old, obsolete exchange rate, based on the gold standard.

Could it be a reflection of Henry Ford's personal views on economy? According to Ford, production of "real" things was positive, while wealth obtained only by interest rates and capital investments was negative. Consequently, he looked with disdain on the world of banking and finance. It would be tempting to see the use of an exchange rate based on the gold standard, instead of an intangible and potentially speculative market rate, in this light. But while not totally unsubstantiated, this interpretation is weakened by the fact, that during the same period, Ford was using actual market rates when calculating sales prices of the Model T.

A more plausible explanation would be that it is a reflection on Fordist thinking about the nature of wages. It was the duty of any enterprise, Henry Ford argued, to pay wages that represented a "fair" remuneration of the workers' contribution to production.

Whether or not this was the case, the end result was at least one that would fit in with the intentions from Detroit. Transferring the American pay rates using the actual exchange rates of the day would have resulted in excessively high wages, 30–40 percent above the actual ones. By using the seemingly arbitrary selection of exchange rate, the result would be more modest, but nevertheless in line with Ford's stated principle of high wages.

When evaluating the wages paid at Ford Motor Company A/S, the working hours should of course be considered. Ford had transferred its 8-hour working day from Detroit to Denmark. But due to a successful struggle by Danish unions around 1918–1919, the 8-hour day had become standard in Danish industry around the same time.[197] There was, however, a difference when it came to the number of working days. During the first few months of production, it was Monday to Saturday at Ford, leading to a 48-hour work week, just as in the rest of Danish industry. At some point in the spring of 1920, however, Saturday was turned into a half day, meaning that the work week at Ford was now 44 hours. This was unchanged until sometime between 1928 and 1930, when the work week was reduced further to 40 hours, which could be placed by management on any days from Monday to Saturday.[198]

Taking differences in weekly working hours into account, wages at Ford Motor Company A/S were still significantly above what could be expected at any other workplace. Furthermore, these wages were earned working 4 to 8 fewer hours per week than normal.

When comparing wages at Ford Motor Company A/S with other workplaces, it should be remembered that work hours at Ford tend-

	Ford Motor Company A/S		Copenhagen metal industry
	Minimum	Maximum	Average on piecework
Unskilled	122	146	66
Semi-skilled	122	156	n/a
Skilled	122	166	84

Table 3 Weekly wages in Danish kroner, as stipulated in the agreement at Ford Motor Company A/S, compared to the average wages paid in the metal industry in Copenhagen, 1922. Calculated from daily or hourly wages, based on a 44-hour working week at Ford and 48 hours in other industries. Sources: KB: Overenskomst, October 1922, *Statistisk Aarbog*, 1923

ed to fluctuate significantly during the year. This was a reflection of the seasonal shifts in demands for cars, which was considered a normal and unavoidable feature of the auto industry. Workers could be fired and rehired more than once during a year, sometimes with a day's notice or less. Unfortunately, there are no exact figures available for the number of work hours for each year of the period.

At the end of the 1920s, a standard work year at the Copenhagen Ford plant was around 200 days, which was only roughly two-thirds of the possible maximum of around 295 days in other industries.[199] So while a Ford worker would be able to make up to roughly 100 percent more than in other Copenhagen industries on a weekly basis, the wage premium compared to a full year of occupation at another employer would possibly have been closer to around 50 percent—which, of course, is still very noticeable.[200]

That made the relationship between Ford wages and wages paid in similar industries roughly the same in Denmark as it had been in Detroit when the 5-dollar day had originally been introduced there. In that respect, using the "par value" exchange rate actually made sense. But as described above, when the 5-dollar day was introduced in early 1914, America was at the beginning of a period of severe inflation. This meant of course that the real value of $5 was undercut, and even though the Detroit minimum wage was raised to $6 in 1919, that would still amount to only $3.36 at the value of the dollar in 1914.[201]

As the $6 minimum wage was transferred to Denmark in 1919–1920, the context was completely the opposite. Inflation had been high during the years of war in Europe, but from 1920 the situation was reversed. Despite fluctuations, consumer prices were generally decreasing, so that in 1930 they were at a level less than two-thirds of that in 1920.[202] While prices dropped, the nominal wages were at the same time raised a bit at Ford Motor Company A/S throughout the 1920s: the minimum daily wage from DKK 17.60 in 1920 to DKK 18.75 in 1930, and the maximum from DKK 25.20 to DKK 28.70 during the same period.[203] Taking deflation into account, the net result was a substantial increase in real income for Ford workers in Copenhagen during the 1920s. Even the communist newspaper *Arbejderbladet* wrote in 1928 that whatever else was wrong with Ford Motor Company A/S, at least they were paying high wages.[204]

The way that wage classes and levels were implemented in Denmark is also telling: in March 1920, not only were the American classification of jobs and wages meticulously copied from Detroit, so was the principle of calculating the total payment as a combination of wage and bonus. This was, however, more a nod to Fordist ideology than a "profit sharing" in the real sense, as the amount was settled and made part of the regular paycheck long before anything could be known about the real profits made that year.[205]

Surprisingly, since the Copenhagen management had gone through so much trouble to align the Danish wages with Detroit principles, only a few weeks after the introduction of the wage scheme it was adjusted, based on local negotiations between unions and management. The resulting change in wages was not very significant in itself, but the process testifies that there was actually some leeway for decisions by the Copenhagen management, despite the explicit intention of following the American model.[206]

As already mentioned, when changes were made in 1922, wage levels were again closely matched to Detroit, still using the 1914 exchange rate. The new wage scheme also copied the American model in the sense that the bonus system was now done away with, in favour of a general readjustment of wages, just as in Detroit. The unskilled workers were given the ability to rise above the minimum wages, just as the other two groups—the difference being, that the maximum was higher for semi-skilled and skilled. And wage rises were now dependent primarily on seniority, and not so much on individual merit. Any worker leaving the company on his own initiative would, if later rehired, have to start again from the lowest wage level.

At the beginning of the 1920s, so-called investment certificates were introduced by the American Ford company. These certificates were popular among workers in the USA and some overseas Ford companies, with 80 percent or more of workers buying them at some factories.[207] Such certificates were also offered to the employees at the Copenhagen plant from March 1920. But they were much less popular among the Danish workers than they were in Detroit. Despite repeated appraisal of the investment certificates by the local management, less than one-third of the employees in Copenhagen—blue- as well as white-collar—had bought one or more certificates in 1924.[208]

One reason why the certificates were not as popular in Denmark as elsewhere might be the existing system of unemployment insurance. Following the substantial layoffs at Ford in Detroit in 1921, many workers saw investment in the certificates as a way of saving up for periods of unemployment. However, even though unemployment certainly was an issue in Denmark too, there was already a system of unemployment insurance funds, administered by unions, paid into by its members and subsidised by the state.

Another likely reason was that unions in Denmark were critical in general towards employer-administrated saving schemes, which to them were reminiscent of earlier times, when paternalistic factory owners had used such schemes to tie workers to their companies and avoid unionisation. When a similar system was established by General Motors in Copenhagen in 1928, it was denounced by the unions.[209] There are no signs, though, that the unions at Ford denounced the saving certificates in principle, but they did not seem to have endorsed them either.

Unions and collective bargaining

Shortly after the opening of Ford's very first European assembly plant in Manchester in 1911, Henry Ford took a personal initiative to stifle union influence, by sending over his most loyal trouble-shooter at that time, Charles Sorensen. Sorensen employed a tactic of divide and rule, by offering benefits to selected workers while getting rid of those who had union sympathies, and shortly after he could proudly declare that "the unionism which has always been cropping up heretofore has been absolutely broken up".[210]

Historians seem to have taken for granted that the British experience also applies to the rest of Europe. For instance, Wilkins and Hill wrote in their pioneering work on Ford's international expansion, *American Business Abroad*, that

> Although workers in Europe were demanding unionization, all employees there in Model T assembly plants were strictly denied the right to negotiate with Ford management.[211]

Furthermore, they mention Denmark as an example, as they refer specifically to the memo from the managers' conference in June 1920, quoted above. In Wilkins and Hill's interpretation, the words "American plan" in the memo should be understood as synonymous with "Open shop", e.g. the politics of refusing to recognise unions and collective bargaining that was prevailing among American employers in the aftermath of World War I. This could be a feasible interpretation, as "American plan" was in fact sometimes used in the USA instead of the more widely used "Open shop".[212] But as we have seen above it cannot be correct. The "American plan" in this context must be taken literally, as the plan for categorising jobs, workers, and wages.

The management of the Ford Company in Copenhagen did not take any steps to counteract the unions as such. On the contrary: while trying to enforce the "American plan", they were at the same time negotiating with the unions, and thereby *de facto* recognising them. A formal recognition came in December 1920, when the Ford management wrote to the metalworkers' union, accepting their elected shop steward as legitimate representative of the workers.[213]

In fact, the Copenhagen management did not only accept the presence of unions; they went one step further and agreed to formal collective bargaining. The first agreement between unions and management over terms of work and payment at Ford Motor Company A/S was reached in October 1922.[214] In certain aspects it was in continuation of the 1920 wage scheme, as the first paragraph stated that the agreement was "based on Detroit regulations".[215] Just as in this scheme, the three categories "Skilled", "Semi-skilled", and "Unskilled" workers were laid out, with the job types assigned to them.

The most interesting points of the agreements were of course those that differed from Detroit practice. For instance, it was agreed that overtime as well as work on late shifts should be paid extra. For overtime, 30 percent extra was paid for the first two hours, 50 percent for the third hour, and 100 percent for subsequent hours. While this reflected what was considered normal by Danish standards, such extra payments were rarely made in Detroit, and certainly not of this magnitude.[216]

Moreover, the company agreed to recognize the elected shop stewards as the workers' legitimate representatives, and the right of union officials to take part in negotiations over "issues of disagreement". But most important from the point of view of the workers was the formal recognition of their unions and of collective bargaining, as manifested in a written agreement resulting from the negotiations. This would have been completely unimaginable in Detroit in 1922. Collective bargaining and the existence of an agreement did not mean, however, that conflicts between labour and management ceased to occur.

Battle of the beer and other disagreements

The early 1920s were a period of much unrest in the labour market in Denmark. The Confederation of Danish Employers[217] pursued a rather aggressive tactic in their attempts to roll back some of the advances that labour had made in the previous years, such as the eight-hour working day and improved wages. In both 1921 and 1922, the employers demanded substantial wage reductions in connection with renewal of several national agreements, and as the unions refused, a nationwide lockout was declared. In 1925 there was a combination of lockout and nationwide strikes in many trades, including docks and transport.[218]

Since Ford Motor Company A/S was not a member of the employers' confederation, they did not take part in the lockouts, and neither the company nor the workers were directly affected by these rather dramatic conflicts—apart from a small episode related to the dockworkers' strike in 1925.[219] But Ford and their workers had their own disagreements, many of which can be ascribed to attempts to implement "Detroit principles".

Some of these disagreements seem minor in relation to the larger issues at stake in the rest of the labour market, but to the workers at Ford they were important enough, partly because they had a symbolic meaning reaching far beyond the specific issues. This was especially the case in the 'battle of the beer'.

On 31 December 1924, management introduced a regulation banning smoking as well as consumption of beer and other alcohol for any employee on the premises of the company. In the regulation it was stated that this was "in strict compliance with the principles of Ford Motor Company, such as they are enforced all over the world".[220] According to manager George Carlson, such a ban had been requested by Detroit, since auditors visiting Copenhagen had seen beer bottles present at the plant.[221] This was during the years of prohibition in the USA, and Henry Ford himself was known to be in favour of temperance. In Denmark, on the contrary, it was an established custom that workers could have a beer with their lunch.

Furthermore, workshop regulations had been an issue for unions since the 1890s, when they first started to effectively question the employers' right to dictate such regulations as they saw fit. In particular, the Danish Metalworkers' Association, had been actively and successfully fighting to make matters regarding work and the workplace a subject for negotiation between unions and employers—the quest for so-called "parliamentarism in the workplace". In 1903 the Association of Employers in Metal Industries and the Metalworkers' Association jointly agreed upon a set of "Common Workshop Rules", which was meant to be adopted as a standard throughout the industry.[222] In other words: the management's unilateral ban on alcohol did not go against only the workers' customary rights, but also their understanding of proper union-management relations. As one of the workers explained when interviewed by a newspaper: "...it is a matter of principles, pure and simple. We will not be ordered into living under prohibition. That's all."[223]

As the unions realised they could not persuade the management to withdraw the ban, they turned to the established procedures for handling grievances, and took the question before the Permanent

Board of Arbitration. At the preliminary meeting of the Board, the plaintiffs were represented by no fewer than 10 people, including the vice-chairman of the Danish Confederation of Trade Unions, senior representatives of five national union associations as well as two shop stewards from Ford. On the other side of the table sat the deputy manager of Ford Motor Company A/S, H.C. Møller, as well as the production manager and the company lawyer V. Falbe-Hansen.

The Board of Arbitration finally ruled that the regulation was in violation of the principles of the agreement between the unions and Ford, insofar as it had been unilaterally declared by management without negotiation. The management then suggested a compromise, in which serving and drinking of beer would still be allowed in the canteen but forbidden elsewhere at the factory—but on the condition that such a compromise could be accepted in Detroit. Consequently Edsel B. Ford, as president of Ford Motor Company, got involved. He was quite dismissive and unable to relate to the demands from these impertinent workers in Copenhagen. Nevertheless, a compromise was finally reached, according to which no beer or other alcohol would be sold in the factory canteen, but workers could each bring one beer for their own lunch.[224]

Another source of dispute was the numbered badge that every Ford worker was obliged to wear visibly on their work clothes. During the height of Ford's social programmes, thousands of workers in Detroit—most of them unskilled, many of them immigrants who barely understood English—had not only found a job, but also received vocational training, attended language courses, etc. at Ford Motor Company. As a result, many identified themselves so much with the company, that they were even seen wearing their Ford work badges on their Sunday dress.[225] When the badges were introduced in Denmark, the reception was markedly different.

In July 1925 management decreed that, on request from Detroit, it would be compulsory for all workers to wear a visible badge with a number. Not only had Ford's original social programmes in Detroit long vanished by that time, they had never been introduced in Denmark. To the Danish Ford workers, the badge was therefore not associated with anything positive. Instead, the obligation to wear a number was considered dehumanising and humiliating. At a union meeting, the badges were denounced as "slave signs", and it was decided to refuse to wear them.[226] Instead, workers would carry badges in their pockets with a number, which they would use as deposits when picking up hand tools at the tool cribs. Management accepted that but maintained that if a worker's individual badge was lost or his tools not returned to the tool crib in a proper state, a fine had to be paid.

This led to the next disagreement. It started in October 1925, when a union meeting decided to protest against the way that the management administered the fines for not treating tools properly, by collectively withdrawing the contracts each worker had been made to sign about responsibility for and return of tools. But the company refused to recognize such a collective withdrawal of individual signatures. A period of prolonged negotiation followed during the next months, involving most of the unions and several meetings.

During the negotiations, the management made the concession that any worker who could give an immediate and satisfactory explanation for losing a tool would not be fined, but that fines had to be paid in all other cases. In June 1926, after more than eight months of meetings and discussions, the unions informed Ford Motor Company that they still opposed the fines in principle, but since there was no prospect of reaching another solution through continued negotiations, they would accept the position of the management for the time being.[227]

On a general level, these disagreements are examples of a clash between a Danish workplace culture and a Fordist approach. This was also how it was interpreted by *Jærn- og Metalarbejderen*, journal of the Metalworkers' Association, in 1928. Looking back on the experiences with Ford Motor Company as a workplace since 1919, the journal acknowledged the high wages being paid, but at the same time noted what were from its point of view the negative aspects of the "Ford system": the increased pace of work and—with reference to the examples given above—the grievances arising from

> 'House Rules' and 'Regulations', contrived by some bright heads in Detroit and supposed to be implemented all over the world, no matter if it was white, black, yellow, or brown people who worked for the mighty man, everything had to be standardised.[228]

Reflecting common stereotypes of its time, the journal also found it appropriate to remind Ford that "the Danish worker is independent and skilled at his work and should not be treated as a Hottentot or a savage Negro".

None of these disagreements led to open conflict in the form of a strike. There were, however, a few strikes during this period, related to other issues. The first, of course, was the aforementioned strike in February 1920, caused by unskilled workers performing jobs that the skilled workers felt belonged to them. Two other short strikes, lasting one or two days each, concerned workers being dismissed or disciplined. The first, in December 1920, was a protest against a worker being fired "and other disagreements". The nature of these "disagreements" is unknown, but work was quickly resumed, as management acknowledged most of the workers' demands.[229] The other one, in February 1925, was caused by a painter being given 14 days' suspension from work by a foreman, after accidentally spilling paint on a newly painted car body.[230]

A fourth episode took place in late May or early June 1925, during the nationwide dock and transport workers' strike. Even though Ford was not formally part of the conflict, some of the workers at the company had stopped the unloading of parts for the factory from a Ford ship, as it was considered work affected by the ongoing national strike.[231] And finally, there was the aforementioned strike in June 1926 by the painters, against the heat and foul air in the paint shop.[232]

Craftsmen versus workmen

The outcome of the conflicts between craftsmen and workmen at Ford Motor Company A/S in 1920 had been a fragile equilibrium. The scarcity of conflicts in the following years can be attributed to the pragmatism of the local management. But the increase in the overall number of jobs also dampened the competition among the workers.

In Danish industry in general, disputes between groups of skilled and unskilled workers were not an unknown phenomenon in these years. The issues were not just about who had the right to certain jobs, but also about the much more intangible questions of mutual respect and recognition.[233] In order to cope with these potential conflicts, and in an attempt to resolve them inside the framework of the union movement, a so-called Committee on Boundary Disputes, *Udvalget for Grænsestridigheder,* was established by the Danish Confederation of Trade Unions in 1911. The committee was supposed to mediate between two or more unions in case they both claimed the right to certain jobs for their own members exclusively.[234]

The Fordist production process, however, represented a more radical challenge to Danish industrial workers in this regard than what could be experienced in most other workplaces. There are no sources as to the precise ratio between formally skilled and unskilled workers at Ford in Copenhagen, but the existence and relative strength of several unions for skilled workers is an indication that quite a large proportion of the workers at Ford—probably more than half—were craftsmen of some sort: machinists, painters, upholsterers, etc. In other words: "deskilling" was far from the level seen in Detroit.

As we have seen, the unions worked together in negotiating a common agreement with the Company in 1922. Their cooperation was further formalised when the combined union club was finally established in October 1924.[235] Nevertheless, the tensions were still there; in late 1924, the chairman of the unskilled workers complained that some of his members had been "driven back" by the skilled workers.[236]

Relations between skilled and unskilled workers were especially tense in relation to painting. A major reason for this was the changes in methods of painting that took place during this period. In the early stages of the auto-industry, painting of car bodies had been done by hand, more or less in the same way as horse-drawn coaches had been painted. Coach painting was a highly skilled job, carried out by craftsmen. As Ford established its production in Copenhagen, changes to the painting process had already been introduced, to eliminate the bottleneck in production it had turned into.

Methods such as dipping parts in paint by machine or flow-painting had already partly undermined the need for traditional skills. But the radical change came at the end of this period, around 1927–1928, with the introduction of a whole new type of cellulose-based spray paint. Since the effects of this technology were most notable from 1928 onwards, we shall just make a note of it here though and return to it in the next chronological period.

Despite changing technologies, the skilled members of the Coach Painters' Union tried eagerly to hold onto any type of job in the paint workshops. The management would honour that to some degree but, especially during the late 1920s, they came under pressure: as the number of auto assembly plants in Copenhagen grew, the number of workers needed for the various paint-shops became too large to be recruited from the rather small group of skilled coach painters alone. Even the union had to reluctantly admit this, and accept unskilled workers doing paint jobs.

In January 1926, the issue was raised at a general assembly of the Coach Painters' Union, as the shop steward from Ford suggested the possibility of forcing unskilled workers at the paint shop to join the Union. This prompted a lengthy discussion in which the chairman warned against such a move, since not only did unskilled workers do paint jobs at Ford, but the opposite was also the case: members of the painters' union doing workmen's job, in periods with no painting jobs. The issue was raised again during 1926, without a conclusion being reached.[237]

In April 1927, the situation escalated, as unskilled workers, joiners, and office clerks were assigned to work at the paint shop. The Coach Painters' Union demanded their removal, in favour of some of their own unemployed members. But management refused, according to the Union protocol with a remark about some of these skilled painters being "utterly useless". In the face of this scorn, the painters reacted immediately by declaring a strike.[238]

At first the strike was not recognised by the other unions, and therefore not only the workmen, but also the metalworkers and joiners took up work in the paint shop. But very soon the situation was reversed: a joint meeting for all skilled workers—but without the unskilled—decided to support the painters in their claim, and not take up any work at the paint-shop as long as the strike was in effect. The unskilled workers, in contrast, maintained that the strike was illegal, since it had not been called for properly through the unions, and that it was an illegitimate attempt by the craftsmen to "monopolise" work in the paint shop. After a few days of strike, the painters went back to work without getting their demands fulfilled.[239]

At the general assembly of the workmen's union, held in late April, the conflict with the skilled workers at Ford was the dominating issue. The general feeling among the workmen was that the craftsmen sought to keep for themselves jobs that could just as easily be done by unskilled workers. The meeting adopted a resolution, stating that the workmen "by all means appropriate" would fight against "any attempts [...] to reduce the possibility of jobs created by the specialised ways of production being offered to the unskilled worker".[240]

The craftsmen, on the other hand, responded by isolating the unskilled workers from their joint meetings, and the disagreements reached a climax at a meeting of the Combined Union Club in May. The chairman of the club, who was a member of the unskilled workers' union, was not re-elected, which prompted the workmen to withdraw, and the Combined Club thereby to cease to exist.[241] Relations among craftsmen and workmen were at breaking point. But soon they would have a new, common issue to worry about.

The agreement is terminated

Clearly, there were disagreements and conflicts between workers and management, and among the workers themselves, in this period. But in the larger perspective of Fordism vs. Danish labour market traditions, one could argue that, in these years, the Ford workers in Copenhagen managed to achieve the best of both worlds: from Detroit they got the high wages associated with Fordism, and from Denmark they got collective bargaining, with all the advantages following from that. And it all happened in a period of rising employment. In this sense, the early 1920s were the golden years for the workers at Ford Motor Company A/S; but the golden years were coming to an end.

Despite any conflicts on the shop floor, the output of the factory was steadily increasing during the early 1920s. But this was only possible due to widespread use of overtime, which has already been noted above. This of course accentuated the issue of overtime payment. It was not just an economic issue; paying extra for overtime went against Henry Ford's overall principle of deploying the workforce in whatever way the management saw fit. As overtime became widespread, the management therefore made a first attempt in 1922 to lower the rates for overtime payment, but the unions successfully resisted.[242]

Overtime payment was nevertheless to become a recurring issue. In 1926 the management terminated the 1922 agreement, with the explicit intent of having the extra payment for overtime and working in shifts removed, or at least reduced. The subsequent bargaining resulted in a new agreement, where the extra payment was maintained but with a small reduction.[243]

Sometime during early 1927, the Copenhagen management received an order from Detroit to cancel the agreement once and for all. According to H.C. Møller's reminiscence, the order came from Charles Sorensen. Why the order was given at that time is not known, though a remark from the management made during later negotiations offers a clue: according to the protocol of the workmen's union, they had been told that Ford

> … would have no agreements with unions, as long as it was not compulsory by the law of the country, otherwise wages and work conditions should be set according to the orders that came from Detroit.[244]

"The law of the country" might be a reference to Germany, where the laws of the Weimar republic made it compulsory for any larger company to establish a *Betriebsrat* (Works Council), in which workers were given a consultative status. Apparently, it came as some surprise to Ford Motor Company that they were required to have formal worker representation, and the company fought hard against this but ultimately had to give in to German law.[245] Charles Sorensen played a key role in the quarrels with the Germans. Sorensen's way of dealing with things is illuminated by a postcard, once sent to him by an Italian business associate. The card featured a picture of Mussolini, and a handwritten note: "M is to Italy what you are to the Ford Motor Company."[246] And in fact, not only did Sorensen have a certain physical similarity with the Italian *duce*, but he was also known to be acting like a short-tempered dictator in his treatment of practically anybody who did not immediately bow to his will.[247] It is therefore not unlikely that the German defeat had prompted Sorensen to find an outlet for his rage, by at least making sure that things were running according to Detroit principles at other foreign plants, such as Copenhagen.

Whatever the reason for the order, we know for certain that the Copenhagen management was not thrilled; in the later words of Møller the cancellation of the agreement was "perfectly silly"[248]. Møller tried to appeal directly to Edsel Ford to have the decision recalled. In a handwritten document called "Notes on the labor situation", he presents the situation as seen from Copenhagen. The document is not dated, but judged from its content, it was written sometime in the first half of 1927, most likely as Møller's preparation for his talk with Edsel Ford.[249]

In the notes, Møller starts by establishing some basic facts about the labour market in Denmark, such as practically all industrial workers being members of a labour union. The agreement, he writes, had been in effect for 4–5 years, and if it were recalled by management by 1 March 1927 (which date must have been set from Detroit), it would surely provoke a strike.

As an alternative, Møller proposes a long-term strategy: the agreement should not be cancelled before September 1927. The reason for Møller's proposal of September is of course that the plant was planned to be closed down anyway at that time, for the retooling needed to go from Model T to Model A production. He also suggested giving the impression that there would be no significant change in pay and other conditions, even if there was no longer a formal agreement. Later, when things had settled down, the payments for working in shifts and overtime could then gradually be done away with. Edsel Ford maintained that the agreement had to be cancelled, but must have been convinced by Møller's plan, since this was more or less what happened afterwards.[250]

On 28 September 1927, the unions received notice from Ford that the company considered the agreement terminated, effective from 1 November.[251] At first, the unions reacted as if this were an invitation for negotiation, but Ford made it clear that no new agreement could be made, "since it is required that certain principles inside our organisation should be enforced". Nevertheless, Ford was willing to meet the unions for talks for "further review" of the situation.[252]

During these talks it was made clear to the unions that the Danish management was acting on orders from Detroit. Soon the national union associations were involved, but no real progress was made during the following months—a period when most workers were temporarily dismissed as planned. Finally, the local unions made a request to the Danish Confederation of Trade Unions, to bring the case to the Permanent Board of Arbitration. But the DSF was reluctant and suggested further talks. Even though Ford Motor Company A/S had previously agreed to follow a ruling from the Board of Arbitration, they were not forced to do so from a strictly legal point, since they were not a member of the Confederation of Danish Employers (DA). This was probably why the DSF hesitated: having a ruling even in their favour that they would not be able to enforce afterwards would be a loss of prestige.[253]

In July 1928, when normal production was resumed and workers rehired, they were each individually handed a new set of work regulations. Like the previous agreement, this was based on Detroit regulations. But the important modifications toward Danish practice found in the agreement had been omitted: there would be no more extra pay for overtime or working in shifts. There was no recognition of shop stewards; instead, workers were obliged to take any grievances to the management on an individual basis. Furthermore, the regulations contained a large number of detailed obligations and prohibitions, which the workers had to accept and observe.[254]

But what was principally most important from the point of view of labour was, of course, that the regulation as a whole was in disregard of the practice of collective bargaining. But the unions were still unable to come up with a clear and united response. During the autumn of 1928, the issue was discussed intensely by each of the unions at Ford, often at several meetings. The possibility of a strike was raised, but there was fear that it would be difficult to prevent strike-breaking. The chairman of the metalworkers' union was against "closing the plant, since our own members out there are definitely not in favour of a strike, mainly because of the high wages".[255]

What made most unions decide against a strike in the end was the old issue of craftsmen versus workmen. At a general meeting of the upholsterers' union, the claim was made that ...

> … the reason why there is no longer an agreement, and why a new one could not be obtained, is that there is an awfully bad relationship between the skilled and the unskilled worker. One might fear that the workmen would take over the jobs of the skilled workers, if they went on strike.[256]

At a similar meeting of the metalworkers, the shop steward from Ford took the floor and declared that the situation at the plant was "skewed, since the unskilled workers were acting against the others in all possible ways".[257] Likewise, a potential strike discussed by the workmen was dismissed due to a fear that skilled workers would utilize the situation to take over the jobs of unskilled workers.[258]

At a meeting on 8 November for all workers at Ford, the vast majority decided to accept the new work regulations for the time being. The only exception was the upholsterers: despite concerns about lack of support from other workers, the board of the Union of Upholsterers declared a strike from 15 November.[259] Contrary to the social democratic orientation of the other unions, the upholsterers had a communist leadership. Consequently, the conflict was immediately inscribed in the overall conflict between social democrats and communists. The strike was condemned by the chairman of the DSF as a "dictatorship of the minority" and received no mention at all in *Social-Demokraten*, the dominant newspaper of the labour movement.[260]

On the other hand, the upholsterers were strongly supported by the communist paper *Arbejderbladet,* with an emphasis on the main principles involved in the conflict:

> It may well be that Ford is tempting [the workers] with wages that are not usual in this country, but that should not decide the matter. The crucial point is that the right to codetermination that the unions have achieved through a generation of struggle has been taken from them with the stroke of a pen.[261]

Despite such appeals, the upholsterers were isolated and even their own members at Ford were reluctant in following the union leadership. Consequently, after twelve days the strike was called off. From now on, there would be no formal agreement between the unions and the Ford Motor Company in Copenhagen.

In the Eye of the Public

> The ship heads straight into harbor
> at shadowy dusk.
> Her megaphone bellows salute to the city,
> the electric searchlights
> level their five-splintered beams
> up in the air like a comet's tail
> and scrawl in firescript on the clouds:
> BUY A FORD[262]

These lines are from 'The Show Boat', first published in Danish in 1922 by the young Danish poet, Otto Gelsted. In a stark, sarcastic mix of expressionism and the language of commercial advertising, the poem depicts capitalism and consumerism as a showboat coming to town, possibly from America. The story ends dramatically, in an act of poetic terrorism: a man described as "an ordinary blond Danish student" pushes a button and blows up the whole ship.

'The Show Boat' speaks in a strong, literary voice, and is still considered an important example of Danish modernist poetry. However, back in its own time its scepticism towards Ford and Americanism was largely overpowered by other voices.

In November 1919, a few weeks after the assembly line had turned out the first car, a journalist from the newspaper *Politiken* turned up at the new Ford plant in Heimdalsgade. The result of the visit was an article under the headline "America in Copenhagen". The new plant, the paper informed its readers, might be modest compared to Ford's facilities in Detroit, but nevertheless worthy of attention, since the American principles of production were now put to use in Copenhagen for the first time. A picture of one day's production of Ford Model T's lined up outside the factory adorned the article.[263]

A few days later, *Social-Demokraten*, another major newspaper, made a report from Heimdalsgade. Actually, there was a new article in *Politiken* the same day, and there was a certain resemblance between the reports, which suggests that the two papers had been invited to the same press tour. Both papers expressed admiration for the new plant: *Social-Demokraten* noticed the use of USA-made specialised machinery that "carries out the work at exceptional speed and with great ease, in a fraction of the time needed at other places", while *Politiken* foresaw that both employers and workers in Denmark would learn a lot from these novel methods of production. But while *Social-Demokraten* was mainly interested in the plant as a workplace, *Politiken* saw it as a potential provider for its readers too—as the headline read: "This is where our Christmas car is assembled".[264]

Also among professionals, the assembly plant was an object of interest: in March 1920, the Danish Society of Engineers arranged a members' tour of the facilities. The visiting engineers were duly impressed—especially by the assembly line, a technology so new that it had not even been given a Danish name yet but was referred to by the English word "conveyor".[265]

From silence to war

When Gelsted chose Ford as his prominent symbol of consumerism and Americanism, he must have been prompted by a general awareness of the brand and the company, not the specific marketing done by the Danish Ford Company, since Ford Motor Company A/S did next to no print advertising in the first few years of its existence.

In early 1917, it had been decided in Detroit that Ford as a company would no longer do any advertising. From now on, this would be done only by the dealers, at their own initiative and expense. This advertising-free period lasted until 1923, when competition had become so intense, that Ford found it necessary to start actively promoting its products again.[266]

Was this policy of no company advertising imposed on the Danish company too, for the years 1919–1922? A look at the magazine *Motor*, published by the Federation of Danish Motorists and being the main auto-magazine of the time, would initially confirm that it was. From early 1920, the magazine contains a relatively large number of Ford ads, but only from dealers. The most and the largest are from F. Bülow, the main dealer of the time, but even ads from dealers in small and larger provincial towns such as Herning, Aalborg, and Elsinore can be found—up to about 20 in one issue of the magazine, including those in the classified section. But not a single advertisement appears from Ford Motor Company A/S itself before early 1924.[267]

However, looking at newspaper advertising, the picture gets more complex. *Politiken* was the daily newspaper with the largest circulation in the 1920s. Moreover, it was a proponent of modernity and modern lifestyle. In 1902, the newspaper had asked its readers to come up with a useful word for the new phenomenon hitherto known as the horseless carriage. This was how the Danish word for car—"bil", as short for "automobil"—was invented. It was also in the pages of *Politiken* that motor-journalism was pioneered by Alfred Nervø, an enthusiast of everything connected with high speed, who wrote for *Politiken* from 1905.[268] Nervø died in 1921, but *Politiken* continued its positive interest in these issues. Finally, as a small but revealing detail, the paper offered insurance against traffic accidents as a free supplement for subscriptions during the 1920s.[269] *Politiken*'s readership at the time can be roughly characterised as the modern middle class, and it was a preferred medium for advertising for car manufacturers and distributors of all kinds.

It is, however, not easy to establish when the first advertisement from Ford Motor Company A/S appeared in the pages of *Politiken.* The first one published explicitly in the name of the company is found in early 1925.[270] But as early as 1921 we find a small handful of ads, which might or might not have been published by the Company. They all carry the word "Ford" as a headline, featuring drawings of one or several cars and feature a list of dealers, either in Copenhagen or in the entire Zealand area, in small print at the bottom. All in all, they look similar to later ads, signed by the company. A typical example can be seen in Figure 10 on p. 68. It could be that these ads had been initiated and paid for by the dealers in common, despite the fact that the dealers were not exactly known for their ability to cooperate in this period.[271] But it is just as likely that these ads were a circumvention of Detroit's no-ads policy by the Danish management. Looking into the company accounts only adds to the confusion: no advertising expenses can be seen for 1919–1921, but in 1922, when Ford USA was still not doing any advertising, the Danish company recorded having spent DKK 29,234 for that purpose.[272]

Advertisment 1919–1928

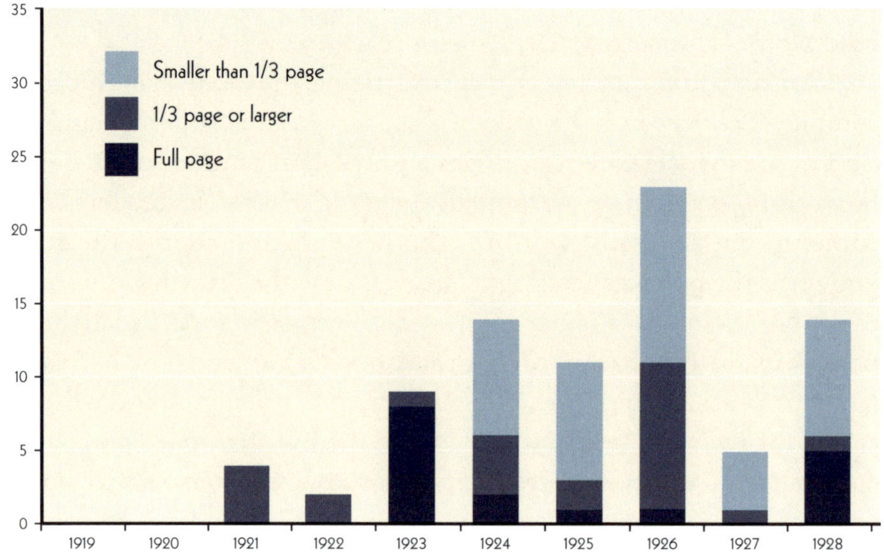

Figure 16 Number of newspaper ads by Ford Motor Company in *Politiken*, 1919–1928. See text below for selection criteria. Source: Online archive at www.politiken.dk

On one hand, the fact that Ford Motor Company A/S, even being newly founded and therefore in need of publicity, did not do any advertising on its own in at least two years from its opening, confirms that Copenhagen was under the no-ads policy dictated from Detroit. On the other hand, the Danish company slowly started advertising at least one or maybe even two years before the policy was lifted. Apparently, the Danish management did what they did on several other issues: followed Detroit policies in principle, but surreptitiously circumvented them when they felt a need to do so.

Company records also reveal that, from 1922 onwards, expenditures for advertising rose very rapidly, reaching a first peak at DKK 448,420 in 1926. For comparison, this roughly equals one-tenth of the amount paid in wages that year.[273] We may gain insight into the volume and character of the Danish Ford company's advertising by looking at the number and character of ads featured in *Politiken*. The number of ads and their distribution on full page, medium size, and smaller sizes through the 1920s can be seen in Figure 16.

Note that ads from 1921–1924 are included. Despite the dubious origin of the 1921–1922 ads, based on the content it should be safe to assume that, at least from 1923, the ads counted here are Company ads. From 1925, only ads specifically signed Ford Motor Company A/S are counted.

As can be seen, the company intensified its advertising greatly in 1923, with no less than 8 full-page ads in *Politiken*. The number further increased in 1924, albeit diversified over a greater variety of sizes. This was also the year the first ad from the company appeared in *Motor* as noted above. Why did the company suddenly become so interested in advertising in the mid-1920s?

The most obvious answer is competition. In September 1923, the company Hans Lystrup became general agent of the Chevrolet brand in Denmark, General Motors' competitor to the Ford Model T.[274] In Denmark, it was still significantly more expensive than a Ford, but at the same time also a much more modern car.[275] Lystrup immediately started advertising their new brand, with one ad per month on average in *Politiken*—more than the number of Ford ads.

The competition from GM became much fiercer in 1924, when the company established its first European assembly plant in Copenhagen, with Chevrolet as its main product. Following this, General Motors shifted its marketing into an even higher gear: in the second half of 1924 alone, it had 22 ads in *Politiken*, of which by far the majority were for the Chevrolet brand. This was supplemented by a handful of dealer ads, mainly from the former Ford dealer F. Bülow & Co. who had become a highly active promoter of GM. Ford tried to follow suit, but on a more modest level with a total of 14 ads for the whole of 1924.

In the USA, the competition between Ford and GM had set off an advertising war between the two brands, which was now also reflected in Denmark. It reached a temporary climax in 1926 with more than 60 ads from GM in *Politiken*, compared to a more modest 23 ads from Ford.[276] In 1927, the number of Ford ads declined rapidly, which is no surprise as there were very few products to sell, due to the closing down of Model T assembly. The French company Citroën, which had likewise established an assembly plant in Copenhagen in 1924 and which could be considered Ford's main European competitor, also took part in the dogfight, but with a little less intensity.

Compared to other ads, those from the car companies were significant not only in number, but also in their size and overall appearance. They are an early example of an advertising war between multinational brands, fought on the pages of a Danish newspaper.[277]

Danish and down to earth

In 1907, Ford in Detroit hired a new sales manager, by the name of Norval Hawkins. Summing up his philosophy in a later book, Hawkins wrote: "The salesman does not really sell goods. He sells ideas about goods."[278] Commonplace today, this was a new and advanced way of thinking about advertising at the beginning of the 20th century. Until he left the company in 1919, Hawkins would create advertising for Ford that would not only describe the cars produced, but tell a story of the comfort and pleasure that owning one would bring into your life. Neither did the company shy away from more or less discreet hints to how owning a car would add to a young man's attractiveness vis-à-vis the opposite sex.[279] However, at the same time, there were ads that pointed to the automobile as an instrument for the independent and liberated female. An American sales brochure titled *The Woman and the Ford* concluded in 1916: "The car is a real weapon in the changing order."[280]

Compared to Ford's American advertising, the ads we find in *Politiken* and other Danish print media in the early 1920s are remarkably simple. As typified by Figure 10 above, they would typically consist of a straightforward drawing of one or more cars in profile and information about prices and dealers—as if the simple fact that the Ford Model T was available for purchase was enough. In the later '20s, the ads became more graphically appealing, often with more elaborate drawings of cars or trucks in a specific setting, and longer textual appraisals. But still, the arguments used were mainly centred on the economy of buying and driving a Ford Model T, and its alleged sturdiness and reliability. Only in two or three ads out of the 68 published in *Politiken* in this period can the spirit of Norval Hawkins be felt in a presentation of the Ford Model T as a vehicle for an upper-middle-class lifestyle.[281]

Figure 17 The style and specific type of border of this advertisement, with small vignettes, was also used in France and maybe elsewhere in Europe. But in the Danish versions the vignettes always show national sights, in this case the Gefion Fountain, the Town Hall tower and the Glyptotek, all in Copenhagen. *Politiken*, 14 September 1926

In Denmark, Ford Motor Company A/S became a client of the advertising bureau Sylvester Hvid & Co.. In the early 1920s, this was the first and, so far, the only full-service advertising bureau in Denmark. The company made ads and campaigns for Ford not only in Denmark, but also for some of its export markets. It even worked for General Motors too for a while.[282]

The cooperation with Sylvester Hvid shows that at least some of Ford's Danish advertising was produced locally. That does not exclude the possibility that others had been copied from American sources. But while it is impossible to establish the definite origin of every ad, several leads seem to suggest that the majority, if not all, were either devised in Denmark or at least heavily adapted for a Danish context. Text and illustrations were sometimes decisively Danish, and for most of the rest at least European in style.[283]

Only in one instance is there a resemblance across borders: in a period around 1925–1926, a number of Danish ads were based on a common template, which included a frame with small vignettes enclosed in an elaborate framework of leaves, reminiscent of art nouveau.[284] The same type of border and style of advertisement was used at least in France and maybe in other European markets. However, a closer inspection reveals a telling difference: in the Danish ads using this frame, the vignettes are showing well-known Copenhagen sights such as the Town Hall, the main railway station, or characteristic church towers.[285] If these particular Danish ads were inspired by the French or vice-versa, or if they both were inspired by a third, maybe American source, they were at least adapted to the national context.

In fact, national themes and illustrations were commonplace in Ford's marketing. In the newspaper ads, the Model T was occasionally shown in front of landmarks such as the Gefion fountain or a runestone. The fact that the Ford cars were American in origin was very seldom mentioned in advertising, and if it was, mostly in a casual or indirect way.

Events and presence

On an otherwise lazy Sunday afternoon in the summer of 1924, a cheering crowd gathered on the central square of the small provincial town of Nykøbing Falster. The occasion was the return of a local family, who had left the town two weeks earlier for a grand tour around Denmark in a Ford Model T.

At least this is the story we are told in the booklet *En Tur gennem Danmark med Ford* (A Trip through Denmark with Ford), published by Ford Motor Company.[286] The head of the family is presented as a local veterinarian by the name Bramsen, and the anonymous narrator as his old friend. The "marvellous trip" of the Bramsen family is told through 12 illustrated pages, and ends with the friend heading straight to the nearest Ford dealer to buy his own Model T. Despite being presented as a personal recollection, with all its lively details, the story of the trip around Denmark is fiction.[287] But in reality, Ford did put quite a lot of effort into arranging tours and events of different kinds and used them skilfully to get publicity.

The first time a procession of Ford cars was driven through the streets of Copenhagen was in January 1924, to mark the opening of a joint exhibition by Copenhagen Ford dealers. In September that same year, a procession of trucks was arranged. In April 1925, 50 Model T's were driven from the South Harbour to the central Town Hall Square in Copenhagen, where a crowd of 3–4,000 people had assembled, and there was quite a commotion. The event was referenced in major newspapers, including *Social-Demokraten* and *Politiken,* the latter under the headline "Ford sensation yesterday". But the most extensive tour was that in November 1926: to celebrate the production of car no. 100,000 assembled in Denmark, a procession of Ford cars was driven throughout the whole country, visiting dealers in most provincial towns of any importance.[288]

Another popular type of event was the exhibitions. The one in January 1924, arranged in cooperation with the Copenhagen dealers, has already been mentioned above.[289] This first exhibition was very favourably received by the public and attracted more than 20,000 visitors.[290] Two years later, the Association of Automobile and Bicycle Wholesale Dealers erected a large exhibition hall called *Forum* in Copenhagen, to house the first international car exhibition in Denmark. In contrast to the USA, where Ford made their own exhibitions alongside, but separate from, those of the Automobile Manufacturers Association,[291] Ford in Denmark took part in this joint exhibition. And as *Forum* became a place for recurrent national and international car exhibitions, Ford would usually appear prominently.[292]

Events and exhibitions were of course not limited to Denmark. Similar activities took place in different export markets. For example, during 1926 alone, there was a car race in Sweden, an automobile show in Poznań, Poland, and a parade of Ford cars through Helsinki.[293]

An event of a slightly different type was the grand opening of the new South Port plant. It took place on 15 November 1924, a sunny autumn day, and it was a celebrity event. *Social-Demokraten,* the major newspaper of the labour movement, wrote:

> A breath of air from the USA was clearly felt in the South Port yesterday morning when the solemn inauguration of the Ford factory was about to take place. Long rows of automobiles rolled up along the factory [...] there was no doubt that this was a distinguished event [...] the huge, bright, and airy factory was the object of exclusive admiration, due to its dexterity and practical setup.[294]

The social-liberal newspaper *Politiken* was impressed by the factory too, calling it "a model for any modern factory". The event was attended by a large number of Ford dealers from Norway, Sweden, Finland, the Baltic States, Germany, and of course Denmark. Among the guests were also several representatives of industry and finance, government officials, and members of parliament—including Thorvald Stauning, newly elected social democratic Prime Minister.[295]

The official opening ceremony took place in the central assembly hall. Here, all machines were at rest, while hundreds of men stood ready at their posts. Jens Jensen, chairman of the Copenhagen city council and former president of the Danish Confederation of Trade Unions, stepped up on a platform and declared his hope that the plant would be to the pleasure and benefit of the nation and for anyone working in it. Then he pushed a button:

> ... and a bell resounded through the room. In the exact same second all the sounds of the factory came to life, and all the wheels began to sing. Pneumatic hammers started to bang, the cranes whistled, and the one-hundred-meter-long belt that brings the cars from work team to work team was slowly moving forward.[296]

As the first car left the assembly line, it was driven away by the oldest remaining Ford dealer in Scandinavia, A.M. Gjestvang from Oslo, while the crowd shouted hurrahs. Later in the evening, a festive banquet was held in the *Tivoli* gardens. Prime Minister Stauning delivered a speech at the banquet, promising in the name of Denmark to take good care of this new "foster child", for the benefit of the country and its workers.[297]

The South Port plant was also used actively in marketing. It was frequently depicted or mentioned in advertising; a notable example is a full-page ad in *Politiken* on 1 October 1924, depicting a drawing of the new, not yet officially opened assembly plant seen from above, surrounded by drawings of different versions of the Model T and crowned by a portrait of Henry Ford. The text details the accomplishments of Ford in Denmark, such as the numbers of cars produced and exported, and states that "this is the most modern factory in Scandinavia".[298] From the start, the factory was open for visitor groups: they could be received three times a day, and an employee was permanently appointed as guide. The visitors were celebrities and royalties, members of engineering associations, technical students, and ordinary members of the public. Public interest was huge during the first period after the opening, were there would be up to 1,800 visitors per month. But the visitor program existed throughout the lifetime of the factory and was later expanded to include primary school classes.[299]

Apart from the cars roaming the streets, the South Port plant was by far the most spectacular symbol of the physical presence of Ford in Denmark. But there were also the dealers, spread across the country. Many of these had been general repair shops, bicycle dealers, etc.

Sylvester Hvid 48.

before becoming car dealers, and were still housed in very modest buildings. As the dealers were independent contractors, Ford Motor Company A/S had little formal say over the appearance of the dealers' facilities. But the company tried to exert an influence, for instance by giving praise to especially well designed and modern dealerships.[300] As for decoration, the company offered illuminated signs with the Ford logo in different sizes as standard equipment from late 1924. In addition, as part of a "Service Campaign" in 1928, Ford asked its dealers to keep their workshops tidy and suggested that they had their mechanics wear clean and uniform clothes—which could be bought from Ford—so that "customers visiting the shop will get a good impression and become faithful that they will receive the best service".[301]

The politics of Fordism

In the USA, it was almost impossible to distinguish between Ford as a car brand and the attitudes and ideas of Henry Ford as a person. For part of the 1920s, even the formally independent dealers were obliged to help spread the political ideas of Henry Ford, as distributors of his weekly newspaper *The Dearborn Independent*. In Denmark, Ford Motor Company A/S did not make much effort to associate itself with the person Henry Ford in its general marketing. His picture was sometimes used in advertising, but quite rarely. There was one medium, though, in which the Company made an effort to present the wider ideology of Fordism: its own company magazine.

The first issue of *Ford Nyheder* (Ford News) appeared in August 1924. According to managing director Georg Carlson, Ford in Denmark had now reached a point in its development where the publication of a magazine like those circulated in the American, Canadian, and English companies had become relevant.[302] The magazine was primarily for internal use: according to its masthead, it was published for the staff and workers of the company.

Figure 18 Poster for the 1924 Ford exhibition. The graphic artist, Sven Brasch, was well known by the time, not least for his posters for cinema. The woman might have been inspired by a movie star. With her dress, short hair, and slender body, she brings more than a touch of glamour to the much less colourful Ford T. Photo: Pernille Klemp / Design Museum Denmark

Following this first issue, the magazine would appear monthly, with 4 pages in black and white, quite modern in its layout and well-illustrated for its time. True to its objective, it did not contain advertising or any other direct marketing, but it did indirectly provide an insight into the marketing activities of the Company, through numerous small reports of activities such as car parades, shows, and races. Ford cars used for special purposes, such as for taxis in Berlin or fire-fighting in Riga for example, were other popular subjects.[303] Overall, the magazine provides a picture of many lively activities by either the company or its dealers for promoting the product.

But part of the magazine was also dedicated to the thoughts and ideas of Henry Ford. From the very first issue, there was a dedicated column on page two containing a quote from Ford or a passage from one of his books. In form and partly in content, these columns were derived directly from the American *Ford News* magazine.

The Danish company magazine also carried repeated invitations to become a subscriber of *The Dearborn Independent*, which was presented as a magazine "inspired by and devoted to the acknowledged progressive ideas that characterise all Ford companies", offering "an abundance of informative content, but absolutely no propaganda". The last claim in particular was hardly in line with the truth.[304] Subscriptions were offered by the marketing department of Ford Motor Company A/S, which may be seen as a local variation of the obligation imposed on the dealers in the USA to distribute the magazine.

It is not known if this resulted in any subscriptions to *The Dearborn Independent*, but there must have been few at best, since the magazine went almost unnoticed in Danish public debate. Undoubtedly, the Copenhagen management must have realised that the chances of soliciting subscribers to an English-language magazine of this character among the employees of the Danish company were very slim.

Both the endorsements of *The Dearborn Independent* and the repeated appearance of Ford himself may be a fulfilment of an obligation to make the Danes acquainted with the broader views and visions of Henry Ford—whether it was by request from Detroit or on the local management's own initiative. However, the impact was limited by the modest readership of *Ford Nyheder*. It was a smaller piece in the larger puzzle, which was Fordism in Danish public debate, and which was fostered mainly by other means, independently from Ford Motor Company A/S.

Henry Ford's views on industry and society were met with some, if sometimes sceptical, interest in Danish public debate. His anti-Semitic viewpoints, which featured prominently in *The Dearborn Independent,* seem to have gone largely unnoticed in Denmark.[305] What attracted somewhat more attention were his arguments for promoting growth through mass production and consumption. They were treated rather cursorily by economists,[306] but the reception of his books indicates that there was a certain public interest.

The three books that were ghost-written by Samuel Crowther but published under the name of Henry Ford were all made available to the Danish audience through a commercial publishing house with no known ties to Ford Motor Company A/S, economic or otherwise. The first one, *My Life and Work*, appeared in Danish in 1923, within a few months of its publication in the United States. It became quite a success, published in three editions and a total of 7,000 copies.[307] It was followed by Danish versions of *Today and Tomorrow* in 1926 and *Moving Forward* in 1932, but contrary to the first book, these were only published in one edition each.[308]

As far as this decrease in editions may be interpreted as a fading interest in Ford's ideas, this was reflected in *Ford Nyheder* too: at the end of the 1920s, Henry Ford was featured less intensively in the company magazine. Meanwhile, however, Ford's argument that industry had to create its own consumers had made an impression on at least one important figure in Danish politics. In his speech to the congress of the Social Democratic Party in 1927, party chairman Thorvald Stauning was criticising those leaders of industry who wanted to counter recession and unemployment by lowering wages. Industry had to lower its costs by rationalising production, and to keep up wages to ensure demand for its products, Stauning argued. And to underpin his point, he made a reference to Henry Ford, whom he quoted as stating that "the unemployed man is a customer who has been put out of the game".[309]

The English were desirable Lords

H.C. Møller, managing director

1928–1940
Time for Change

PRODUCTION

Volume and Diversity

On 17 July 1928, a fundamentally new Ford car rolled of the assembly line in Copenhagen for the first time since production had begun almost 9 years earlier. It was the Model A, which was now finally replacing the aging Model T.

The change from Model T to Model A had been an almost nightmarish experience for Ford in Detroit. Henry Ford's stubbornness and unwillingness to abandon the Model T had had the result that, when the green light for developing a new model was finally given, it took place in a feverish and haphazard way, in which important changes to the construction were introduced alongside with the production of the first cars. But more importantly: the volume strategy which had proved its worth in making the Model T such a success initially now turned out to be a major constraint on new developments. Reconfiguring and retooling of the highly specialised production apparatus had taken months, during which not a single car could be produced.

Towards diversity

The changeover from Model T to Model A was a wake-up call for Ford. Whether it was due to better planning or more flexible production technologies, subsequent model changes were executed without such radical breaks in production. This was the case in Copenhagen too. During the change from Model T to Model A manufacturing in 1927–1928, production at the South Port plant was halted for eleven months.[1] Most of the time was used for re-tooling the factory but other factors, such as lack of parts from Detroit, may have contribut-

Figure 19 Two cars being assembled in sequence. Differences in appearance, such as a split rear window and a more rounded curvature of the rear part of the body of the car in front compared to the one behind, reveal that they are two different models. The one in the front is a Model V8 ca. 1939, while the one in the back is hard to identify from the photo. Unknown photographer. Ford Motor Company / Nordfoto / Ritzau Scanpix

ed as well. Later model changes—such as the introduction of the Model B and Model V8 in 1932—caused nowhere near the same disruption, and production was either not discontinued, or only stopped for such a short time that it went practically unnoticed.

Furthermore, during the 1930s the Copenhagen factory learned how to produce not just one single model at a time, but different models in parallel. This was made necessary by the considerable broadening of the product portfolio of Ford Motor Company A/S. In a photograph from the late 1930s, titled "Finished Cars leaving the Factory", three different models in a row are seen driving out of the assembly hall. This might have been staged for the photo, but on another photo from the actual assembly hall, we see two different models on the line at the same time.[2] This is consistent with the general change towards a productive model combining volume with more diversity, which Ford Motor Company undertook in this period as a response to the "Sloanism" of General Motors.[3]

The orientation towards diversity was based on several changes in the production technology. One of them was in body construction; the original Model T bodies were made up of sheets of steel, attached to a wooden frame. While some other manufacturers, such as Chevrolet and Dodge, had started using all-steel bodies from as early as 1915, Ford was reluctant to go in that direction. Nevertheless, all-steel bodies had advantages not only for the final product, but also in production; for example, the wood in the bodies made drying of paint at high temperatures impossible. Consequently, Ford gradually lowered the wood content, until the Model T touring bodies effectively became all-steel in 1925.[4]

Perhaps as early as 1925, but at least from the introduction of the Model A in 1928, body assembly was now done by welding: the parts were placed in a large jig and welded together by electric spot-welding.[5] At that time, welding was not a completely new technology in Danish industry, as it had been used for special purposes, mainly in shipyards and boilermakers. But electric welding in particular—as opposed to acetylene gas welding—was still a relative novelty in other industries.[6] It was nevertheless put to widespread use at Ford, where at least 36 electric welding machines were installed during the 1930s.[7]

While earlier body assembly, apart from the use of pneumatic tools, had resembled traditional methods known from coach building, welding was a completely different work-process, requiring different skills. According to one contemporary observer, one of the benefits of arc welding was that this "is not an art [and] the training of an electrical welder takes only a short while".[8]

Colour is back

The most eye-catching change in car-making technology in the late 1920s was related to painting. Broadly speaking, the early age of mass production led to a decrease in colours of consumer products, due to the need for standardisation and the lack of suitable paint technologies. One observer of this development claims to have found that, in 1917, 95 percent of all fountain pens available in America were black and 88 percent of blankets were white.[9] As we have seen above, Ford was no exception to this general trend, as Ford Model T's from at least early 1915 onwards were available only in black.

From the early 1920s, however, the chemical industry introduced new dyes, paints, and pigments suitable for use in mass production. And as corporations acknowledged that colour certainly had a marketing value, consumer products became more colourful.[10] Ford finally moved away from the "any colour you like as long as it is black" policy in 1924, with the introduction of a grey Model T.[11] But it was not Ford but General Motors that led the way in reintroducing colours in the mass production of automobiles.

In 1923 General Motors launched the "true blue" Oakland 6-54, which received its striking blue appearance from a new type of paint, developed by the DuPont chemical company in close cooperation with GM. Instead of oil, this new paint was based on nitrocellulose and it could be made in a vast range of colours. General Motors started using DUCO—the tradename of the new paint—throughout their complete model range during the mid-1920s and introduced it at their Danish assembly plant in 1925.[12]

But the most important reason for changing to nitrocellulose-based paint was not the range of colours that became available, but the remarkable reduction in the time needed for painting that it offered.

Figure 20 Electric welding together of a car body, with body parts mounted in a jig. The photo is not dated but must be from the late 1930s. Compare to earlier methods of body assembly, as seen in Figure 8. Unknown photographer. Thalbitzer: *Ford Motor Company A/S gennem 25 Aar*, 76

While a complete paint job with traditional oil-based paint would require more than 8 days of consecutive sanding, painting, drying, and polishing, it could be finished within 8 hours using DUCO paint, spray guns for applying, and hot air for drying. Furthermore, it was remarkably more durable than the traditional varnishes GM had previously used to give its high-end models, such as Cadillac, a colourful, hand-painted finish.[13]

Although DUCO was a trademark of the DuPont Company, it soon became the household name for this type of paint, regardless of its origin. This was also the case among Danish car painters.[14] But inside the Ford organisation, it was normally referred to as Pyroxylin, which is another name for nitrocellulose—probably because DUCO had too strong an association with General Motors.

Ford's first attempt to strike back against GM's new colours was the "empire grey" of the improved English version of the Model T, which was also launched in Denmark in 1924. It is not clear how it was painted, and it could still have been done by traditional methods. Ford did not take up the use of Pyroxylin paint in Detroit before August 1926, when the American new Model T was launched in different colours.[15] According to Thalbitzer, spray painting with Pyroxylin was first introduced at the Copenhagen plant in 1928, coinciding with the retooling for Model A production. This is plausible, but in fact it was announced by the Danish company in February 1927 that all passenger cars would from now on be delivered in Pyroxylin paint.[16]

Starting from 1938, the paint was changed once again, from nitrocellulose-based paint to a so-called synthetic paint. This type of paint required fewer sequential layers of paint—and sanding in between—to acquire a good finish, thereby further simplifying and speeding up the paint process. At the same time, it was supposed to be even more durable than Pyroxylin.[17]

The new methods greatly affected the work of the painters: hand-painting with traditional oil-based varnishes had been a highly skilled job. New methods, such as flow-painting, had already changed this to some extent. But developments were greatly accelerated with the introduction of Pyroxylin paint, applied with spray guns. To achieve a good finish of the final paint job, meticulous preparation was required, in the form of sanding, filling, and polishing with pumice and water between layers of paint. Some of this still required considerable skill.[18] But the spray-painting in itself was another matter. According to an expert responsible for in-service training of painters, to do the actual spray painting:

> ... you do not need a skilled painter; any reasonably intelligent person can learn how to do this in a short time. With a few hours of training, an unskilled worker or even a girl can very well learn how to spray paint.[19]

Consequently, unskilled workers or employees with other vocational training than painter were increasingly put to work in the paint shop at Ford Motor Company A/S.

The hazards of painting

A general effect of the so-called second industrial revolution was that the industrial workplace changed in character: increased mechanisation did away with some of the physical hardship on one hand; rationalisation and scientific management introduced a new level of repetitive work and long-term fatigue on the other. Electric power gradually replaced steam and transmission belts for driving machinery, with no less potential for causing harm than the previous technologies, but in less obvious ways. And last but not least, new chemical substances and compounds came to play an increased role in production, compounds that were often known under fancy trademarks, with the actual content hidden as a commercial secret.[20]

The nitrocellulose-based and synthetic paints used in the auto industry, as well as the solvents and thinners, were typical examples of the latter. The painters had a feeling that their health might be negatively affected by exposure to these substances, but they had no chance of knowing what they actually contained, and much less their long-term medical effects.

During the 1930s, medical professionals increasingly became interested in issues related to industrial work environment and workers' health. In 1934, cooperation started between the Coach Painters' Union and the physician and haematologist Jakob Jakobsen. Through the union magazine, Jakobsen was searching for volunteers among spray painters, who would submit blood samples for his research. Jakobsen's interest in the issue developed into a rather intensive research program, which resulted in him being awarded the degree of Doctor of Medical Science for his dissertation on spray painting hazards in 1939.[21] Meanwhile, Jakobsen was consulted several times by the Coach Painters' Union and was one of two medical professionals who contributed to the union magazine.[22] The union, on the other hand, contributed financially to Jakobsen's research, and helped him get in contact with members who had symptoms related to spray painting.[23]

For his doctoral thesis, Jakobsen carried out various examinations of blood cells, exposed rabbits to the fumes of various solvents and thinners—after which they did not fare very well—and made clinical observations of paint shop workers. Two different paint shops were included, but the names of the companies were not disclosed. However, according to the description, at least one of the shops must have been at an assembly plant. Furthermore, at an early point the painters' union had asked Jakobsen to include Ford in his research. It is therefore most likely that at least some of the workers examined are from Ford Motor Company A/S. But in any case, the paint and the methods used were fairly comparable across the auto industry, and therefore so too were the health effects.

A painter, who had started his apprenticeship at the age of 14 and had been working with cellulose paint for roughly 12 years, is daily coughing up ...

> ... a good deal of strongly coloured mucopurulent lumps. He further complains of dryness of the mucous membranes of the nose and throat, excessive crust-formation in the nose and usually a dry cough, especially when the spraying work is rather intensive [...]. Frequent attacks of dizziness under intensive spraying work, but it subsides rapidly when he goes out in the open. Sometimes also a sensation reminding of alcoholic intoxication, feeling at first animated and then drowsy. [...] He always feels very sleepy, and often he falls asleep in the evening immediately after supper. He is always very tired, but he hesitates to admit thathe is irritable—something those close to him have noticed.[24]

Figure 21 Spray painting. Unknown photographer. *Ford Nyt,* no. 2, 1931

Another worker was described as looking poorly: "Complexion dirty-greyish". A third worker reports himself that he is "able to stand cellulose lacquering about middling well, but no better", and that the main reason for him to keep the job is that it pays well. He experiences discomforts such as:

> … irritation of the mucous membranes of the eyes, nose and throat, with lacrimation, crusts in the nose and production of an expectorate coloured according to the lacquer solutions employed. Generally the appetite is poor. Dizziness and exhausting tiredness are common sensations. Now and then he is troubled greatly by itching and pricking localized to the anterior surface of both legs. All these phenomena subside rapidly during vacation.

Jakobsen concluded that it was not so much the pigments of the paint, which are with a few exceptions such as lead fairly harmless, as the inhalation of volatile components, such as benzene and toluene, that caused changes in the blood composition, as well as symptoms such as fatigue, dizziness, and lack of appetite. He also observes that both the change in blood composition and the visual symptoms disappear gradually when the worker is not exposed to paint for several days, such as during vacation. But he hesitates to make any final conclusions as to possible long-term effects of spray painting.

It was a widespread notion among the workers that the best cure for the negative effects of spray painting was to drink large amounts of milk. But Jakobsen's research made him conclude that while milk might make some of the symptoms feel less annoying, it would have no real effect. Instead he called for measures to prevent inhalation of the volatile components of paints and thinners. This could be done with masks, but these are not always effective, and the workers tend to resist them, as they are cumbersome to wear. A better solution was therefore spray booths with exhaust vents or simply better ventilation of the complete paint shop. He also points to the need for better regulation and control of the working environment by the authorities.[25]

Jakobsen's dissertation was one of the first on the subject of occupational health in Denmark, and in this sense a pioneering work.[26]

It was part of a general effort to incorporate scientific, medical research into the prevention of occupational hazards. Studies have shown how the initiative for this came from a few dedicated members of the medical profession, who found political support from the social democratic / social-liberal government, and whose work was even sponsored by some private enterprises.[27]

But as the cooperation between the Coach Painters' Union and Jakob Jakobsen shows, this was not the whole story. The workers themselves were also involved, and took initiatives to point the attention of the medical professionals in certain directions.

In parallel with the scientific research, the painters at the shop floor at Ford Motor Company A/S were demanding practical solutions. As mentioned above, it had come to a short strike in 1926, as workers were protesting against heat and fumes in the paint shop. But the company management was not completely unresponsive to the complaints from the workers. During the 1930s, an air-conditioning facility with the ability to "wash" the air, as it was blown into and exhausted from the paint shop, had been installed. This had proven effective in greatly reducing the amount of dust in the air, but unfortunately not in removing the fumes from solvents and thinners.[28]

MARKETS AND MODELS

A Broader Portfolio

In the late 1920s, Ford Motor Company's position as the largest manufacturer of automobiles in America, and thereby also in the world, had been overtaken by General Motors. Ford even had a hard time defending its second place against the upcoming Chrysler Corporation.[29]

But when the new Model A was released to the American market in December 1927, Ford once again finally had a car that was able to stand up to competition. The Model A was not a revolutionary car, in the same way that the Model T had been in 1908. It was not pushing technology forwards—for instance it featured a four-cylinder engine, where many competitors offered six cylinders, and the brakes were mechanical, where other brands had already introduced hydraulic brakes.

But at least the Model A was up to the standards of its time including a gearshift, clutch, and gas-pedal in the layout, that had now been established as a convention by the industry. And perhaps most importantly: it was backed by Henry Ford's personal reputation as a car maker.

In the United States, the Model A became a great success. But when it arrived at the much more diversified European markets in the beginning of 1928, reception was mixed. Generally, it was considered too large for the lower-end markets, which preferred smaller and more economical models, but still not able to compete with the more luxurious models of the upper markets. It did especially poorly on the important British market, where it was also hampered by the way that taxation was calculated, in the same way that the Model T had been. In an effort to counteract this, Ford introduced the Model AF to the European market: a Model A with a smaller cylinder volume. This, however, made the output of the engine drop to a point where the performance of the car became sluggish.

From A to V8

In contrast to the UK, the Model A fared quite well in the Nordic and Baltic markets. At the time of introduction, the price of a Model A ranged from DKK 2,625 for the open version, now called Phaeton, to over DKK 3,250 for the two-door sedan, to DKK 3,575 for the four-door sedan.[30] For comparison, a Chevrolet two-door sedan sold for DKK 3,400 and a Dodge four-door sedan for DKK 5,800.[31] Ford's offering was still cheap, compared to its competitors, but the gap had become smaller since the days of the Model T.

Assembly had started in Copenhagen in July 1928, and therefore sales for that year only reached about 6,600. But in 1929–1930, total sales were as high as 18–20,000.[32] This was almost as good as the golden years of the mid 1920s and gave ground for optimism. But then two things happened: yet another Ford model was introduced; and the economic conditions for selling cars changed drastically.

The new model was actually two different cars, called Model B and Model 18. But the two were basically identical, except for one crucial part: the engine. While the Model B was equipped with an updated version of the four-cylinder engine of the Model A, the 18 sported a newly developed V8 engine. With the introduction of these new models, the Model A had been replaced after only about four years, compared to the almost 19-year lifespan of the Model T.

Furthermore, by introducing an eight-cylinder engine, Ford took a leap forward from its competitors, which had previously overtaken Ford's four-cylinder engine by introducing six-cylinder models. The new engine was to become a huge success for Ford, and consequently a range of frequently updated models that were to follow during the 1930s would be known by their engine, and marketed as "V8", even though they were formally identified by model numbers such as 40, 48, etc. The four-cylinder Model B, on the other hand, was so overshadowed by the V8 that it was discontinued in 1934.

At its introduction, the V8 sold at prices ranging between DKK 3,950 and DKK 4,755 depending on version. When the revised V8 was presented in June 1933, the price of the cheapest version was DKK 4,975. This was arguably not an unreasonable price for a car in this class. But at the same time, the cheapest Chevrolet was offered at DKK 4,550.[33] The days when Ford was always a cheaper alternative to its closest competitors were now definitely gone.

What had the greatest impact on the sales of the V8 was, however, that it had the bad luck of being introduced just as the Great Depression was hitting Europe. In Denmark, this led to companies closing and unemployment peaking in 1932. This of course seriously affected not only the sale of commercial vehicles, but also the ability and willingness of private buyers to acquire expensive consumer goods such as a car. Ford's sales plummeted, as seen from Figure 41 in the Appendix.

From 1933 onwards, sales began climbing upwards again, although at a moderate pace. But at the same time the board had realised that the company was losing market share, especially to General Motors. A warning sign had already been raised the previous year when a well-established Ford dealer on the island of Falster had defected to General Motors. The board reacted by taking the unusual step of investing company funds directly in a new dealership on Falster—which might also be seen as a signal to other dealers contemplating a similar shift: that they could face a similar counterstrike. At the same time, it was decided to intensify marketing activities.[34]

During the latter half of the 1930s, sales were on the rise again. A major reason for this was undoubtedly the general improvement of the economy; but another development might have contributed: the broadening of Ford's product portfolio, both upwards and downwards.

Since 1923, Ford had offered the Lincoln luxury car, which was initially marketed under its own brand and sold in very small numbers. In 1936, the Lincoln-Zephyr was introduced, as a more modern and slightly more affordable version of the very traditional and very costly Lincoln. Its sale was limited to 30–40 per year, delivered mainly to royalty, diplomats, and high-ranking businessmen.[35] In 1939, the Mercury brand was introduced, aimed at the market in between the Lincoln-Zephyr and the Ford V8.

That same year, the Danish Crown Prince and Princess were on an official visit to the USA. The program included a tour of Ford's enormous River Rouge manufacturing facilities, with Henry Ford as tour guide. At the end of the tour, a Ford Mercury, fresh off the assembly line, was presented to the Crown Princess as a gift. As the Crown Princess answered Henry Ford's question regarding colour that she preferred dark blue, Henry Ford immediately ordered the originally black car to be repainted, before it was shipped to Denmark, where it was prepared for final delivery at the South Port plant. Until sometimes in the 1950s, the Crown Princess and later Queen would drive a Ford Mercury as her personal car, while the King would prefer Cadillacs.[36] During 1939 a total of 499 Mercurys were delivered from Copenhagen, mainly to customers in Denmark and Sweden.[37]

With the Lincoln-Zephyr and especially the Mercury, Ford had gained a foothold in the market for expensive cars. But from a sales perspective, what happened at the opposite end of the market was of much more interest.

A Ford for Europe

In May 1929 construction work began on a new Ford production facility in Dagenham, adjacent to the river Thames, south of London, England. The new facility was to become not just an assembly plant but a complete production facility, capable of producing all the components needed for cars, complete with its own iron and steel works. Not only would Dagenham become the supplier of cars for Britain, it was also to take over Dearborn's role as supplier of parts for the other European assembly plants—in Henry Ford's own words, to become a "Detroit of Europe". The plan was to take advantage of economies of scale in order to lower costs and become more competitive, just as had been done at River Rouge.[38]

Dagenham stood ready to take up production in 1931. But by that time, the miserable sales figures for the Model A in England had already become a threat to the whole logic of the new plant as a large-scale production facility. This finally made it possible for the British Ford management to achieve what they had tried for years: persuading Detroit to let them design a car, especially adapted for the European market.

The result was the Ford Y, a small and cheap car, but technically up to date and modern in its design. In fact, the sleek looks of the small car were so successful that some of its design elements, such as the sloped radiator grille, were reused for the 1933 update of the larger V8. Production of the Model Y began at Dagenham in August 1932, and by the end of the year assembly was started in Copenhagen. On the markets served from Denmark, the car was named Ford Junior.[39]

From London, six of only 19 prototype Model Y's had been shipped to Copenhagen, to be used for display in various ports around the Baltic Sea, and the first cars for sale arrived in Copenhagen only two days after production had commenced in Dagenham—indicating the relative importance that was given to the markets under Ford Motor Company A/S. The Model Y / Junior was priced rather competitively in Denmark: DKK 3,075 for a Tudor Sedan.[40]

While the Model Y / Junior was officially designed for Europe, it was aimed quite specifically at the British market, where it was to compete with other small cars from Morris and Austin. It did so with great success and sold in large numbers. In some other parts of Europe, it was not so well received. In Sweden for instance, the Junior was nicknamed "Jojon"—Swedish for "the yo-yo"—as a tribute to the way it handled the long and often unpaved main roads of this country.[41]

Juniors for Sweden were supplied directly from Dagenham. The sales figures were less than 2,000 in total for the period 1932–1937.

Finland (and from there Estonia) was also supplied from Dagenham and sold fewer than 300 units during the same period.[42] Juniors for the rest of the Nordic and Baltic area was assembled in and sold from Copenhagen. From there 2,608 units were delivered between 1932 and 1937 to Denmark, Poland, and the Baltic states. This was roughly 10 percent of Ford's sale in these markets;[43] again, a figure that was not exactly staggering, but also not insignificant.

Just as important as the sales numbers of specific models was the fact that Ford Motor Company A/S, by the late 1930s, was able to offer a broad portfolio of cars, aimed at different segments of the market, from budget to luxury.

The immense popularity of the Model Y in the UK—with more than 150,000 units sold between 1932 and 1937—was confirmation for Ford Motor Company that the decision to make a "European Ford" had been the right one. Consequently, it was followed by several similar smaller models, the first one being an updated version of the Y with a slightly bigger engine, called Model C in England. In Denmark it was called Junior de Luxe, while the original Junior was renamed Junior Popular. Through another update, the Y also evolved into the Ford Anglia in 1939 and the Ford Prefect which differed from the Anglia only by having four doors instead of two. These were also delivered from Ford Motor Company A/S by the end of the 1930s.

Ford in Britain had high hopes that with the Model Y and its successors it would finally be possible to achieve the volume of production at Dagenham that this facility was originally built for. But the aftermath of the economic crisis in the early 1930s brought rising nationalism and economic protectionism to most parts of Europe. This was not least the case for the important German market. As the Nazis came to power, it became increasingly difficult, bordering on impossible, to sell any "foreign" cars in the country. In an attempt to meet the political challenges, it was decided that the Ford plant

Figure 22 Car models offered by Ford Motor Company A/S, ca. 1940. To these models should be added the Lincoln and Mercury luxury models, as well as vans and chassis for trucks. Unknown artist. Thalbitzer: *Ford Motor Company A/S gennem 25 Aar*, 59

Junior
23 HK

Junior de Luxe
32 HK

Prefect
34 HK

Eifel
34 HK

Taunus
34 HK

Royal V-8
60 HK

in Cologne, which was originally designed for assembly only, should be upgraded to a fully-fledged manufacturing facility, in order to be able to present German-made cars to the German market. A redesigned Model Y, with an engine manufactured in Cologne and bodies supplied by German subcontractors, was launched under the name Ford Köln.

Taking up manufacturing in Cologne was of course to go against the original plans for Dagenham but was seen as necessary for Ford to remain in the German market. According to promotional material, the engine of the Köln was made "durch die Arbeit deutscher Werkmannshände zu Stahl und Eisen", and the car was characterised as "der Wagen für jedermann", with the cheapest version designated "Volkstyp"—a homage to Hitler's request for the auto industry to create a "Volkswagen".[44]

More popular than the Köln was the Eifel, which was built on the same platform as the Anglia but with German-made bodies, and was manufactured between 1935 and 1940. It was succeeded by the Taunus, the first model that was independently developed by Ford in Cologne.[45] The Köln was also marketed by Ford Motor Company A/S, and assembly took place in Copenhagen 1937–1939. Even the Taunus made its way to the Danish market in the short period between its launch in June 1939 and the outbreak of war.

The Köln, Anglia, and Eifel were also the start of a symbolic new marketing trend, which would become long lasting, of combining the all-American Ford brand with names that had a decidedly European connotation.

MANAGEMENT

Under English Lords

In the beginning of 1929, Ford Motor Company A/S was effectively made a subsidiary of Ford in the UK under the leadership of Percival Perry. Perry had been in charge of Ford's British operations in the pioneering years but had fallen out with some of Dearborn's executives and had left the company in 1919.

Meanwhile, Ford's position in the UK had deteriorated drastically, as already described above.[46] A combination of bad management, the lack of a product specifically suited for the British market, and political animosities against American products had reduced Ford from a major to a minor player in the British market in the mid-1920s. "We have been defeated and licked in England", the company vice-president Ernest Kanzler wrote in early 1926.[47]

In the spring of 1928, contact was re-established between Henry Ford and Perry on the latter's initiative. Soon Ford became convinced that Perry was the person he needed to remedy the situation in the UK. Without much hesitation, he decided to put Perry back in charge of the whole British Ford organisation.[48]

Perry immediately engaged himself in developing a plan, together with Detroit, for reviving Ford's position in England. The plan, however, soon developed into a complete restructuring of Ford's European operations. This plan included the construction of a new, major plant in Dagenham, south of London, as already mentioned. Such a plant had actually been on the cards since the early 1920s but had never been realised. But within a year of his re-instatement, Perry had turned intention into action and started construction at Dagenham. His ambition was that it should become not just a manufacturing centre for Ford in England, but for the whole of Europe, delivering parts to all assembly plants on the continent.

Perry also laid out a plan for a complete restructuring of the ownership and management structure of Ford in Europe. European subsidiaries should no longer be owned and managed directly and individually from Detroit. Instead, Perry suggested that ownership of all European subsidiaries should be transferred to Ford in the UK, which would then be owned by the American Ford company. As head of Ford in the UK, Perry himself would also assume responsibility of the other European subsidiaries.[49] The plan was approved by Henry Ford.

In 1938 Percival Perry was knighted, and so were several others of the top executives of the British Ford company in the years to come.[50] The "American years" of Ford management in Europe had now turned into the reign of the English lords.

New leadership

According to the new plan, Ford Motor Company would own 60 percent of the shares in the British Ford company, which would in turn own 60 percent of the shares of each of the other European subsidiaries. Percival Perry, chairman of the English company, was also to be chairman of every other European company. But for some reason, the Swedish company was to be 60 percent owned by Ford in Denmark, and the Finnish company 60 percent owned by the Swedish.[51]

In terms of ownership, the Swedish company was now a subsidiary of Ford Motor Company A/S, and so was the Finnish company indirectly. All three companies had Percival Perry of Ford in Britain as chairman. From the point of view of Copenhagen, they were seen as off-shoots of Ford Motor Company A/S.[52] In practical matters, there was a close cooperation, partly based on personal ties as key executives in Stockholm had been recruited from Copenhagen. Likewise, the Swedish and Finnish companies had the same manager for a period. And after all, both the Swedes and the Finns were mainly dealing with cars assembled in Copenhagen.

This was a major principal step away from the previous policy of keeping almost complete ownership. The vast majority of shares of Ford Motor Company A/S had been in the personal possession of Henry Ford and his family from the beginning, with only a few symbolic shares allotted to the other board members. But in several European markets, it was increasingly becoming a problem, marketing-wise and even sometimes politically, that Ford was seen as a foreign company, and thereby an outside competitor to national industry. Perry and others succeeded in convinced Henry Ford that broadening the ownership base would be one way of integrating the various subsidiaries better in their national environment.

The minority shares, however, were not given completely free. Firstly, shares worth DKK 10 million were bought back by the company at par value, paid for by the reserves.[53] This was in reality a transfer of value to the Ford family in Detroit, as they still owned the vast majority of shares. Secondly, shares worth DKK 12 million were acquired by Ford in Britain. They would later be transferred to a holding company in Luxembourg, Société d'Investissements Ford, created by Percival Perry for the purpose of collecting dividends from all European subsidiaries.[54] Then, finally, the remaining shares with a nominal value of DKK 8 million were offered to investors. However, only 18,500 shares, representing a nominal value of DKK 2 million, were sold to the general public. The rest were reserved for special interest groups, such as Englishmen (25,000), certain distinguished firms and managers (15,000), dealers (10,000), Danish employees (10,000), and Norwegian employees (1,500). There was a great interest in acquiring shares, and somehow both dealers and employees managed to get hold of a far higher number of shares than originally planned for, as these two groups ended up owning almost 24,000 shares each. Of the employees, it was mostly managers and white-collar workers who acquired shares—H.C. Møller personally bought 1,820—but even a dozen blue-collars managed to become shareholders.[55]

However, the principal goal of a 40 percent external ownership was not reached in the first place, due to the decision to buy back DKK 10 million worth of shares. After the release of shares to the public, only 27 percent of the shares were actually owned by investors outside Ford.[56] It is not clear what the management or the board had in mind in the long run for the shares that Ford Motor Company A/S owned in itself. But in 1930 the Danish Companies Act was revised, making it illegal for a limited company to possess shares in itself of that magnitude. Ford was given some years to comply, but in 1934 it was decided to use the reserves to simply cancel those DKK 10 million worth of shares.[57] The ratio between internal and external ownership would then finally be the 60/40 originally planned, as shares worth DKK 12 million would belong to Ford of England and the other DKK 8 million would belong to external investors.

Another part of the plan for rooting the various European subsidiaries more firmly in their respective national context was to invite distinguished local representatives of business and politics into the boards. In March 1929, the general meeting had routinely re-elected the board, whose active members were H.C. Møller and two other Danish company executives, with Edsel B. Ford and B.J. Craig in the passive role of representing Detroit from a distance. But in May an extraordinary general meeting was called, which completely reshuffled the Danish board. Out went H.C. Møller and the other two company executives, K. Rahbek Lyhne and Mortensen, along with B.J. Craig. The only member of the old board that remained in the new was Edsel B. Ford.[58]

Instead, V. Falbe-Hansen made a comeback as a board member. And with him, the well-connected lawyer brought some of his personal acquaintances: former Minister of Foreign Affairs Count Carl Moltke, editor and member of the board of the National Bank Carl Thalbitzer, and Professor P.O. Pedersen, rector of the Technical University of Denmark[59]. The election of Pedersen as a board member would initiate a tradition of close ties between Ford Motor Company A/S and the Technical University.

B.J. Craig was replaced by Charles E. Sorensen, and finally Percival Perry was elected to the board, and without further ado became its chairman. The inclusion of Charles Sorensen on the board seems rather surprising, given the official line of "de-Americanisation"; but Sorensen clearly had a responsibility for keeping an eye on things in Europe in these years, even if this was not indicated by his official position. He regularly travelled with Perry and visited Denmark several times.[60]

The composition of the board was now distinctly different from how it was prior to March 1929. No company executives were members anymore, even though Møller attended all meetings without voting rights. And in March 1936, Møller was again elected as a regular board member in place of count Moltke, who had passed away in September 1935.[61]

But in general, the people who made up the board were separated from the daily routine of running the company. Instead, they engaged themselves actively in discussions of a more strategic nature, and of the general financial matters. Agendas of the board as well as general meetings expanded, indicating that the new leadership took an active interest in the company. Another indication of the active role of the board was the fact that Percival Perry took a personal part in most of the meetings from his election as chairman in May 1929 until early 1938. But from then on, his participation started to wane considerably, reflecting the fact that, relative to other parts of Europe, things were running rather smoothly in Denmark.[62]

Detroit, on the other hand, was not very present. As mentioned above, Edsel B. Ford had taken part in the board meeting called in Detroit in 1923 to decide the expansion of share capital needed for building the new factory. The next meeting in which he took part was some 14 years later, in August 1936. According to the minutes this was a relatively short meeting, with nothing special on the agenda, so it was mostly a courtesy visit.[63] Sorensen was a bit more present, as he took part in three board meetings between 1929 and 1940 but was also monitoring the situation in Denmark from a distance.[64]

But even if the discussions of the board became more substantial after 1929, and the board members more involved in decision making, there was never any doubt about who was ultimately in charge. Never did the board actively try to counteract recommendations received from above, be that from London or—less often—from Detroit. On the contrary: the board reacted swiftly to any British request. One of the more drastic demands from London was that the Danish company should buy back 40 percent of its shares from the investors at face value. This was received and discussed by the board on 7 December 1933, resulting in an extraordinary general meeting, held on 28 December, to make the formal decision requested. The buyback was completed in June 1934, following the six months' legal notice required.[65]

The reason for this manoeuvre was to be found in Dagenham. Due to the deteriorating market situation, London was in need of cash for the completion of the building project, and since Ford in the UK was a major shareholder in Ford Motor Company A/S, a buyback of shares would mean a transfer of money from Copenhagen to London. Similar requests were made towards Dutch, Belgian, and Spanish Ford companies.[66] This was of course helpful to the economy of the Dagenham project, but it did not solve the main problem: that Dagenham never reached the level of production it was conceived for. While the European economy started to revive, protectionism and political turmoil were on the rise, creating trouble for Ford in several markets, such as Germany, Spain, and France. This also led some European branch managers to circumvent Ford in the UK, trying to solve problems in direct communication with Detroit, thus undermining the authority of Perry and his European leadership.[67] There are, however, no indications that Copenhagen was anything but loyal to London.

Relative to Detroit, London was closer to Copenhagen not only geographically, but also mentally. The Americans might be more efficient, but the British understood better what was going on in Europe. Perry would assemble all the European managers and directors for a yearly dinner in Paris. In contrast to the earlier years, these managers would now mostly be of European background, and with a few exceptions their cooperation went well.[68] According to veteran board member Falbe-Hansen, Percival Perry was open to discussion, even on a detailed level, and would listen to advice.[69] H.C. Møller was on good personal terms with Perry and considered him and his executives "desirable lords" in comparison to the Americans.[70]

Shareholder value

With 40 percent of the company now belonging to outside investors, Ford Motor Company A/S had to take shareholder value into consideration. Continuously reinvesting all the profit in the company, as had been done up to then—with the year 1924 as one major exception—was no longer feasible. The shareholders would expect to be paid a dividend in return for their investment.

And so, they were. The profit before tax for the year 1929 was DKK 5.2 million. At the general meeting of shareholders in 1930 the board proposed a dividend of 10 percent, meaning that DKK 3 million would be paid to the shareholders. DKK 1 million of this would, however, return immediately to the company, as it was the owner of one-third of the shares. Another DKK 2 million was to be set aside as a reserve, and the rest of the profit was transferred to the following year's account. All in all, out of the DKK 5.2 million profit, roughly DKK 3.2 million would be kept in the company. The shareholders were nevertheless content with their 10 percent dividend, and appreciation of the year's result was expressed at the general meeting.[71]

A 10 percent dividend was also paid to the shareholders in 1930. But then the waves set in motion by the crash of the Wall Street stock market reached the shores of Denmark. In the beginning, this was not necessarily bad for the Danish economy, since it made the prices of imported raw materials drop. But as the economy deteriorated in still more European countries, the sale and export of cars began to decline too. The Danish home market went into a state of economic depression, reaching its lowest point in 1932.

Some of the political measures that were introduced to combat the crisis were hitting the car industry especially hard. In 1931 the tax on automobiles was raised,[72] and for the first time since 1920 the total sale of cars was in decline. Like in other nations, the Danish government reverted to protectionist measures, and from 1932 onwards import became heavily regulated and restricted, making it difficult to obtain the parts needed for production. The situation was no better on the export markets, and as can be seen in Figure 41 in the Appendix, both production and sales figures were low during the first half of the 1930s. This was of course reflected in the annual accounts, which hit rock bottom in 1933 with a loss of DKK 310,000. Consequently, in the years 1931–1933 the shareholders received no dividend at all.

From the mid-1930s, things started to brighten up a bit again. Production was gradually rising and stabilised at a little over 10,000 units per year at the end of the decade. That was still far below the maximum production capacity of the plant. Nevertheless, profits were reaching higher levels, typically hovering around roughly DKK 4 million per year during the last half of the 1930s.[73] From 1934 dividends were paid again, starting at 8 percent but reaching a peak of 20 percent in 1937.[74]

The dividend was, however, to be calculated based on a diminishing amount of share capital. The cancelling of DKK 10 million worth of own shares, and the subsequent buying back of 40 percent of the rest, meant that the total amount of share capital was reduced from DKK 30 million to DKK 12 million in 1934. Consequently, the 20 percent dividend of 1937 resulted in a payment of DKK 2.4 million to the shareholders, which was less than the DKK 3 million that had been the result of the 10 percent dividend in 1929.

All in all, despite the turbulent years of crisis around 1931–1933 and the subsequent continuous currency and import restrictions, the 1930s were not necessarily bad for Ford Motor Company A/S. As profits stabilised during the latter part of the decade, it at least partly made up for earlier losses. And compared to other European Ford subsidiaries, Copenhagen in fact did well in relative terms. During the early 1930s, when Denmark managed to stay in the black with 1933 as the only exception, Ford in Britain and Germany experienced losses of a far greater magnitude.[75]

No data has been found that permits a comparison between the Danish company and other Ford subsidiaries for just the 1930s. But after the war, an account was made up of the returns on capital invested in Ford's European companies for the whole period of 1922–1949. This could have been skewed by the fact that Denmark was less damaged by the war than most other European countries. Nevertheless, it showed that during this period, Ford's average return on its investment in Denmark had been 13.3 percent. This was far above England (3.9 percent), Germany (0.7 percent), and France (a loss of 4.3 percent). Only Belgium (14 percent) and Portugal (23.1 percent) could display a higher return on investment. But the return in Belgium and especially Portugal was from a considerably smaller investment than in Denmark.[76]

Other car manufacturers invested in the Danish and associated markets too. Around 1930, General Motors moved its production from the smaller premises in the South Port to a newly constructed, modern plant at Aldersrogade in Northern Copenhagen. As part of its move into Europe, GM had bought the British Vauxhall in 1925 and German Opel in 1929. The latter was now also assembled in Copenhagen, while other GM sub-brands, such as Buick, Pontiac, etc. were imported as built-up from USA.[77]

The last of the "big three" American car manufacturers joined the others in Copenhagen when a plant for assembling Chrysler cars was established in 1930. It was not established by Chrysler itself, but by the Danish company Bohnstedt-Petersen A/S, the official distributor of the brand. This plant was placed in the North Port area, at Sundkrogsgade. It was smaller than the others, with around 300 blue-collar and 20 white-collar workers producing between 25 and 30 cars per day during the 1930s.[78]

Finally, assembly of a smaller American brand, Willys-Overland, was started around 1935. Again, the company was Danish, started and owned by Jens Yde, who had been European sales manager for Willys. It was situated at Frederiksholms Havnevej in the South Port area, near to Ford and Citroën, but was considerably smaller than these plants.[79]

According to the Statistics of Industry, Commerce and Transport, 971 blue-collar and 288 white-collar workers were employed in the car-making industry in Copenhagen in 1935. Despite expansions and new companies, this was no more than in the last count ten years before. But in contrast with 1925, which had been a boom year, 1935 was a year of slow recovery from the crisis of the early 30s.[80]

Ford becomes organised

It was Henry Ford's ideal that government should leave the regulation of business to the free market alone. However, this was far from the reality of Denmark in the 1930s. While Denmark had not been actively involved in the First World War, it had been economically strongly affected by it. And just as in several other European countries, this had led to state interventions into the private sector. Commissions had been set up for that purpose, in which government officials cooperated with representatives of industry and commerce in regulating production as well as distribution.[81]

After the war, these regulations were partly and gradually dismantled. But the times of laissez-faire had permanently been replaced by a new era, in which political intervention into the economy for the sake of the public good had become legitimate. In particular, the Social Democrats, when they came into power, pursued a policy of public intervention in favour of economic growth and industrial development. This was further reinforced during the early 1930s, as a reaction to the economic crisis. Most notably, the so-called Currency Committee was established in 1932, with the authority to regulate and limit import.

The work of the Currency Committee included representatives of industry in both administrative and consultative positions.[82] This was part of a general tendency to involve trade and employer's organisations in what was essentially public administration in the form of commissions etc. during the 1930s.[83] Parallel to this, it had also become customary to consult such organisations as well as labour unions before preparation of legislation. These "semi-corporatist" traits of the Danish political system—within the framework of liberal democracy—meant that it was increasingly difficult for a company like Ford Motor Company A/S to take care of its political interests alone.

To start with, Ford would start to informally coordinate with General Motors, the other large Danish car manufacturer, before negotiations with the authorities. But in 1932 the board decided that Ford Motor Company A/S should join the Industrial Council, *Industrirådet*.[84] The Industrial Council was the main representative of industry in relation to the government and parliament in general, and especially in matters regarding trade policy—including the aforementioned Currency Committee. Since trade policy and the decisions of the Currency Committee were vital to Ford, joining the Industrial Council was a natural move.

Another political issue of great importance for Ford was the taxation of cars. This was changed several times during the late 1920s, including the introduction of both a sales tax and a tax on gasoline, supplementing the yearly duty already in force. As a result of this, but also an increase in the number of cars, the total revenue of taxes paid by car owners had risen from DKK 22.6 million in the fiscal year 1927–1928 to DKK 41.3 million in 1929–1930. The Association of Automobile and Bicycle Wholesale Dealers therefore approached the government with a demand for lower taxes. Ford was not a member of the association, but nevertheless the situation regarding taxes was discussed in detail at a board meeting. The conclusion was, however, that since the revenue of the taxes was directed towards improving and maintaining roads, and thereby indirectly furthering auto mobility, the company had no interest in taking part in any political action against it.[85]

But the management must nevertheless have felt a need for political representation that was closer to and more involved in the car industry than the Industrial Council, which was influential but at the same time broad in its scope, representing all types of manufacturing industries. Consequently, in 1940 Ford joined the new Association of Car Manufacturers and Importers, *Sammenslutningen af Automobil-Fabrikanter og Importører*, created that same year.[86]

This was at a time when Henry Ford's staunch individualism was still the order of the day in Detroit. Consequently, Ford refused to join such organisations as the American Automobile Manufacturers Association.[87] The decision of the Danish management to do otherwise was approved by Percival Perry, but in retrospect Møller expressed his doubt as to whether Dearborn was ever informed about it.[88]

Slowly Towards Normal

From the point of view of labour, two things defined the 1930s in Denmark more than anything. The first one was the economic depression. Denmark was hit by the economic crisis in late 1930, the effect of which reached its most extreme in 1932, when average unemployment levels reached almost 32 percent of registered workers.[89] Those workers who fell victim to unemployment would experience a severe decline in living conditions, which in turn would lead to political unrest.

On the other hand, this was the decade when the Social Democrats established themselves as the country's leading political force. In 1929, party chairman Thorvald Stauning formed his second government, after the short-lived and somewhat feeble first social democratic government of 1924–1926: this time in an alliance with the smaller Social-Liberal Party, which would prove to be successful throughout the 1930s. In 1935 the Social Democrats, campaigning under the slogan "Stauning or chaos", received their best parliamentary election result ever, with 46 percent of the votes.[90]

Average real wages actually increased slightly during the early part of the period, before declining again in the later part, resulting in a level in 1939 very close to 1930. But when the social reforms carried out by the Stauning-government, such as two weeks' paid holiday (in 1938) and improved housing conditions, were added to this, those workers who did not lose their jobs had reason to feel that social conditions had actually improved, despite the depression of the early 1930s.[91]

Payment under pressure

During the years of deflation in the 1920s, Ford Motor Company A/S had not been part of the general attempt by employers in Danish industry to push down wages. On the contrary, Ford's high wage regime had actually survived the 1920s in Denmark much better than back home in Detroit.

But in December 1929, the Copenhagen management for the first time declared an intention of lowering wages, effective from 1 January 1930. This came as some surprise. 1929 had been a very good year saleswise, profits were on the rise, and Denmark had not yet been hit by the depression following the Wall Street crash. Granted, wages were high at the Danish company, even compared to other European Ford operations, but so was productivity: in both 1930 and 1931 Percival Perry, in his capacity as chairman of every European Ford company, including Denmark, confirmed that the Copenhagen plant had the highest wages but the lowest production costs per unit of any in Europe.[92]

It might have been a primarily defensive move from the management: with the seniority system used, workers would more or less automatically reach the highest levels of payment, as long as they were able to hold on to their jobs at Ford for long enough. The new wage scheme proposed by the management was specifically targeting the topmost wage levels, suggesting a wish to prevent further gravitation towards the highest wages.[93]

However, instead of just cutting wages, the management entered into prolonged negotiations with the workers, and no actual cut in wages was carried out until two years later, in early 1932. Meanwhile, Denmark had been hit by the depression, car sales were going down and overall unemployment was steeply on the rise. In other words: the unions were now on the defensive.

From a declared wish to cut all wages by 10 percent, the management lowered its proposal to around a 5.6 percent reduction, which was finally enacted in January 1932. The workers grudgingly accepted. But just a few months later, in June the same year, management demanded another 10 percent reduction in wages. The demand was followed up by 25 workers, all receiving the highest pay rate, being laid off. When union representatives asked for negotiations, the answer from production manager Georg Frederiksen was that "he failed to see that there was anything to negotiate about".[94]

The unions now brought out heavier artillery: following threats that the company might be victim to a general union blockade, which could potentially stop the transport of goods to and from the plant, a meeting was set up. However, on the day, no representatives of Ford Motor Company A/S showed up. The unions reacted by presenting the management with a range of conditions for accepting decreased wages, including the setting up of a proper agreement, like the one that had been terminated six years before, and the re-hiring of the 25 workers that had been laid off.[95]

Ford Motor Company A/S dismissed these demands. Nevertheless, the management went into *de facto* negotiations with the unions, and a compromise based on reduced wage cuts was reached. But when this compromise was presented in a meeting on 5 November 1932, it was rejected by a majority of the workers present. Further negotiations resulted in another compromise, which was finally accepted by a 60 percent majority of the workers on 29 November. Unfortunately, the details of the compromise are not known, but apparently the lower wage levels were left untouched, while the highest wage level was cut substantially. The 25 workers that had been fired would be given priority as job openings became available. And finally, a personal promise was given by general manager H.C. Møller that there would be no more wage cuts within the next 12 months.[96]

Figure 23 shows the development of average real wages at Ford compared to average real wages for male industrial workers in Copenhagen during the 1930s. It is based on hourly wages, multiplied by 40 hours for a standard week for Ford and 48 hours for the industry in general. The actual wages have been turned into real wages using the official price index, and finally normalised so that the wages of the general industry in 1929 equal 100. The starting point of 173 for Ford reflects that the average weekly wage paid there was that much higher than in the Copenhagen industry that year. In absolute numbers: DKK 130.40 at Ford versus DKK 75.36 in the industry in general.

The rise in real wages from 1929 to 1931 for both Ford workers and the average industrial workers was mainly due to deflation; wages were almost constant in absolute terms. From then on, inflation sets in. But while wages in absolute terms are still relatively constant for the average industrial worker, this is when the Ford management succeeds in pushing down the pay rate—from DKK 3.26 per hour in 1931 to DKK 2.73 in 1935. The result is that real wages at Ford are going down faster than in the industry in general, thereby narrowing the gap between Ford wages and those of the rest, even if Ford wages are still a respectable 44 percent higher in 1935.

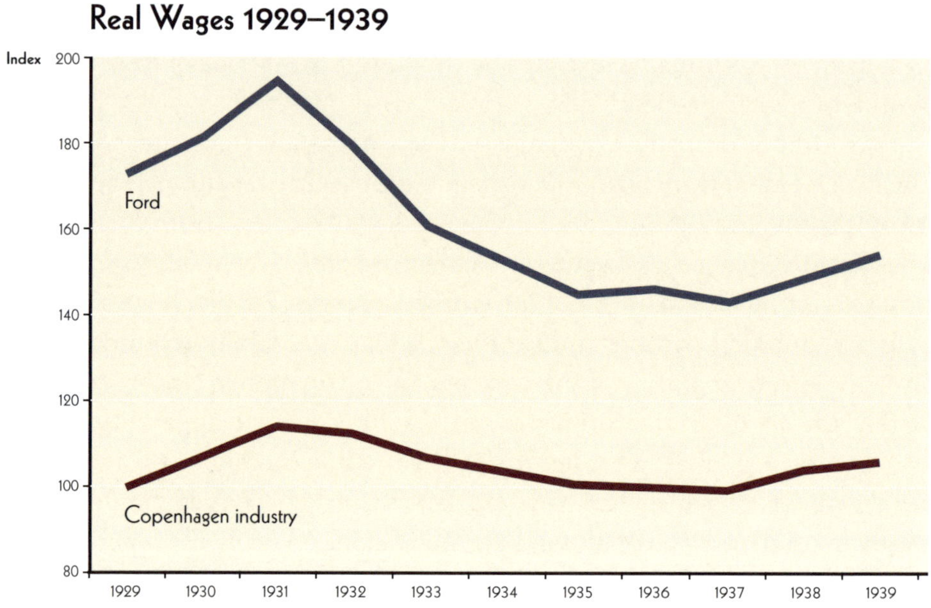

Figure 23 Development in real weekly wages 1929–1939, for Ford Motor Company A/S relative to average for male workers in Copenhagen industry. See text for detailed explanation. Source: FMC: Balance Sheets and *Statistisk Aarbog*, relevant years

In early 1935, Ford workers intensify pressure for higher wages. This and other issues were raised by the unions at a meeting with the management in March, but with no result. On 1 April approximately 450 out of 600 Ford workers attended a common union meeting. Union representatives were met with accusations of being too passive, and a resolution was adopted, demanding a minimum wage of DKK 2.80. This was, however, not achieved.[97] Not until April 1938 was the hourly wage finally raised by DKK 0.10.[98]

A time to work ...

In 1930, four members of the workmen's union at Ford Motor Company A/S decided to switch to another union, that of Specialised Workmen.[99] Despite the similarities in name, the latter was a small union, primarily organising semiskilled workers at the Copenhagen shipyards. It was not part of the Danish Workmen's Association, the national association for unskilled workers, to which the workmen's union at Ford belonged.[100]

As often happens in such cases, the workmen's union was not inclined to let another union organise workers on what it considered its own turf. Consequently, it made a formal protest through the national association to the Danish Confederation of Trade Unions, whose so-called Committee on Boundary Disputes made a ruling in January 1931: the Specialised Workmen's Union had no right to organise the four workers in question, and their membership was to be transferred back to the Union of Workmen in the Metal Industries.[101] But while this was accepted by both unions, the four workers brought the case to civil court, demanding that the workmen's union should be ordered to let them go. The court, however, resolved that since the four workers had not been denied membership of a union as such, their right to freely seek occupation had not been jeopardised. And since it was not up to the court to interfere with the internal organisational structure of the union movement, the plaintiffs' claim was dis-missed.[102]

In the scheme of things, this was a rather trivial case. But what makes it illuminating in this context is the four workers' main reason for insisting on changing their union membership and even going to court: the Specialised Workmen's Union was able to offer them a higher level of unemployment benefit than the union they were already members of. The risk of unemployment—and the possible level of compensation—was certainly an issue to the workers at Ford Motor Company A/S.

Work at Ford Motor Company A/S was well paid, but for most of the period it was also more or less insecure. Firstly, there was the inherent fluctuation in employment during the year, reflecting the seasonal shifts in demands for cars, something that was considered a normal and unavoidable part of work in the industry. Typically, blue-collar employment would rise steadily from the beginning of the year, peak during spring, decline a bit during summer, reach a low point during autumn, and finally go up again a bit by the end of the year. Employment in the high season would often be more than double that in the low season.[103] What this meant was that employment at Ford did not guarantee work all year round: a standard work year at Ford was in fact around 200 days,[104] which was only around two-thirds of the possible maximum number of workdays in industry in general.

Secondly, there were the long-term fluctuations, caused by general economic developments. These are illustrated by the yearly employment numbers for the period of 1919–1964, shown in Figure 42 in the Appendix. Surprisingly, the significant drop in sales and production during the economic depression of the early 1930s is not reflected in a similar decrease in employment. This, however, could be due to a limitation in the source material, since Figure 42 is based on end-of-year employment. This might conceal the fact that employment had dropped in the form of a lower peak during high season. The ongoing concern about lack of employment, displayed by the unions in various ways during the 1930s, also indicates that jobs were actually at stake in this period.

Finally, to these two types of fluctuation in employment we should add those caused by model changes. As seen above, the changeover from Model T to Model A caused an almost complete stop in blue-collar employment for several months in 1927–1928. But as already discussed, Ford learned a hard lesson from this, and was able to shorten the period considerably for later changes in model, both in the production of parts in Detroit and Dagenham and in the assembly in Copenhagen. As a result, changes in production might still have an impact on employment, but it became almost negligible, as the company became more and more proficient in assembling several models simultaneously.[105]

While work at Ford could be scarce at times, it could be very intense at others. In early 1935, a record-breaking work week of 76 hours due to overtime was recorded.[106] While this was probably an extreme example, there were without doubt periods of extensive overtime. Since extra pay for overtime had been cancelled together with the agreement in 1927, management had no economic incentive to limit its use. The unions were in an ambivalent position: on one hand, overtime meant a higher weekly pay-check; on the other, it was at the expense of general employment and working conditions. The policy of the unions was therefore to accept only 4 hours' paid overtime per week and demand any excess of that to be compensated with time off in lieu. But without an agreement, they had no way to enforce that, except for appeals and complaints to the management.[107]

In 1938, all Danish workers won the right to two weeks of paid holiday by law. Apart from being primarily a welfare reform, a secondary reason for this was also to improve employment. Before the passing of the law, some workers had been able to secure local agreements about paid holiday. At Ford, the issue was first raised in late 1931, when the unions suggested paid holiday as a compensation for the wage cuts demanded by management.[108] Nothing was resolved then, but in 1936 an agreement on paid holiday was reached, two years before this became mandatory by law.[109]

The unions at Ford did not only work on the company level to secure steady and stable jobs. They also took political action to secure as much production as possible for the car industry. In 1936, the Economic Council of the Labour Movement was established. According to Prime Minister Thorvald Stauning, the aim of the council was to improve the possibilities of the workers and their representatives to influence political decisions regarding trade and employment.[110] The previous year, Johannes Kjærbøl had been appointed Minister of Trade. Kjærbøl came from a post as chairman of the Danish Metalworkers' Association (DSMF), and having a former union leader appointed to a political post central to regulating import and export gave auto workers hope of political sympathy towards the industry.

Shortly after the appointment of Kjærbøl, the metalworkers' union at Ford approached the former chairman of their association, asking him to make sure that foreign currency allotted to car manufacturers through the Currency Committee was used to import parts for local assembly, and not complete cars. Such addresses—formal or informal—from the unions to the minister were repeated several times during the rest of the decade. Some of them went through the Economic Council of the Labour Movement, which also held meetings with both unions and workers from Ford and other assembly plants, discussing issues of trade and import.[111]

There are no indications that these union initiatives were coordinated with the initiatives from the Ford management about the same matters, which were taken around the same time. But the union initiatives and the initiatives from management had at least one thing in common: they did not cause any immediate political change. Matters of currency and import were decided in the framework of bilateral agreements between Denmark and other nations, leaving very little room for the Minister of Trade to make specific concessions to the auto industry, even if he had wanted to do so. When the metalworkers' union repeated the request to the minister to stop the import of finished cars in favour of local assembly, it was forwarded to the Currency Committee. The Committee politely but firmly denied the request, telling the union that "according to trade agreements with other countries, we are obliged to import a certain number of finished cars".[112]

New deals

The crisis of the early 1930s was, in important ways such as diminishing wages and a possible decline in employment, a setback for the workers at Ford Motor Company A/S. But at the same time, this experience fostered a strengthening of fighting spirit among them. It was rather unusual that the rank and file should reject a compromise negotiated and accepted by their own union representatives, as happened at the meeting on 5 November 1932. While not only related to the issue of wage cuts, discussions at the general assemblies of the local metalworkers' union in both May and November 1932 became so heated that the meetings had to be broken off and resumed a week later.[113]

The disagreements of 1927–1928 has previously been described by Knud Knudsen, who concludes: "In the conflict with Ford the unions had to abandon old and time-honoured principles of organisation."[114] This is true in the sense that not having a negotiated agreement was an important defeat for the workers and the unions. But despite that, the unions were still functional at Ford. There is no sign of a loss of membership; on the contrary: in November 1932 the combined union club, which had fallen victim to disputes between the skilled and the unskilled workers in 1927, was reorganised as a direct response to the wage cuts.[115]

The union members would also continue to elect shop stewards. When the names of these were forwarded to the management, as was standard practice, the routine response would be that recognising shop stewards were no longer part of the "jurisdiction" of the company.[116] Nevertheless, the management found it practical to uphold some sort of communication with the unions. Its declared intention of cutting wages in 1929 was followed by talks with union representatives, as detailed above. This continued during the 1930s, when management were ready to accept elected spokespersons on an *ad hoc* basis, while still officially adhering to the principle of not recognising shop stewards.[117]

Industrial relations at Ford Copenhagen during the 1930s can thus be characterised as a sort of semi-official collective bargaining. In his reminiscence, H.C. Møller explained in retrospect: "We had to have a union. What happened was that unions in the Ford Denmark plant were tacitly approved."[118] A key result of these developments was that wages now *de facto* became subject to negotiation. During the period when a formal collective agreement had been in place, the basic wage level scheme had been set up by the management as a more or less direct copy of the wage scheme in effect in Detroit. The unions would accept what was in principle a dictate on these issues, without doubt because the scheme put forward by the management resulted in wages well above what could be obtained in other, similar parts of industry. Instead, the unions saved their strength for other issues. But at least from the crisis in the early 1930s, high wage levels could no longer be taken for granted. And since the change in 1928, the Danish management had been able to secure itself more leeway in setting the wage levels. The overall result was that on the important issue of deciding wages, Ford Motor Company A/S was now coming much closer to what was the normal procedure in Danish industry.

Speaking of industrial relations in general, the local management in Copenhagen tried to find a compromise between their obligations to Detroit on one hand, and what they themselves judged to be the best way of handling things, based on the local context, on the other. And they did so with some success, as the level of conflict was low for the rest of the interwar period—there were sometimes heated negotiations, but no strikes after 1928. As such, industrial relations at Ford Motor Company A/S evolved quite differently from in the UK during this period. As head of the British Ford company, Percival Perry pursued a strict anti-union policy, much like in Detroit. An extensive spy system, arbitrary sackings, and foremen "driving" the workers would ensure that Dagenham would in this respect also resemble River Rouge, and become known as the "place of fear".[119]

PRESENCE

On the Road to Modernity

On the 28th of November 1927, a rather unusual advertisement could be seen in every single English-language newspaper in the USA. It had the form of a personal letter from Henry Ford himself, announcing the new Model A. Apart from a small portrait of Henry Ford and his signature, the ad consisted of nothing but text, explaining the thoughts and ideas behind the new car. There was no picture, no specifications, or even price mentioned of the new Model A—these were only revealed gradually through other full-page ads in the following days. This campaign, devised by the company N.W. Ayer & Son, went into marketing history, as it created a huge impact while at the same time disregarding all the established advertising principles—and clichés—of its time.[120]

When the Model A was introduced in Denmark two months later, the number of consecutive ads was reduced to three, but apart from this the campaign was faithfully reproduced in several Danish regional and national newspapers, including of course *Politiken.* The first ad in the series—the message from Henry Ford—was a direct translation of the American original.[121]

The car as lifestyle

These were, however, the only ads by Ford Motor Company A/S during this period that we can say for certain were moulded directly over an American model. While it is impossible to establish the definite origin of every Ford ad, it is evident from their form that most of them were either devised in Denmark or at least heavily adopted for a Danish context, just as in the previous period.[122]

A prominent example is a 12-page special advertising section of the company magazine, published in 1931. Under the headline *Med Ford gennem Danmark* (*With Ford across Denmark*), it depicts various versions of the Model A in front of typical Danish landscapes or well-known landmarks—including Skamlingsbanken in South Jutland, a traditional site for patriotic manifestations.[123] National themes and symbols were less pronounced in newspaper ads but, even if not decisively Danish, there was nothing overtly American about the text and illustrations either; nor is there any sign that advertising was co-ordinated on a European level.[124]

But while there were no direct American references in the text and symbols of Ford's Danish advertising, it may be argued that they reflected American ideas in a more subtle and indirect way. The straightforward, common-sense content of the earlier ads was now supplemented by loftier appeals. A typical example is one of the earliest ads for the new Ford Model A, from the summer of 1928. With its black and white drawings and praise of the technical qualities of the Ford engine, transmission, etc. it resembles earlier advertising; but its main message is something else, as can be seen from the illustration and read from the first paragraph:

> The longing for being a car owner is probably never stronger than when summer announces itself, and every part of you yearns for a trip into the open countryside, to enjoy the sun, the air and a refreshing swim together with your family.

As described above, Norval Hawkins had pioneered modern marketing at Ford in Detroit at the beginning of the 20th century. In 1928, it was almost 10 years since Hawkins had left Ford. But it was as if his dictum, that sales appeal must be made to the heart rather than to the mind, had now finally been taken up by the Danish Ford Company.[125]

Ford was not alone in its appeal to lifestyle from the late 1920s and onwards. In particular, GM was going in the same direction. This reflected the fact that the market for cars for the broad middle class was now maturing in Denmark in the same way as it had in the USA some years before: owning a car, whatever its brand, was no longer prestigious in itself. The market was differentiating, and the function of the ads was now also to place a specific car on the right level in the hierarchy of brands and models.

Figure 24 "What more can you expect?". An example of a Ford advertisement appealing to lifestyle. Full page in *Politiken*, 11 July 1928

The visual appearance of Ford's advertising was changing during the 1930s. The ideal was a contemporary and modern look. But compared to other European markets, Danish newspaper ads appeared a bit more graphically and artistically restrained. One example would be the use of the V8 logo. Launched in 1932 the number 8 enclosed in the letter V became widespread, parallel to the success of the V8 line of cars. It was used in Denmark too. But from the mid-1930s, the original logo was diversified in the USA into versions where the V was tilted, or even turned 90° to resemble the head of an arrow, to signify high speed. This new, dynamic logo was also used for instance in France and the Netherlands, but was almost never seen in newspaper advertising in Denmark.[126]

Ford's main adversary in advertising, General Motors, got a boost when the leading American advertising bureau J. Walter Thompson established itself in Copenhagen. This was a direct result of the growing automobile industry: J. Walter Thompson had an exclusive contract with GM for its international marketing, which stipulated that the bureau had to have offices in any country where GM had an assembly plant.[127] The feud between Ford and GM over newspaper ads continued during the late 1920s, reaching a peak in 1930 with 35 Ford ads in *Politiken,* compared to around 30 from GM. But from then on, the number dropped significantly, reflecting the economic depression of the early 1930s. Ford's management was in a bit of a dilemma: on one hand it would be sensible not to spend money on advertising when the potential customers were out of money. On the other hand, something had to be done, as sales were plummeting.

At a lengthy board meeting in September 1933, it was decided to reinforce marketing efforts. As manager, H.C. Møller was authorised to spend an extra DKK 200,000 on "direct advertising", above the amount already allocated for that purpose.[128] But as can be seen from Figure 25, the money does not seem to have been spent on newspaper ads.

The number of newspaper ads did not start to rise again until the very late 1930s. And at that time, the character of Ford's advertising had changed. Gone were most of the large, full- or half-page ads of ten years before. Instead, the number of smaller ads had grown. This

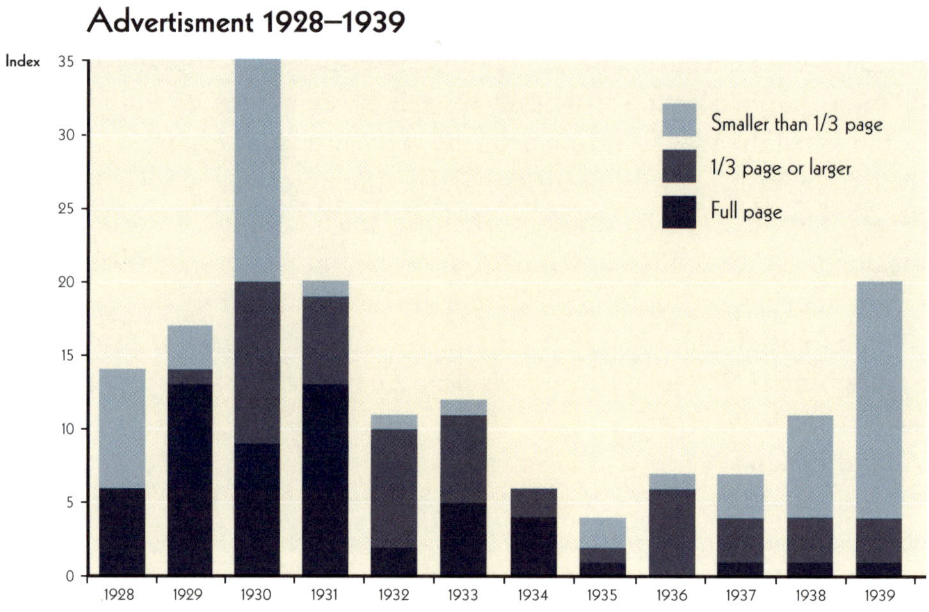

Figure 25 Number of newspaper ads by Ford Motor Company in *Politiken*, 1928–1939. Source: Online archive at www.politiken.dk

reflected the company's changing product portfolio. The growing number of ads from 1937 onwards were promoting the Eifel, Ford's new low-cost model which was launched that year. Apart from being numerous, these ads distinguished themselves by being small and placed on the last pages of the paper, close to the classified ads. Furthermore, the ads for the Eifel were all identical. The large, individually crafted ads used for the V8 would not have been consistent with the Eifel's appeal to the cost-conscious buyer.[129]

Fashionable Ford

A substantial part of the extra money that the board decided in 1933 to use for marketing, was probably invested in the company magazine. In January 1931 it had been relaunched under the new and somewhat fancier name *Ford Nyt*.[130] While the original *Ford Nyheder* had been published primarily for employees, the new version was oriented towards the general public. It was distributed through dealers, but it was also possible to subscribe.[131] It was enlarged considerably from 4 to 28 or more pages per issue, with larger illustrations.

In 1933 it was revamped once again, with larger pages, even more photos, and a layout that was clearly inspired by contemporary illustrated magazines, including the use of colour on the front page. The photographers were generally anonymous, but at least one cover photo can be attributed to Jonals Co., the first advertising photo studio in Denmark and generally recognised as a pioneer in modern commercial photography. From now on, the magazine was primarily a marketing platform. However, the ambitions had clearly been set a bit too high, as the rate of publication was lowered from monthly to quarterly in 1935[132]

Parallel to this, Ford abandoned Sylvester Hvid as their partner in advertising. In 1934 Frantz Harlang, a former employee at Sylvester Hvid, teamed up with Frithjof Toksvig, who had worked in advertising in the USA, to form a new full-service advertising bureau. Under the name Harlang & Toksvig, this bureau would become a leading proponent of modern methods of marketing in Denmark.[133] Harlang and Toksvig took over production and distribution of *Ford Nyt,* but also other PR activities for Ford, such as the production of brochures.[134]

The circulation of *Ford Nyt* is unknown, but it must have reached a considerably smaller audience than the ads in the nationwide newspapers. On the other hand, the magazine offered Ford Motor Company A/S an opportunity to paint a more extensive and coherent picture of itself, in the way it wanted to be seen by the public.

The content was a broad selection of issues related to being a car owner in general and owning a Ford in particular, such as technical hints and explanations, the use of Ford cars in different situations from utility to race and spectacular travels, celebrities driving Ford—and even regular fashion reports about selecting the right dress for driving. Just as in the newspaper ads, Americanism in the magazine was mostly indirect, in its appeal to a certain lifestyle. Especially during the 1930s, the way Ford cars were presented, and tied together with celebrity drivers, events, and fashion, evokes connotations of modernity and a contemporary lifestyle even more than in the newspaper ads. But at the same time, the appeal to common sense and the

FORD NYT
Nr. 2 - 1939
Ford Motor Company A/S
SYDHAVNSGADE 27 — KØBENHAVN V.

framing of Ford as the car that delivers most for the money, which are so clearly present in the newspaper ads, are also found in *Ford Nyt*, even if in a more subdued form.

The previous columns and quotes from Henry Ford were now a thing of the past. Henry Ford would still appear in the pages of *Ford Nyt* every now and then, but as a celebrity among celebrities, not as a social visionary.

Part of the landscape

In 1931 a so-called foxhunt took place on Funen, where 50 private drivers were chasing a "fox" in the form of an aeroplane. The same year so-called "reliability races" were held in Denmark, Norway, and Sweden.[135] These were new types of events, replacing the traditional processions of cars, which had lost some of their attraction by the end of the 1920s.

But the most spectacular of all events were undoubtedly the Scandinavian "Ford Rodeo", which took place just outside Copenhagen in July 1931. An enthusiastic crowd of 25,000 watched as drivers raced on a track filled with moats, ditches, ramps, and other obstacles. A special women's competition took place on flat terrain covered with balloons, and the winner was the one who burst most of them. Between races, the public was entertained by a live band. There were extensive press reports of the rodeo, which was also filmed. Encouraged by the success, Ford was determined to make the rodeo into a yearly event. But by the following year, 1932, the economic depression had hit with full force and, symbolically, on the day of the event, it poured with rain. The public stayed away, and no attempt was made to repeat the event.[136]

Ford also prominently took part in the recurrent national and international car exhibitions, which were held in the *Forum* exhibition hall, built in 1926 on the initiative of the Association of Automobile

Figure 26 Dad is home from the office in his shiny Ford V8, and greeted by his wife and son, while the neighbours look over the fence in envy. Elements such as the functionalist bungalow and the striking colour of the car add an aura of modernity to the otherwise traditional family scene. Unknown artist. Cover of *Ford Nyt*, no. 2, 1939

and Bicycle Wholesale Dealers.[137] But Ford also continued making occasional separate exhibitions, such as a jubilee exhibition in *Tivoli* in March 1939, which drew a crowd of 33,000.[138]

There were also public displays of a more lasting character. At the same 1933 board meeting where a decision was taken to intensify print marketing, it was also decided to use DKK 200,000 to set up a new showroom, "centrally located" in Copenhagen.[139] And the showroom that opened in June 1934 was indeed centrally located, on one of the city's most fashionable streets: H.C. Andersens Boulevard, opposite to the Town Hall Square. It was built in a decisively modern, almost art deco style, with a large glass facade. In the evening, its strong, horizontal lines were emphasised with neon lights in red and blue, topped with a large, glowing Ford logo. The showroom was built by Ford Motor Company A/S, but run by one of its major dealers, A/S Scaniadam.[140]

In early 1931, all European Ford companies were encouraged to establish service stations "of uniform appearance" within their territory, and the possibility of setting up one or two such stations in Denmark was discussed by the board, and DKK 1 million was reserved for the purpose. However, later that same year it was decided not to pursue this further, as it was deemed unnecessary by the standards already reached by the independent dealers.[141]

Nevertheless, Ford dealers around the country continued the gradual renovation and expansions of their garages and showroom, on their own initiative. Many chose to do so in a modern, functionalist style.[142] The most impressive example was that of Aarhus Motor Compagni, the main Ford dealer in Jutland. Aarhus Motor Compagni had been growing considerably since its modest start in 1925, and in 1937 a completely new service and sales building was opened in the port area in central Aarhus. It was a two-storey building in concrete, with a facade characterised by straight lines and large areas of glass, in an unmistakably functionalist style. At the time of its grand opening, with 4,000 guests in attendance and personal greetings from Henry and Edsel Ford sent by telegram, it was said to be the largest Ford service and sales facility in Europe.[143]

Figure 27 Showroom, established by Ford in 1934 on one of the most fashionable streets in Copenhagen, just opposite to the Town Hall Square. Unknown photographer. Thalbitzer: *Ford Motor Company A/S gennem 25 Aar*, 90

National importance

At a board meeting in 1931, a somewhat peculiar issue was on the agenda. Percival Perry outlined

> ... Mr Henry Ford's thoughts in regard to the advisability of combining farm and industrial work, eventually by establishing a system where after industrial laborers should have an opportunity to operate simultaneously with his industrial occupation a small farm, which he could by and by acquire ownership of.[144]

One of several paradoxes in Henry Ford's social vision was that, despite the fact that he had built his industrial empire based on an extreme division of labour, increased rationalisation, and urbanisation, he was at the same time romanticising the coherent lifestyle of small-town America. The idea that industrial workers should also become farmers had previously been put forward in 1922 in *My Life and Work*.[145]

Based on Perry's recommendations, the board now discussed whether the Danish company could contribute to the realisation of Henry Ford's ideas in this regard. Considerations were raised about the necessity of a substantial reduction of the plant's 40 hour working week. Nevertheless, the board decided to investigate the possibilities further, and the manager was authorised to start looking for a suitable piece of farmland that could be acquired. But the board also pointed out that land should only be purchased when it was "considered justified from an investment standpoint". A few months later, Denmark was hit hard by the economic recession. No more was ever heard about plans for buying farmland.

This was the one and only time during the 1930s that what could be called Fordist issues of a grander scale were on the agenda of the board. For the rest of the time, the board was directing its attention towards issues of a more immediate and specific nature, such as political and economic concerns directly relevant to the company.

One of the reasons why the board of Ford Motor Company A/S had been changed in 1929 was to include members from different Danish sectors of commerce and public life, thereby rooting the company more firmly in its national context. As it would turn out, they would not only lend their name and reputation to the company, but also become active partners to manager H.C. Møller in representing the company. One example is a meeting between the Minister of Trade and Industry C.N. Hauge, and Ford Motor Company A/S represented by H.C. Møller and board member P.O. Pedersen. Not only was Pedersen rector of the Technical University and a respected professor in electrical engineering, his political and managerial skills would prove to be of great benefit to the company.

The backdrop of the meeting that took place in January 1932 was of course the economic crisis. The government was contemplating various initiatives to safeguard Danish export and to restrict import in order to protect home industry. In this situation the board decided to ask for a meeting with the Minister of Trade, to present the company's view on the situation. The meeting was granted, and it took place on 7 January.

What the representatives of Ford Motor Company A/S aimed for was not to obtain any specific concessions for the company. Instead, they aimed at convincing the minister on a more general level that the activities of the company—based on its extensive imports and exports—were of benefit to the country. The main arguments had been set out in a letter sent to the minister before the meeting, in which Ford presented the figures seen in Table 4.

According to H.C. Møller's report from the meeting, which was translated into English and sent to Detroit, the minister at first appeared reticent, referring to Ford Motor Company A/S as an American company, due to its ownership. Pedersen and Møller countered this with several arguments, such as the fact that the company was purchasing some of its materials from Danish subcontractors. They also stressed that the value of the exports of the company was almost as large as its imports, claiming that in this way the company was earning most of the foreign currency it needed to pay for its import. All in all, Pedersen and Møller made a thorough attempt to present Ford Motor Company A/S as an enterprise of Danish national importance, despite its American ownership.[146]

Another point put forward by Ford was that, due to the finishing of the Dagenham plant, it was to be expected that the company's imports from the USA would diminish in favour of increased imports from the UK. This was good news for the minister, as Denmark was under a certain political pressure to increase its import of industrial goods from Britain, in return for its large export of mainly agricultural products.[147] The Ford management and board were clearly well aware of the current political issues and tuned their argument towards them.

According to Møller, he and Pedersen felt that "our visit to some extent influenced the Minister's judgement of our Company's activities".[148] That could very well have been the case, but it is unlikely that the meeting had any direct impact on government policy: only a few weeks later, parliament passed the law that established the afore-

Item	Number	1,000 DKK
Import value of car parts		65,541
Freight		3,764
Export value finished cars		61,245
Material purchased in DK for production		7,875
Manufacturing expenses (Excl. wages and salaries)		3,475
Wages and salaries		10,528
Average no. of payroll employees during peak season	715	
Average no. of payroll employees all year	377	
Average no. of salary employees	67	
Commercial expenses (Excl. wages, salaries, and taxes)		**4,165**

Table 4 Economic activities of Ford Motor Company A/S 1929–1931, as presented to Minister of Trade and Industry, C.N. Hauge, January 1932. Source: BFRC: Charles E. Sorensen records series, Hauge

mentioned Currency Committee. The Committee would impose several restrictions on import and export that was found by Ford Motor Company A/S to be "considerably handicapping" to its sales.[149]

The Ford management would continue to underline the company's contributions to the Danish economy: for instance, at the 1932 general meeting, at which it was reported that Ford Motor Company A/S "as far as possible endeavours to purchase its supplies in Denmark in order to support Danish industry and trade", and that during 1931 a total of DKK 3,620,000 had been paid to Danish suppliers.[150]

Møller and other board members would have other meetings with government authorities and "various parties" about these issues in the following years.[151] Nothing came of these initiatives, however, in the form of specific import or export privileges for Ford, and much less in the way of any significant changes in the economic and trade policy of the government.

In 1926 Henry Ford had expressed his discontent with Denmark's "labour government" in no uncertain terms.[152] But local management at the Copenhagen Ford plant took a less ideological and more pragmatic stance, taking note of the fact that the Social Democrats had become the leading political force of the country. Neither the management nor the board agreed with all aspects of the tax and trade policies pursued under social democratic government. They tried to influence them, but within the framework of a working relationship.

Neither did the Danish Ford Company voice any public criticism of the "labour government" *per se*. On the contrary, as seen above, newly elected social-democratic Prime Minister Thorvald Stauning was invited as a prominent guest at the opening of the South Port plant in 1924. The Social Democrats, on the other hand, developed a similar pragmatic attitude towards Ford as a company of economic importance, as a creator of well-paid jobs and as an inspiration for industrial modernisation, as we shall see in more detail later.

Difficult years

Most European states reacted to the crisis with some sort of protectionist measures, often combined with political nationalism. One way an export-oriented company like Ford could react to this was by strengthening its direct appearance in those national markets affected and making a stronger presence inside the protectionist walls that were being built. As a response to diminishing sales in Poland in 1931, Ford Motor Company A/S started researching the possibilities for establishing an assembly facility in that country. The main purpose of the plant would be to circumvent the high tax levied on imported cars.

H.C. Møller was authorised by the board to negotiate the purchase of a site in Gdynia for that purpose. According to the plan, which was supported from London, a Polish company would become a subsidiary of Ford in Denmark, in the same manner as the existing Swedish and Finnish companies. However, the plans for Gdynia proved to be too costly. The possibility of renting a site somewhere else was investigated, parallel to negotiations with the Polish government on tax conditions for imported car parts. But this was a nut too tough to crack, even for Ford, and after 5 years of investigations and negotiations, the plans for expansion were finally given up in May 1936.[153] Sales in Poland continued to be low throughout the 1930s.

The attempt for Norway was more successful. During the mid-1930s, sales in Norway were deemed to be unsatisfactory. After a visit to Oslo, Percival Perry found that there was a potential for better market penetration, if a Ford company were established in Norway. But car import was limited by a quota system, in which import companies were given permission to import a certain number of cars, partly based on their sales in previous years. To obtain a quota, a deal was struck with the largest existing Ford dealer in Norway, Gjestvang Automobilforretning A/S, which sold 90 percent of its shares to the Danish Ford company, thereby effectively becoming its subsidiary. In the same process, the name of the Norwegian company was changed to Fram Motor Kompani A/S.[154] Following this, sales in Norway increased by 30–50 percent compared to previous years.

Increasing political tension in Europe in the late 1930s was also beginning to affect Ford Motor Company A/S. The civil war that broke out in Spain in 1936 would cause great difficulties and losses for Ford and its Barcelona assembly plant, despite an attempt to side with both parties.[155] But for Ford in Denmark, the war in Spain went by rather unnoticed.

But when the Soviet Union attacked Finland in November 1939, thereby initiating the so-called Winter War, Ford Motor Company A/S became involved. In early 1940 it was decided to supply the Finns with 200 V8 trucks for the war effort on favourable terms. At first, they were to be sold by Ford in Denmark to Ford in Finland at cost price and with 12 months' credit, but this was later changed to a sale directly to the Finnish government. The trucks were to be delivered from Dagenham and assembled at a provisional plant set up in Northern Sweden, near the Finnish border. However, the trucks were not ready for use until the war was almost over. At the end of the war, it was also decided to donate DKK 100,000 to the rebuilding of the Finnish Technical High School.[156]

The fact that there was a special relationship between Ford in Finland and Denmark, as the first was partly owned by the latter, was most certainly part of the explanation why Ford Motor Company A/S decided to support Finland during the war. But at the same time, it was in line with the general politics of the Danish government —and public opinion. In contrast to the civil war in Spain, where the

Danish government had supported the policy of "non-intervention", Denmark took a clear stance in favour of Finland in the Winter War. No direct military aid was sent, but private support, including enlisting as volunteers to fight on the Finnish side, was accepted, and several Danish organisations and companies supported "the Finnish cause". Being one of these companies also placed Ford in the political mainstream.

In September 1939, Germany invaded Poland. The collapse of Poland as an independent country led to a loss of DKK 77,000 to the Danish Ford company's activities in that country, which was considered "modest" considering the circumstances.[157] But clearly the board was aware that this might only be the beginning of even graver circumstances. In late 1939, precautions for keeping the plant going in circumstances other than "normal line of business", as well as procedures for dealing with employers in case of mobilisation, were discussed and adopted.[158]

With the great German victories that have struck the world with astonishment and admiration, a new era has arisen in Europe

Declaration by the Danish government, July 1940

1940–1945
Interregnum

PRODUCTION

Keeping Things Going

In the early hours of 9 April 1940, Denmark became occupied by Germany. Military resistance was brief and there was no significant loss of life or destruction of property. A coalition government was formed by the four major parties in parliament which, for the time being, was allowed by the Germans to manage the country under the rules of occupation.

From the beginning of the occupation, the Danish government pursued a policy of cooperation with Germany, partly motivated by an interest in safeguarding Danish economic interests. The Danes in general adapted to a situation that seemed inevitable. As Germany expanded its power in Europe, Danish farmers and industry were politically advised to seek advantage from this new geopolitical situation, and a great number of them did so.[1]

However, as Germany started to lose momentum in the war, especially on the eastern front, relations with and attitudes towards the force of occupation started to change. Resistance, including armed sabotage, was slowly emerging. In late August 1943, the policy of cooperation came to an end, and the government stepped down. From then on, Denmark was in principle ruled directly by the German authorities. However, large parts of the civil administration kept working until the end of the occupation on 5 May 1945.

The period from April 1940 to May 1945 was an interregnum for Ford Motor Company A/S: not only in the general sense that it was a period where normal political, government, and economic relations were suspended in Denmark, but also in the more specific sense that production was not so much dictated by the company's inherent plans for further developments of car assembly, as it was an *ad hoc* adaptation to whatever was possible during the external circumstances.

Now falling within German occupied territory, the Copenhagen plant would of course cease to receive car parts and other supplies from Dagenham.[2] It would in principle have been possible to receive parts from Cologne, and even from Dearborn until the end of 1941, but if such deliveries took place at all, they were insubstantial. In 1940, the production of cars and trucks was already reduced to 1,555 units, compared to more than 10,000 the year before. The following years it was reduced further, until it came to a complete stop in the spring of 1943.[3]

To supplement the declining production of cars, Ford Motor Company A/S would embark on several new types of production, gradually leading farther away from its area of expertise. In May 1940, just a few weeks after the occupation, an agreement was made with Imbert Generatoren GmbH, a company in Cologne, Germany, producing wood gas generators for cars based on their own design. Due to a lack of petrol, gas generators were in high demand in most of Europe, and Ford's V8 engine had proven very suitable for being powered by wood gas. Initially, Ford was to produce generators on license from Imbert for the Danish and Norwegian markets. However, it turned out that to sell generators in Norway, they had to be produced within that country. Furthermore, getting raw materials for this production became more and more difficult as the war dragged on. By the end of 1941, only spare parts for service could be produced.[4]

Instead, it was agreed that the Danish Company should start producing gas-generators to be delivered to the Ford plant in Cologne, with which Imbert already had a close cooperation. For such production, raw material could be obtained from Germany. This time the Copenhagen factory was not just producing according to designs from Imbert but was involved in testing several types of improved generators. Since deliveries from Germany were also delayed, this order could not be fulfilled before September 1943. By that time, Ford in Cologne was not able to receive the 4,000 generators produced, and they were delivered directly to Imbert instead. The same was the case for a later order for 5,000 sets of filters and coolers.[5]

Figure 28 Advertisement for the Imbert wood gas generator. The generator is fitted on the rear of a pre-war Ford V8. *Social-Demokraten*, 24 September 1943

The quest for alternative production continued, and in early 1943 an agreement was made with Niessen Werke in Vienna for the manufacture of 300 so-called disinfectors. Niessen Werke was a supplier of technical equipment for bomb-shelters, and the disinfectors were probably meant for that purpose. By the end of 1944 about 180 units had been shipped.[6]

Gas-generators, filters, and coolers were of course different from the regular production of a car assembly plant. But even if the reconfiguration of the production line took some time, it clearly was manageable. However, in late 1943 Ford Motor Company A/S took a step further into a hitherto unknown type of production. In August that year, Ford was approached by the German company Gebrüder Sachsenberg A/G, producers of light transport material for land and sea ("Land und See Leichtbau"). This resulted in an agreement, according to which Ford was to produce a total of 132 boats, based on drawings and specifications delivered by the German company.

Producing boats was of course an area in which Ford Motor Company A/S had absolutely no experience, and one may wonder why they took on the order. But Gebrüder Sachsenberg would supply Ford not only with drawings for the boats, but also with fixtures and special tools. With these aids, it could be argued that constructing a small boat would not be that different from assembling a car body. And Ford needed orders to keep the factory going.

Nevertheless, the boats turned out to be a dubious adventure for Ford. It was agreed that construction of the first few boats should be considered a test. Following the approval of the Danish authorities, the construction of the boats progressed at a relatively slow pace. The first one was almost ready for testing by 1 November 1944 as scheduled; but then it was destroyed by sabotage, as described in more detail below.[7] Construction of the remaining boats commenced, but due to further sabotage and the final defeat of Germany in May 1945, only 21 were built and 12 were partly finished.

Taking up these various types of alternative production allowed Ford Motor Company A/S to keep the factory going all the time during the occupation, but with a diminished workforce. The number of blue-collar working hours dropped significantly from more than 900,000 in 1939 to around 200,000 in 1940 and 1941. But in

1942–1944 it was a bit higher, at around 350.000.[8] The total number of both blue- and white-collar employees by the end of the year was as low as 90 in 1940, climbing to 305 in 1944.[9]

MARKETS AND MODELS

Unfamiliar Products

Even if Ford had had the possibility of producing cars in the same numbers as before the occupation, they would have had a hard time selling them. War and occupation were cutting off the company's export markets one by one. And on its domestic market, rationing of petrol had effectively curtailed the private use of cars from as early as September 1939.[10] Consequently, of the 3224 cars produced 1940–1944, only 1822 were actually sold.[11]

At least some of the cars were sold with gas-generators, meaning that they could in principle have been for ordinary, personal use—at least for a time, until it became impossible to obtain tyres for cars. Others were sold without, meaning the customers must have had one of the rare special permits to buy gasoline.

The types of products of which Ford Motor Company A/S took up the manufacture, to compensate for the loss of its car market—such as gas generators, equipment for bomb shelters, and even boats—have already been presented above. To those should be added an agreement with the company Nordisk Køleteknik A/S for 1941–1942, according to which refrigerators produced by that company would be distributed by Ford Motor Company A/S and sold by its dealers. This last arrangement did not imply any production from Ford.

But across this remarkably diverse range of products, the overall challenge for Ford Motor Company A/S was a profound change in market relations. Only four days after the occupation, an office of the German *Wehrwirtschaftsstab* (Military Economy Staff) was established in Copenhagen.[12] The *Wehrwirtschaftsstab* was an administrative body, referring directly to the high command of the German army. Before the war, it had already been gathering considerable amounts of information, partly with the help of military intelligence, about production of strategic interest in countries that Germany might plan to invade or occupy.[13]

The overall task of the *Wehrwirtschaftsstab* was to procure any products that would sustain the German war effort. In some occupied countries, this was done by directly taking over industries. But in Denmark, where the government was still in force, cooperating with German authorities, the *Wehrwirtschaftsstab* generally operated by setting up business agreements between Danish export companies and buyers in Germany.

Since there was a risk that the considerable demand from Germany could result in raw materials being diverted away from production for the domestic market, an agreement was made between Denmark and Germany in June 1940 about so-called "extraordinary deliveries". The basic principle of this agreement was that, whenever the *Wehrwirtschaftsstab* placed an order in Denmark, it was obliged to allow for export of the necessary raw materials etc. from Germany to the Danish company in question. On the other hand, the order could be paid for by a credit account in the Danish National Bank.[14]

Deliveries under this agreement were highly regulated. At first, the *Wehrwirtschaftsstab* (renamed *Rüstungsstab* in February 1943) would place an order. Then the company in question would have to obtain permission to fulfil the order, at a certain price and expected profit rate. The permission would be granted by the Industrial Council, a trade organisation representing all major industries, but only after approval by a special department of the ministry of foreign affairs. This department would consult, among others, the Directorate for Product Supply, a government body for the regulation of trade, which had replaced the former Currency Committee in 1940. Coordination of the whole process was delegated to the Industrial Council.[15]

Practically all the contracts signed by Ford for production for export during the occupation were a result of this procedure.[16] As part of the process, the expected profit for each delivery had to be calculated in advance and submitted for approval. But this could be difficult as the war progressed, and military and political circumstances changed. For the production of boats, for instance, a profit of between 8.3 and 9 percent of the production cost had been calculated, but since the delivery was never finished due to the end of the war, it turned out to be only 1.9 percent, or DKK 12,422.[17]

But not all products had such low profit rates. The average profit rate for Ford's deliveries to Germany was 18 percent, compared to an average profit rate of 12 percent for the period 1940–1944. While these might be considered acceptable profit rates, it should be remembered that the turnover, and thereby the profit, in real figures were exceptionally low: roughly DKK 3 million in total, during the four years of occupation. Of these roughly one-third was earned from export to Germany.

MANAGEMENT

Dealing with Germany

On the day of the occupation, news about the events was travelling from Denmark to Dearborn at great speed. A hastily convened board meeting of Ford Motor Company A/S was held at 10 a.m. local time—equivalent to 4 p.m. in Denmark—at the Ford headquarters at River Rouge. The only two board members present, Edsel B. Ford, and Charles E. Sorensen, decided to immediately transfer a sum of $161,340, deposited by the Danish company in a New York bank, to the American Ford Motor Company; an *ad hoc* measure, meant to minimise any potential loss of assets in Denmark.[18]

The German occupation created a special situation regarding leadership. In other occupied countries, such as France, Belgium, and the Netherlands, local Ford plants were subsumed under the leadership of Ford in Cologne, whose manager, Robert Schmidt, became *Wehrwirtschaftsführer* of all these operations, and appointed as formal custodian of the Ford Werke by the Nazi government. As the war progressed, there was an increased coordination of production, which mainly consisted of trucks for the German army.[19]

In Copenhagen, German officials, most likely from the local office of the *Wehrwirtschaftsstab*, showed up at the South Port plant just a few days after the occupation. They conducted a thorough inspection of the plant, including drawing maps.[20] For H.C. Møller and the management, the question was of course whether this was the preparation of a German take-over of the company.

But it was not. As the only Ford company in the Nazi-occupied part of Europe, Ford Motor Company A/S could continue under its own leadership. No German custodian was appointed in Copenhagen and

H.C. Møller kept his position as manager. Likewise, Percival Perry was formally chairman of the board throughout the whole period of the occupation. However, since he could not travel to Denmark and communication was limited, it was the deputy chairman, V. Falbe-Hansen, who acted as *de facto* chairman in his absence.[21] This was possibly a result of the special political conditions of the occupation in Denmark, in which the Germans were officially only taking care of the military "protection" of the country, while its political and economic institutions were allowed to continue—at least for a while.

Deciding how to deal with the German requests, and how to keep the company running, were the two major issues that the management of Ford Motor Company A/S was now faced with. And decisions had to be taken without any possibility of consulting London. The local management did not only have to act under the conditions of occupation—they were practically on their own.[22]

The Danish members of the board kept up their meetings at regular intervals throughout the occupation, just as the yearly shareholder meetings were held. But interestingly, according to the minutes, the challenges of dealing with the forces of occupation were never brought up at board meetings. Of course, there is the possibility that they were discussed, but that under the circumstances it was thought best not to put the deliberations down in writing. But it was basically left to H.C. Møller and his staff to make the decisions, and thereby also to carry the weight of responsibility.

In July 1940, shortly after the capitulation of France, the Danish government issued a declaration regarding Denmark's relations to Germany. It stated that …

> With the great German victories that have struck the world with astonishment and admiration, a new era has arisen in Europe that will bring about a new regime in political-economic terms under the German leadership. It will be Denmark's task to find its place in a necessary, mutual, and active cooperation with Greater Germany.[23]

Consequently, Danish companies were urged to seek business opportunities with Germany. By that time, Ford Motor Company A/S had already begun its cooperation with Imbert Generatoren GmbH. Ford's dealings with German companies were limited in the beginning, and production was intended for the home market, not for Germany. But as it became impossible to sustain car production, Ford became gradually more dependent on other possibilities, and gradually but steadily drifted towards producing for Germany.

The war also affected the relationship between Copenhagen and the Swedish and Finnish companies. The two Danes in charge of Ford in Stockholm, Brøndum as general manager and Beck as sales manager, were able to obtain Swedish passports. That allowed them initially to visit Copenhagen, and even travel abroad. But from 1943 onwards, travels to Denmark became severely restricted.[24] The board in Copenhagen still received business reports from Sweden and Finland. And each year the Danish board would, as it had done also before the war, appoint an employee residing in Stockholm to represent it at the general meeting of the Swedish company.

In reality, though, the Swedish and Finnish companies were left to act with a great degree of autonomy, as they strove to keep up production. The Swedish Ford company established a production of charcoal gas generators, independently of the Danish production of wood gas generators, and made a business out of renovating and selling used trucks. The Finnish company started an import of Swedish gas generators. Its business seems to have thrived, especially after Finland became allied with Germany, and it was able to import spare parts for trucks from Cologne for delivery to the Finnish army. The decision to do so was taken locally in Helsinki.[25]

During this period, two members of the board passed away. The first was Professor P.O. Pedersen, who died in August 1941. A new member of the board was elected, Professor Anker Engelund, who had also succeeded Pedersen as rector of the Technical University.[26] In May 1943 it was the president of the international Ford Motor Company and son of Henry Ford, Edsel Ford, who died at the age of 49.[27] Due to the circumstances, no replacement for him was elected, and for the rest of the occupation, Charles E. Sorensen was the only representative of Detroit on the board, but of course without the ability to attend its meetings.

Growing Impatience

Despite the so-called "peaceful occupation" of Denmark, top officials of the Labour movement feared that the labour unions would fall victim to a forced Nazification, as had been the case in Germany—and as had happened in other occupied countries. Therefore, they almost instantly decided on a strategy of appeasement towards the German authorities. In August 1940, the Danish Confederation of Trade Unions (DSF) made a joint proposal to the government together with the Confederation of Danish Employers (DA), suggesting that both strikes and lockouts should be declared illegal. Instead, any industrial disputes that the two parties were not able to solve by themselves should be decided by a commission of economic experts. This was immediately adopted by parliament.[28]

In May 1940, the indexation of wages, which had been part of most national agreements between employers and unions, had been abolished. The indexation stipulated that wages were to be regulated in relation to prices. Indexing was put into effect again in late 1941 though, but only with a partial compensation. Without the right to strike and with prices rising without wages being fully indexed relative to that, there was a general decrease in real wages in Denmark of around 20 percent on average from April 1940 to the spring of 1942.[29]

At Ford Motor Company A/S, management introduced a split pay scheme from June 1941. Those blue-collar workers assembling cars would be paid the same as before, but those employed in the alternative productions that were taken up were to be paid according to a new pay rate. While the average hourly wage for car assembly was DKK 3.38, it would be only DKK 2.58 for other work. As a sort of compensation, Ford offered to increase the pay rate in relation to prices, as stipulated in the national agreements, of which they were not otherwise part. But since indexed wages had been put on hold in the national agreements, and were only partially resumed from late 1941, this had a minor effect.[30] The pay rates were raised a couple of times during the period. The end result was that, with both categories combined, there was a slight increase in the hourly pay rate for blue-collar workers at Ford of about

8 percent for the period 1939 to 1944—but during the same period, prices increased by 54 percent on average, according to the official index.[31] In other words: as did most others, Ford workers experienced a significant drop in real wages throughout the occupation.

The type of bargaining that had developed through the late 1930s was taken a step further. Not only did management meet with representatives of the unions, but it also *de facto* acknowledged the leading shop steward and chairman of the combined club as the main representative of the workers. And at least from 1942, the results of these negotiations over pay rates and other issues, which had been informal at the beginning, were now put down in writing and signed by both parties.[32] In reality, formal bargaining had now been reinstated.

The workers at Ford had grudgingly agreed to the lower pay rate for non-car production in 1940, at a time when unemployment was high, unions on the defensive, and the political situation insecure. But as time went on, they started demanding better wages. That was in line with the general mood within the working class: from around 1942 employment had vastly improved, not least due to a lot of construction work being undertaken for the Germans. Despite being illegal, the Communist Party was not without influence in some work-places, and generally workers were becoming more active in a mixture of protests against the occupation and demands for better living conditions.

In late 1942, the combined union club at Ford Motor Company A/S was pressing for a return to normal wage rates for all workers and asking the national union associations to support them. After some fierce negotiations, the lower wages for non-car work were maintained, but raised. But the local union representatives were dissatisfied, as a higher-ranking official of the metalworkers' union had settled the agreement without consulting them.[33]

A few months later, the management provoked anger among the skilled workers as they directed a workman to do some work that had hitherto been done by a skilled metalworker. Apart from causing the old animosities between skilled and unskilled workers to resurface, this also led to a general demand from the unions for a complete removal of the work directive that had been in place since the 1930s, in favour of a properly negotiated agreement.[34] That did not happen. But the mood between the workers had clearly become more impatient.

The resistance against the occupation, which had been slowly developing throughout the country, did not of course go unnoticed by the Ford workers. Sabotage against companies producing for the Germans and retaliation from Nazi paramilitary groups escalated in the summer of 1944. By the end of June 1944, German authorities declared a nightly curfew in Copenhagen. Workers at the Burmeister & Wain shipyard reacted by leaving their jobs at 12 noon in protest and were soon followed by workers from other major workplaces. During the following hot summer days things escalated, with barricades and shootings in the streets, leading to deaths and casualties. More German military were brought to the city, and supplies of gas, water, and electricity cut off. What would later become known as the "Copenhagen popular strike" lasted for about a week, before the Germans agreed to loosen their grip on the city, and work was resumed.[35] The popular strike also included Ford, where both blue-collar and white-collar employees took part in it. The management afterwards decided to pay them their wages for two days of the strike.[36]

PRESENCE

Dilemmas

25 June 1944 was the 25th anniversary of Ford Motor Company A/S. It was also the day when bombs planted by Nazi terrorists shattered parts of the famous *Tivoli* amusement park, and when the German authorities declared the curfew that would lead to the dramatic days of the popular strike. These gloomy circumstances did not encourage any grand and festive celebration. A banquet was held for dealers and employees, but the main initiative directed towards the general public was the publication of a book on the history of the Danish Ford company. The text of the 106 richly illustrated pages was written by board member and editor Carl Thalbitzer. The occupation was barely mentioned, but its effects was clearly, if indirectly visible: the cars shown as contemporary were all 1939 models.[37]

During the early years of the occupation, some newspaper ads appeared, mainly marketing gas generators for private cars. However, as Ford soon had next to nothing to offer to private consumers, and no car-buying public existed, there was no real need to advertise. But

Ford Nyt was published sporadically, about once a year. The June 1944 issue was dedicated to the anniversary, including a text by the author Johannes V. Jensen, who would be awarded the Nobel prize later that same year, in which he declared his everlasting love for the Ford car.[38]

But the greatest challenge for Ford Motor Company A/S in these years was not how to market its product. What would come to affect Ford's relationship with the public most was how its relations to the Germans was perceived. In the beginning, it was not that difficult: not only all significant political forces, but also the great majority of the population, saw cooperation with the German authorities at all levels as something inevitable. Danish industry was urged by the government to seek business opportunities with Germany.

According to H.C. Møller, the Danish Ford company in the beginning tried to avoid working directly for the Germans, answering requests from the *Wehrwirtschaftsstab* to do so by stating that its limited production of cars was of national interest to Denmark, since part of the production was used for compensation deals with other countries. This might be correct—or it might be an afterthought, since it was written in late 1944, when, in contrast to 1940, it was clear to everyone that the Germans were rapidly approaching defeat.

During this time, political and public attitudes towards Germany had also been gradually changing. Resistance towards the *Wehrmacht* and German authorities slowly emerged and was fuelled by Germany's first major defeats in the war. In late August 1943, the Danish government resigned, officially leaving the rule of the country to the forces of occupation. Acts of sabotage became widespread against companies, which according to the resistance movement were aiding the German war effort.

Meanwhile, Ford had gradually become more and more involved in business with German partners. And while initially meant for the home market, products were exported to Germany at least from 1943. Writing in late 1944, H.C. Møller was keen to emphasize that the contracts that he and the company entered into with German partners were all "instigated" by the Germans. That might be true, or it might be a case of self-justification. But given the authority vested in the *Wehrwirtschaftsstab*, it seems plausible that turning down a business proposal from their side was not something that was done lightly.

Very many Danish companies delivered goods and services to German civil and military customers during the occupation. Some did it enthusiastically, taking the opportunity to profiteer from an otherwise dire situation. Others, like Ford Motor Company A/S, drifted gradually in that direction, as the economic and political situation made it seem inevitable.

An important question many companies had to face after the war was whether the products they had delivered to Germany were helping the Nazi war effort. According to Møller's 1944 memorandum, he and his co-managers had made a decision early on during the occupation, not to produce "real war supplies". And clearly, the type of goods first delivered from Ford in Copenhagen were not directly for warfare. Wood gas generators were not military equipment *per se*. But it could of course be argued that their use in civilian transport helped preserve gasoline for military purposes. This is probably why the Imbert factory in Cologne was bombed several times by allied air forces. During the last part of the war, the factory was kept going using forced labour and prisoners of war.[39]

But with the production of boats, Ford Motor Company A/S took a step further. At the time of production, as well as later, the character of these boats was partly shrouded in mythology. Internally, they were referred to as "motor-tugs".[40] But in some circles outside the company, rumours circulated that Ford had started manufacturing motor torpedo boats for the Germans.[41]

Tugs as well as motor torpedo boats are, however, of a size that would normally require a slipway and other facilities, which were not present at the South Port plant, as well as some experience in shipbuilding. It is therefore most unlikely that any of these claims were correct. Fortunately, the FMC archive contains hitherto unpublished photos of some of the boats, taken after one of the acts of sabotage. These photos provide an indication of the real nature of the boats.

Judging from these photos, the boats would have been approximately 5–7 meters in length, which is also consistent with the fact that they were transported to Germany by rail. According to the application for production licence, they were fitted with an engine of approximately 100 HP, which could have been a Ford V8.[42]

Figure 29 One of the boats manufactured by Ford Motor Company A/S for the German contractor Gebrüder Sachsenberg A/G, shortly after it had been sabotaged on 21 November 1944. Unknown photographer. Ford Motor Company A/S photo collection

The size and shape of the hull, the rather long propeller shaft, and the type of engine all point towards the boats being so-called *Sprengboote*. This was a type of weapon devised by the German Navy late in the war. As the name implies, *Sprengboote* were carrying a load of explosives. They were small, fast-moving vessels, meant to be rammed into enemy ships, with the driver jumping off at the last minute.[43]

In the end, *Sprengboote* would prove to be an inefficient weapon, born out of German desperation during the last phase of the war. But nonetheless, it was a weapon. In judging the Ford management's decision to take up its production, it cannot be ruled out that they were unaware of the intended use of the boats. The Germans would not necessarily have revealed what they were meant for, and in all internal documents they are referenced as tugboats or just boats. Maybe that is what H.C. Møller honestly thought them to be, or maybe he simply decided to believe so.

The boats soon attracted the attention of the resistance. On 17 October 1944, shortly after it had been finished, the first test boat was blown up, fixtures and tools were destroyed, and a couple of trucks supposedly belonging to the Germans were sabotaged too. This was carried out by the communist resistance group BOPA, known for its bold actions against several industrial plants during the last part of the occupation.[44]

A few weeks later, on 21 November, two other boats were sabotaged, this time simply by punching the hulls.[45] It is the result of this that can be seen in Figure 29. This was done by another group, consisting of a handful of employees from within the factory itself. In contrast to BOPA, this group was connected to the national-conservative wing of the resistance and to underground military groups. The actual operation was probably carried out by Torben Fischer-Madsen, Hans Vilhelm Lind, and Palle Moe.[46]

Finally, on 8 March 1945 a boat was blown up and three others were slightly damaged when they were stationed on the Copenhagen rail yard, waiting to be transported to Germany. This was a dramatic episode, as it came to a gunfight between saboteurs and a German army patrol, resulting in one dead on both sides.[47]

Apart from the three mentioned above, at least two other Ford employees were active in the resistance: Knud Otto Jensen and Viggo Schiørring. Jensen had been absent from the company since 17 October, the day of the first sabotage, indicating that he might have been involved in this operation, despite not being a member of BOPA. Schiørring had already been incarcerated for other activities from 15 July.[48] As far as their occupations at Ford can be ascertained, all five were part of the technical and administrative staff.

One of the saboteurs who took part in the first raid against the boats on 17 October, Otto "Thomas" Carlé, has given a lively account of what happened. According to him, H.C. Møller and the Danish ambassador to Berlin, O.C. Mohr, who was a personal friend of Møller, suddenly appeared on the scene, as the group was preparing to blow up some trucks in addition to the boat. Møller was "all in a fluster", claiming that the factory was American property, but was told by the saboteurs to "get lost".[49]

But the management was at least to some extent aware of the sentiments and activities of some of its employees. On a meeting in October 1944, the board was informed that two employees, Jensen and Schiørring, were missing for "political reasons"—a euphemism for being caught by the Germans. The board decided that the two would receive their usual wages during their absence. In June 1945, shortly after liberation, Fischer-Madsen, Lind, and Moe each received a donation of DKK 1,600 from Ford Motor Company A/S. No official reason was given, but according to Fischer-Madsen it was in recognition of the way they had carried out the sabotage in November 1944, without damaging the rest of factory.[50]

Following the liberation, there was a political focus on those companies that had in some way done business with the occupiers. They were many, since the Danish government at the beginning of the occupation had encourage economic cooperation with Germany, as mentioned above. But now, public sentiment had changed. One of the results was the establishing of a special Auditing Commission, with a mandate to go through all cases of economic cooperation with the Germans, and to establish if some companies had taken the opportunity to earn "excessive profits". Regardless of what level of profit had originally been approved by the authorities, a maximum allowed profit of 5 percent was now retrospectively decided for all industrial products.[51]

The Auditing Commission went through around 50,000 cases and passed a sentence in 10,030 of them. One of these many cases was Ford Motor Company A/S. It was established that the company had made a total profit of DKK 1,081,297 from selling to German companies, of which DKK 822,781 was considered excessive and had to be refunded to the state. But compared to other companies this was considered a minor offence, and no criminal charges were brought against the company.[52] The refund was made in silence and without discussion, and the issue does not seem to have had any effect on Ford Motor Company's reputation in the public eye.

This is an American company and it's going to be run from America

Henry Ford II

1945–1958
New Expectations

PRODUCTION

Working the Same Way, but Faster

On 5 May 1945, the occupation of Denmark came to an end, and a few days later the capitulation of Germany brought an end to war in Europe. In October that same year Percival Perry—now Lord Perry—made a round trip of the Nordic countries to evaluate the situation. His report to Dearborn was quite optimistic:

> Considering the general consequences of the war in Europe my view is that the position of the Company is much better than could have been reasonably expected. We have met good spirit everywhere amongst the various persons and a determination to re-establish Ford business more firmly than ever before.[1]

In March 1946, cars started rolling off the assembly line in Copenhagen again, but production was well below pre-war levels. Despite Perry's initial optimism, it would actually take several years before conditions were normalised. Due to lack of parts, as well as restrictions on the private purchase of cars, assembly came to an almost complete stop again in 1948–1949. It was not until May 1950, five years after the end of the occupation, that assembly could finally continue on a regular, if somewhat limited basis. But then, from the mid-1950s, as the economy recovered and restrictions were lifted, the demand for cars started growing steeply, leading to a remarkable growth in both the range and the numbers of cars assembled.[2]

Not only were relatively few cars produced before the mid-1950s, but those that were assembled were basically pre-war models. Assembly could be done with the same methods and equipment as before, and consequently Ford had no incentive to make large investments in new production technologies. Any improvement made in tools and machinery during these years was gradual, and more about expanding existing technologies than introducing new ones. One example is the increased use of spot-welding. In 1943, when the number of spot-welding tools was first counted, 36 such tools existed. In the next count, in 1960, around 70 spot-welding tools were in use for body assembly alone.[3]

Another investment in improving the plant was the DKK 1 million spent in 1950, primarily on new spray-painting booths and a facility for phosphate coating, both for use during body assembly.[4] Nevertheless, there were still no paint booths for repair work on preassembled cars, and during the early 1950s the lack of proper facilities was a recurring reason for complaints from the painters.[5]

The need for space

The Copenhagen management acknowledged the problems related to painting. The rising number of cars that were received pre-assembled had not only to be cleaned and tidied up upon arrival, but often also to have their paintwork repaired. The lack of paint booths for this purpose made the work "unhealthy and inefficient", they wrote in 1954 in an internal report, directed towards Ford's European leadership.[6]

That was, however, only a minor part of the overall problem: the general lack of space. Not only for assembly, but even more so for keeping spare parts for the growing number of different models, and for the increase in administrative work associated with sales and service of a growing number of cars. For the white-collar staff, working in cramped offices, "noise of all kinds causes disturbance and the mental overcoming of noise is tiring, and business calls and conferences about the performance of the work disturb all people in the vicinity."[7]

A final issue regarding space was caused not by production, but by legal regulation of the working environment: the Company was unable to live up to requirements regarding the number of toilets available to the employees. This was all made clear to Ford's European management in the report.[8]

In fact, expansion of the facilities had already been briefly discussed before the war but had been abandoned due to lack of land suitable for construction in the immediate vicinity of the existing facilities. The situation was now changing, as local authorities had started further development of the harbour area to the south-east of the Ford factory. In 1947, a plot of land to the east of the Ford Basin was rented for a period of up to 50 years, while rights for renting another adjacent plot were acquired.[9]

Arguments finally had an impact on the European Ford management and, in January 1956, the Danish board was able to confirm plans for leasing new land and constructing a new office building, a parts and accessories warehouse, the relocation of car conditioning space and garages, and the purchase of new equipment, at a total cost of DKK 11,233,630.[10] But before construction could commence, it was literally blocked by a crossing train, as the Danish State Railroad Company were making plans for a new railroad line, while the Copenhagen municipality had decided to extend Sydhavnsgade, the main road going past the factory. Both the railroad line and the road were to pass through the area originally designated for Ford's expansion. Instead, the Company was offered another area, and in 1957 work on the new facilities could finally go ahead.[11]

The entrepreneurial work that had to be done in preparation of the building site was quite extensive, including establishing sewers, water and other installations, as well as a new road.[12] The new facilities would not be ready for use until winter 1958–1959. The effort could be well justified by the fact that the car market was already on the rise and further expansions of sales were to be expected in the future. But in hindsight it was a harbinger of things to come. Most of the capital invested and labour spent was in facilities related to administration, sales, and service. Only a minor part went to improving the assembly plant.

Figure 30 New administrative building (centre) and warehouse (right) under construction, January 1958. Unknown photographer. The National Museum of Denmark

Speedup

While no radical changes were made in production technology, another means was introduced to make assembly more effective. In the spring of 1952, a meeting was called at the combined union club to discuss the fact that time studies had been introduced at the plant. While time studies had been used at General Motors for several years, it was something new at Ford, primarily related to the introduction of new models.[13] In the immediate post-war period, Ford is however known to have increased its use of time studies substantially at its American plants, as part of a general modernisation combined with an effort to increase work speed.[14] And apparently, from the mid-1950s, standard assembly times for different models, American as well as European, were sent to Copenhagen from Detroit.

Whether or not the times were the same as those used at the American assembly lines is not known, but at least the Danish workers found them "manageable for the most part".[15]

Fewer Markets, More Demand

The war and the subsequent political changes in Europe had cut of some of the pre-war markets for Ford Motor Company A/S. While no attempts were made to hold onto the Baltic markets after 1945, Ford apparently still had some hope for regaining its position in Poland. In 1946, 17 units were sold on the Polish market, the next year a possibility for delivering cars in exchange for coal was discussed, and as late as April 1950 the company took part in a car show in Poznań[16] But as the Iron Curtain was pulled tighter, this hope came to an end.

At the same time, initiatives were taken to start assembling cars locally for both the Finnish and the Swedish markets. During the last years of the war, plans for a truck assembly plant in Finland had been discussed between Brøndum in Sweden and Rydman, the manager of the Finish subsidiary. It was to be financed by the substantial profits that the Finnish company had made during the war, and the project received backing from H.C. Møller in Copenhagen. The Finnish plant, built on a small peninsula south of Helsinki, started production in 1946.[17]

The formal decision to establish assembly in Stockholm was taken at a board meeting in Copenhagen at the beginning of 1946.[18] The reason was market conditions more than economy of production. There was a belief that, by producing locally, there would be fewer negative sentiments towards Ford as a foreign brand in Sweden, and consequently the market share vis-à-vis domestic brands like Volvo and emerging Saab would grow bigger. These assumptions proved wrong: the Stockholm plant started assembly in 1949, but unlike the one in Helsinki, it never became economically viable. The final nail in the coffin was a change in import tariffs in 1959.[19]

This combination of political developments and internal decisions meant that geographically the market for cars assembled in Copenhagen had become much smaller. But on the other hand, from the early 1950s onwards, demand for cars would soar in those markets remaining.

Post-war problems

The later upsurge in the mass market for private cars was however not immediately foreseeable in 1945. On the Danish home market, the years immediately following liberation constituted a harsh economic and political environment. The effects of the occupation had been scarcity, repression, and anxiety. Now, there were hopes and a popular demand for better times. Repression was over, anxiety had been lessened, but scarcity would drag on for several years.

Import of consumer goods, cars included, was heavily restricted during the late 1940s and early 1950s, as foreign currency, especially US dollars, was reserved primarily for raw materials and capital goods. The Directorate for Product Supply would continue in effect until 1960, even if its role in regulating and restricting import would gradually diminish.[20]

Buying a car required a special permission from the Directorate, or from its sub-committee for distribution of cars, established in 1949. In 1950, the committee turned down 90 percent of the applications received—3,934 permissions were granted.[21] From 1952 onwards, it was possible to buy a car without permission, provided that a percentage of the price was paid in US dollars—an arrangement colloquially known as the "Dollar premium". While still restricting sales, at least this gave a competitive edge to locally assembled cars.[22] In 1957 all restrictions on the sale of cars were lifted, in favour of an increase in the already existing sales tax.

In 1948, Denmark started receiving favourable loans in US dollars through the Marshall Plan. A considerable part was invested in mechanising agriculture, which boosted the market for tractors. In the down-period of car sales in the late 40s, the company management expressed hope for an increasing market for tractors.[23] The Fordson tractor, which had been a marginal product in the interwar years, was receiving more attention, and there was even an attempt to establish production of a locally designed trailer and other farming equipment.[24] The latter was no success, but the sale of tractors did rise considerably, and during 1950–1952, when car sales had resumed but at a very modest level, the income from the tractor business was roughly equal to that of car sales.[25]

In May 1950, cars were finally rolling off the assembly line again in the South Port. The ones produced were British Anglia and Prefect models, based on a pre-war design.[26] Despite the fact that parts for these cars could now be obtained in limited numbers from Dagenham, import was still not free and importation from Detroit in particular was hampered by restricted access to US dollars. For a period in 1950–1951, the Danish company had to resort to unconventional methods to get hold of American cars, such as barter transactions: Frozen fish, ham, and bacon were sent to the United States in exchange for automobiles.[27]

The total yearly sale of cars in Denmark had been very modest during the late 1940s, reaching an all-time low of only 2,844 in 1949. But as the market was partly liberalised in 1952 and as the economy gradually improved from the mid-1950s, total sales of cars on the Danish home market started to rise steadily again: from 19,212 in 1952 to 42,778 in 1958.[28]

Ford Motor Company A/S took a fair share of this expanding market. Figures from the early 1950s show that Ford's market share in Denmark grew from roughly 10 percent in 1950 to 16 percent in 1953. That made Ford third on the market, behind Opel (24 percent) and Volkswagen (18 percent).[29] Unfortunately, comparable figures for the last part of the period have not been found.

In Norway, Ford's sales were also rising, settling around one thousand passenger cars per year in the early 1950s, equalling a market share of roughly 11 percent.[30] In Sweden, Ford's relative share of the market was diminishing in the 1950s, due to increased competition from domestic brands. It was, however, a diminishing share of a market that was growing even faster than in Denmark: the total number of registered cars in Sweden more than quadrupled during the ten-year period 1946–1956, from around 203,000 to over 855,000.[31] But as already noted, from 1949 onwards, cars for Sweden were no longer assembled in Copenhagen.

All in all, by the end of the 1950s Ford sales had finally surpassed pre-war levels, with almost 17,000 units sold in 1958.[32]

British, German, or American?

Before the war, most of the cars sold by Ford Motor Company A/S had been American models, supplemented with an increasing number of British and, in the very late 1930s, a few German models. Now the relationship was reversed. When the assembly line in Copenhagen started running again in earnest in May 1950, the cars that came off it were of British origin.[33]

The two models offered to the buying public in 1950 were not only rather similar, the Prefect being a slightly beefed-up four-door version of the Anglia. They were also essentially the same as those that had been sold before the war, 15 years earlier. But as the car business was a seller's market, even such older models were welcome anyway. In 1953, a new and much more up-to-date version of the Anglia / Prefect was introduced, and the Anglia especially became popular in the Danish market following that. Parallel to the Anglia, which was designed for the middle to lower end of the market, the newly developed Consul / Zephyr range for the middle to higher end market had been released in Denmark in 1950. Unlike the Anglia, these cars were heavily influenced by American design, and relatively expensive. The six-cylinder Zephyr in particular was mostly sold as a business car.[34]

The fact that the cars assembled in Copenhagen in the early post-war period were British is a sign that Dagenham was finally fulfilling the role it had been originally designed for, back in the late 1920s: to become the main supplier of Ford cars for Europe. During the 1930s, Dagenham had been challenged by the growth of the Cologne plant, which also led to the import of Ford cars of German origin to Copenhagen. But Cologne had been hit hard during the war and in the late 1940s Dagenham was unquestionably the main European Ford producer.

Unfortunately for Dagenham, its position was soon to be challenged once again. The Germans were able to restart production within a few years. Just as in England, what first emerged from Cologne in 1948 was a pre-war model: the Taunus. But as soon as 1952, a new Taunus 12M was released, and a few years later the 15M, which was the same model but with a larger engine. Furthermore, a larger model, the 17M, was launched in 1957, and by this time the range of

Taunus versions that were to be offered for the rest of the period was almost in place.[35]

With these models, Cologne was ready to challenge Dagenham as the main supplier of Ford cars to Copenhagen. In 1953, 64 percent of the Ford passenger cars sold from Copenhagen were of British origin and 28 percent of them German. But the Germans were catching up, and five years later, the British share was reduced to 52 percent while the German share had grown to 40 percent.[36]

The relative sales figures of the different Ford models were a result of supply and demand. Considering the first last, British and German Fords had somewhat different images. Especially with its models for the lower end of the market, British Ford had a reputation for offering no-nonsense cars, such as the Anglia, at relatively low prices.[37] The German models, on the other hand, were often more innovative, both technically as well as in their design. This is clear from an internal report from 1954, which talks about "the public's disappointment with the quality" of both the Consul and the Zephyr, and the competitive pricing being the reason why sales of British models had not declined further. In contrast, the popularity of the Taunus is explained by its "modern lines, luxurious interior, and fine service record". In a list of "non-competitive features" of different models in the same report, the British models figure prominently. For instance, it is noted that the Consul lacks a modern style instrument panel, that it has a noisy rear axle, and that there is too little space between the front seat and the steering wheel.[38]

American Ford cars were now supplemental to the European models. Due to the import restrictions, very few private buyers—if any—had the option of legally obtaining an American car. But some were delivered to special customers, such as the royal family and the US embassy.[39] Until 1953, the couple of hundred American cars sold each year were all delivered to Copenhagen pre-assembled from the USA.[40] Local assembly of American cars was resumed in 1953. In that year, a total of 402 US models were sold, equalling 8 percent of the total number of passenger cars. In 1958, the total number was a little higher, but due to the overall expansion in sales, the relative proportion was less, at only 5 percent.[41] The sale of the American Ford models was stagnating, and even diminishing in relative terms.

Finally, there was the Vedette, built in France. The idea behind this was to offer a car for the middle to higher end of the market, with an engine based on the proven and popular American Ford V8 but wrapped in a continental European design. On paper this might have seemed like a winning idea. But despite being a technically good and elegant car, the Vedette never really caught on outside France. It was imported as preassembled by the Danish company for a period, but sales figures were negligible. In 1954, Ford sold its French plant and with it the Vedette brand to French automaker Simca. It was however still distributed by Ford in Scandinavia as Ford Vedette during the following years.[42] In 1958, 236 were sold.[43]

Only passenger cars have been mentioned above. But Ford Motor Company A/S continued to assemble and sell vans and trucks as well. Immediately after the war, these actually made up the largest part of the company's activities. Out of the 5,011 units sold from Copenhagen in 1946, almost two-thirds were commercial vehicles, such as British vans and American V8 trucks.[44] But this was a special situation of the immediate post-war years, when it was easier to obtain a permit to buy a commercial vehicle than a passenger car for private use.

MANAGEMENT

This Is an American Company

"This is an American company and it's going to be run from America." Henry Ford II stated his intentions in no uncertain terms at the international managers' conference in Dearborn in June 1948.[45] Ford II had become president of Ford Motor Company three years earlier, when his grandfather Henry Ford finally stepped down.

Before that, other top executives of the pre-war period had left the organisation, including Charles Sorensen, who had resigned in 1944. Ford II brought in a new leadership and embarked on the road to a complete overhaul of the outmoded forms of management within the company. Some of the new managers had proven their capabilities in organising military production and logistics during the war; others were recruited among current or former employees of General Motors. GM had at that point been the undisputed leader among the "big three" American automakers since the late 1920s, and Ford was currently only number three, behind Chrysler. Apparently, Henry Ford II felt that bringing executives with experience from the leading company into his own would help Ford Motor Company in its strategic effort to regain its position as number two of the big three.[46]

Detroit reaches for control

Having concentrated on the company at home for the first couple of years, Henry Ford II and the new leaders of the Ford Empire started looking at Europe. They did not like what they saw. The new leadership felt a need to reform European management along the same lines as they were modernising management back home in the USA.[47]

Early in 1948, Ford II made a tour of Europe to assess the situation, including a stopover in Copenhagen on 4–7 March. He was accompanied by several top managers. One of them was G.K. Howard, a former GM senior executive who had been appointed by Ford II as a special advisor on international matters. In his early career, Howard also happened to have been manager of GM in Denmark in 1924–1925[48]. In Copenhagen, Ford II and his escort were given a tour of the South Port plant, and meetings were held with dealers, the board, and representatives of the press. The visit was concluded with a large dinner party with selected representatives of Danish business. In the company magazine *Ford Nyt* the visit was presented almost as a friendly family gathering, in a four-page illustrated report.[49] Howard, on the other hand, would later refer to the European round trip as the "shakedown cruise".[50]

Observations from the trip were presented at the aforementioned managers' conference, where Henry Ford II announced that for the future "we are going to formulate the overall policies right here" in Dearborn.[51] One of the decisions made in Dearborn was to create a subsidiary company by the name of Ford International Incorporated, with G.K. Howard as director.[52] Howard had very ambitious plans; apparently too ambitious to be realised, since within a year the international company was scaled down and made a division of the Ford Motor Company again, and the leadership passed over to A.J. Wieland, another former GM executive.[53] With this, Ford's international management was stabilised, at least for a period.

Nevertheless, the overall plan of doing away with indirect ownership of the European subsidiaries, which Howard had laid out, would be realised. In January 1950, Ford USA took over the majority of shares in all European Ford companies, including Ford Motor Company A/S. But for some unknown reason, the Swedish and Finnish companies were still indirectly owned through the Danish subsidiary.[54]

The leadership of Ford in Europe was now firmly back in American hands. In one respect, this was a centralisation. But in fact, its aim was also to create more room for the European subsidiaries to manoeuvre and take initiative. Dagenham could manage its own product development and the need for different products for different parts of Europe was recognised.[55] As part of the preparations for reorganising in Europe, a balance sheet had been drawn up in 1949, showing the relative profitability of the European Ford subsidiaries between 1922 and 1949. Apart from Portugal, where the return was highest in percent but low in absolute numbers, the average return on investment was by far the highest in three countries: Denmark, Belgium, and the Netherlands.[56] With a history of average return above 13 percent so far, prospects seemed good for Ford Motor Company A/S.

Changing of the guard

Despite the vigour and optimism with which Lord Perry had assumed his responsibilities in Denmark after the war, his leadership was coming to an end. In April 1948, shortly after the visit of Henry Ford II and G.K. Howard, Perry had resigned as chairman of Ford UK. One month later, he also resigned as chairman of Ford Motor Company A/S, and his post was taken over by another Englishman, Sir Stanford Cooper.[57]

But the reign of this new English lord would be short lived. During 1949 the board was actively engaged in working out the practical transfer of majority ownership from London to Dearborn, and in December 1949, a new set of cooperation agreements with Ford USA as well as with the other European companies was adopted at an extraordinary general assembly. In March 1950, the practical consequences of the liquidation of the British ownership for the Danish company were resolved by the board without further ado.[58] Ford Motor Company A/S was now a *de facto* American company again.

This was reflected in the composition of the board. As soon as normality had been restored in 1945, Edsel B. Ford, who had passed away in 1943, and Charles Sorensen, who had retired from the board, were replaced by Henry Ford II and B.J. Craig, the latter being one of Dearborn's chief financial executives.[59] Craig was soon replaced again by G.K. Howard for a short period in 1949–1950, until he was again replaced by the new director of the Ford International Division, A.J. Wieland.[60] In 1952, Stanford Cooper, who had kept his position as chairman, left the board as the last remaining Englishman. Instead, another Dearborn representative, regional manager for Europe W. McKee, was elected to the board, and immediately made chairman. Not only were the Americans now firmly placed in the board, but both Henry Ford II and Wieland also made it clear in writing that on important matters they expected "to be kept informed through Ford International and have an opportunity of expressing their view before decisions were made".[61]

It was not only the board but also the daily management of Ford Motor Company A/S that was changed thoroughly. In December 1948 it was announced that H.C. Møller, who had been managing the company for 22 years, would retire, effective 30 June 1949.[62] This was a direct result of the "shakedown cruise". Henry Ford II did not make a secret of the fact that he generally wanted younger men in management positions. G.K. Howard wanted a former GM man to take over management in Denmark, but instead Arthur Beck was chosen.[63]

Beck had been with the Danish company since 1919 and helped starting up initial production in Heimdalsgade as a mechanic. He was soon promoted to other jobs, such as purchase agent and later service manager. During the 1930s he became sales manager of the Swedish subsidiary, and in 1945 he was appointed assistant manager.[64] In other words: the new managing director had a thorough understanding of the company and the Scandinavian market.

Møller was allowed to stay on the board and a large dinner party was given in his honour on the day of his retirement, with Ford representatives from the UK and the USA.[65] Less than three years later, in April 1952, assistant manager Hjalmar Mortensen retired as well. Just as in the case of Møller, this was presented to the public as his own decision—but in fact he had "agreed to tender his resignation" at the request of the chairman of the board.[66] Finally the company had lost a third key executive, production manager Georg Frederiksen, in 1949, just a fortnight before Møller's retirement. Frederiksen had been with the company since its start in 1919, and served as production manager since the early 1920s. But in this case the decision was made by authorities above Dearborn: Frederiksen did not retire, but died.[67] As a combined result of the retirement of Møller and Mortensen, and the death of Frederiksen, the three men who had formed the core management of Ford Motor Company and the South Port plant for more than 20 years were now history.

Further changes to the board were made in 1957. In that year A.J. Wieland died, and his position as head of Ford's International Division was taken over by Tom Lilley. Consequently, Lilley replaced Wieland on the Danish board. Furthermore, two Danish members left the board. One was V. Falbe-Hansen, the last remaining of the initial founders of the company and member of the board since 1919, except for a period between 1922 and 1929. The other was Carl Thalbitzer, board member since 1929. With this, manager Arthur Beck was the only person left within the board and management who had a history with the company reaching back more than a few years. The replacement of the old guard was almost complete.

Under American leadership

The relationship between Ford Motor Company A/S and its Swedish subsidiary was also influenced by Detroit's changing plans for Europe. In the beginning there was a bit of confusion: in 1947, the Danish board agreed in principle to sell all its Swedish shares to Ford Investment Company Ltd., the holding company of Ford UK. But this decision was nullified at the next meeting, a few months later. No explanation was given for any of these decisions.[68] A few years later, Ford Motor Company A/S actually made further investments in Sweden. This happened in 1950, when the share capital of the Swedish company was increased, and Ford Motor Company A/S bought a portion of these new shares at the price of DKK 4.7 million, maintaining its 60 percent ownership.[69]

But the whole structure of the Danish Ford Company owning the Swedish, which in turn owned the Finnish, was of course contrary to the declared intentions from Detroit, of eliminating the chains of indirect ownership of its subsidiaries. It is unknown why this structure was allowed to proceed, even after Detroit had bought the majority of the Danish company back from Ford UK. But in July 1955 it finally came to an end, as an extraordinary general meeting unanimously approved the sale of shares at a nominal value of 6 million Swedish kroner to the American Ford Company for a total sum of DKK 26.2 million, of which DKK 11.2 million would be paid to the Ford Motor Company A/S, while the rest would be distributed among the shareholders of the Danish Company—of whom Ford Motor Company in Dearborn constituted the majority.[70] From now on, Ford Motor Company A/S was no longer controlling Ford in Sweden and Finland.

According to Arthur Beck, there was more independence for smaller subsidiaries, such as Ford Motor Company A/S, under the reign of Henry Ford II. For instance, retail prices and rebates could be decided more freely. Beck also comments on the change of internal culture in the Ford Motor Company, away from the "no smoking, no cocktails" spirit of "the old man" Henry Ford. Beck was clearly more in sync with Henry Ford II, with whom he claimed to have had a good personal relationship.[71]

The continued efforts by Ford USA to streamline its foreign operations nevertheless led to a gradual change in managerial culture. Depending on viewpoint, it could be described as either more rational procedures or more top-down bureaucracy. Around 1949, a procedure called Appropriation Requests was introduced. It was meant to standardise the way in which the board approved new initiatives and the associated costs. A few of the projects put forward for approval in this way required large investments, such as DKK 11.2 million for the lease of land and construction of new office and warehouse buildings in 1956.[72]

Most of them were smaller projects, however, such as retooling required on the production line when a new model was to be assembled. The cost of these projects was in the region of DKK 100,000 or less.[73] Before the war, such smaller investments due to changes in production had seldom been put before the board but had just been decided by management at its own discretion. From now on they had to be specified as projects, and given an adequate project number, before they could be considered.

The shift of ownership from British to American in 1950 also led to a more formalised way of remunerating Dearborn for technical and other assistance. A so-called service fee agreement was made for each year, typically by Dearborn requesting a certain amount to be paid and the Danish board complying without discussion. The amount was raised rather considerably, from roughly $25,000 in the early 1950s to $350,000 in the mid-1960s.[74]

But the Danes did not accept just any suggestions from Detroit. In particular the aforementioned sale of shares in the Swedish company led to some discussion. Formally, what the Danish board received from Dearborn was an offer to buy the shares under certain conditions. In the pre-war period, such an "offer" would most likely have been accepted without further ado. But at this instance, the board meeting had to be adjourned and reconvened over a period of three consecutive days before a decision could be made. What troubled the board was not the sale in itself or the price offered by Dearborn, as much as the distribution of the payment between the company and its shareholders. During the negotiations, the board suggested to Dearborn that the portion of the total sales price of DKK 26.2 million paid directly to the company should be raised from DKK 7.7 million to DKK 11.2 million, and the portion paid to the shareholders lowered correspondingly.

With Ford USA being the major shareholder, what the board requested was in effect that a greater part of the money should be invested in the Danish company, instead of being transferred to Dearborn. This was around the time when the planning of the substantial enlargement of the Copenhagen facility went into its final phase. Undoubtedly the board had in mind that bolstering the assets of the company in this way could be beneficial in promoting its building plans. The Dearborn representatives accepted the board's proposal, thereby closing the deal.[75]

This was also a period when minority shareholders raised their voices at general meetings; most prominently at the 1949 general meeting, when Mr. Berg Madsen, a minority shareholder who was also representing the newly formed Danish Shareholders Association, questioned the dividends paid. This was a delicate question, which had been touched upon at previous general meetings, but in a rather subdued manner. But Berg Madsen brought the Ford family into the discussion, as he pointed out that, as majority shareholders, they *de facto* decided the size of dividend paid. He suggested that more of the profit should be paid to the shareholders and less be carried over to the next year's account. Furthermore, he suggested a new method of electing the board—by vote in proportion to number of shares—which would in principle give the minority shareholders representation.[76]

The criticism was dismissed by Falbe-Hansen as representative of the board, and the report was approved, and the board re-elected by majority as usual. Minority shareholders also took the floor with questions at later general meetings, but in a less critical way, probably because the dividends were actually raised gradually, during the following years.

INDUSTRIAL RELATIONS

New Hopes

As Henry Ford II took over the presidency of Ford Motor Company in 1945, one of his first acts was to fire the notorious Harry Bennet. Bennet, who at the time of his dismissal was general supervisor of all labour relations and a member of the board, had been the symbol of Ford's militant and sometimes violent anti-union policy in America since the early 1920s.[77] Following this, Ford II publicly announced his wish to implement a new vision for industrial relations at Ford. In a way, he was maintaining the basic idea of his grandfather that labour and management had a common interest in promoting productivity. But while Henry Ford saw unions as an outside interference in his company and an obstacle for higher productivity, his grandson now declared them legitimate representatives of the workers.

Since 1941, Ford Motor Company in the USA had accepted union agreements, but only grudgingly and under pressure. Henry Ford II now committed the company wholeheartedly to collective bargaining, primarily with the United Auto Workers. But it came at a price: unions on the other side would have to accept the task of keeping discipline within their own ranks, and help prevent so-called "illegal" or unauthorised strikes, collective work speed lowering, etc.[78]

In many European labour markets, this could be considered nothing new or noteworthy. In Denmark, acceptance of collective bargaining in return for union commitment to securing peace in the workplace had been a generally accepted strategy among employers since the beginning of the 20th century. But in the USA, Henry Ford II's new policy was met with great interest from both unions as well as the general public.

A swing to the left

In Denmark, industrial relations in general were affected by the political and ideological developments of the post-war period. Like in many other European countries, the end of war and German occupation was followed by political upheavals in the labour movement. Social democratic hegemony was challenged by the rising support for the Danish Communist Party (DKP). During the summer of 1945, there was a short but unsuccessful series of talks about a merger between the two parties. At the parliamentary election in October 1945, the social democrats and the Communist Party received 33 and 13 percent of the votes respectively. In Copenhagen, with its above-average number of industrial workers, the communists gained noticeably higher support of 25 percent, with 38 percent to the social democrats.[79] For both parties, however, the outcome of the election was a disappointment, as the office of Government was taken over by the centre-right Liberal Party.

As the Cold War grew more intense, events in Eastern Europe would take their toll on the support for the Communist Party in Denmark, and eventually lead to a split and gradual marginalisation of the party during the late 1950s. The Social Democratic Party, on the other hand, regained its position in Government, first from 1947 to

1950, and then from 1953 onwards, supported by and partly in coalition with the smaller Social-Liberal Party.. In many ways this was a restoration of the political hegemony established by the same two parties during the 1930s.

Despite the fierce rivalry between the two parties, the trade union movement would stay united across political divides, with social democrats and communists competing for influence and positions within the same union. Several communists were elected as shop stewards and union officials, and in the post-war decade industrial workplaces with a strong communist support were not uncommon, especially in Copenhagen.[80]

These developments were of course reflected at Ford Motor Company A/S too. They were even embodied in the history of one person: Axel Sjølander, who played a central role as activist during the 1940s and 50s. Sjølander was first elected leading shop steward at Ford in early 1943, and for more than a decade thereafter he occupied various union posts, including chairman of the combined union club, leading shop steward, and chairman of the metalworkers' union club.[81]

Before getting a job at Ford Motor Company in the mid-1930s, Sjølander had already been a union activist at other workplaces and had also been a member of the Social Democratic Party since 1929. But in 1945, like quite a few others, he joined the Communist Party. For the first time ever, the unions at Ford were now headed by a communist and not a social democrat.[82] At an extraordinary general meeting of the Union of Automobile and Bicycle Mechanics, which took place in the late summer of 1945 when the two labour parties were discussing a merger, Sjølander took the floor and spoke emphatically about the need for political unity between communists and social democrats.[83]

Sjølander would leave the Communist Party again after a few years. After leaving the party, he explained his membership as a tactical move, in order to safeguard his position as chairman of the combined club.[84] This might be a case of hindsight, but whether his communist affiliation was heartfelt or tactical, it was a sign that there was a support for the Communist Party—or at least for its union strategies—among the Ford workers at the time: a swing to the left among the rank and file.

Wages and memoranda

During the occupation, real wages had diminished, and now it was time for the unions to recoup some of the loss. In April 1946, the lowest wage rate was raised from DKK 3.03 per hour to DKK 3.30, and the highest from DKK 3.63 to DKK 3.80. Supplementary to that, extra payment was agreed upon for working overtime, and future wage increases were guaranteed every six months, should the official price index move upwards.[85] Generally, the late 1940s and early 1950s were characterised by a rather rapid upsurge in hourly wages for the Copenhagen Ford workers. But when looking at hourly wages it should still be remembered that a standard working week at Ford was 40 hours, while it was 48 hours in most industries. A skilled worker would now have a fair chance of getting a higher weekly paycheck at another workplace than by working for Ford Motor Company A/S. For an unskilled worker, payment could be under or above the industry average, depending on whether he had reached the maximum pay level at Ford or not.

Whether or not a worker at Ford still considered himself being high paid would come down to how he valued his 8 hours of extra spare time per week. But comparing weekly pay to weekly pay, Ford was now paying an average salary.

The new leadership that had come into place in Detroit had led to a change in industrial relations in Ford Motor Company globally. Contrary to pre-war conditions, when Ford had sought to impose on its European subsidiaries its American policy of not recognising unions and not—until 1941—entering into collective bargaining, these were now left free to handle industrial relations according to local conditions. In the mid-1950s, both Ford in England and in Germany had entered into union agreements, although labour relations were significantly different: poor in Dagenham, with periods of open conflict, but more peaceful and cooperative in Cologne.[86]

In Denmark, however, no principal changes took place in relation to the system of bargaining. The semi-official bargaining system that had been established during the late 1930s and strengthened during

Year	Copenhagen industry, all male workers	Copenhagen, skilled metalworkers	Ford Motor Company A/S	
			Min.	Max.
1946	138	149	121	145
1953	211	233	200	216

Table 5 Weekly wages in DKK paid at Ford Motor Company A/S, 1946–1953, compared to Copenhagen industry. Source: ABA: SSMF, correspondence, file 4583 & 5315. *Statistisk Aarbog*, 1947 & 1954. Based on a working week of 40 hours at Ford and 48 hours in the industry in general

the war continued. It was consolidated in a two-tiered system, rather particular to a Danish context.

In 1946 as well as in 1950, management would issue updated versions of the existing non-negotiated work regulations, as previously they were more or less directly translated from American sources, with a few minor adaptations.[87] Especially the 1946 version was characterised by a rather paternalistic voice, reminiscent of the pre-war period. Nothing is mentioned of shop stewards or bargaining procedures in these regulations. But in reality, union representatives were recognised by management and collective bargaining took place on issues such as hourly pay rates, rates for overtime and night shifts, rules for hiring and firing of workers, etc. The results of this bargaining would be put down in documents, often several pages long, and signed by both parties. At least from around 1950, such documents were negotiated on a yearly basis.[88]

The negotiated documents would have the headline "Memorandum" during the 1940s, and "Amendment to the work regulation" from around 1950. The unions would rather consequently refer to them as agreements[89], the term generally used for the outcome of collective bargaining in the Danish system of industrial relations. However, the management of Ford Motor Company A/S would tenaciously refuse to call them that. Commenting on the outcome of negotiations with the company in 1947, a national union official wrote to a local union chairman:

> We have noticed that instead of 'Agreement' or 'Contract' the word 'Memorandum' is used as heading, but such is of course not unknown when we are dealing with Ford Motor Company.[90]

Despite the sarcasm, the unions found that they had gained most of what they wanted, in regard to union recognition and collective bargaining rights, and decided to reconcile themselves to the absence of an agreement in the formal sense.

"Part of the social machinery"

Industrial relations came into general political focus in Denmark in the aftermath of the war, and claims were raised for "industrial democracy" by different parts of the labour movement. In its new programme, *Fremtidens Danmark* (Denmark of the future), adopted in August 1945, the Social Democratic Party had called for the establishing of factory councils. While the party lost ground at the general election that same year, the labour market was still characterised by much unrest, culminating in large strikes in connection with negotiations for new national agreements in 1946. It was in this situation that the union movement raised the question of factory councils again, even if in a more moderate form. And in 1947 the Danish Confederation of Trade Unions (DSF) and the Confederation of Danish Employers (DA) agreed that cooperation committees, with a right to be consulted but not to make decisions in matters of management, should be introduced in any enterprise with more than 25 employees.[91]

In the internal debates of the labour movement, cooperation committees were linked to a wider vision of driving democracy forward into the realm of production. But as an agreement was reached between unions and employers, this aspect was pushed to the background. Both sides concentrated on two central aims which they had in common, even if the emphasis and interpretations was slightly different. One was to further cooperation between workers and employers. In the words of the employers' confederation:

> … [to] do away with some of the mistrust, which is fertile ground for a campaign for unrest and dissatisfaction […] As the partners enter a trustful relationship, the workers will become more engaged in their jobs.[92]

The other aim was to involve the workers actively in the process of rationalisation and industrial modernisation, to gain a higher level of productivity and economic growth. In a resolution adopted in May 1946, DSF declared as its goal to have "productive committees" implemented, which might lead to an increased production of social goods by heightening the interest and the confidence of the workers in the process of production.[93]

It was in this context that Ford Motor Company A/S took the step to establish a so-called Committee for Information and Cooperation, which held its first meeting in July 1946.[94] This made Ford a first mover when it came to this new type of cooperation, setting up its committee more than a full year before the national agreement on the matter became effective.

At first sight, it was a bit surprising that a company that had been reluctantly dragging its feet for years on the subject of collective bargaining suddenly overtook the rest of the industry by establishing a formal body of cooperation at this early point. But the reasoning behind this move closely reflected the new ideas about industrial relations emerging in the USA at the time. Whether the initiative came from Detroit or the decision was taken locally in Copenhagen is unknown.[95] But in his introductory speech at the first meeting of the Committee, manager H.C. Møller echoed not only the arguments of the Danish debate, but also the new ethos that had emerged within the global Ford company under the leadership of Henry Ford II, when he said:

> Any enterprise is part of the social machinery. It is the purpose of the meetings of the Committee for Information and Cooperation to avoid misunderstandings, insecurity, and friction, caused by lack of information.[96]

Sixteen people took part in the first committee meeting at Ford Motor Company A/S, of whom eight or nine represented the blue-collar workers, apparently one from each union plus the leading shop steward. The other seven or eight represented white-collar workers and management. The relative size of each group did not matter for decision-making though, as the committee was set up along the same principles as would also be the basis for the later national agreement: it was for the dissemination of information and for counselling only and had no right to make formal decisions.[97]

The leading shop steward was Axel Sjølander. He was at the time still a member of the Communist Party, and as such it might be expected that he would have been somewhat reluctant to the idea of a committee with the aim of promoting production through cooperation between workers and management. On the contrary, Sjølander expressed his agreement with H.C. Møller and declared his hope that the work of the council would become "part of the efforts to secure peaceful and positive working conditions at the factory".[98]

Not only did Sjølander express his appreciation for the committee, but he would also become highly engaged in its work. At one meeting alone he suggested setting up a workplace security committee, establishing a holiday lottery subsidised by the company, arranging study trips to Dagenham for workers (in order to "encourage them") and to have a joint picnic for blue- and white-collar workers (in order to "improve the understanding between them").[99]

The study trip to Dagenham was undertaken in 1947, and led to a suggestion for another trip to the USA the next year. H.C. Møller was very doubtful if that would be possible. He took the matter with him on his next visit to the Ford Motor Company headquarters—and came back with a polite but firm rejection.[100] Møller himself very rarely reacted to a proposal put forward to the committee by turning it down right away. His favourite method of counteracting a request he was reluctant to meet was to defer it for further investigation. Sjølander, on the other side, could be persistent. One of his proposals had been to install loudspeakers in the workers' cloakroom and the canteen, so that information could be given this way. H.C. Møller was against it, but Sjølander kept pushing for it, and after more than a year it was carried out.[101]

While most of Sjølander's initiatives came through, one way or another, it was not always as planned. When he suggested the joint picnic for blue- and white-collar workers, Møller was positive, adding that the event should have a "manly character". But whatever the final character of the picnic, something apparently went wrong; according to a later meeting the picnic "had not been completely satisfactory" and some "unfortunate episodes" had taken place. Maybe the event became too manly after all? But Sjølander did not give up: he suggested that a picnic should be held again next year, but this time with volunteer marshals. This was approved by Møller.[102]

Shifting allegiances

The new line in industrial relations that had been introduced in Detroit was followed with close interest by the shop steward of the Danish Ford workers. In the Cooperation Committee, Sjølander declared the "statements put forward by Ford in the USA" about the "human factor" to be of great importance, and Ford II's ideas about "the spirit of cooperation" very "illuminating".[103]

When the Company President visited the South Port plant in March 1948, as part of his first grand European tour, Sjølander had a chance to chat with Henry Ford II himself. A photo of the meeting between the shop steward and the president of the Ford Motor Company was later featured in *Ford Nyt*.[104] It is symbolic of the change of attitude regarding industrial relations that had come about in the American Ford leadership. The older Henry Ford never visited Denmark in his capacity as president of Ford Motor Company, but had he done so, the idea of him chatting with a union representative would have been unthinkable.

When they met, Sjølander delivered a letter to Ford II, informing him about the workers' concern about the very limited level of production in Copenhagen at the time.[105] A few days later, Henry Ford II sent a personal answer to Sjølander from his hotel in Stockholm. There might be "some obstacles", he writes, but then he assures the shop steward of his intention to make the Copenhagen plant "a better place to work and keep it abreast of all manufacturing in Denmark".[106]

In this period, Sjølander also became acquainted with Svend A. Godfredsen, an American of Danish descent who held the office of labour relations officer at the US Economic Cooperation Administration, Special Mission to Denmark—the administrative body of the Marshall Plan.[107] In 1949, Sjølander wrote a personal letter to Godfredsen, in which he expressed his personal faith in Henry Ford II, and his will to realise a "new policy in regard to labour". He furthermore applauded the Marshall Plan as a "grand attempt to strengthen the ties between America and the old world".[108]

At that time, Sjølander had left the Communist Party, and would rejoin theSocial Democratic Party a few years later. But he kept working together with other union activists, some of whom were still members of the Communist Party, such as the chairman of the metalworkers' club and vice-chairman of the combined club. The cooperation continued, even after he was toppled as chairman of the combined club in 1952, according to him by the Communists. And he would not refrain from supporting the more militant opposition inside the Metalworkers' Association (DSMF) from time to time.[109]

From the outside, Axel Sjølander's mingling with both communist principles of class struggle and Fordist ideas of cooperation seemed incoherent. But that is not necessarily how it was seen from the shop floor at Ford Motor Company A/S. After all, Sjølander was re-elected time and again as shop steward by his fellow workers, right up until he left Ford due to age in March 1961.[110]

During the late 1940s and early 1950s, the workers at Ford found themselves in a rather unstable situation. Production—and thereby jobs—fluctuated significantly, and the future of the workplace was not immediately predictable. In that situation, union activists as well as rank-and-file workers reached out for whatever means they thought available, in order to get a grasp of the situation and secure as much influence as possible, no matter where they had invested their political sympathies in the world outside the Ford plant. Communist shop stewards might interpret the basic relationship between workers and management as one of class struggle, but that would not prevent them from trying to get results through the Cooperation Committee. And those who, like Axel Sjølander, became enthused by the prom-

Figure 31 Leading shop steward Axel Sjølander (front right) chatting with Henry Ford II at the South Port plant, March 1948. Unknown photographer. Rødovre Municipal Archive, Axel Sjølander personal archive

ises of cooperation, delivered by Henry Ford II, would not necessarily refrain from more militant tactics if they saw fit.

Overall ideological orientations would certainly influence the way, the workers interacted with management. But ideological orientations were infused with, informed by, and had to be adapted to the day-to-day experiences on the shop floor, in production and in worker-management relations. And as the realities of production changed, so did the workers' perceptions of such things as cooperation, and what could be gained by it.

Waning visions

Shortly after the establishing of the Cooperation Committee, its work was discussed at a general meeting of the painters' club. The consensus was that it had already led to several improvements.[111] Indeed, improvements did come in this period, even if they were not all due to the Cooperation Committee. In fact, some of them were the result of one of the very few strikes at Ford in the post-war period, which took place in the spring of 1946, just prior to establishing the committee.

The primary reason for the strike, which lasted two and a half days, was work insecurity. The workers at Ford had accustomed themselves to the fact that production would sometimes be stopped for various reasons, and they would be temporarily dismissed without pay. In some years, production would go on for only nine or ten months. But what the workers could still not accept was that they might be sent home in the middle of a workday, without getting paid for a full day's work.[112]

One day in March 1946, 37 men were laid off without notice in the middle of the day. This led to all other workers going on strike. The demand was that any workday should be considered a full day, and an end to temporary layoffs without notice. Managing director H.C. Møller at first offered a raise in hourly pay, as well as higher extra payment for overtime and various other benefits. However, in the end, workers' demands regarding temporary layoffs were also accepted. These gains should be seen in the context of the spring of 1946 being a period of unrest in the labour market in general, with rising militancy from several unions.[113]

Both unions as well as management surely had these events in mind as they started work in the Cooperation Committee in the summer of 1946. As already described above, several issues were pushed forward by the unions and many of them were accepted by management. But there was one problem looming above anything else, and in relation to which all the other issues became insignificant: that of keeping up production and securing jobs.

An important strategic reason for the Danish Confederation of Trade Unions to push for cooperation councils on a national level in 1946–1947 had been the assumption that they would give the workers more insight into the economy of the enterprises, and thereby also some *de facto* influence on decisions regarding production, including hiring and firing.[114]

A recurrent issue that the Cooperation Committee at Ford had on its table was the immediate outlook for production. In the late 1940s, production was both limited and fluctuating. H.C. Møller was quite keen to deliver trustworthy and updated production plans. He also shared some of his concerns about political issues that might affect the possibility of import and the demand for cars[115]—but only to an extent. When a request was raised for deeper insight into the economy of the company, he resorted to his well-proven tactic of deferring: the yearly financial statement was public, Møller declared, and any questions regarding it would be answered by the same procedure as questions from shareholders.[116] The matter was never raised again within the committee.

Arthur Beck, who replaced H.C. Møller as manager in 1949, had a more straightforward way in his cooperation with the unions and was more inclined to flat-out refuse suggestions he did not agree with.[117] And even if some information about production plans were still given, the union representatives found it to be too superficial. At a meeting of the painters' club in 1957, the chairman was questioned by members about future production. He regretted that he was not able to answer the question satisfactorily, since he "was not able to get the full truth from the management".[118]

In the end, what mattered most to the union and the workers was not lofty talk about cooperation but hard facts about the production, what was done to secure it, and the possibility of still having a job the day after tomorrow. But as uncertainties grew about the future of the plant, management did not deliver that in a way the unions felt was reassuring. Not necessarily because they did not want to, but just as much because they were not able to.

Disputes at the shop floor

Occasionally, the disputes between skilled and unskilled workers, which had been a burning issue in the 1920s but had since been reduced to a simmer, would flare up again—mostly when changes in production disturbed the established balance. This was the case for instance with the increased use of electric welding, which would lead to a scarcity of skilled welders in the early 1950s. Unskilled workers were therefore offered training as welders.

From the point of view of the workmen's union, that could be considered a favourable situation since it offered a route to more qualified jobs for its members. But it was at the same time a risk, since such trained welders could be considered qualified to an extent where they would have to be transferred to the metalworkers' union . The workmen's union decided to support the training of some of its members as welders, provided they were allowed to stay in the union. But then the metalworkers' union Metalworkers' union decided to open its doors to membership for unskilled workers with a certificate as welders.[119] This potential conflict never erupted, however, since it was overshadowed by other matters.

In the 1950s, the issue of work speed resurfaced. In early 1952, Ford was introducing time studies, which prompted a meeting in the combined union club. There was a bit of confusion about the scope of the time studies, but apparently it was in relation to the introduction of new models. The unions decided not to resist time studies as such, but to demand a proportional increase in wages, should they lead to higher productivity.[120]

The introduction of time studies was an echo of developments in Detroit, but it resonated differently in Copenhagen. A wave of strikes against "speed-ups" swept through Ford plants in Detroit and elsewhere in the USA during 1949. And despite agreement in principle between Ford and the United Auto Workers, spontaneous, unauthorised strikes against work pressure were not uncommon throughout the 1950s.[121]

In Copenhagen, no such strikes occurred against time studies or speedups. In fact, the issue was not raised again until 1957; in that and the subsequent year, it was discussed at union meetings. But once again the workers decided not to protest against time studies as such, but to demand that representatives appointed by the workers themselves should be allowed to take part in the timing and, if necessary, be trained to do so at the expense of the company.[122]

This was in line with the general politics of the labour movement, in relation to rationalisation and time studies.[123] Whether or not the demands raised at the union meeting were actually met by the management, and in what way, is not known, but the matter was not raised again.

The reason why this issue did not generate as much complaint and conflict in Copenhagen as in Detroit could be that, even if speedups occurred at the Danish plant, it was simply on a less intense level than in the American plants. But this cannot be known for sure, based on the sources available.[124] What we do know for sure is that the contexts were different: during the inter-war period, when there were no unions at Ford in Detroit, there were no effective instruments for workers to resist speedups. In fact, speed-ups and related issues were the main reasons for American autoworkers to finally start organising during the 1930s. Consequently, how to handle working speed inside the framework of bargaining between unions and management was still a new and partly unsettled matter in post-war Detroit, while formal or at least informal bargaining already had been the mutually accepted way of handling such issues for a long time in Copenhagen.

Beyond Copenhagen

On an early autumn day in 1955, union representatives of all the Copenhagen auto plants were gathered in the headquarters of the Danish Metalworkers' Association. Among them was H. Henriksen, leading shop steward at Ford Motor Company A/S, and Axel Sjølander, at that time chairman of the metalworkers' club at the company. The occasion was a visit from the USA by Jack Conway, personal assistant to Walther P. Reuther, president of the United Auto Workers.[125]

While contact between the Danish and the American labour movements had been sporadic at best before the war, the situation changed significantly after 1945. Under the general auspices of the Marshall Plan, several trips for Danish labour representatives to the USA were arranged. A breakthrough in this regard was a delegation of union leaders, including Eiler Jensen, chairman of the Danish Confederation of Trade Unions, who travelled across the USA for a month during 1949. The delegation visited industrial workplaces, had meetings with Paul Hoffman, the administrative leader of the Marshall Plan. They also took part in the national congress of the American Federation of Labor, and met with Walther Reuther, president of the United Auto Workers, and attended a meeting of the local 600 of the UAW, organising workers at Ford's Detroit plants.[126] During the following years, up to 1956, around 158 Danish union leaders on various levels would take part in delegations to the USA. But rank-and-file union members were also offered trips to America, such as the 42 Danish workers who took part in the *Work Study Training Programme* in 1952.[127]

But remarkably, no union representatives or rank-and-file workers from Ford Motor Company A/S took part in any of these trips. As noted above, Axel Sjølander, in his capacity as leading shop steward, had been in personal contact with Henry Ford II during his visit in 1948, and was on friendly terms with the American labour officer in Copenhagen. In 1953 Henriksen, who had succeeded Sjølander as leading shop steward, had a meeting with an American Ford representative visiting the Danish company, with whom he apparently discussed issues regarding the already existing pension fund for the workers in Copenhagen. Subsequently, he wrote some letters to Detroit on this matter, as well as on the possibilities of a pay raise. But none of these contacts included American union representatives or the UAW.[128]

A chance for Danish autoworkers to have a direct exchange of experiences with American colleagues came in 1950 when an international conference of autoworkers was called for. Even though it took place in Paris, it was initiated from America. Denmark was represented by the chairman of the branch no. 14 of the Metalworkers' Association, which was also the branch organising metalworkers at Ford Motor Company A/S. At the conference he would most probably have met UAW representatives, but whatever was discussed it had no immediate impact in Copenhagen. No union representative from Ford took part in the conference.[129]

Consequently, despite the steep rise in union connections across the Atlantic since 1949, the meeting in the autumn 1955 was the first time union representatives from Ford in Copenhagen met an official of the American autoworkers' union. Mr. Conway's visit to Denmark was part of a larger journey around Europe, arranged by the International Association of Metalworkers. At the meeting he talked about how the American autoworkers had successfully fought for higher wages in recent years, as a reaction to automation and rising productivity in the industry. The questions and remarks that followed reflected an interest by the Danish union representatives in the conditions of their American colleagues. The Danes were duly impressed by the results that the UAW had gained. But not all things American were impressive. Both parties were aware that, even though industrial productivity and the wages paid in USA were on a higher level than in Denmark, some things were not. Most notably the American welfare system—or lack thereof. "Even though we may be a poor country", the secretary of the Metalworkers' Association remarked, "we have been able, due to our work, to accomplish several things, for which we are happy".[130]

In retrospect, the meeting on that day in September stands out as a courtesy visit mostly. It did not lead to an increased cooperation between Danish and American unions. In fact, there are no signs of direct contacts between union representatives at Ford in Copenhagen and the UAW other than this one. But later that same year, a delegation of Danish union representatives, including the leading shop steward from Ford, was in the UK and Belgium, to visit American assembly plants there.[131]

Apparently, the fact that the Danish plant was part of a global corporation, and any attempts by Ford to foster a corporate identity, did not promote any very strong need for cooperation across the Atlantic among the workers at Ford Motor Company A/S.

Cars for Freedom

"Now the cars are rolling again—from the Danish Ford factory." This was the headline of a Ford advertisement in *Politiken* in May 1950. The occasion was that regular assembly had been resumed for the first time since the short-lived instances immediately after the war. Ford now had a proper product to offer that segment of the public that had been able to obtain a permit for buying a car.

During the late 1940s, Ford was publishing next to no newspaper ads. This of course made sense since they also had next to no products to offer. But in 1950, six ads appeared in the pages of *Politiken* during the year, most of them advertising Anglia and Prefect, but the Taunus was also featured. In 1958 the number of ads in *Politiken* had risen to 11, out of which two were the size of about half a page, while the rest were a quarter or smaller. Still not very much though, compared to some of the pre-war years.

The publishing of *Ford Nyt* resumed in 1946, with two issues. Most of the rest of the 40s saw two issues per year, rising to typically three per year in the 50s. While both newspaper ads and the company magazine were still barely catching up to the heights of the pre-war years, a third channel of marketing saw a rather steep rise: brochures. More than 60 brochures and leaflets were published in 1946–1957, compared to about 39 in 1930–1939.[132] But not only did brochures grow in number: while many of the earlier ones were simple leaflets, they generally became larger, glossier and more colourful over time during the post-war years. This was clearly a medium into which Ford was putting an increasing amount of effort and resources.[133]

As cars became available for sale, and customers were able to afford them, Ford Motor Company A/S gradually resumed exhibitions again. At first, these were in the form of smaller presentations of new models, or as part of the joint exhibitions arranged by the Association of Car Manufacturers and Importers. But in 1955 it was decided that the time was ripe for a bolder move: a grand exhibition was set up in Copenhagen, and later sent on tour around the country. More than 150,000 visitors in total came to see the latest Ford cars.[134]

Figure 32 "Now the cars are rolling again—from the Danish Ford factory." Newspaper ad celebrating the start of assembly of English Anglia and Prefect models in Copenhagen. *Politiken,* 8 May 1950

Working against restrictions

Managing director H.C. Møller was following the political situation closely, as restrictions on both import of car parts and sale of finished cars made the immediate post-war years difficult for Ford Motor Company A/S. His mood was changing by the month during the late 1940s: the introduction of the Marshall Plan in 1947–1948 gave hope for economic and industrial renewal, and therefore also a possibility of expanding the market for cars. In early 1947, Møller informed local union representatives about "the positive attitude" of the authorities regarding import. Later that year, he seems to have lost his previous faith in the Marshall Plan leading to renewed demand for commercial vehicles. Then he found now hope in the plan, as well as in a trade agreement with the UK during 1948.[135]

Despite his concerns, H.C. Møller did not approach the political decision makers directly, as he and the board had done in the 1930s; but that does not mean that he was politically passive. Møller had since then become much more involved in various trade organisations: he was now a member of the Industrial Council, the board of the Association of Car Manufacturers and Importers, and the representative committee of the Society for Industry.[136] He would have had good reason to believe that he could have more political impact via these positions than by acting on behalf of Ford Motor Company A/S alone.[137]

Arthur Beck, who replaced Møller in June 1949, was less well connected. It might therefore be expected that he and the board would consider taking direct political action as the import and export restrictions dragged on, especially since the situation of the car assembly plants—Ford, GM, and others—was actually on the general political agenda several times during the early 1950s. But this did not happen.

Strangely enough, despite its very direct implications for the company, the political situation regarding import and sales was not a central issue for the board during the early 1950s. It was on the agenda only once, without leading to any discussions or initiatives.[138] Considering the level of detail by which other, sometimes rather trivial matters were treated by the board, it is unlikely that Arthur Beck as manager was involved in any political initiatives on his own, without the board at least being informed.

The lack of political interest displayed by both board and management through the early 1950s may be a result of the somewhat tumultuous changes in leadership: within a few years, a whole new group of people had taken the driver's seat of Ford Motor Company A/S—people recruited mainly from the international Ford organisation, without the same insight—or interest—in the local context, as the ones they replaced. The board became increasingly preoccupied with affairs relating to the reorganisation of Ford in Europe. That included changes in organisation and ownership directly relevant to the Danish company, such as the sale of the Swedish subsidiary, but matters like the reorganisation of Ford Iberica and the sale of Ford in France to Simca were also discussed in some detail by the Danish board.[139] The outlook of the new board members was clearly that of being part of Ford in Europe, just as much as being a Danish company.

However, during the summer of 1957, Ford Motor Company A/S finally took part in meetings between representatives of several car assembly plants and relevant trade unions on one side, and members of parliament and the minister of trade on the other.[140] But the Ford management arrived late to a game that had already been played for some time, in the form of political negotiations. In November 1957, the last remaining restrictions on car sales were removed, following a decision in Parliament.

American dilemmas

The post-war years in Denmark were marked by an increasing interest in and even fascination for all things American—and the car was perhaps the object that symbolised American culture and lifestyle more than anything else. While 2.6 percent of Danes owned a car in 1948, the figure for the USA was 22.5 percent.[141] But not only was car ownership much more widespread in America, the American cars of the late 1940s were also very different from the typical European models, mostly of pre-war origin, that roamed the streets of Denmark.

In these years, American cars grew bigger and developed a distinctive style, typically with a large grill at the front and tailfins at the back, and with elaborate use of chrome and colour. The wide chrome grill was the reason why American cars became known as "Dollar Grins" in Danish slang of the late 1940s. And typically of the ambivalent attitudes of the Danes towards American consumerism and popular culture, Dollar Grin could have both positive and negative connotations.

While some were impressed by the American cars, looking at them with envy and admiration, others were sceptical. In 1949 *Motor*, the magazine of the Federation of Danish Motorists, featured an article under the headline "Rebellion against the Dollar Grin".[142] Generally, the press became increasingly critical towards American car trends during the 1940s and '50s. In a dichotomy of style versus function, American cars were framed as being excessively into the former and ignoring the latter.[143]

But even if they had been attracted by the style, not many Danes would have been able to buy an American Dollar Grin in the immediate post-war period due to import and currency restrictions. Sales of American-made Fords were low and most were delivered to special VIP customers.[144] But it did not go unnoticed inside the company when Ford lost one its most prominent VIP customers: the Danish Queen Ingrid. The Queen had been driving her own Ford Mercury since 1939, with a couple of updates to newer models. But in 1957 she decided to abandon Ford. According to company lore, the reason was that the new Mercury presented that year had simply become too American in its design. The opulent chrome grill and tailfins had made the Queen turn away from her otherwise favoured brand, choosing a more conservatively styled British Jaguar instead.[145]

Finding a way to tap into popular fascination with American culture, without being associated with its excesses, was a challenge that Ford had to face in its post-war marketing and PR. And it was accentuated by the profound changes in the company's product portfolio. By origin, Ford was an American company, selling and marketing a product made in America, even if it was assembled and finished in Copenhagen. During the 1930s, the American Ford models had been supplemented by cars of European origin and design. But from around 1950, the European models were no longer just a supplement: the cars that were assembled and offered to the customers were from then on predominantly of British and German origin.

A newspaper ad from 1958 illustrates how Ford was dealing with these dilemmas. The ad features a drawing of a British Anglia being assembled in Copenhagen, and the text reads:

> The best of two continents. Once the flow of cars was only one way—from America to Europe. Today, it is an interaction, and Ford manufacturers around the world are all contributing to the grand, common image of Ford quality.

Figure 33 With its tailfins, large front grill, and elaborate use of chrome, the 1957 Ford Mercury was the archetypical Dollar Grin. Here it is being photographed at the South Harbour, with the Ford assembly plant as backdrop. Unknown photographer. Ford Motor Company A/S photo collection

> It is impossible here to do justice to each nation in this important development. But generally, we may talk about American luxury, English solidity, French elegance, and German precision.
>
> It is with these features from two continents the Ford car is being built today.[146]

In other words, if a potential customer felt somewhat appalled about the opulent appearance of American cars, he did not have to worry when buying a Ford, because even if the company was American, its cars were European in their solidity, elegance, and precision. And on the other hand: if you were actually looking in envy at an American Mercury or Fairlane, but could only afford an Anglia or a Taunus, you could at least comfort yourself with the fact that even these models had the magical touch of American luxury to them.

American cars only made up a minor part of Ford's newspaper advertisement in the post-war period, compared to models of European origin. But in contrast with earlier periods, Ford became more explicit in highlighting the origin of its American models in marketing during the 1950s.[147] On the face of it, this was a strengthening of the company's American profile. But on the other hand: until 1932, any Ford, and during the rest of the 1930s, most Fords advertised were of American origin. And since this was well known, there had been no special need to highlight that fact in advertising. From the 1940s onwards, this was no longer the case, and as Ford cars became increasingly European, Ford had to make the American origin of specific models explicit, to make use of it in marketing.

America, as the land of the future, was also present in the company magazine. The fascination of new technology was displayed in articles about the use of nuclear technologies in industry, spacecraft, and futuristic car designs. More content was related to America and American lifestyle, including car-related events, races, and ordinary celebrity news. People related to Ford Motor Company, from VIP customers to leading managers, appear frequently: most prominently Henry Ford II, whose trips to Denmark in 1948 and 1952 were covered as if he were a head of state or a Hollywood star.[148]

Producing freedom

On 4 March 1948, the weather was unusually bad in Copenhagen. Only in the last minutes did the fog over Copenhagen Airport clear up a bit, allowing Henry Ford II and his entourage to land in a chartered plane from Berlin as planned. This was part of Ford II's first European roundtrip, to provide him with a first-hand impression of a part of the industrial empire he had now become head of.[149]

Henry Ford II was received in Denmark as a true celebrity. He stayed three nights in Copenhagen, before continuing to Stockholm.

During his stay, he resided in a suite at d'Angleterre, the city's most prestigious hotel, where he also gave a very well-attended press conference. Among other media, he was interviewed for radio by the popular journalist Gunnar "Nu" Hansen.

Apart from visiting the plant and being present at a board meeting, Henry Ford II took part in a lunch with 150 Danish and Norwegian Ford dealers, and a dinner party for especially invited representatives of Danish industry and commerce and other VIPs, such as the American ambassador to Denmark and director of the National Bank and former minister of finance C.V. Bramsnæs.

At the dinner party he gave a speech, in which he chose to talk extraordinarily little about industry as such, and not about car manufacturing at all. Instead, the topic of his speech was freedom: "Freedom for humanity and for private enterprise", against the "slave state". While the slave states—none was mentioned by name—are reactionary and curb the initiative of the individual, freedom is a mighty source of energy for creation and progress. Ford II emphasised as his conclusion: it is everyone's obligation to consider how his or her freedom is best used. And businessmen in particular should contribute to greater harmony within as well as between states, a growth in world trade, and an overall expansion of production. The speech was later printed in Danish as a four-page booklet and distributed as part of the April 1948 issue of the company magazine *Ford Nyt.*

For Henry Ford, the car had not just been a means of transportation. It was the embodiment of a social vision: an affluent society, based on mass production and consumption, but also based firmly on a free market. His political and ideological had been expressed primarily in books and media, but during the 1920s, his company had also been mobilised for that purpose. The Danish Ford company had felt committed to promoting Ford's social ideas, to a certain degree. But during the 1930s, the openly ideological dimension of Fordism waned, and played almost no role in the public presence of the company.

The speech of Henry Ford II in 1948 marked a return to ideology. Just as it had been in the 1920s, the purpose of Ford Motor Company A/S was still, above all, to run a business and make a profit. But as the Cold War gathered pace, this basic raison d'être was encapsulated in a narrative of a more altruistic nature: that of contributing to the defence of the free world.

When Henry Ford II made the explicit connection between free enterprise and human freedom, he was not just echoing his grandfather. He was also very much in line with the basic ideas behind the Marshall Plan, which was about to be launched at the same time. Political freedom and individual enterprise would foster industrial growth—and industrial growth would foster material welfare, thereby safeguarding freedom against the lures of Communism.

The connection between freedom and industrial production recurred several times in the Danish company magazine throughout the following years, either implicitly or explicitly. A new centre for space research, established by Ford in the USA, is presented as an example of how the company strove to "further technical and human science on responsible, democratic grounds"[150]. And when Dagenham was expanded in 1958, it was presented to the Danish readers as "more than just one firm, in need of higher capacity for production —it is an example of the expansive economy of the whole western world".[151]

In 1949, a year after Henry Ford II had given his speech on the ideal of freedom through productivity, another American visited Copenhagen, bringing with him the same ideals. This time it was not the president of the Ford Motor Company, but an ordinary autoworker from Detroit. His name was Thøger Eriksen, and as his name implies, he was of Danish descent.

Eriksen was invited as "the Christmas guest of honour" by the newspaper *Berlingske Tidende* and the Scandinavian airline company *SAS*. He had been selected by a special committee, among a large number of nominees. Arriving in mid-December, Eriksen would take part in a number of banquets, meet the mayor of Copenhagen and the Prime Minister, tour the country, and visit family and old acquaintances in Jutland, before finally returning to Detroit just before New Year. His visit was covered intensely by *Berlingske Tidende,* but largely ignored by the labour press.[152]

But even if they were not reading the conservative newspaper, the workers at Ford became familiar with Eriksen's visit anyway. Since he had for a long time been employed by Ford in Detroit, the

Danish Ford company also became actively involved in his visit. Manager Arthur Beck was part of the welcome committee, as well as H.C. Møller, and a visit to the South Harbour Plant was of course a part of Eriksen's program. When Eriksen arrived at the plant, work had been stopped, and all the workers had gathered to meet the guest. Eriksen gave a speech in which he detailed the standard of living that he had been able to obtain as an autoworker in America: by working five hours he could earn enough to buy a pair of shoes, in 30 hours a set of clothes, and in 500 hours a good second-hand car. According to *Berlingske Tidende*, the Danish workers sacrificed their lunch break in favour of "learning more about life at the grand factories in the metropolis of the automobile".[153]

Standing next to Eriksen during his speech was leading shop steward Axel Sjølander. Sjølander was also among the invited guests at the lunch that Ford gave in honour of Eriksen in *Tivoli*, and he was among the last to say farewell to Eriksen at the airport when he returned home to Detroit. Later Sjølander would write to Svend A. Godfredsen, at the American special mission to Denmark of the Marshall Plan, expressing his admiration of what he had heard from Eriksen about the standard of living of American workers.[154]

I am able to inform you today, that Copenhagen has been chosen as a centre for production of Ford construction equipment

Robert M. Rice, 24 January 1966

1958–1966
Expansion and Decline

PRODUCTION
Just Not Enough

In January 1959, the new American Ford models Custom and Fairlane were presented in the showroom that was part of Ford's new administrative building. This was also the closest thing to an official inauguration of the facilities. In contrast with the festive inauguration of the South Port plant in 1924, the new buildings were put to use gradually, as they became ready, without much ado. But the press nevertheless took the opportunity to comment on the office building, designed by Danish architects, which was found to be "stylish" and "bold", while the adjacent storage hall was "modern" and "rational".[1]

The new administrative headquarters, consisting of approximately 1,600 m^2 over two storeys, had been erected just south of the Ford Basin, and behind that to the east was a 6,600 m^2 large hall for storage of cars and spare parts.[2] In relation to the existing factory, this was an extension by roughly 75 percent of the area under roof. Supplementing the buildings was a large open space for additional storage of cars.[3] An impressive extension of the facilities, leaving no doubt about Dearborn's conviction that its Copenhagen Company was an asset worth investing in for the future. But the big question was: would the future also include production in the form of assembly?

Clearly, what had been built in 1957–1958 was primarily for the purpose of importing, selling, and servicing a growing number of cars. The new warehouse was filled to the brim with racks and shelves, with a combined length of two kilometres. It was testament to the need of rational storage of an increasing number of parts necessary for servicing a portfolio of cars growing not only in absolute numbers,

Figure 34 New storage facilities for spare parts, 1958. Unknown photographer. The National Museum of Denmark

but also in the number of different models and in the complexity of each model.[4]

While being stylish, the new administrative building was not only made to show off; it also contained several new, bright, spacious offices for the growing number of sales and administrative staff. Parallel to the enlargement of the facilities, investment was made in office technology. A punch card system, delivered by IBM, was used for managing stocks and sales, and a fully automated pneumatic tube system for handling internal communication.[5]

While most money and effort were put into storage and office facilities, the 1958 expansion did affect assembly too, even if only on a small scale. In the original plant, space became available as offices were moved out, and some rearrangement took place. During the late 1950s, the workers had made increasing complaints about the painting facilities: not only because of the lack of proper ventilation, but also because of the cramped space, which made work difficult and, in the words of one of the painters, "made the joy of doing a good job disappear".[6]

It was not just the workers, who were complaining about the paint facilities. The Working Environment Authority was not pleased with the situation either, and was putting pressure on the company to improve matters. The same authority also pointed to an issue of a prosaic, but in a certain sense pressing, nature: the insufficient number of toilets available to the employees. To meet the demands from the authorities, it was decided in 1959 to make a further investment in the assembly plant, mainly in renovation and renewal of the painting facilities. During the next couple of years, new paint booths were installed, and more space was set aside for repairing paint damage on built-up cars. As a result, the frequent complaints about the painting facilities came to an end during the early 1960s.[7]

Expansion in assembly

Parallel to the decision to renew the painting facilities, it was also decided in late 1959 to make the investment necessary for assembling the Taunus Model 17M, the reason being that a change in customs had made local assembly profitable. Part of the investment was in new tools and fixtures specific to the Model 17M, but another part was into a necessary expansion of the overall capacity of the assembly plant from 28 units per day to 38.[8]

What was done specifically to achieve this raise in production capacity is not known, but part of it was the expansion of the upholstery shop in 1960. Upholstery was relocated into some of the areas made available as offices had been moved to the new administrative building, and production was reorganised around a newly installed assembly line.[9] The total amount invested in expanding production facilities and renovating the assembly plant around 1959–1960 cannot be assessed precisely, but it was somewhere between DKK 1.0 and 2.2 million[10] This was of course a substantial sum, but never the less rather modest compared to the more than DKK 11 million spent on the 1958 expansion.

Considering that part of the investment was for other purposes, this does not seem to be a high price to pay for a raise in production capacity by more than 30 percent.[11] The keyword here is "rearrangement", as the process was referred to in the minutes of the board. This was not an investment in completely new production technologies, but rather a refinement, rearrangement, and partial expansion of an existing production process.

The fact that a production process whose main elements had been fairly constant since the 1930s could still be used for car assembly in the early 1960s could of course be seen as proof of the relatively rigid and change-resistant Fordist system of mass production. But that would only be partially true. From another perspective, the unchanging character of the main elements of the system could also be seen as a testament to its ability to accommodate any necessary change. When for example assembly of the Taunus 17M was started in 1959, most of the investments had to do with the general increase in production capacity. The funds directed towards new tools and fixtures, specifically needed and developed for assembling the new model, were limited to only about DKK 160,000. The same relatively low amounts were spent on tools for other models introduced in this period.

Not only was the adaption of production relatively cheap, but it also seems to have taken place rather swiftly, as no major halts to production due to model shift have been recorded. On the contrary: the production system was able to handle several models simultaneously and change smoothly between them. The Copenhagen plant had come a long way from the efficient, but inflexible, production methods of the 1920s, and was now perfectly able to combine volume and diversity in assembly. This was illustrated in a description of the production process in *Ford Nyt* in 1960. The company magazine proudly notes how "this or that engine will turn up [at the assembly line] at just the right moment, so that it will end up in the corresponding chassis". Production was running like "a well-planned puzzle".[12]

Figure 35 A Ford Cortina, assembled in England, is driven ashore in Copenhagen from Ford's own transport ship Dyvi Anglia, ca. 1964. Unknown photographer. Ford Motor Company A/S photo collection

Diversity but too little volume

On 2 May 1963, car number 300,000 rolled off the assembly line in Copenhagen. It was a Taunus 17M.[13] This specific model had become exceedingly popular, and the investments made into its assembly and in the general increase in production around 1959–1960 had paid off. But locally assembled cars were becoming a minority among the total numbers sold; during the early 1960s, roughly two-thirds of all cars sold by Ford Motor Company A/S had arrived at Copenhagen in a complete state, so called built-ups, by ship from England or by train from Germany.[14]

The South Port assembly plant might have evolved into a modern and flexible production system. But the irony was that while the plant had gained in diversity, it was now lacking in volume. At first glance, an output of 6–9,000 cars per year was no small number. It was a little below the level of the 1930s, but then the cars had also become more complicated and the product portfolio wider than then.

But the playing field had changed significantly since 1930. During the immediate post-war period, Dagenham was still Ford's only complete production facility in Europe, and relatively little was invested in Cologne. But due to market changes, this was revised by the late 1950s. Cologne was now to become the second major Ford plant in Europe, alongside Dagenham, and made profitable by large-scale mass production.[15] The result was that, around 1960, there were now not one but two large-scale Ford production facilities in Europe, the output of which dwarfed that of smaller plants, such as the one in Copenhagen.

Questions about the profitability of the Danish plant were raised in 1963, and in 1964 a closure of assembly seemed unavoidable. For reasons detailed below, production was nevertheless allowed to go on, with a reduced workforce.[16] But finally, in January 1966, it was announced that Ford Motor Company would no longer assemble cars in Copenhagen. The production facilities were still to be used by Ford, though, even if not by Ford Motor Company A/S. The original 1924 South Port plant was to be sold to a new company, Ford Industrial Equipment A/S, established for producing farming and construction equipment for the European market.

After 47 years and a total of more than 323,000 units produced, the very last Ford car rolled off the assembly line in Copenhagen on 15 July 1966.

MARKETS

The Germans Are Coming

The sale of cars, and especially passenger cars, was booming in Denmark from the mid-1950s. During the ten years from 1956 to 1966, the total number of registered cars almost tripled.[17] The car was starting to become a general commodity, as not only the upper and middle classes, but even some of the more affluent members of the working class could now afford one. In 1964, Ford's share of this expanding market was 16 percent, which happened to be exactly the same as in 1953. But in absolute numbers, Ford's yearly sales in Denmark had risen from around 4,000 units to 15,000 units per year in that same period.[18]

Developments in Norway were parallel, if a little later, as the restrictions on car sales were completely lifted in 1960. In 1964, Ford's relative share of the market was 21 percent in Norway, higher than in any Nordic country, but with 12,000 units it was below Denmark in absolute numbers. In Sweden, Ford's relative share of passenger car sales had diminished during the 1950s, due to increased competition from domestic brands, and in 1964 it was 13 percent, the lowest relative figure among the Nordic markets. But it was a diminishing share of a large and growing market, so the absolute number was 32,000 units, making Sweden the largest market for Ford within the Nordic countries. In Finland, Ford's market share in 1964 was 16 percent, equal to 13,000 units.

But in contrast with earlier periods, far from all these cars were delivered from Denmark. The Swedish company was no longer part of Ford Motor Company A/S and was importing and assembling on its own. However, from 1959, assembly would stop in Stockholm, as it was no longer considered economically viable. From then on, at least some of the cars for the Swedish market were again assembled in Copenhagen,[19] but the bulk of Ford cars for Sweden were imported directly as built-up units from Dagenham and Cologne, circumventing Copenhagen.

In 1960, a new Ford company was set up in Norway. Until then, Norwegian dealers had been cooperating directly with Ford in Copenhagen, but there was now a political desire for a national company. Furthermore, investigations carried out by Ford had shown that, in relation to duty and taxation, a Norwegian subsidiary would be beneficial to Ford Motor Company A/S. Consequently, such a company was established, with 99.9 percent of the shares owned by the Danish company.[20] The Norwegian company would also import some of its cars directly.

Consequently, of the roughly 72,000 Ford cars delivered to the Nordic countries in 1964, only 24,989 were sold by Ford Motor Company A/S.[21]

Taunus versus Cortina

The spring 1960 issue of *Ford Nyt* contained what was labelled a "representative sample" of the company's offerings. Presented in bright colours and cheerful settings, there were cars for different market segments, and of diverse origins: British (Anglia, Consul, Zephyr, and Zodiac), German (Taunus 12M and 17M) and American (Fairlane, Thunderbird, Mercury, Galaxie, and Lincoln Continental).[22]

But the presentation did not necessarily reflect the sales potential of each different model. The British models had regained some popularity, as in 1964 the British-made Fords had a total market share of nine percent in Denmark, compared to seven percent for the German-made. On the Swedish market, which at that time was getting some of its cars from Copenhagen, the German models were much more popular. In Sweden, the total market share of British Ford models was four percent, compared to eight percent for the German models.[23]

In the early 1950s, the biggest hindrance to selling more German Ford cars had been Cologne's failing ability to swiftly follow the fluctuation in demand. The Ford leadership in America had been reluctant to invest too much in renewed production in Cologne, which would potentially undermine the role of Dagenham as its main European facility. But during the late 1950s, two competing trade associations was emerging, and the EEC, including Germany, was established in 1958 and EFTA, including Britain, in 1960. For fear of being left without any bridgehead into the EEC, Dearborn decided to revise its position on Cologne. The strategy towards the European market pursued by Ford in this period has been dubbed "the two fishing lines": the British and German Ford companies were now each allowed to develop their own distinct product line, and essentially to compete against each other on the rest of the European markets.[24]

This was reflected in the development of the Taunus models. From around 1960, they took a new and more independent direction. The 17M was completely redesigned in a radical departure from American chrome and tail-fin styling, with a "form follows function" approach. The new version, with the official designation P3, was affectionately nicknamed *Badewanne* (bathtub) by the public. Two years later, a new

Figure 36 Representatives of various European Ford companies gathered in Cologne for a presentation of the 1960 Taunus 17M. The somewhat skeptical look on their faces may be attributed to the radical new design of the car, which nevertheless became quite a success. The two people at the front left are Orla Larsen, sales manager of Ford Motor Company A/S, and his son Ben Larsen, who was at the time working for Ford in Cologne. Unknown photographer. OEL private collection

12M (P4) was presented, offering technical novelties such as front wheel drive and a completely new V4 engine. Both cars were received favourably by the press, and the 17M was the best-selling Ford model for Ford Motor Company A/S in the early 1960s.[25]

One of the ways the British answered the German challenge was to launch the Cortina in 1962. It was based on the Consul (also marketed as the Consul Cortina for a short period), resulting in a car that was middle-class in size but at a much lower price point than the original Consul. It became one of the best-selling cars on its home market, but also an export success.[26]

In 1962, a total of 9,463 Ford passenger cars of British origin were sold and distributed from Copenhagen. The British cars represented eight different models, from the Anglia to the Zodiac. However, only 21 percent of these, mainly Anglias, had been assembled locally, with the rest being delivered as built-ups. Compared to that, of the 6,206 units of the two versions of the German Taunus, the 12M and the 17M, that were sold the same year, 75 percent had been assembled in Copenhagen.[27]

While Taunus and Cortina were picking up customers, the American Ford models kept falling behind. 527 American passenger cars had been sold by Ford Motor Company A/S in 1958, but in 1962 the number had dropped to 343, roughly two percent of the number of passenger cars sold that year. Of these cars, typically only a handful each year were of the most expensive models: Mercury and Lincoln.[28] The fact that the sales figures for American cars were diminishing, even after the import restrictions had been lifted, indicates that it was not the restrictions alone that were responsible for their low sales in Denmark. The American models did not fit the needs and taste of the market well, and were not that well received, either by the motor press or by the public.[29] And perhaps just as importantly: they were expensive.

MANAGEMENT

American Leadership

When the Norwegian Ford company was established in 1960, it marked a novelty in management: the general manager appointed was an American, Robert M. Rice. Rice came from a position as financial manager at the Danish Ford company.[30] This would prove to be a sign for the future management of Ford Motor Company A/S, as the relatively quick succession of board members and managers that had been introduced in the post-war period now continued.

In 1960, Arthur Beck retired as general manager of Ford in Denmark. At first, he was replaced by his assistant manager, Einar B. Jensen.[31] But Jensen's career as general manager was to be rather short, and quite unsuccessful. Clearly, he did not live up to the expectations of the American owners, who presented his written resignation to a board meeting in July 1963, in which Jensen did not take part himself. In a statement, the American board members declared it to be "in the Company's true interest" that the board accepted Jensen's "request for permission to resign"—which the board did, followed by the appointment of Robert Rice as the new manager of Ford Motor Company A/S.[32]

Not only did the company now have an American general manager for the first time since the short period under James Harrington in 1919–1920, but the assistant manager, in office since 1961, was also an American: C.V. Barion.[33] With two Americans as top executives and the manager of Ford's European operations as chairman of the board, Ford Motor Company A/S was now firmly under American leadership.

In 1959, board member Anker Engelund had resigned as rector of the Technical University and was replaced in this position by Eggert Knuth-Winterfeldt, who was promptly elected to the board of Ford Motor Company A/S as well, where he and Engelund sat together until the death of Engelund two years later. Knuth-Winterfeldt thereby continued a tradition, by being the third rector of the Technical University to become a board member.[34]

When Professor Engelund died in 1961, he had been a member of the board since 1942 and served as its chairman since 1957. Another board member, James van Luppen, was elected chairman in his place. Van Luppen was a Belgian, who had been appointed manager of Ford's European operations under the International Division in 1959, and who had also been a member of the Danish board since then, replacing Tom Lilley.[35]

Van Luppen was chairman until 1965, when he retired from the board. In his place, Robert Rice was elected chairman.[36] As both managing director and chairman of the board, Robert Rice was now undisputedly the person heading the Copenhagen Ford plant. But at that point he must also have known that, in all likelihood, he would be leading it towards closure.

Profits and reserves

The general boom in car sales made the 1960s very profitable for Ford Motor Company A/S. This is reflected in the dividend paid to the shareholders, which was 20 percent for each of the years 1959–1965. For comparison, only two other companies registered at the Copenhagen Stock Exchange paid such high dividends during that period, and most others paid between 8 and 16 percent.[37]

While the dividend was constant, the pre-tax profit fluctuated. It was typically around DKK 6–8 million, but in the years 1959–1960 and 1964 it was only around DKK 2.3–2.6 million.[38] This was, however, not a reflection of bad years for the business. On the contrary, in 1959 Ford had exhibited substantial increase in both production and sales, and the turnover of DKK 256 million was the highest ever in the history of the company. But the next year broke that record: turnover was DKK 290 million, based on sales that reached 28,837 units, more than in any previous year since 1919.[39]

But during these two years, the board had also decided to put aside extraordinarily high amounts in reserve, at least partly for the purpose of reducing tax payment. Furthermore, the reorganisation of business in Norway into a separate subsidiary also influenced how the accounts were structured and presented. Both issues lead to a rather fierce internal debate in 1961–1962. The two main questions were how to present the results of the Norwegian business, and how detailed the published account should be, especially concerning the reserves.

The board of Ford Motor Company A/S was keen on including information about the results of the Norwegian company in the Danish annual report, to make the report more comparable with the years before creating a separate company. The Norwegian management on the other hand was expecting a decrease in profit from 1961 to 1962, and therefore advised that the information regarding Norway in the Danish annual report should be kept to a minimum, in order to avoid "a serious stockholder relations problem".[40]

Ford International was inclined to support the Norwegians. But at the same time, they were requesting for the Danish Board to give considerably more details about the accounts in the annual report than required by Danish law. In particular, they wanted the total amount of reserves stipulated and specified to the shareholders.

A similar request had actually been made by a shareholder at the 1960 annual meeting. Mr. Hertz of the stockbrokers Hofgaard & Hertz had voiced his concern that the proposed 20 percent dividend might "hit [...] the public eye". He therefore suggested that the dividend should be stated also as a percentage of the company's net capital, including reserves. But the board did not want to publish numbers that would indirectly reveal the amount of reserves, and his recommendation was politely but firmly discarded.[41]

For the 1961 annual report, the directors were now asked to give the same information, not by a minority shareholder but by Ford International. The Danish management reacted with astonishment. They made it clear that, in that case, the company would be "officially admitting" that its reserves were more than DKK 78 million, or more than 6.5 times its capital. It would, they argued, not be in the interest of the company to reveal such information, especially not to the Labour Unions nor the Dealers Association. They also reported to Detroit that the local auditors and legal advisors were "astonished and disturbed" by the suggestion by Ford International to reveal this information.[42]

Following a number of letters and telegrams between Detroit and Copenhagen, and between Copenhagen and the London office of the company's auditors Coopers & Lybrand, the matter was settled: Ford Motor Company A/S would add the information requested by Detroit to its annual report for 1961, but in a subdued form and with additional explanatory remarks. When presenting the report at the 1962 shareholders' meeting, O. Bondo Svane declared on behalf of the board that, in this year's account, the company had "put all of its cards on the table". This was reported favourably in the financial newspaper *Børsen*.[43] By way of accounting, the reserves had been reduced to smaller, but still sizeable amount of DKK 30 million in the final report. But contrary to the initial fears of the Danish management, neither unions nor the dealer's association took any notice of the fact that the company had such an amount of money set aside for a rainy day.

The end of assembly

In late 1963 Robert Rice, newly appointed general manager in Copenhagen, was summoned to a meeting in Ford's European headquarter in Brussels.[44] The one and only point on the agenda was this: should assembly in Copenhagen be closed down?

There were several reasons why this question was asked. Generally, trade among the Western European countries had been liberalised during the post-war period, and tariffs had come down. Transport and communication had become cheaper too. But following the establishing of two major zones of economic cooperation, EEC and EFTA, Ford had been compelled to strengthen and concentrate production not only in Dagenham, as originally planned, but also increasingly in Cologne.

Now, Rice was asked to make an analysis of the consequences of closing assembly in Copenhagen. Rice made a report, presenting various arguments for and against a closure, tending towards the latter. In January 1964 he informed the board that assembly in Denmark had become increasingly unprofitable, and that it might even have to end that same year. The board expressed its understanding of the situation.[45]

The closure was not enacted in 1964, though, because of political events: the prospect of a trade war between Denmark and Britain made a rise in customs duty on built-up cars from Dagenham a possible scenario for 1965, making local assembly relatively more profitable. Production was allowed to go on in Copenhagen, but in April 1965 the workforce was cut down from 950 to 700.[46]

In 1965, the profitability of assembling cars in Copenhagen was questioned once again. Ford's Regional Finance office for Europe came up with calculations, based on four scenarios: The conclusion was that only under the most optimistic scenario, which included an unlikely increase in production from 28 cars per day to 64, would it be possible to make a profit from assembly in Copenhagen. But even then, it would still be more profitable from an overall corporate point of view to assemble all German Ford cars in Cologne, since the scale of production there would make assembly cheaper.[47]

Another condition for the most optimistic scenario was that the duty rate for built-up cars would be raised from 12 to 15 percent. But as trade negotiations between Denmark and Britain yielded a positive outcome, the prospect of a trade war and higher import tariffs vanished during the summer of 1965.

Copenhagen manager Robert Rice challenged the calculations made by Ford's regional office in Brussels. Applying opportunity cost principles, he found that production would break even at a rate of 32.5 cars per day. He also pointed to the fact that General Motors was making a business out of employing 1,200 men and producing 150 cars per day in Copenhagen. But he readily admitted that the situation was volatile, and that in the not unlikely event that tariffs would be lowered in the future, assembly activities would likely become unprofitable.[48]

Another consideration was the damage that ceasing assembly in Denmark could do to the public perception of the Ford brand. But in the meantime, the Copenhagen plant had caught the attention of Ford Motor Company's Tractor Division. They saw a potentially growing market in Europe and especially in the EEC, for which Denmark would be a perfect bridgehead. If the Tractor Division took over the assembly plant, Ford Motor Company A/S would not have to bear the cost associated with closing it down, including employee termination costs, and would avoid the possible negative PR that would come from letting the workers go with no alternative.[49]

That settled the question. A new company, Ford Industrial Equipment A/S, was established, which bought the assembly plant for $1.95 million, of which $1.45 million was paid out to shareholders. At the same time the former Citroën assembly plant nearby was bought and added to the production facilities of the new company.[50] Ford Motor Company A/S continued operating as a sales and service company, occupying the newly built office building and warehouse.

INDUSTRIAL RELATIONS

In the Mainstream

While Ford workers during the previous period had oscillated between a strong concern for lack of production and high hopes for a new, American spirit of cooperation, the late 1950s marked a transition to a period of relative tranquillity. On the labour market in general, the unrest of the immediate post-war years had somewhat settled down after reaching an apex with large strikes in connection with negotiation of new nationwide agreements in 1956, in which militant union activists played a leading role. From around 1957–1958, the boom in the western economy could be seen in Denmark too, with unemployment going down and real wages rising significantly. The prospect of a new, more affluent society began to assert itself, even to the working class. Characteristically, the Social Democratic Party went into the parliamentary elections in 1960 under the slogan "Make good times better"—and gained the largest percentage of the vote since the war, enabling them to continue in government.

Wages below average

For Ford workers, this meant that the prospect of getting a job with decent pay somewhere other than at the Ford plant was now more real. Furthermore, from 1958 the standard work week in industry was gradually reduced, so that it was 44 hours in 1966, reducing the difference from Ford's 40-hour week from eight to four hours. But not only was Ford gradually losing its distinctiveness and much of its special appeal as a workplace; in fact it was lagging behind in one key aspect: wages.

It was not that wages were not raised at Ford anymore. Generally, the negotiations between unions and management that took place regularly would result in wages being improved year on year. Sometimes the workers had to push a little harder, as in 1960 when a short strike of only a few hours—the only one in this period—resulted in a pay rise. And paradoxically, the general economic upturn of the early 1960s also became an impediment to higher wages at Ford. In 1963 the social democratic government feared that the rapid expansion of the economy, which included higher wages, could become a threat to national competitiveness on the export market. Therefore, several initiatives were taken to moderate both prices and wages, including a two-year extension by law of the national agreements between unions and employers.[51]

Ford Motor Company A/S was not covered by any such nationwide agreements, but nevertheless the company management referred to these political decisions as a reason for not being able to raise wages in both 1963 and 1964. The unions reacted with anger, and in both years, negotiations actually led to a rise in pay.[52]

But wages in absolute terms are one thing; the relative development in wages at Ford, compared to other, similar workplaces is another. Developments in this regard since 1957 were summed up in 1965 in a note to the combined union club. In 1957 the average hourly pay

Year	Danish metal industries, skilled workers	Skilled auto-workers in Copenhagen	General Motors	Ford Motor Company A/S
1957	300	295	284	266
1958	310	300	299	274
1959	322	317	311	292
1960	357	336	337	307
1961	365	376	365	322
1962	410	413	416	357
1963	446	448	449	390
1964	477	490	485	413
1965	533	529	530	457

Table 6 Average weekly wages in DKK paid at Ford Motor Company A/S, 1957–1965, compared to workers at GM and skilled autoworkers in Copenhagen and all Danish metal industries. Source: Combined Union Club Ford, 28 December 1965 in ABA: SSMF, correspondence, no file number. See also comments in text

at Ford was still notably higher than in comparable industries. But when the shorter work week—40 hours at Ford and 48 hours at most other industrial workplaces—is factored in, the picture changes: the weekly payment at Ford is below the average for skilled metal-workers. In fact the wage gap actually widened during the period, while the work week in industry in general was shortened, diminishing Ford's relative advantage in that respect.

Most frustrating to the Ford workers was probably the fact that, while they saw wages diminish relatively, they could also observe that their colleagues working in comparable jobs at General Motors were able to have their wages raised more or less in the same ratio as the industry in average.

It should be noted, however, that the figures compiled by the unions are exaggerating the situation in some respect. It is not completely fair to compare wages at Ford, where the workers are a mixture of skilled and unskilled, with only skilled workers in the rest of the industry.

We may take that into account and compare the average Ford worker's weekly pay in 1965 with that of an unskilled and a skilled industrial worker in Copenhagen, which were DKK 451 and DKK 547 respectively during a 45-hour workweek.[53] In other words, the average weekly pay at Ford was now only very slightly above that of an unskilled worker. Granted, the Ford worker would only need 40 hours to earn that payment. In the end, it was a matter of personal preference if having the whole Saturday off, instead of only half of it, was worth the relatively low weekly pay. For those who thought so, paychecks at Ford could be considered no better and no worse than other workplaces. For those who did not, they were below standard.

The end of exceptionalism

In August 1962, a worker was fired after nine years of employment. The workmen's union found the sacking of their member unjustified, and it became a matter of principle. As no solution could be found locally, the union decided to involve the national association. After half a year of negotiation, Ford maintained the decision, but agreed to pay the worker DKK 600 in compensation.[54]

What provoked the union in this case was the fact that the workman had been fired despite having worked for the company for so many years. This was a breach of the tacit understanding that seniority was taken into consideration when layoffs were taking place.

Another incident the following year further strained relations between workers and management. An electric welding machine had become overheated, leading to a serious accident and a worker being hospitalised, with second-degree burns on both thighs. The unions saw this as evidence that the workers were being pressed too hard. According to their formal complaint, the worker tending the machine had actually warned the foreman that it was running hot, but had been ordered to continue, to get the car he was working on finished in time. Furthermore, the unions claimed that this particular foreman was known for pressing the workers, causing at least one previous incident of a welding machine running too hot and breaking down, but without any casualties.[55] The Working Environment Authorities and the police were involved, but did not find sufficient evidence to press charges against the foreman or the company.

The layoffs in April 1965 did not exactly improve relations between unions and management. All of those fired were production workers. This led to bitter reactions from the workers, not just because of the number of jobs lost, but also because of its timing. It was announced as effective from 1 April, just before the Easter holidays. The workers accused the management of choosing this specific date only to avoid paying the holiday compensation that the workers would otherwise be entitled to. Management, on the other hand, referred to the fact that production had already been running low for several months.

Regardless of whether the accusations by the workers were justified or not, the incident is a testament to the distrust that had grown between the workers and their unions on one hand, and the company management on the other, as the future of the assembly plant became still more uncertain.

Fluctuation in employment was nothing new to the workers at Ford. The risk of being laid off for a shorter or a longer period had always been part of working in an industry sensitive to both seasonal and structural changes in demand. But the context was different now. In earlier periods, job insecurity had been compensated to various degrees by factors such as higher wages, a shorter working week, and lack of better alternatives; not so anymore. Wages at Ford were now only mediocre, the working week was becoming shorter in the rest of industry too, and in a period of economic upswing there were plenty of other workplaces to choose from. The exceptionalism of Ford as a workplace had come to an end.

The workforce gradually diminished as it became clear that assembly would be discontinued. At the time of the final closure in April 1966, 420 remaining workers lost their jobs. 120 were immediately rehired by Ford Industrial Equipment, the new company that was taking over the production facilities. It was estimated that a total of 270 jobs would become available as production increased. Anyway, finding a new job as an industrial worker was not particularly hard in 1966. At the same time as Ford was closing down, General Motors announced that it was going to expand its activities in Copenhagen, and roughly 150 former Ford workers found a new job in assembling Opel Kadetts for export. Regardless of whether they were immediately rehired by another company or not, all Ford workers were offered compensation for the layoff, ranging from DKK 500 to DKK 5,000, depending on seniority.[56]

Given this, the unions took a positive stance towards the closure of car assembly, in favour of the new production. They saw it as a possibility to renegotiate wages and working conditions. Maybe it would even be possible to sign a proper collective agreement with the new company?[57]

PRESENCE

Fireworks Before Closure

On a summer night in 1959, the Copenhagen sky suddenly burst open with a shower of glittering stars, shimmering lights, and cascades of fire. It was the biggest display of fireworks seen in the city since the commemoration of the King's 75th birthday in 1945, and more than 40,000 had gathered around the Ford headquarters in the South Port, to watch the spectacular sight up close.[58]

The day was 25 June, exactly 40 years since the formal incorporation of Ford Motor Company, and this was of course the reason for the event. But the celebration had begun in the morning, when 500 guests attended a reception in the newly built main office and showroom, which had been converted into a flower garden for the occasion. Later, a lunch was held for specially invited guests. Among them were social democratic Minister of Finance Viggo Kampmann and Knud, hereditary prince of Denmark. They were also among the speakers, offering their congratulations to the company.[59]

The subtle presence of America

The Danish Ford company's American heritage was not a prominent feature of the celebration, but it was not forgotten. Among the distinguished guests were Tom Lilley, vice-president of Ford Motor Company, and Val Peterson, US ambassador to Denmark. But the person who drew most attention was undoubtedly Vivi Bak, a young Danish actress. She arrived at the scene in a Model T, but soon began posing for photographers in a "shiny new Dollar Grin".[60] So America was nevertheless subtly present among the fireworks, the flower show, and the lunch in *Tivoli.*

American Ford models were also featured in the company's general advertising and made up the greatest number of different models in the presentation made by Ford in the spring issue of *Ford Nyt* in 1960, as mentioned above. At a first glance that was odd, since the American models counted for a steadily diminishing part of the total sales, as seen above. Why would a company put that much emphasis in its advertising on a product that accounted for less than three percent of its sales? Probably in the hope that the aura of affluence and luxury that surround the American Ford models would shine on the more mundane European models too. The argument of the 1958 newspaper ad quoted above, that Ford represented "the best of two continents", was still valid. And in order to underpin the image of Ford as a combination of American luxury with European solidity and precision, American models of course had to be part of the advertisement.

Ford also continued to make its presence felt in the physical environment. As we have seen, it had already started in the interwar period, as dealers were urged to modernize, and to equip their facilities with signs delivered from Ford, including the official company logo.

But in the post-war period this was taken a step further, as Ford Motor Company A/S began to put up their own advertising, in the form of signs and neon lights. Prominent examples included a large, animated neon sign visible for anyone traveling along the lakes surrounding central Copenhagen, and another one along the main northern exit road from the capital. The largest neon sign, however, was placed on a newly built water tower in the provincial town of Roskilde, near the main highway stretching across Zealand. According to Ford, the six-metre-high lettering made this one of the largest neon signs in Europe.[61]

But the largest physical manifestation of Ford in relation to public presence was still the South Port plant. It had more than 3,000 visitors per year, and the organised visitors' program continued during the 1960s, probably right up to the closing down of the assembly plant.[62]

Figure 37 The 1924 South Port assembly plant being demolished in 2006.
Photo: Lars K. Christensen

Making the closure public

In January 1966, Ford Motor Company A/S went public with the most important message from the company since its start in 1919: the cessation of all car assembly in Copenhagen. However, the company chose to present the news not as a closure, but as a new beginning.

In his statement to the press on 24 January, Robert Rice started by declaring that Ford was going to establish a new industrial facility in Denmark: its first European factory for construction equipment. The focus of his presentation was about the positive impact the new company and its export activities would have on the Danish economy. The fact that the new company was to replace the assembly of cars was mentioned only in passing. But current and future customers were assured that sales and service of Ford cars in Denmark would not be affected.[63]

The public reaction to this message was undoubtedly influenced by the fact that Denmark was in the middle of a period of strong economic growth. As seen above, the reaction from the unions and the labour movement was remarkably calm, since finding new employment for those laid off was unlikely to be a problem. Likewise, for the general public, cars had now become an everyday commodity, and likewise the fact that they were imported from all over the world had become commonplace. For the average Dane, for whom owning a car had now become a realistic option, what was interesting in relation to Ford were the features and the prices of next year's models—not so much where and how they had been manufactured.

Ford Motor Company A/S would continue as a sales and service company and remain owner of the office building and warehouse along Sluseholmen. It even expanded its sales-related facilities: in 1966, 60,000 square meters were acquired in the port town of Esbjerg, for receiving and preparing built-up cars from England, and in 1979 the warehouse in Copenhagen was doubled in size.[64] But in 1991, Ford's Danish headquarters were finally relocated from the South Port, first to Glostrup and later to Ballerup, a Copenhagen suburb.

Ford Industrial Equipment A/S gave up production in the South Port another 10 years later, in the mid-1970s. The former assembly plant was used for other purposes for a number of years, but was demolished in 2006, after an unsuccessful attempt to have it listed as an industrial heritage landmark. The showroom and parts of the other buildings from around 1958 still exist but have been heavily modified.

Today, the Copenhagen South Port mainly consists of IT and media companies, university departments, and upscale apartment buildings. But the Ford name lives on, as the part of the harbour adjacent to the former car factory is still known as the Ford basin.

Hegemony here is born in the factory

Antonio Gramsci, *Americanism and Fordism*

The Transformation of Fordism

On the preceding pages it has been established how Fordism was transformed, as it expanded in time and space from Detroit to Denmark —and how different the Fordism of Copenhagen in the 1960s was from that of Highland Park during the 1910s and River Rouge during the 1920s.

But two partly intertwined questions still need to be considered in more detail. The first question regards the causes and effect of this process. While it might be aptly named as a transformation, and has been so called before, this is still an overly broad term.[1] Can we perhaps untangle the process a bit more, for a more precise description?

The second question regards Ford Motor Company A/S as an example for the general process of bringing Fordism, or perhaps even Americanism, to Denmark and to Western Europe. Are there grounds for claiming that the Danish Ford Company represents general features of this process, and that there is something to be learned from its history, which reaches beyond Copenhagen and Denmark?

A Case of Hybridisation

Throughout the preceding narrative, developments in the history of Ford Motor Company A/S have been related to the concept of productive models, as introduced in the first chapter of this book. The original Fordist productive model was adapted to a volume strategy, in which profit was realised by basically selling as many units of the same car as possible. As this strategy came into crisis because of changing market conditions in the USA, it was adjusted towards the strategy originally developed by General Motors, known as volume and diversity: a strategy aimed at offering a broader portfolio of cars, aimed at different strata of the market, and to promote consumption by making regular upgrades to the product, while still maintaining as many of the benefits of rationalised mass production as possible.

This adaption of Fordism towards volume and diversity shows that, as a productive model, it is not static over time, even within its original national context. But transferring a productive model in space, from one national context to another, adds a new dimension of transformation. Studies of the diffusion and transformation of productive models in the car industry suggest that a direct transfer without any adaptation to local context has been exceedingly rare and generally not successful.[2] One such example would be the attempt to directly transfer the Fordist model to the UK from 1911 onwards which, after a promising start, led to almost total failure.[3]

Most transfers have therefore resulted in some sort of hybrid, adapting the productive model to its new context through a process of trial and error. The need for such adaptations could be found in different traditions in production, different market situations, different industrial relations, etc.

According to Robert Boyer, what determines the outcome and the character of hybridisation is basically the strength and rigidity of the original model, versus the strength and rigidity of the national institutions of its new context. Within this overall understanding of the process, he identifies several variations. For instance, if the original firm's productive model has strong principles and routines, while the receiving country has weak institutions, the result might be an almost direct *transplantation* (which, as already mentioned, is rarely the case). At the other end of the spectrum, we find the situation where a firm without strongly implemented routines and principles moves into a country with strong and coherent institutions, resulting in it *becoming similar* to the firms of the host country.[4]

Somewhere in the middle sits what Boyer terms a *functional equivalent*, where flexibility in the routines of the original firms as well as in the institutions of the host country allows for the creation of a true hybrid. In fact, Boyer proposes a total of nine different principal outcomes of the process of hybridisation. But instead of going further into a principal discussion of these variations, it seems more productive to turn to the real, empirical history of Ford Motor Company A/S, and review it from the standpoint of hybridisation. In the following, the five areas into which the preceding narrative has been structured will be considered in relation to the rigidity versus the flexibility of both the Fordist model and the Danish context.

Production

The tools and techniques used for assembling cars in Copenhagen in 1919 had been transferred almost directly from Detroit. The volume of production was considerably smaller, and the effective use of American production technology was hampered by the lack of space and the inefficient layout of the buildings in Heimdalsgade. Nevertheless, the general principle of serial mass production was employed. And not only the assembly line, but also other technologies such as flow-painting and electrically powered hand tools were put to use straight away.

The South Port plant would provide a much better framework for the principles of Fordist production. The building, with its overall layout designed to facilitate a straight-line production process, as well as the unrelenting use of functionalist principles, was an impressive piece of factory technology in itself. Inside, the use of assembly lines and conveyers was greatly enhanced, as was the use of electrically and pneumatically driven hand tools and specialised machinery.

The South Port Plant, while built by a Danish construction company, was designed by the same architect who had designed the Highland Park plant, and its completion was monitored in detail from Detroit. It was meant to function just as any of Ford's American Model T assembly plants. And from the beginning it performed well, rivalling Manchester as Ford's largest European operation.

The complicated and time-consuming changeover from Model T to Model A assembly in 1927–1928 was testament to the fact that the same rigid and specialised technologies that were used in Detroit had been employed in Copenhagen. But during the 1930s, the production process was gradually and successfully turned towards a combination of volume and diversity. This happened along with the introduction of new technologies, such as spray painting and electrical spot welding. And the productive model of combining volume and diversity was fully realised in the post-WWII period, when assembly of new models could be taken up relatively fast and simultaneously with existing production. The alleged inflexibility of the Fordist model of production should therefore not be overstated.

The driving force behind these changes was however not located within Ford Motor Company A/S or its national context. It was a reflection of how Ford in general was changing its productive model from volume only to a combination of volume and diversity. This started in the USA in the 1930s and was intensified because of the new market situations in Europe during the post-war period. But whether the Danish plant was adapted for assembling different American Ford models at the same time, as in the 1930s, or British and German cars along the same assembly line as in the 1950s, the impetus in both cases came from outside.

Only in one instance, the extension of the South Port plant during the 1950s, did the Copenhagen board and management actively push for technical modernisation on a larger scale, based on local conditions. The main arguments were, however, related not to assembly, but to the need for better office and storage facilities, office automation, etc., reflecting the fact that a proportionally increasing number of cars were imported as built-up, and not assembled locally.

There is nothing to suggest, though, that assembly in Copenhagen was falling behind from a purely technical point of view. Based on limited investments in assembly, mainly for retooling, it was able to swiftly take up the assembly of new models as needed. It was not a lack of technology for diversification that led to the closure of assembly in Copenhagen. It was a growing demand for volume, prompted by developments that were beyond the reach of the Danish management, and even to some extent of Ford in general, such as market developments and the emergence of new transnational trade associations in Europe. The Copenhagen operation simply became too limited, and thereby too costly, relative to the much higher output of Dagenham and Cologne.

In the process of hybridisation, we may safely conclude that production technology formed a rigid part of the original Fordist model —not in the sense that it was unchanged over time, but in the sense that these changes were decided and brought about mainly from the outside of Ford Motor Company A/S. Technology is, however, only one part of the production process. The other part is how production is organised. And for this part, Ford had to make concessions to Danish customs literally from day one.

In Detroit, the Fordist model was based on the use of a primarily unskilled and unorganised labour force, which could be utilised and allocated with only minimal constraints or restrictions. In contrast with this, the labour force in Copenhagen to a much larger degree comprised skilled workers. Furthermore, the workers were all unionised, and there was a connection between skill and union membership, which was enforced on the workshop floor. Consequently, the workforce in Copenhagen could not be utilised in the same way as in Detroit. Even if the Danish management was instructed from Detroit to transfer the "American plan" for work organisation, it was not able to do so in an unchanged form, due to resistance from the local workforce.

To further complicate things, there is the temporal aspect. When Ford Motor Company A/S installed its assembly line in Heimdalsgade in 1919, it was heralded by the press as something completely new, never seen in Denmark before.[5] Very few Danish companies had embarked on serial production around that time. But that would change over time, beginning with an increased interest in rationalisation during the 1930s. The real boom, however, was in the post-war years. Programmes for technical aid to industry were an integral part of the Marshall Plan. In 1949, a Productivity committee was set up under the Ministry of Trade, which would become a nexus for an extensive effort to further industrial productivity. A great number of technical specialists, employers, and labour representatives would travel to the USA to study American methods of production and report back.[6] Companies would invest in new production technology, partly financed by the Marshall Plan. And efforts to increase labour productivity, mainly in the form of time and motion studies, swept through industry.

Much of what made the production process at the Copenhagen Ford plant stand out in 1919 had become commonplace in Danish industry 1966. There were of course several technologies applied at the

South Port plant that were specific to the assembly of cars. But general Fordist technologies such as the assembly line, and production principles such as a high degree of division of labour, a hierarchical organisation, and a systematic attempt to rationalise every part of the process were now widespread. Everywhere in industry, focus was now on productivity. In relation to the production process, Ford Motor Company A/S had become mainstream, not because of internal changes, but because the surrounding industry had developed in the same direction.

Markets

The products that Ford Motor Company A/S was offering its primarily Nordic, Baltic, and Polish customers were initially exactly the same as on the American market: the Model T and later the Model A and the V8. The Model T was sold in large numbers from the beginning, giving Ford a market share in Denmark in the early 1920s that was presumably the highest of any car brand at the time. One reason for this initial success was undoubtedly that Ford was expanding the market by offering cars at a very low price, thereby reaching potential customers who could not or would not pay the price of the models offered by other manufacturers. In this aspect, Ford's profit strategy based on volume, a standardised product, and low price was well suited to Ford Motor Company A/S.

The Danish company also benefitted from the lack of competition from domestic car brands. This was in contrast to the UK, where British car makers offered a range of models, including some that were able to compete with the Ford Model T on price. Therefore, the volume strategy was not as effective in England, and this was a main reason why Ford's share of the market plummeted. The volume strategy came into a crisis in America too, during the 1920s, due to a saturation of the market for cheap, low-end cars and a diversification of the demand among the middle class.

But the volume strategy would also start to show signs of weakness on the markets catered to from Copenhagen. Even from the mid-1920s, General Motors in particular, but also European brands like

Citroën, were offering models for the Danish market that were only slightly above the Ford T in terms of price, but considerably more modern in terms of technology and design.

The Danish company, however, could present respectable sales figures for the Model T until its discontinuation in 1927–1928. Unfortunately, that was in part due to aggressive competition on price, which resulted in the revenue per car sold becoming unsustainable by the late 1920s.

But apart from intensified marketing there was not much Ford Motor Company A/S could do. As an assembly plant and *de facto* subsidiary, it had no way of developing its own models, adapted to its specific markets. In this sense, it would be correct to say that from a purely Danish perspective, there was no real hybridisation when it came to models and markets. But from a wider European perspective, there was in fact hybridisation going on. Developments in other markets, primarily the UK, finally persuaded Detroit of the need to launch new models that were more competitive in a European context. By introducing these models on its own markets, Ford Motor Company A/S was able to offer a broad range of models by the end of the 1930s, from the inexpensive Junior to the Lincoln luxury car.

This was further enhanced during the post-war period, as the international Ford organisation developed its strategy of "two fishing rods" for Europe. Situated in each of the two trading associations, EEC and EFTA, Dagenham and Cologne were gradually given more freedom to develop their own range of cars, and even compete against each other. And the cars assembled in or sold by Ford Motor Company A/S were now mostly of European origin, developed specifically for that market, while American cars had become a niche product.

Ford's market share in Denmark in the 1960s was well below that of the 1920s. But it was a market share based on a more sustainable strategy for the growth of the post-war period, when the demand for cars was not only rising, but diversifying further to new customers, even within the working class.

Industrial relations

In 1919, the labour force in American mass-producing industries was quite diverse, consisting of workers with very varied background in relation to skill, ethnicity, and culture. And most companies, not least Ford, were operating on strict principles of industrial relations, excluding unions and collective bargaining. In Denmark, at the same time, the labour market was quite coherent and homogenous. Most industrial workers were organised in unions, and a system of collective bargaining and agreements was in effect, accepted by both unions and employers and backed by the state. This could have caused an open conflict between the Fordist model and the national institutions, just as had happened previously in the UK.

But Ford Motor Company A/S instead chose to adapt to the local context and accept union membership and collective bargaining. The agreement that was made between the unions and Ford Motor Company A/S in 1922 was literally a hybrid, as it took Detroit regulations as its starting point, but added to it a number of paragraphs reflecting the standards of the Danish industrial labour market. Other examples, such as the "battle of the beer" shows how the Danish workers successfully contested Detroit's unilaterally imposed regulations.

This period ended dramatically when Detroit ordered the collective agreement abolished in 1927, against the wish and advice of the local management. But the order was nevertheless carried out, and internal disagreements among the workers made them unable to resist. The events of 1927–1928 were a blow to the labour unions, as they were not able to formally uphold the most crucial element of the Danish labour market model: an agreement based on collective bargaining. But this apparent victory for the Fordist model of industrial relations, would soon prove to be ambiguous.

Within a relatively short period, management realised the benefits of securing the consent of the unions in matters relating to working conditions, and collective bargaining was tacitly reintroduced, without Detroit being informed. The process was gradually codified into a system resembling the yearly negotiations of local agreements on wages, working hours etc. taking place in the rest of the industry, but for one thing: the word *agreement* could not be used. The resiliency of Danish labour market practices had resulted in another hybrid. And the internal relations between skilled and unskilled workers, which had been strained to breaking point during the 1920s, were gradually improved.

Due to the way that the 6-dollar daily wage had been transformed into Danish kroner, wages at Ford Motor Company A/S had initially been remarkably high—probably even relatively higher than in the USA, when compared to average industrial wages in Denmark. And unlike in the USA, where Ford's high wages were soon undermined by inflation, wages at Ford Motor Company A/S kept their value throughout the 1920s. Consequently, hourly wages, which were a central part of collective bargaining in the rest of Danish industry, were of little concern to the unions during the negotiations that took place at Ford Motor Company A/S in the 1920s.

But in the aftermath of the economic depression, the gap between average industrial wages in Copenhagen and payment at Ford started diminishing, even though the difference was still substantial. This made the unions bring up the issue of payment in the then still rather informal bargaining with the company management. These developments continued and accelerated during the post-war period. As the unions in industry were recovering what had been lost during the occupation, wages at Ford were falling behind in a relative sense, even if they were still increased year by year in nominal terms. In the 1960s, wages at Ford Motor Company A/S were at best on a par with other comparable workplaces, and in some instances lower. While the Ford workers of the 1920s and 1930s had grudgingly accepted industrial relations that were somewhat peculiar in a Danish context in return for high wages, the situation had changed fundamentally by the time of closure. Wages at Ford Motor Company A/S were no longer exceptional compared to the rest of industry, and neither were their industrial relations in general.

In terms of hybridisation, what happened to industrial relations over the years in Copenhagen could be characterised as a case of *becoming similar*, in the sense that Ford Motor Company A/S was forced to gradually move away from Detroit principles and adapt to local customs. It should not be forgotten, however, that the Detroit principles were not static, but also themselves changed throughout the period. If it had not already, this became clear when the American Ford company, under the presidency of Henry Ford II, embarked on a new strategy for industrial relations in the post-war period, giving the unions concessions such as the right to collective bargaining in return for their cooperation in keeping peace at the workplace and striving for higher productivity. The context of this reorientation was the emerging Cold War, and a wish to secure the support of the working class behind American politics. But the actual seed of this change was planted back in the 1930s, when workers in Detroit had started to challenge the Fordist hegemony at the workplace in an organised way, leading to Ford grudgingly entering into its first collective agreement with the United Auto Workers (UAW).

Consequently, while Detroit still had a strict set of principles for industrial relations, these were from the late 1940s much more compatible with Danish practice. Now, Ford Motor Company A/S, which had been reluctant at best when it came to following Danish industrial relations, could suddenly become a first mover by establishing a Cooperation Committee in 1946, about a year before it was made compulsory.

Initially, the new attitudes expressed in Detroit were received positively by the Ford workers in Copenhagen, who also engaged very actively in the new Cooperation Committee. However, as it became clear that the most important matter for the workers, that of securing production and jobs, was beyond the power and influence of the committee, the initial enthusiasm gave way to more pessimistic attitudes. This was enhanced by the developments in both production and wages.

In the 1920s, Ford Motor Company A/S had been a special workplace, unlike most others in Denmark. By the 1960s, hybridisation had turned it into a workplace like any other, for better or worse. When car assembly was finally closed down in Copenhagen in 1966, jobs were readily available in other parts of industry under similar or perhaps even better conditions. Therefore, the closure was accepted without grief from either the unions or the workers at the shop floor.

Management

From a formal point of view, management of Ford Motor Company A/S can be divided into three distinct periods: 1919 to 1928, when all principal decisions were made in Detroit, and Copenhagen had to follow the same rules and principles as any American Ford assembly plant and the board was intended to act merely as a rubber stamp; 1929 to 1949, when the Danish company was under the rule of Ford in the UK, with a close cooperation between Copenhagen management and "the English Lords", a larger degree of freedom, and a board that played an active role in company management; and finally, from 1950 until assembly was discontinued in 1966, when Detroit took back control, managers and board members were replaced in rapid succession, increasingly often with Americans, and the board became gradually more preoccupied with the integration of the Danish company into the new, more streamlined Ford organisation.

It would be easy to identify these three periods of management with one type of hybridisation each: the first one as a mere transplantation of Detroit principles and routines, the second one as a real hybrid of Detroit and Copenhagen, with a certain degree of freedom for the latter, and then again, a return to transplantation or at least just a partial hybridisation, with America in the leading role in the last period.

Nevertheless, what this study has shown is that the actual history was somewhat more complicated and with more nuances than that. This is probably most evident during the 1920s. It was clearly Detroit's expectation that the Danish plant could be run in the same way and by the same directives as any American assembly plant. Manager J.J. Harrington was loyal to these expectations, even when they seemed out of touch with local realities, such as the peculiar transformation of the 6-dollar daily wage. But even he made concessions to Danish customs, especially in his dealings with the unions.

Within less than a year, Harrington was succeeded as manager by George Carlson. Carlson also followed and implemented directives from Detroit when necessary. But he also managed to secure considerable leeway for decision-making at his own discretion, most strikingly in his relations with the unions, but also when it came to dealership structure and other issues. In this way Carlson initiated a management culture characterised by a certain pragmatism, which sought to implement Fordist principles but with deference to the local context. Clearly Carlson was aware of the social and cultural differences between Denmark and the USA, and the need to take them into consideration. H.C. Møller continued along the lines laid out by George Carlson, actively trying to bridge between the demands made from Detroit and Danish customs. In the end, though, when given a direct order from Detroit, such as the one to cease collective bargaining, Møller would obey.

When the formal ownership changed in 1929, so did the formal structure as well as the praxis of management. The board was enhanced and allowed to play a much more active role, both in dealing with the internal matters of the company, as well as representing it externally. Board and daily management were divided into separate roles, as H.C. Møller and other executives were no longer members of the board. However, this only lasted for a few years before Møller was reinstated.

During this period, a close cooperation developed between the Copenhagen management and the formal European management, personified by Percival Perry in London. Interference from Detroit, on the other hand, was minimal. The outbreak of war meant that the ties between Copenhagen and both London and Detroit were temporarily broken. During this period, the Danish management was left to act on its own, but at the same time its decision-making power was limited by the constraints of the German occupation. As soon as the war was over, close cooperation with London was resumed. This was a period when the board and management were able to, and often did, act on their own initiative, on matters important to the Danish company.

Henry Ford II's declaration that "This is an American company and it's going to be run from America" marked the beginning of a re-Americanisation of Ford Motor Company A/S from the late 1940s onwards. A rapid succession of managers and other executives, as well as board members, meant that the existing management culture was broken up. Around 1960, key board members as well as the General and Assisting Manager were all Americans.

Formally, the company was now more under American control than even during the "American years" of the 1920s. However, the context had changed in several ways. American investments in Europe and in Denmark had grown, and so had the interest in, and partial implementation of, American methods of management.[7] Being an American company under American management was not necessarily that unusual anymore.

Presence

Not only as a productive model, but just as much as a social vision, Fordism was based on the idea of a free market, with minimal state interference. But in 1919 Denmark was significantly different from USA in that respect. During the time of the First World War, strong elements of corporatism and state regulation had been introduced. And while some of these were rolled back during the 1920s, state intervention into the economy was reinforced as a response to the economic depression of the early 1930s.

Ford Motor Company A/S would not have been able to function without adapting to national institutions and regulations, both legal and informal. In contrast with Detroit praxis, Ford in Denmark gradually became involved in collective efforts to safeguard its interests, as a member of relevant trade and employers' associations—not the least the Industrial Council, in which manager H.C. Møller came to play an active role. Moreover, the company soon developed a proactive praxis in relation to political decision makers. The board elected as part of the changes in 1928 played a part in that. The logic behind the new composition of the board was to root the company more firmly in the national business and political context, by electing already well-connected Danes as members. This was accomplished, as board members such as editor Carl Thalbitzer and Professor P.O. Pedersen became active ambassadors and spokespersons for the interests of Ford Motor Company A/S. From then on, Ford Motor Company A/S became fully immersed in the quasi-corporatist Danish model for political decision-making, with both formal bodies for cooperation and informal consultations between industry, unions, and politicians.

From the beginning of its existence in Copenhagen, Ford Motor Company A/S was viewed by the press and the public as a symbol of modernity. Sometimes its American ancestry was mentioned, at other times it was just implicit. In its own public appearance through advertising, the company magazine, and even in its physical presence through the buildings of its dealers, Ford Motor Company A/S confirmed this image. It was always clearly in line with shifting trends of modernism, but also blending into whichever style was in vogue, incorporating national symbols in the 1920s, making use of functionalism and even art deco in the 1930s, and connecting to technological futurism in the 1950s.

During the 1920s, Henry Ford was sometimes featured in newspaper ads, but most explicitly his viewpoints were presented in the company magazine. It is likely, however, that this was mostly for the benefit of Detroit. After all, the readership of the magazine was quite limited in its early years. Fordism as a social vision was much more effectively communicated by the books of Henry Ford, such as *My Life and Work* which appeared in Danish in 1923. But that was of course outside the purview of the Danish Ford company. And in general, Americanism was mostly implicit in the public communication of Ford Motor Company A/S, such as the pictures of Hollywood stars driving Ford cars appearing in the company magazine. Waving the Stars and Stripes as an explicit cultural and political banner happened very seldom.

The early years of the Cold War formed an exception, symbolised by Henry Ford II's speech in favour of political freedom and market economy during his 1948 Copenhagen visit. But Henry Ford II was speaking into another global context, compared to his grandfather. In 1948, the USA was well on its way to establishing a political hegemony in the western world. What once had been Henry Ford's personal advocacy of Americanism as the goal for all civilisations, was now political mainstream in most of Western Europe.

The economic and cultural impact of America was widely accepted in Denmark after the Second World War, and even welcomed by many. That is not to say that it was without its critics. But the criticism against Americanism did not come down on Ford in any particular sense, probably not just because the Americanism of Ford was no longer exceptional, but also because Ford was perceived as less American than ever. Not only were most of its products of European origin, as the company itself was keen to emphasise in advertising, but Ford Motor Company A/S had a Danish history stretching back more than a generation. It had become a part of the heritage of Danish industry and Danish modernity.

Cause and effect

Adapting the concept of hybridisation to the case of Ford Motor Company A/S confirms that the company was indeed a hybrid between Denmark and Detroit, between local customs and institutions and the principles and routines of Fordism, as developed in the USA. But the case of Ford Motor Company A/S also clearly demonstrates that hybridisation cannot be understood as a simple linear process from A to B.

Firstly, while it is possible in theory to construct several distinct types or variations of hybridisation, as suggested by Boyer,[8] a company may in reality belong to more than one of these, depending on what aspects of its practice and activities we focus on. For instance, based on production technology, products, and formal management, Ford Motor Company A/S in the 1920s was close to a direct transplantation of the Fordist model. But focusing on how production was organised, the character of industrial relations, and the actual praxis of management, it was what Boyer would term a real, functional hybrid.

Secondly, to determine the type of hybridisation of a company at any given time, it is not enough to look at the formal characteristics, such as the management structure or the official principles of industrial relations. While Ford Motor Company A/S during the 1920s was instructed by Detroit to manage its workforce according to the "American plan", that was not what actually happened on the shop floor. And while the Danish board of directors were supposed to, and largely did, function merely as a rubber stamp, at the same time the management was in practice able to secure a certain leeway for decision-making of its own.

Thirdly, the type of hybridisation may change significantly over time, and not necessarily in any linear way. For instance, focusing on management, the implementation of Fordism in Denmark in 1919 was intended by Detroit to happen according to precisely defined principles and routines. Even without taking the Danish reactions into consideration, the changes around 1928 marked a shift towards greater flexibility. But from around 1950, there was a shift back towards stricter implementation of Detroit principles.

Fourthly, over time, developments in both the company of origin as well as in the receiving country may lead to a new balance. Henry Ford II's renewed focus on American leadership, and his very explicit declaration of that in 1948, lead to a formal shift back to stricter implementation of Detroit principles. But at the same time, developments in both countries worked towards diminishing the differences. In industrial relations, Ford in the USA had come closer to a European position, and Danish industry was emulating American methods of production and management to a much larger extent than before the war. In other words, both the Danish and the American labour market had moved towards each other, thereby making it possible to adhere to the new and revised principles of Fordism in a still strongly coherent Danish context, without causing any major conflicts.

In broad terms, taking the most important developments in each period into consideration, the hybridisation of Ford Motor Company A/S could be described as going from a *transplantation* of Fordism in the 1920, through a period of true, *functional hybrid* in the 1930s and 1940s, to *similarity* in the 1950s and 1960s. But to reach a coherent and comprehensive understanding of the process, we would still have to add all the complexities and contradictions mentioned above.

There are therefore also several causes, some of them partly intertwined, that we may point to in explaining why the transformation of Fordism from Detroit to Copenhagen took place as it did. One of them is technological developments. The whole raison d'être for setting up an assembly plant in Copenhagen in the first place was rooted in fundamental technological changes in the way automobiles were produced. After production had been set up, changes in technology might have been incremental and evolutionary, such as the introduction of spray painting and electric welding, but they did take place, and they affected the production process and industrial relations, including relations among the workers themselves.

Another cause was adaptation to changing market conditions. Right from the start, the company's main and almost only product, the Ford Model T, seemed well suited for its markets. But soon it came under pressure, as Ford did on other European markets. The economic crisis and political changes during the 1930s led to increasing protectionism and nationalism. During the post-war period, markets were again liberalised, but the emergence of two competing trade associations presented a new challenge. The overall result of changing market conditions was a widening of the product portfolio, as well as a shift from American to predominantly British and German cars.

But what is common to these causes for development is that they were mostly induced from outside Denmark. Spray painting and electric welding were largely a means to accommodate the need for a transfer from a volume strategy to a strategy of combining volume and diversity, first undertaken in the USA. The introduction of the first Ford model designed especially for Europe was mainly a reaction to problems on the British market, and the rising star of the Taunus in the post-war period was a function of trade policies on a European level.

These were all important developments, but even if they may have been enacted in a specific way, they were not unique to Ford in Denmark. Looking for causes for hybridisation that were specifically rooted in a Danish context, one thing does stand out: relation to labour. Not only in the specific sense of having to deal with a workforce that was different in its composition and far better organised than what was the case in Detroit; but also in the sense of a labour market with already well-established institutions and procedures, and even in the broad sense of a national political context, in which organised labour played a significant role. Despite Detroit's expectations that things in Denmark should be done according to the American plan, management in Copenhagen had to adapt to this local context on all levels, from shop floor negotiations to meetings with government officials.

Denmark was not the only European country into which Fordism was transformed that had a labour movement that was much stronger than in the USA. However, the Danish working class was not only unusually well organised, but it had also managed to establish institutions for securing influence on its working conditions, as well as a high degree of political participation. That, combined with the fact that Ford Motor Company A/S was established very early, as only the second Ford assembly plant in Europe, is what makes the Danish case especially interesting and important for the transformation of Fordism.

Labour and Fordism

Labour movements reacted differently to Fordism within different European nations, but often with positive interest. Most remarkable was the "infatuation with Fordism" that swept through Germany during the 1920s, as already described in the beginning of this book.[9] It affected most of the political spectrum, including the German Social Democratic Party, labour unions and left-leaning public intellectuals. The German labour movement was leading in Europe, and historically the Danish Social Democratic Party had always been strongly influenced by its big brother just south of the border. To assume that the Danish labour movement was infatuated with Fordism to more or less the same extent therefore seems obvious—but that would be a mistake.

A pragmatic embrace

In 1920, a book on America was published in Danish under the title *Amerikanske Tilstande: En Rapport til unge Nordboer* (American Conditions: A Report to Young People in the Nordic Countries). The author was Herbert Iversen, a socialist academic who had lived in the USA for some years. Tragically, Iversen died young from the Spanish flu, and his book was published posthumously.

Iversen's book is not about Fordism, and in fact it does not contain much about industry as such, despite the fact that Iversen had actually earned a living as an industrial worker during his studies. But the book offers a detailed account of American economics, politics, and society. Iversen wrote the book based on the conviction that America, due to its economic strength, had the potential to become a power of global magnitude. And this was not necessarily positive; Iversen found America to be still "in its youth", in a process of transformation from brutal "robber capitalism" towards a more centralised and monopolised economy. Consequently, from a social point of view:

> America is not a "land of the future". Its relative economic immaturity leads to political habits, social ideals and concepts, and an intellectual life or "consciousness" which in many ways may appear old fashioned to us.[10]

Iversen struck a chord, which would resonate through social-democratic assessments of the USA during the inter-war period. The prevailing picture of the USA was that of an immature teenager: bursting with economic energy but socially and culturally under-developed.[11]

Actually, Danish social democrats displayed a remarkably meagre interest in America in general and Fordism in particular during the interwar period. Thorvald Stauning, renowned party chairman and prime minister during the 1920s and 1930s, never visited the USA. Neither did any other senior party or union representatives.[12] Very little was published about Fordism or America in general in party or union magazines,[13] and the few articles which did appear were mainly critical, such as the aforementioned article dismissing the working conditions at Ford's Detroit plants, published by the magazine of the metalworkers' union in 1927.[14]

Roosevelt's presidency would lead to a slight increase in social-democratic political interest in the USA during the 1930s. The New Deal was met with critical appreciation, but also depicted as a long-overdue attempt to reach a level of social civilisation already known in Europe. And warnings were issued not to put too much faith into what Roosevelt and the Democrats could and would do for the working class.[15]

Party chairman Thorvald Stauning only commented on Ford in public on two occasions.[16] The first was when he took part in the official opening of Ford's South Port plant in November 1924 as newly elected Prime Minister. As already noted above, he gave a speech at the banquet in which he promised to take good care of this new "foster child" of Denmark.[17]

The second was at the Social Democratic Party congress in 1927, at which Stauning in his main speech referred to Henry Ford, quoting him for saying that "the unemployed man is a customer, who has been put out of the game".[18]

In the first instance, Stauning was explicitly speaking in his capacity as Prime Minister, not as chairman of the Social Democratic Party. And he was welcoming a plant that had brought industrial jobs to the country, not embracing Fordism *per se*. The other instance, however, was of an undeniably political character. Not only was it part of a speech held at the party congress. It was also an endorsement of a key element in Henry Ford's socio-economic thinking: the necessary relationship between mass production, mass employment, and mass consumption.

During the early 1920s, several nationwide lockouts and strikes had occurred in Denmark, resulting from attempts by the employers to drive wages down. The argument was that lower wages were necessary to make domestic industry competitive against imported goods. The social democrats on the other hand argued that the way forward for Danish industry was not through lower wages, but through raised productivity. They pointed to the fact that there were too many small industrial firms, and that structural rationalisation was needed to create larger, more viable enterprises. They also called for investments in modern production technology.

At the 1927 party congress, Thorvald Stauning also reasserted that increased production was the foremost interest of the working class, and that …

> … it is natural that we stand united behind a policy aimed at this, even if such a policy will have to support a certain capitalist development. We cannot do without such development from small-scale to large-scale capitalist production; it is a necessity for capitalism, but also a precondition for the socialisation that will happen later.[19]

Figure 38 Official inauguration of the South Port assembly plant, 15 October 1924. Jens Jensen, trade union veteran and president of the Copenhagen City Council, is about to push the button that starts the assembly line. The bald, bearded man standing close to the podium is Thorvald Stauning, newly elected social democratic Prime Minister. Unknown photographer. Thalbitzer: *Ford Motor Company A/S gennem 25 Aar*, 72

It is in this context that Stauning embraces Henry Ford's argument that industry needs to create its own customers by paying the highest wages possible and by providing stable employment.

A few years later, not Henry Ford, but Ford Motor Company A/S is brought up in the same discussion, by the national Metalworkers' Association, (DSMF). In 1930, Percival Perry had presented the result of a survey of profitability within Europe, at the general meeting of Ford of England. According to the survey, the Danish company paid the highest wages of all the European Ford subsidiaries, but had the lowest production costs per time unit, making it one of the most profitable.[20]

These remarks inspired an editorial in the union magazine, discussing wages in Danish industry in general. Ford was presented as proof that the future of industry depended not so much on low wages as on modern production facilities. The magazine noted with regret that there were too few "large, modern, and rationalised companies, capable of competing on the world market and at the same time pay a decent salary" in Denmark.[21]

During and after the economic crisis in the early 1930s, employment became the number one priority for the labour movement. The few critical articles about Henry Ford and Ford Motor Company A/S, that had been posted by union magazines, now disappeared altogether. Instead, a laudatory article on Ford Motor Company A/S was published in *Jern- og Metalarbejderen* in 1932, as part of a series on industrial enterprises in Denmark called "Our workplaces". It was mainly a description of the modern production facilities in Copenhagen, which was presented as an "expression of the world-famous ideas and initiatives of the Ford organisation". Not a word was written about working conditions and the lack of union agreements.[22]

These signs of a slightly more positive view on Fordism should not be exaggerated. Labour's embracement of Fordism was both tactical and limited. Tactical in the sense that it was used in a specific context, to argue that employers should modernise their facilities instead of lowering wages to decrease production cost; and limited in the sense that it was never an unconditional endorsement of Henry Ford's social visions. On the contrary: social democratic political thinking of the interwar period not only deviated from but was contrary to Fordism in important ways.

The latter was exemplified by an opinion article written by Thorvald Stauning in 1929 and featured prominently in two consecutive issues of the daily newspaper *Social-Demokraten*. Under the headline "Industry and the workers", Stauning called for structural rationalisation and technological modernisation, to safeguard employment and raise the standard of living of the workers. "I absolutely believe that industry can be the saviour of society", he emphatically declared.[23] But to this he immediately added that:

> I do not believe in industrial strength and great progress without the hastening of development by political measures. [...] when industrial production has become a vital condition for society, it can no longer be left to a few thousand capitalists to decide whether there should be work or unemployment in the nation.[24]

This was very far from Henry Ford's stated opinion, that government was "essentially negative", and the only positive thing it could do to industry was to remove any obstacles and, for the rest of the time, stay out of the way as much as possible.[25] Unlike Ford, the social democrats- were determined to use the state apparatus as an active instrument for industrial modernisation, in ways beneficial to the working class.

America is different

Compared to the relative indifference of the interwar period, the upsurge of interest in the USA within the Danish labour movement after 1945 is striking. The overall framework for this renewed fascination with America was of course the Cold War, in which the Danish Social Democratic Party committed itself firmly to the West.

But apart from an anti-communist sentiment and the lofty ideals of freedom and democracy, what was motivating the labour movement, and especially the unions, more than anything was the pressing task of securing jobs, paychecks, and goods for consumption. The means of production were worn down, machinery was out of date, and there was a shortage of raw materials. Labour was therefore looking towards rationalisation in a broad sense, both technological as well as in relation to organisation of work.

This was not without conflict, as time and motion studies were intensified from the late 1940s, and "the man with the stopwatch" became a common sight on the shop floor. Rank and file workers sometimes reacted negatively, based on the well-founded assumption that time studies could lead to increased work speed and a deterioration in working conditions.[26]

But for the majority within the labour movement, heightening productivity was still a necessary precondition for a better standard of living for the working class. Any problems created by rationalisation had to be taken care of by involving the workers themselves in the process. This was the common ground from which the Danish Confederation of Trade Unions (DSF) was able to reach an agreement about compulsory Cooperation Committees with the Confederation of Danish Employers (DA). While originally seen by the unions as an instrument for workers' co-determination in a broader sense, it was argued more narrowly by the employers that their main function was to pave the road towards higher productivity, by avoiding misunderstandings between workers and management.[27] By the time Cooperation Committees were instituted nationwide, one had already been at work for a year at the South Port plant. Ford Motor Company A/S had now become a first mover in this new line of cooperation between labour and management.

It was also the quest for higher productivity that made Danish labour movement look towards USA. As already mentioned above, a delegation of high-ranking union officials headed by the chairman of DSF Eiler Jensen, visited USA in 1949. An important part of the trip was a meeting with Paul Hoffman, head of the ECA, the administrative body of the Marshall Plan. The delegation also met UAW president Walther Reuther, took part in the congress of the AFL, and visited several industrial workplaces. The trip was financed partly by the DSF itself, and partly by the ECA.[28]

During the following years up to 1956, around 158 Danish union leaders on various levels would take part in delegations to the USA.

Figure 39 Danish union leaders meeting with officials of the ECA during a study trip to the USA in 1949. DSF chairman Eiler Jensen shaking hands with Paul Hoffman, head of the ECA. Unknown photographer. Library and Archive of the Workers Museum

But rank-and-file union members were also offered trips to America as part of the *Work Study Training Programme*.[29]

As such, the turn towards the USA was saturating most of the labour movement, from rank-and-file union members to Social Democratic Party leadership. And as most governments of the post-war years were headed by the social democrats, the labour movement's interest in America blended with Danish official policies. It was the Ministry of Trade that organised or promoted many of the above-mentioned study trips—as well as some for technical specialists, farmers, and others—and published their findings in official reports, often in co-operation with the Ministry of Foreign Affairs.[30]

While Danish workers and union leaders were fascinated by what they saw coming from the USA, in terms of productivity and material goods, they also maintained a critical eye towards other aspects of the American society. During the study trip by trade union leaders to the USA in 1949, one of the participants, "Big Kai" Lindberg, secretary of the Danish Confederation of Trade Unions and Member of Parliament, gave an interview to the Danish newspaper *Politiken.* In the interview he was quoted as saying that "nothing we have seen here is better than at home" and that in America "the gifted individual" has better chances, but "the average middleman is better off at home". Lindberg also hinted that these views would be expressed in the final report.[31]

This interview was the direct cause for a letter from George Marshall himself to the Danish Ministry of Foreign Affairs, in which Marshall politely, but in no uncertain terms, requested that the contributions of every participant of the delegation be thoroughly evaluated before the final report was published.

When the report was published, under the somewhat ambiguous title *Amerika er anderledes* (America is different), Lindberg's remarks were not included. But other critical remarks were. The high level of productivity and the corresponding high wages in industry featured prominently in the report. But the working conditions in American industry were a cause for concern. The report specifically refers to the strikes that the UAW "had to establish" at Ford earlier in 1949, in order to prevent the work-speed becoming "too unreasonable". And despite the strikes being a success, intensity of work was still high—too high, according to a local union representative. Seen through Danish eyes:

> ... it was not a very inspiring sight to wander through the large Ford enterprise and watch the monotonous kind of work carried out by most of the labourers. Raising efficiency and rationalisation is a condition for a satisfying standard of living, but it is important to keep in sight that technology should be supporting the worker, and that under no circumstances should the worker become a mere tool, controlled by the assembly line.[32]

Under the headline "America also has a great deal to learn", the delegation reported from the negotiation of a new collective agreement between Ford and the United Auto Workers, which took place just around the time of its visit to Detroit. The Danes were amazed to hear that one of the things regarded as a great leap forward by the American union was that Ford had now committed itself to paying a limited daily amount for workers who were hospitalised. This, and other examples, led to the remark that ...

> ... it was somewhat peculiar to see that American unions had to resort to strike to obtain social benefits that we at home have considered a matter of course for more than a generation, and which have been secured by law for everybody in our country.[33]

It was the ECA that financed the printing of the report. Initially, it was planned for translation into English and distribution in the USA too. But after reading the report thoroughly, the ECA decided to skip that idea.[34]

A different vision of modernity

Several studies have described how workers and labour movements in certain European countries became fascinated by Fordism during the interwar period, and how even centre-left governments turned towards the USA not only for reasons of security, but just as much for help in modernising industry and raising productivity in the aftermath of World War II. But what has received less attention is how the actual transfer of economic Americanism was shaped by the resistance of workers and unions towards certain parts of it, and by the need to integrate it into a social and political context, in which the working class was much more strongly represented than in the USA. It is probably in this respect that the case of Ford Motor Company A/S is most important and most illustrative for the transformation of Fordism.

As we have seen, it was in its relation to labour that Fordism had to change most, as it was transformed from Detroit to Denmark. This was reflected directly in the organisation of production, which had to be modified literally from day one, due to pressure from the unions. And while Detroit was not without luck in enforcing "certain principles", such as the formal abolition of collective bargaining, unions maintained a strong position, and collective bargaining was later resumed. With variations, industrial relations at Ford Motor Company A/S were always closer to the Danish than to the Detroit model.

But Fordism also had to adopt to conditions outside the factory gates. In *Today and Tomorrow* Henry Ford lamented the effects of "labour government" in Denmark.[35] As noted above, what Ford Motor Company A/S was facing in 1919 was in fact not so much government interference, as it was the effect of an already well-organised labour market. A strong framework for collective bargaining had been a reality since the so-called September compromise of 1899 between the Danish Confederation of Trade Unions and the Confederation of Danish Employers.[36]

But it is true that the working class had strong political and parliamentary representation too. By the late 1920s a period of social democratic political governments started that would last throughout the rest of the period covered in this book, with only a few years of exception. While social democracy was largely hegemonic within the labour movement, political forces further to the left also played a role at certain times, especially around 1919 and during the aftermath of the Second World War. The consequence was a strong representation of labour interests in the class compromise, which determined the political development of the country.

Finally, the political and cultural self-confidence of the working class should not be underestimated. This was institutionalised, for instance, in the existence of a national and several local newspapers, a publishing house, workers' colleges, and an extensive network of clubs and associations within almost all spheres of life, from youth associations through sports clubs, educational associations, and consumer cooperatives to burial services associated with the labour movement.

In terms of hybridisation, this should all be taken into account as types of "rigid" national institutions that directly or indirectly formed an obstacle to the direct transfer of Fordism and forced it to transform and adapt to its local context.

When Antonio Gramsci contemplated the chances of Fordism spreading to Europe, he was sceptical. In contrast with the rationalised culture found in the USA, Europe was bogged down, he wrote, by a "leaden burden" of tradition, hindering the spread of Fordism and Americanism.[37] Given his personal history, Gramsci's rather pessimistic assessment is understandable. He had himself experienced the modernity of the highly industrialised town of Turin, but also how other parts of Italy, not least the *Mezzogiorno,* was dominated by a social stratum of landowners, civil servants, and clerics, promoting reactionary politics and religious traditions, and ultimately forming the basis for Fascism.

The "leaden burden" that Fordism met in Denmark was, however, of a quite different nature. It was not so much that of reactionary traditionalism, rooted in quasi-feudal institutions. On the contrary, it is best described as a form of modernity, but one that was different from that prevailing in the USA. It was the existence of a historically young but already deeply rooted form of organised labour and political mass organisations, adherent to ideologies of a socialist or social-reformist nature.

Therefore, reluctance from Danish labour towards Fordism during the interwar period cannot be written off as just a form of traditionalism. It was generally motivated not by resistance towards modernity as such, but on the contrary by a feeling that in certain social and other aspects the USA was actually not modern enough. The post-war period was characterised by a far greater interest in America and all things American among the Danish public, including the labour movement. But nevertheless, there was still a fair bit of scepticism among both leaders and rank-and-file members when it came to certain issues. What they saw when looking towards America, as well as when experiencing attempts to transform Fordist methods of production and industrial relations to Denmark, was basically a confirmation of the point originally made by Herbert Iversen: that America might be the land of the future in terms of material wealth, but from a social point of view it was too often still in the past.

Fordism as Americanism

The history of one single assembly plant does not tell the whole story of the transformation of Fordism from Detroit to Europe. That would require a comparative study of several national trajectories, that goes well beyond the scope of this book. But we might at least ask the question: how does the history of Ford Motor Company A/S relate to what is commonly known about Fordism in Europe? Does it confirm or contradict any existing assumptions?

In 1926, Henry Ford himself declared that "the essential principles of Americanism are the goal toward which all civilisation is striving".[38] This might be written off as just another example of boastfulness being an integral part of Americanism. But the impact of America on the rest of the world, including the old continent, cannot be denied. If by nothing else, it is confirmed by the long tradition of critical discourse, often amounting to obsession, among Europeans on American influence in Europe; a discourse that goes back long before the advent of Fordism.[39]

Americanisation as a headline may cover a broad range of topics from production, technology, and management through consumption to popular culture, leisure practices, and even politics and ideology.[40] But to a large extent the discourse has been occupied mostly by the latter of these themes. Only to a lesser degree has it been about the economic relations between the USA and Europe, and about America as an idol for European industry. And these two spheres of debate have often run in parallel, without touching each other.[41]

Someone who actually connected economy, culture, and politics was Antonio Gramsci. When he tried to come to terms with Fordism and its implications for Europe in his prison notebooks, he chose to do so under the headline "Fordism and Americanism". While never defining Americanism as such, it is clear from his treatment of the topic that Gramsci considered Fordism to be a core element of the wider concept of Americanism. What he thereby implied was that Americanism has its basis in the economy of mass production and consumption. At the same time, by connecting Fordism to a concept that in contemporary debate was—and is—predominantly connected with issues of (popular) culture and politics, he acknowledged that Fordism was about more than just production. Because of America's relative lack of history and tradition, the "superstructure" of culture, politics, and ideology is dominated by its economic "structure" in a much more immediate way than in Europe, Gramsci found. And as production is rationalised, American society as such is becoming rationalised. Or in other words: "Hegemony here is born in the factory."[42]

What characterised Americanism was therefore not only rationalised methods of production, but also a "rationalised" culture, first and foremost in relation to work, but also in ways of living in general, including family relations, gender relations, and even sexual relations. On the other hand, Gramsci would scorn those Europeans who "as a form of café life" embraced America as just a source of new and enticing cultural forms, without realising the potential of Fordism for transforming the material basis of European civilisation and its social order.[43]

Americanism during the interwar period might have been discussed in cafés, but it was undoubtedly also visible in certain types of consumer products and popular culture. Nevertheless, it was still primarily a by-product of economic activities, such as American export to or investments in Europe. This, again, was an effect of the rise of the USA to its position as the leading industrial nation of the world. While the UK had been the cradle of the industrial revolution, it had been overtaken by America at the end of the 19th century. In 1913, the USA alone accounted for almost half of the world's industrial production.[44] There were several reasons for America becoming such a massive industrial power, but an important one was the development of mass production. However, despite this dominant economic position, the prevailing political line of successive US administrations during the 1920s and 1930s was one of isolationism.

American investments in Europe during this period were unevenly distributed: roughly one-third went to the UK, and another third to Germany and France combined. It was also concentrated mainly within only a handful of industries—one of them being car manufacture.[45] In Denmark, most of the foreign investments during the early 20th century came from neighbouring countries, primarily the UK and Germany. But the auto industry stood out: Ford Motor Company A/S and General Motors represented not only the largest American investments by far in Denmark; they most likely also provided the largest number of workplaces of any foreign company.[46] And as the Copenhagen plant was only Fords second in Europe, and GM's was the company's first, it is fair to see Denmark as a bridgehead for the American car industry in mainland Europe during the interwar period.

From the outset, the Danish Ford company did act as a proponent of a "rationalised" culture. As confirmed by this study, Detroit had the intention of organising production in Denmark using the same technology and according to the exact same rationality as in America, dismissing other concerns, such as local labour market traditions, as largely irrelevant. This was reflected in the initial reports in the Danish press, which mainly focused on the speed and efficiency of the Ford plant.

But as has also been shown, the Fordist principles were moderated by reality from day one. And in its praxis, the Danish Ford company made important concessions in its management, in relation to government authorities and civil society and in the way it marketed its products and presented itself to the public—but most fundamentally, as we have seen, in the realm of industrial relations, including how production was organised and labour was managed. The history of Ford Motor Company A/S thereby confirms the claims of Harm G. Schröter in his study of the Americanisation of the European economy, that workers' resistance to American methods of production were a major hindrance to the adoption of such methods in the interwar period.[47]

Neither was Fordism embraced unconditionally by political decision-makers. As described above, the social democrats were receptive to Fordism as a method of increasing productivity and reaching a higher standard of living, but at the same time embedded their praise for Fordist efficiency in a narrative, in which industrial modernisation would be part of a politically laid out plan for social reform—a vision far from that of Henry Ford.

While Ford Motor Company A/S made an effort during the 1920s to spread the social and political ideas of Henry Ford, especially through the company magazine, it appeared somewhat half hearted, and played a minor role in the 1930s. What was constant, though, was Ford's effort to appear as a proponent of modernity in the eyes of the public. To that end, it would sometimes emphasise its American descent. But just as often, the signs of modernity adopted by the company, in its physical appearance in signs, buildings, etc., as well as in its printed material, were actually closer to a European type of functionalism. And typically, in its marketing, Ford Motor Company A/S was just as keen to associate itself with Danish national symbols as with Hollywood glamour.

Americanisation as strategy

From 1945 onwards, American economic, political, and cultural i nfluence affected Europe in a fundamentally new way, and to a hitherto unseen extent. The overall reason and context for this was of course the emerging Cold War, and an American interest in keeping Western Europe firmly within its sphere of interest. On the other hand, Western European governments were looking towards America for partnership and protection against what was perceived, rightfully or not, as the threat of communist expansion.

The Americanisation of Europe now, for the first time, took place as part of a deliberate American strategy.[48] At its core was the Marshall Plan, designed to increase European industrial productivity, using American technology and production methods. It was a multifaceted initiative, which included financial aid, support from American specialists coming to Europe, and an intensive program of study trips to the USA by managers, specialists, union representatives, and even rank-and-file industrial workers.

The increase in productivity was to be the basis of higher standards of living, which was seen as the best way of keeping the populations—and especially the workers—of Western Europe away from the lure of Communism. The Americanisation of the post-war period thereby combined the economic and the security policy interests of the USA. It was most poignantly articulated by Paul Hoffman, head of the Economic Cooperation Administration of the Marshall Plan, when he said: "The real battle today is between the American assembly line and the Communist party line."[49]

EUROPE
COOPERATION
means prosperity

This strategy could not have been successful, however, without the changing relationship between labour, industry, and state that had evolved in the USA since the 1930s. It was during this period that the most technologically advanced and internationally oriented corporations in mass production, liberal politicians and administrators, and moderate labour leaders came together, as the agents of a new political hegemony.[50] The basis for this new hegemony was a class compromise based on high wages in return for high productivity.

The same political forces were increasingly sceptical towards the traditional isolationism of the interwar period. By the end of World War II, they were united in the belief that it was in the best interest of the USA to be part of, and leading in, a liberal world order. And for that, a stable, productive, and non-communist Europe would be crucial. This was what fuelled the expansion of American political and cultural power throughout Western Europe in the post-war period.[51]

But it was also the concessions made to American labour, such as the right to organise and bargain collectively in major industries, that secured its consent in promoting American interests in Europe. Parts of these gains were undermined by the Taft-Harley Act, which followed a political swing to the right at the 1946 congressional election. But nevertheless, the AFL in particular, but also the CIO became active partners in building the transatlantic alliance during the Cold War. Without these two crucial elements—the active participation of American labour specifically, and the promise of material welfare based on higher productivity in general—it would have been much harder, and maybe not possible, to win over the majority of the Western European working class to the post-war American hegemony.

When Henry Ford II chose to make a thoroughly political speech during his 1948 visit to Copenhagen, calling for "greater harmony" within and among western nations based on free trade and high productivity, he was in a certain sense reinvigorating the ideological statements of his grandfather, sharing with him the notion that high productivity was the key to material welfare and thereby social har-

Figure 40 Poster promoting the Marshall Plan as a means for industrial growth and prosperity in Europe. Louis Emmerick, Netherlands, for the European Recovery Programme, 1950. Courtesy of the George C. Marshall Foundation, Lexington, Virginia

mony, as well as his rejection of class antagonism. But unlike in the 1920s when Fordism as an ideology, despite its popularity in various European circles, had been largely a one-man show, Henry Ford II was now speaking in sync with the dominant ideological view and political interest of the USA, and what was also in the process of becoming the order of the day in Western Europe.

Furthermore, the transformation of Fordism that had taken place in America since the 1930s had made it more compatible with European labour markets and political traditions. That is not to say that the spread of American methods of production in Europe after 1945 took place without problems. The union membership base as well as the proportion of skilled workers were still much larger in Europe than in the USA, meaning that the methods transferred across the Atlantic still had to be adapted to the new context.[52]

Nevertheless, there was generally a positive expectation that the promises of material welfare in exchange for higher industrial productivity would be fulfilled. That was also the case among the workers at Ford Motor Company A/S in the immediate post-war period. And despite the disappointments voiced over stagnating wages and employment, the plant as a workplace was characterised by a low level of conflict during the 1950s and 1960s.

The relative tranquillity at Ford Motor Company A/S during this period was therefore not just due to internal factors. It was just as much a reflection of this being a period when the labour market in general was characterised by increasing wages and almost full employment. Any worker at Ford not satisfied with his conditions would stand a good chance of getting an equally well paid or even better job elsewhere. This also explains the lack of negative reactions from unions or labour politicians when the plant was finally closed down in 1966.

In more general terms, the social and political climate of the late 1950s and early 1960s was one of optimism and relative prosperity of the working class, symbolised by the social-democratic slogan for the 1960 general election: "Make good times better". The need to secure the political and ideological consent of the working class meant that Fordism in Europe was married not only to a vision of material wealth, but also to some sort of political redistribution of that wealth. This was specifically the case in Denmark, where most post-war-governments were headed by social democrats, and where a publicly funded, universalist welfare state evolved to an extent unrivalled by almost any other nation.

But even in countries where conservative political forces had a majority, social reformism and inclusion of the working class were on the agenda. It is an irony of history that Fordism, which, in Henry Ford's original vision of an affluent society built on mass production, had been explicitly anti-union and pro-free market, eschewing any political intervention, now became the productive basis of social-reformist politics, often with a strong labour movement influence.

Resolving the paradox of Fordism

During the post-war era, two lines which originally ran in parallel began converging: on the one hand, the transformation of Fordism that had taken place in Europe, in the course of adapting it to a context where organised labour played a far greater role than in the USA; and on the other hand, the development of a new hegemonic block within the USA, dependent on securing the consent of the American —and, in a broader perspective, the European—working class.

That is why regulation theory, focusing on Europe during the 1950s and 1960s, can rightfully claim that Fordism is connected to the welfare state and based on cooperation with strong labour unions, despite the fact that Henry Ford's own social visions as well as Ford Motor Company's original praxis in Detroit was strongly anti-union, anti-politics, and anti-state. The apparent paradox between contemporary, sociological concepts of Fordism and the empirical realities of Fordism during its years of creation may thus be resolved once we employ proper, historical analysis.

This was also the period when Ford Motor Company A/S gradually began to fit into the mainstream, first and foremost as a workplace, but also in other aspects. Unfortunately, the economic and political changes on a European level, which facilitated this process, also undermined the reasons for production at Ford Motor Company A/S, and finally led to its closure as an assembly plant.

Despite the similarities in outward appearance between the South Port plant and any American Ford assembly plant, the transfer of

Fordism from Detroit to Denmark was not just one of simple export, but of transformation and hybridisation. The tremendous economic, cultural, and political power behind American influence in Western Europe after 1945 should not be underestimated. But the history of Ford Motor Company A/S also confirms what has been emphasised in recent literature on Americanisation: it has never been just a simple, unaltered transfer of American ways and values. The receiving part almost always played an active role in the process, and for Americanisation to be successful in the long run, both consent and comprehension by those affected was needed.[53]

That is furthermore a reminder that, while Americanisation is often also modernisation, not all modernisation is Americanisation. For a great part of the last century, most features of American society were implicitly or explicitly advertised to Europeans as more modern than in the old continent. Some of them might have been, but others were not. The resistance to Fordist models of production and industrial relations that Ford and others experienced in Europe was not just a case of traditionalism versus modernism; it was a clash between different pathways towards modern industrial society. Danish unions were not anti-modern when they insisted on the right to collective bargaining and to elect shop stewards. Theirs was just another modernity—one in which workers were recognised as a class, with interests of their own that did not always coincide with those of the owners of the means of production.[54]

Post-Fordism

The renewed interest in Fordism some fifty years ago, among sociologists and economists, was sparked by the belief that Fordism as a mode of regulation was coming to an end. And Post-Fordism was coined as a term for what was supposed to supersede it. Right from the start, Post-Fordism was a vague and not very well-defined concept, and it has only become broader in its use since then. Originally, new ways of organising industrial mass production, such as lean management or "Toyotaism", were seen as characteristic of Post-Fordism. To these have later been added more general, technological developments, such as robotisation and the spread of the Internet, and political developments, such as the fall of the Soviet Union and the end of the Cold War.

Despite the vagueness of the term, Post-Fordism has entered mainstream sociological and economic theory, and literally tens of thousands of academic publications have been devoted to it.[55] Furthermore, it is used widely in public debate, where specific developments within very different spheres of life—ranging from teaching methods in primary schools to pension reforms—may be deemed necessary with reference to the inescapable logic of Post-Fordism.

Due to its widespread use and many meanings, a thorough and critical approach to Post-Fordism would be a large-scale project, and it would in any case be outside the scope of this book.[56] But a few remarks seem appropriate, based on the preceding analysis.

The first one regards the historically changing nature of Fordism. What we have seen in the almost 50 years of history of Fordism in Denmark is that it changed considerably over time, and that technology was by no means the prime mover. What was much more important as a driver in the transformation of Fordism was human action, directly or indirectly, from the specific actions of organised labour through political regulation to the vague, but nonetheless significant, importance of traditions and cultures. In fact, while Fordism today is mainly associated with inflexibility, it was actually flexible enough to evolve into and maintain its role as the dominating mode of regulation of capitalist economy for a period of about two generations. This is of course due to the fact that Fordism was much more about industrial and social relations in a broad sense than just production technology in the narrow sense.[57]

The history of Fordism is therefore also a warning, not to make too simplistic assumptions, bordering on technological determinism, about social change in general. For instance, the relative de-industrialisation of western economies seen during the past decades might have been an effect of changing technologies in production. But it was most certainly also an effect of deliberate liberalisation of the global economy, whereby the transfer of goods has been made cheaper and new labour markets have been opened for exploitation. It was, after all, not Japanese industrial robots that tore down the Berlin wall, and economic deregulation and precarisation of labour were not invented by computers. The turn from Fordism towards Post-Fordism —whatever its exact content and its present and future implications—is a result of human action and intent.

The second point partly follows from this. Despite differences in evaluation of the precise character and connection between Fordism and the welfare state, it seems without doubt that such a connection exists. It was Fordism, with its coupling between wages and productivity which, for good or ill, established the foundation for the immense growth in material wealth, that characterised Western Europe from the mid-1950s onwards. And it was the need to uphold the hegemony of the Fordist model that led to a relative redistribution of wealth in favour of the working class, hitherto unseen during the capitalist mode of production.

Today's labour movement therefore needs to ask itself: for what reasons have the Fordist model been dismantled? Are deregulation, precarisation of labour, and increased competition between workers across borders an unavoidable effect of globalisation and new technologies—or are they a result of intentional decision, and therefore also something that can be reversed? Are fragile working relations and neo-liberal accommodation of capital investments the only way left to secure at least some jobs in a global economy?

The labour market of the twenty-first century is unquestionably different from that of the 1950s and the 1920s. But some of the principal challenges nevertheless remain: how to secure jobs, obtain a decent wage, and gain as much influence as possible on working condition. When the workers at Ford Motor Company A/S were challenged in 1919 by new production methods and new principles in management, they answered by mobilising their most effective weapon: organisation. And while they experienced both internal splits and defeats along the road, they actually managed, in the long run, to transform Fordism. So, in a wider perspective, did the Western European working class.

This of course happened in a political context quite different from today's. During the Cold War, even if predominantly anti-communist, the Western European labour movement was put in a favourable position due to the existence of an alternative social and political system. Today this alternative system no longer exists, which might be considered a good thing from the perspective of personal and political freedom. But at the same time, the pressure on the economically powerful to make concessions to the working class in order to uphold the existing social order has been eased considerably.

Will Post-Fordism lead to a further weakening of the global working class? Or will labour succeed in reinvigorating its organisations on a transnational level, and create a strong alternative to neoliberalism? If the latter becomes the case, we might even witness a new form of hegemony, growing out of the workplaces of the world.

Appendix

Fordism in Literature

As the books and articles listed under References will reveal, this book has been inspired, informed, and sometimes provoked by a wide body of literature. Some of these texts have already been introduced in previous parts of the book, mostly in the chapters "The creation of Fordism" and "The transformation of Fordism", but also elsewhere. It is not the intention to repeat here what has already been written, but merely to provide a short but hopefully comprehensive overview of the most important literature used. It is also the aim to call attention to some of the texts that have been important as inspiration for the present book, without necessarily having been referenced extensively throughout it.

Much has been written about Ford and Fordism. Disregarding eulogies (or the opposite) to Henry Ford himself, these writings can very crudely be divided into two categories. The first category is empirical accounts of the business history of Ford Motor Company, or the production methods or labour relations characteristic of Fordism, based on primary sources and most often written by historians. The second category is attempts to come to terms with Fordism as concept, epoch or mode of regulation within capitalist economy, most often developed from within social science. There are those contributions that seek to bridge the gap between these two types, but they seem to be quite rare.

From the American System to Mass Production by the historian and museum curator David Hounshell belongs to the first category. Hounshell provides a very thorough narrative of the development of Fordist production principles, within the broader framework of the history of American mass production. His book may have been supplemented by newer contributions, such as Nieuwenhuis and

Wells and others, but it is still by far the most comprehensive work on Fordist production before World War II.

Also belonging to the first category are a couple of business histories, most notably the monumental three-volume history of Ford Motor Company by historian Allan Nevins in collaboration with editor Frank Hill, published between 1954 and 1963 under the common title *Ford* and the subtitles *The Times, the Man, the Company; Expansion and Challenge 1915–1933*, and *Decline and Rebirth, 1933–1962*. These books were commissioned by Ford Motor Company, but they are in no way uncritical in their approach and present the history in great detail based on primary sources.

While *Ford* is still valuable for reference, especially on the history of American Ford, it was surpassed as far as the European history of the company is concerned in 1964, when Mira Wilkins and Frank Hill published *American Business Abroad: Ford on Six Continents*. Wilkins, later a professor of Economics, had worked as an assistant to Allan Nevins, and her work continues in the same empirical tradition. A new edition of the book was published as recently as 2011, giving testimony to its lasting influence.

2003 saw the publication of *Ford, 1903–2003: The European History*.[1] This two-volume book, edited by Hubert Bonin, Yannick Lung, and Steven Tolliday, remains the most ambitious work on the subject. It comprises a number of articles on the general history of Ford in Europe, including methods and theory, as well as articles covering the history from the perspective of ten different European countries, including Denmark.

A contribution to this anthology, which has been of great value to the present book, is Steven Tolliday's up-to-date, overall view of the history of Ford in Europe from 1903 to 1976. Apart from this article, Tolliday has made several other contributions to the subject of Fordism, work, and the auto industry in Europe.[2]

What is also notable about *Ford, 1903–2003: The European History* is that it brings together the tradition of empirical studies with those more theoretically inclined, even if not necessarily in the same contributions. The anthology is partly rooted in the work of GERPISA, the international research network on automobile industry, which again is inspired by the framework of the originally French school of regulation theory. This is most clearly reflected in the contribution by Michel Freyssenet.[3]

Moving to the subject of labour and industrial relations, *Autowork*, edited by Asher and Edsforth, presents several valuable accounts on working conditions and labour-management relations at Ford's American enterprise. Steven Tolliday and Jonathan Zeitlin have made several contributions relating to Fords in Europe, especially in the UK.

Regarding the influence of Fordism on economic, social, and political thinking in Europe, Mary Nolan's *Visions of Modernity* is of central importance. In this, Nolan writes specifically on the case of Germany and mainly in the era of the Weimar Republic. In her later book *The Transatlantic Century,* she covers some of the same topics in less detail, but through a much broader period of time and regarding Europe in general. Harm G. Schröter provides a similar overview, focused on economy but with an emphasis on the relations between economy, culture, and politics.

David E. Nye's *America's Assembly Line* has a somewhat different character. It aims to tell the story of the economic, cultural, and even ideological impact of mass production since the assembly line was introduced at Ford Motor Company in 1913. It does so in a somewhat kaleidoscopic, but also very illuminating way.

One of the books that seeks to bridge the gap between the empirical analysis and the conceptual understanding of Fordism is Mark Rupert's *Producing Hegemony*. Coming from political science, Rupert argues convincingly how America's global power after World War II was rooted in the establishing of a political hegemony, based on Fordism and mass production. Rupert's theoretical inspiration from the works of Antonio Gramsci also forms a link to the present book. This is likewise the case with Nicola Pizzolato's *Challenging Global Capitalism.*

Firmly placed within the second category are the writings about Fordism that have emerged from regulation theory. Jessop provides an overview in *Fordism and Post-Fordism.* A discussion of regulation theory as such falls outside the scope of this book, but a summary may be found in Robert Boyer's introduction to *Regulation Theory*, and some relevant criticism in Ferrucio Gambino's *A Critique of the Fordism of the Regulation School*, as well as in the aforementioned book by Pizzolato.

Inspired by regulation theory, but within the framework of studies of the international automobile industry carried out by the GERPISA research network, Robert Boyer, Michel Freyssenet and others have developed the theory of productive models, which may be used to define Fordism more specifically in relation to other productive models. This has been thoroughly presented in Boyer and Freyssenet: *The Productive Models*, as well as in Freyssenet's contribution to *Ford, 1903–2003: The European History*.

Compared to the vast body of literature on Ford, what has been written specifically about Ford in Denmark is very limited. Some books and booklets have been published by the company itself, in relation to anniversaries, most notably Thalbitzer's *Ford Motor Company A/S gennem 25 aar* (Ford Motor Company A/S during 25 years), which does contain some valuable information and especially illustrations, even if it is typical for its genre.

One of the first times Ford Motor Company A/S is treated in academic literature is possibly in Knud Knudsen's article on the introduction of assembly line production in Denmark. Knudsen's focus is very specifically on the 1927–1928 conflict following the termination of the collective agreement.

The most comprehensive treatment of the company before the present book was the contribution on Denmark by Peter Sørensen et al. to *Ford, 1903–2003: The European History*. It is an important contribution, since it is the first attempt to write an overview of the history of the Danish company from its start in 1919 to the end of assembly in 1966—and even beyond. It is, however, limited to business history as such. Neither developments in production technology nor industrial relations or labour history are included in the narrative or analysis.

Peter Sørensen is also the author of *Ford i Danmark 1919-1966* (Ford in Denmark 1919–1966). The aim of this analysis is to look at Ford Motor Company A/S as an example of foreign direct investments in Denmark, and to assess its importance as well as the role it played in Danish public debate on foreign investments. This is potentially an interesting subject, but unfortunately this contribution is limited by insufficient references.

The role of Ford Motor Company A/S is also touched upon in Per Boje's book on Denmark and multinational companies. Michael

Wagner has written about the public reception of Ford as a brand and a product, and Tobias Bang has made Ford's contribution to post-war consumer culture, especially through its advertising brochures, the subject of an MA thesis.

Americanisation in Denmark in 1945–1947 has been the subject of a research project initiated by the University of Southern Denmark. Despite the rather narrow timeframe, the project has in reality been occupied with the post war period in general—and even with the 1920s and '30s to a limited degree. One of the outcomes, relevant for this book, was the aforementioned article by Michael Wagner. Another one was Niels Finn Christiansen article on social democratic relations to and attitudes towards the United States: 'USA – et socialdemokratisk dilemma' (USA—a social-democratic dilemma).

The most comprehensive treatment of the Danish labour movement in relation to Americanisation is undoubtedly Dino Knudsen: *Amerikaniseringen af den danske fagbevægelse* (The Americanisation of the Danish trade union movement). But apart from focusing on labour unions and treating the Social Democratic Party only peripherally, it is also about the post-war period only. Apart from some remarks in the article by Niels Finn Christiansen mentioned above, very little has been written so far about social democratic attitudes towards America in general, and Fordism specifically, before 1945.

What have been mentioned here are only the most important of the works that have been consulted. A complete list of references can be found below.

Types and Origin of Primary Sources

The present book may be characterised as a hybrid between labour history and business history. It has been an ambition to root both aspects of the study in relevant primary sources.

As for labour at Ford Motor Company A/S, most relevant sources have been found at the Library and Archive of the Workers Museum in Copenhagen (ABA). The bulk of the material is made up of protocols of board meetings and general assemblies of various trade unions, which had members working at Ford Motor Company A/S. Since the membership of these unions spanned several employers and workplaces, discussions relevant to Ford are scattered throughout the densely written pages of the many protocols. Despite lacunas, it has been possible to find protocols from at least two and often more unions throughout the complete time period, and thereby often including different or conflicting views.

Supplementing this material, the archive of correspondence of the Union of Workmen in the Metal Industries has been used. Because it also contains incoming letters and attachments, valuable material originating from Ford Motor Company A/S, but no longer present in the company's own archive, has also been found there.

Unfortunately, none of the workers from Ford seems to have written their memoirs—at least none has been found in the known repositories of such memoirs or in print.[4] However, Axel Sjølander, who was elected shop steward at Ford Motor Company A/S in large parts of the post-war period, has recounted his experiences in his private correspondence, now deposited at Rødovre municipal archive.

For the business side of the history, the most important primary sources are of course those found in the company archive itself. When I started my inquiries into the history of Ford Motor Company A/S, it was the impression among business historians that its archives had been lost during one of its relocations. But with helpful assistance from the staff of the company, I was able to locate them at the present premises of the company in Ballerup, Copenhagen. At the time of finishing the manuscript I have been informed that Ford in Denmark will again move to a new location. Consequently, the historical archive will be transferred to the Ford Motor Company Archive in Dearborn, USA.

While the archive has been kept in good condition, the material is in somewhat random order and no index exists. It has been possible, however, to find a complete set of minutes from board meetings and general assemblies throughout the period. Financial accounts in different forms have also been located. So-called Balance Sheets exist for 1919–1949 (except 1928), which contain key production and financial figures. The figures given, the way they are presented, and the level of detail vary throughout the period. The Balance Sheets are discontinued in 1949 in favour of Financial Statements and Operation Reports (FSOR). The figures given in these are also somewhat inconsistent over time; for instance there are no employment numbers from 1956 onwards. The FSORs seem to have been discontinued in 1962, and no other similar sources have been located for the last years to 1966.

Annual reports[5] have been issued since the company shares became publicly tradeable in 1929. Combining the holdings of the FMC archive with those of the Royal Library, an almost complete series of annual reports has been established, albeit with a few omissions, especially for the late 1950s.

Other important material from the company archive includes various accounts of production, documents regarding the expansion in the late 1950s, and the closure of assembly in 1966, as well as a collection of photographs. Two series of photographs, one from the newly erected South Port plant ca. 1925 and one from the time of expansion around 1956–1958 has been donated to the National Museum.

Another repository of documents relating to Ford Motor Company A/S is the Benson Ford Research Centre (BFRC) in Dearborn, Michigan, USA.[6] The BFRC, which is part of the museum and archive complex known as The Henry Ford, holds a vast collection of historical records. There are no specific files or collections regarding the Danish company, but relevant material may be found for example in the correspondence of Charles Sørensen or elsewhere.

One specific type of material in the BFRC deserves a special mention: the transcripts of interviews that Mira Wilkins conducted with former European managers, including those of the Danish company as well as a few other central actors, before publishing her book on Ford's international history in 1964. She later graciously deposited these at the archive, where they have been a very valuable source for this book, not only on specific topics, but also as a glimpse into the mindset of those who were in charge of running the company.

The actual physical space and the production process inside the assembly plants in both Heimdalsgade and the South Port plant may be documented from two types of sources in particular. One is photographs, such as the aforementioned series from 1925, now in the collections of the National Museum, but also photographs located in the collection of the Copenhagen Museum, The Royal Library, and elsewhere. The other is the risk evaluation reports made for insurance purposes, which contain descriptions and sometimes sketches of buildings and equipment. These are now part of the holdings of the National Archive.

Apart from the sources mentioned here, quite a number of others have been used, and a complete list of archival sources can be found below for reference.

Statistics: Long-Term Trends

For a company history stretching almost 50 years, it is of course of interest if continuous series of data on central issues can be established. As noted above, the holdings of the historical archive of Ford Motor Company A/S are not arranged in any chronological order. And even if series of financial accounts and so on can be pieced together for a longer period, the data are not necessarily presented consistently throughout the years.

Nevertheless, it has been possible to put together statistics of long-term trends in the central areas of production, sales, employment, profit, and dividend. Unfortunately, it has not been possible to establish a similar long-term overview of wages, since consistent and comparable data for the whole period do not exist. Instead, data about developments in workers' pay for shorter periods of time are provided throughout the book.

Production and sales

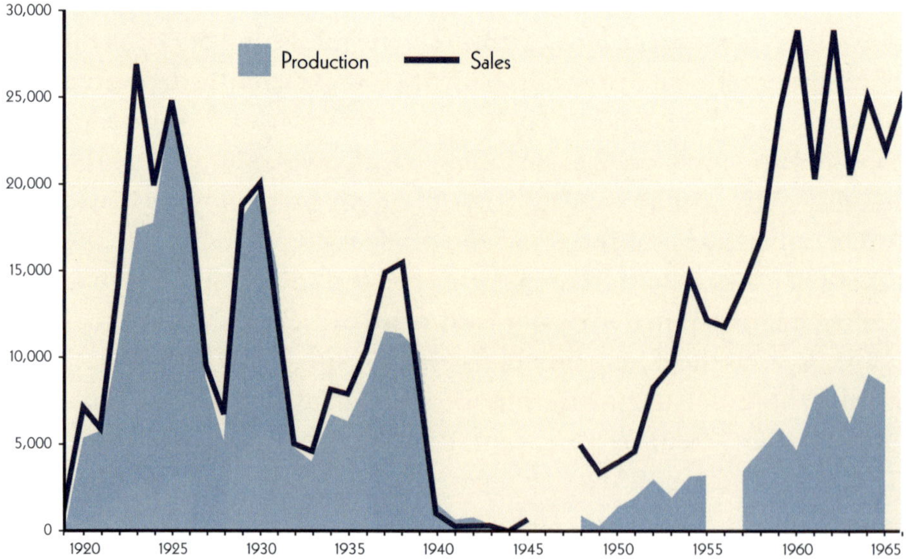

Figure 41 Number of units produced and sold, 1919–1966

All figures for sale and production are from sources in the archive of Ford Motor Company. Figures for production are the total number of units assembled. The sources are: Production 1920- (1919–1943 used), Balance Sheets (1944–1945), Financial Statements and Operation Reports (1948–1955 & 1957–1962), and the Annual Reports (1963–1965). Data is missing for 1946–1947, 1956, and 1966.

The sources for sales are also from the FMC archive: Balance Sheets (1919–1926 & 1939–1945), Deliveries 1927–46 (1927–1938 used), Financial Statements and Operation Reports (1948–1955 & 1957–1959), and the Annual Reports (1960–1966). Data is missing for 1946–1947. For some years, the numbers may be for sales to final customers, and for others the number of units delivered to dealers, but the difference should be negligible.

Employment

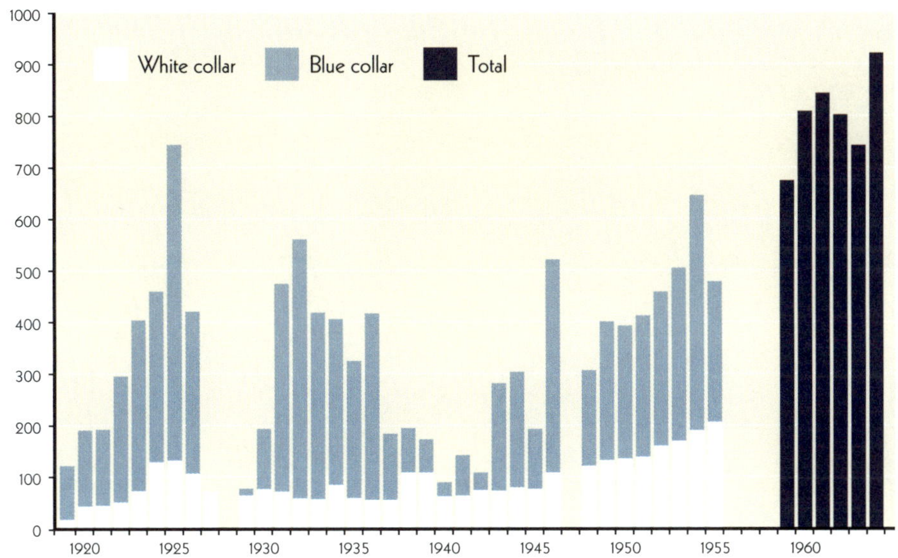

Figure 42 Number of employees, 1919–1964

Sources for employment figures are from FMC archive: Balance Sheets (1919–1927, 1929–1946 & 1948), Financial Statements and Operation Reports (1949–1955), and the Annual Reports (1959–1964). For 1928, 1947, 1956–1958, and 1965–1966 no data has been found.

For 1919–1955, the numbers of blue-collar workers and white-collar employees are stacked together for a total. For 1959–1964 only totals are given in the sources.

The graph depicts the level of employment at the end of each year. Employment would vary significantly from month to month and would have been at a higher level in some months during each year than what is depicted here. But unfortunately, data for maximum or average yearly employment are only available for a limited number of years. Randomly selected samples from these years indicate that employment at the end of the year may be both above and below yearly average, but for the sake of comparison they are used here as a rough approximation. For this reason, the graph probably underestimates fluctuation in employment. Especially for 1927 it should be noted that production was terminated in August that year, and that employment in the first part of the year was therefore far above the low level indicated at the end of the year.

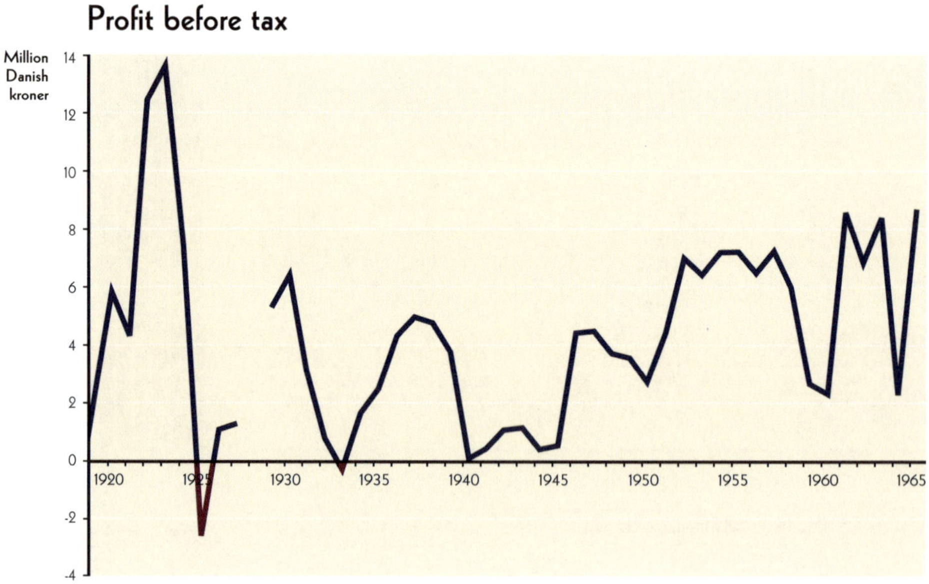

Figure 43 Profit before tax, 1919–1965, current prices

The sources for profit before tax are the Balance Sheets, found in the FMC archive (1919–1948) and the Annual Financial Statements, found partly in the FMC archive, partly at the Royal Library (1949–1965). No data has been located for 1928 and 1966.

Dividend

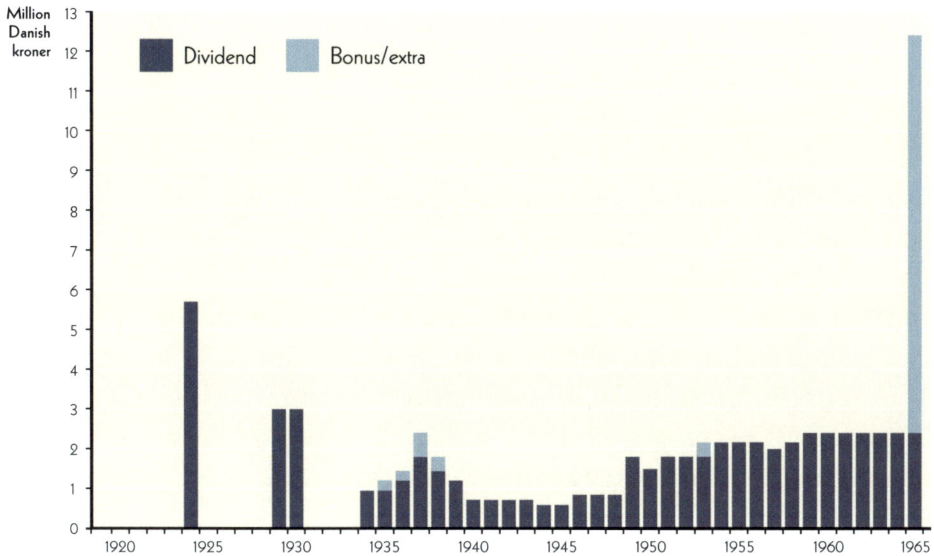

Figure 44 Dividend & bonus, 1919–1965, current prices

Sources for the amounts paid to shareholders as dividend are minutes of the annual general meetings in the Minutes of Board and General Meetings, found in the FMC archive (1919–1965). Data exist for all years; a zero value indicates that no dividend was paid. For the years 1935–1938 and 1953 an extra bonus was added to the dividend. At the 1966 General Meeting, it was decided that the DKK 10,000,000 income from the sale of the assembly plant to Ford Industrial Equipment A/S should be distributed among the shareholders as an extra dividend for 1965.

List of Tables and Figures

Danish Names of Associations and Institutions

Throughout the text, Danish associations and institutions are referenced by name in English translation. Below is the Danish name for each, and an official abbreviation as far it exists.

Labour unions

The term union normally designates a local body, while associations are national organisations of local unions within the same trade. DSF (later LO) was the national confederation of union associations.

Coach Painters' Union: *Vognmalernes Fagforening.*

Danish Confederation of Trade Unions: *De samvirkende Fagforbund*, DSF, from 1959 *Landsorganisationen i Danmark,* LO.

Danish Metalworkers' Association: *Dansk Smede- og Maskinarbejder Forbund,* DSMF.

Danish Workmen's Association: *Dansk Arbejdsmands Forbund,* DAF, from 1959 *Dansk Arbejdsmands- og Specialarbejder Forbund,* DASF.

Joiners' Association in Denmark: *Snedkerforbundet i Danmark.*

Painters' Association in Denmark: *Malerforbundet i Danmark.*

Plumbers' Association in Denmark: *Blikkenslagerforbundet i Danmark.*

Plumbers' Union of 1873: *Blikkenslagernes Fagforening af 1873.*

Scandinavian Upholsterers' Association: *Skandinavisk Sadelmager- og Tapetserer-Forbund*, from 1943 *Sadelmager- og Tapetsererforbundet i Danmark.*

Specialised Workmen's Union: *Specialarbejderforbundet.*

Union of Automobile and Bicycle Mechanics: *Fagforening for Automobil og Cyclemekanikere,* later *Automekanikernes Fagforening, Metal afd. 14.*

Union of Joiners and Chairmakers: *Snedker og Stolemagernes Fagforening.*

Union of Upholsterers: *Sadelmagernes Fagforening.*

Union of Workmen in the Metal Industries: *Støberi-, Special- og Maskinfabrikarbejdernes Forbund.*

Note: colloquially speaking, unions are often referenced just by trade instead of their formal name; for instance workmen's union instead of Union of Workmen in the Metal Industries.

Employers organisations and trade associations

Association of Automobile and Bicycle Wholesale Dealers: *Automobil- og Cycle-Grosserer Forening.*

Association of Car Manufacturers and Importers: *Sammenslutningen af Automobil-Fabrikanter og Importører*

Confederation of Danish Employers: *Dansk Arbejdsgiverforening,* DA.

Industrial Council: *Industrirådet.*

Society for Industry: *Industriforeningen.*

Public institutions and government bodies

Auditing Commission: *Revisionsudvalget.*

Currency Committee: *Valuta-Centralen.*

Directorate for Product Supply: *Direktoratet for Vareforsyning.*

Permanent Board of Arbitration: *Den Faste Voldgiftsret*, from 1964 *Arbejdsretten.*

Sub-committee for Distribution of Cars: *Automobilfordelingsnævnet.*

Political parties

Communist Party: *Danmarks Kommunistiske Parti,* DKP

Liberal Party: *Venstre*

Social Democratic Party: *Socialdemokratiet*

Social-Liberal Party: *Radikale Venstre*

Others

Danish Shareholders' Association: *Aktionær-Sammenslutningen af 1947.*

Economic Council of the Labour Movement: *Arbejderbevægelsens Erhvervsraad.*

Federation of Danish Motorists: *Forenede Danske Motorejere,* FDM.

Royal Danish Automobile Club: *Kongelig Dansk Automobil Klub*, KDAK.

Notes

Introduction
pp. 11–15

1. Elteren, *Americanism and Americanization*, 115.

The Creation of Fordism
pp.17–41

1. Quoted from Hounshell, *From the American System to Mass Production 1800–1932: The Development of Manufacturing Technology in the United States*, 217.
2. Boyer and Freyssenet, *The Productive Models: The Conditions of Profitability*, 50.
3. Ford, *My Life and Work: In Collaboration with Samuel Crowther*, 73.
4. Quoted from Hounshell, *From the American System to Mass Production 1800–1932*, 221. Emphasis in original. This approach, which was also known as "the American system of manufacture", had already been pioneered in mass-producing items such as firearms, sewing machines, and bicycles.
5. Hounshell, 227. For more about body variants, see p. 68.
6. Boggess, 'The Customer Can Have Any Color He Wants – So Long As It's Black: A Study of the Materials and Methods Used to Paint Model T Fords During the Black Era', 27.
7. Boyer and Freyssenet, *The Productive Models*, 48.
8. Hounshell, *From the American System to Mass Production 1800–1932*, 230–33; Hughes, *American Genesis: A Century of Invention and Technological Enthusiasm, 1870–1970*, 207.
9. Hounshell, *From the American System to Mass Production 1800–1932*, 224.
10. Hounshell, 247–56; Nye, *America's Assembly Line*, 21.
11. Freyssenet, 'Developing Analytical Tools to Identify the "Fordian Model" in Europe', 101–102.
12. Ford, *My Life and Work*, 81–82.
13. Freyssenet, 'Developing Analytical Tools to Identify the "Fordian Model" in Europe', 55.
14. Hounshell, *From the American System to Mass Production 1800–1932*, 252; Freyssenet, 'Developing Analytical Tools to Identify the "Fordian Model" in Europe', 49–50.
15. Freyssenet, 49–50.
16. Hughes, *American Genesis, 1870–1970*, 207; Hounshell, *From the American System to Mass Production 1800–1932*, 260; Montgomery, *Workers' Control in America: Studies in the History of Work, Technology, and Labor Struggles*, 119.
17. Ford, *My Life and Work*, 78–79.
18. Ford, 87.
19. Montgomery, *Workers' Control in America*, 117.
20. Montgomery, 117–18.
21. Montgomery, 117.
22. Freyssenet, 'Developing Analytical Tools to Identify the "Fordian Model" in Europe', 102 & 111.
23. Rupert, *Producing Hegemony: The Politics of Mass Production and American Global Power*, 111.
24. Rupert, 113ff; Raushenbush, *Fordism*, 63.
25. Nevins and Hill, *Ford: Expansion and Challenge 1915–1933*, 332ff.
26. Rupert, *Producing Hegemony*, 123.
27. Ford, *My Life and Work*, 126–27, 147. See also Raff and Summers, 'Did Henry Ford Pay Efficiency Wages?', 668.
28. Raff and Summers, 667–68.

29. The concept of scientific management is most often associated with Frederick W. Taylor but cannot be limited to him alone. Ford and Taylor differed in certain key aspects, but they shared the belief that it was possible to determine almost any questions regarding production by applying rational methods. Disagreement between management and labour was largely a product of lack of insight by the latter.
30. Ford, *My Life and Work*, 117, 255, & 262.
31. Rupert, *Producing Hegemony*, 114.
32. Ford, *My Life and Work*, 111.
33. Coopey and McKinlay, 'Power without Knowledge? Foucault and Fordism, c. 1900–50', 112.
34. Coopey and McKinlay, 110.
35. Ford, *Today and Tomorrow: In Collaboration with Samuel Crowther*, 8.
36. Ford, *My Life and Work*, 184.
37. As described in Nolan, 'Productivism and Technocracy in Historical Perspective'.
38. Ford, *My Life and Work*, 184–85.
39. For more on Henry Ford and anti-Semitism, see Link, 'Rethinking the Ford-Nazi Connection'; Eifert, 'Antisemit und Autokönig: Henry Fords Autobiographie und Ihre deutsche Rezeption in den 1920er-Jahren'.
40. Rupert, *Producing Hegemony*, 79–80.
41. Boyer and Freyssenet, *The Productive Models*, 63–64.
42. Hughes, *American Genesis*, 213–14.
43. According to Boggess, the two new colours were introduced into the production at River Rouge in August 1925. There is a connection between new painting techniques and all-steel bodies, and according to both Hounshell and Nieuwenhuis & Wells the production of all-steel bodies began at River Rouge sometime during 1925. But according to Casey, the "new" Model T was not marketed before 1926. Boggess, 'The Customer Can Have Any Color He Wants—So Long As It's Black: A Study of the Materials and Methods Used to Paint Model T Fords During the Black Era', 39; Hounshell, *From the American System to Mass Production 1800–1932*, 274; Nieuwenhuis and Wells, 'Ford, Budd, and the History of Mass Production', 63–64; Casey, *The Model T: A Centennial History*, 92–93.
44. Hounshell, *From the American System to Mass Production 1800–1932*, 264–67; Edsforth and Asher, 'The Speedup: The Focal Point of Workers' Grievances, 1919–1941', 67.
45. Hounshell, *From the American System to Mass Production 1800–1932*, 263–64.
46. Bryan, *Henry's Lieutenants*, 155–156.
47. Nevins and Hill, *Ford: Expansion and Challenge 1915–1933*, 430 & 442.
48. Hounshell, *From the American System to Mass Production 1800–1932*, 267.
49. Hounshell, 294.
50. Boyer and Freyssenet, *The Productive Models*, 68.
51. Nevins and Hill, *Ford: Expansion and Challenge 1915–1933*, 325–30.
52. Nevins and Hill, 592.
53. Asher and Edsforth, 'A Half Century of Struggle: Auto Workers Fighting for Justice', 10.
54. As discussed in more detail later, especially on p. 315.
55. Henry Ford died in 1947.
56. Asher, 'The 1949 Ford Speedup Strike and the Post War Social Compact, 1946–1961', 127.
57. Nevins and Hill, *Ford: Decline and Rebirth, 1933–1962*, 321–22; Asher, 'The 1949 Ford Speedup Strike and the Post War Social Compact, 1946–1961', 128–30. Time study is a way of rationalising a work process, by measuring the minimum time needed for each task involved in the process. It might result in a reorganisation of the process and/or the setting of a standard time for the job, that workers must meet or go below.
58. Asher, 148–49.
59. Nolan, *Visions of Modernity: American Business and the Modernization of Germany*, 21 & 48. The booklet was mostly a critique of Taylor and a commendation of Henry Ford.
60. Nolan, 30ff. Other writers have made similar observations; see for instance Maier, *In Search of Stability: Explorations in Historical Political Economy*, 19ff; Hughes, *American Genesis*, 284ff.

61. Nolan, *Visions of Modernity*, 71.
62. Nye, *America's Assembly Line*, 68 & 91.
63. Pizzolato, *Challenging Global Capitalism: Labor Migration, Radical Struggle, and Urban Change in Detroit and Turin*, 25–27.
64. Even though Gramsci made no direct reference in his own text, he was at that point in continuation of a way of thinking that dates back to Rudolf Hilferding, but also includes Rosa Luxemburg, Nikolai Bucharin, and V.I. Lenin. Sørensen, *Gramsci og den moderne verden*, 232ff. For an introduction to the debate in general, see Kocka, 'Organisierter Kapitalismus oder Staatsmonopolistischer Kapitalismus? Begriffliche Vorbemerkungen'; Hardach, Karras, and Fine, *A Short History of Socialist Economic Thought*, 38–50.
65. Gramsci, *Selections from the Prison Notebooks of Antonio Gramsci*, 279ff; Sørensen, *Gramsci og den moderne verden*, 254.
66. Hobsbawm, *How to Change the World: Reflections on Marx and Marxism*, 314ff.
67. Boyer, *The Regulation School: A Critical Introduction*, 15ff.
68. Jessop, 'Fordism and Post-Fordism: A Critical Reformulation', 49; see also Pizzolato, *Challenging Global Capitalism*, 38.
69. Gambino, 'A Critique of the Fordism of the Regulation School', 43.
70. The studies referred to have been carried out in the framework of GERPISA (Permanent Group for the Study of and Research into the Automobile Industry and its Employees), a French-based international research network. See Boyer and Freyssenet, *The Productive Models*, 119–20. On productive models in general, see also Boyer, 'Hybridization and Models of Production: Geography, History and Theory'; Boyer and Freyssenet, 'A New Approach of Productive Models. The World That Changed the Machine'; Freyssenet, 'Developing Analytical Tools to Identify the "Fordian Model" in Europe'.
71. Boyer and Freyssenet, *The Productive Models*, 8 & 19–20.
72. Boyer and Freyssenet, 60.
73. Boyer and Freyssenet, 19.
74. See for instance Freyssenet, 'Developing Analytical Tools to Identify the "Fordian Model" in Europe', 110–11. 1941 was the year when Ford Motor Company in Detroit finally recognized the union of the autoworkers and signed an agreement.
75. The concept of hybridisation will be presented in more detail in the chapter on the transformation of Fordism.
76. For an overview, see: Elteren, *Americanism and Americanization: A Critical History of Domestic and Global Influence*.
77. Elteren, 102.
78. Nolan, *Visions of Modernity*. See also Nolan, *The Transatlantic Century: Europe and America, 1890–2010*, esp. 84ff.
79. Nye, *America's Assembly Line*, 5–6.
80. Nye, 107ff. & 128ff.
81. Rupert, *Producing Hegemony*, esp. 80 & 92ff.

1919–1928 · Pioneering Years
pp. 43–139

1. BFRC: Ford Motor Company Incorporation records series, Minutes of Meetings of Board of Directors, 13.05. 1919.
2. Tolliday, 'The Rise of Ford in Britain: From Sales Agency to Market Leader, 1904–1980', 10.
3. Tolliday, 8 & 11; Wilkins and Hill, *American Business Abroad: Ford on Six Continents*, 49.
4. Bryan, *Henry's Lieutenants*, 154–55; Engelstoft and Dahl, *Dansk Biografisk Leksikon*, vol. 12:628–29.
5. Wilkins and Hill, *American Business Abroad*, 96–97. When Wilkins and Hill note that assembly started in France in 1913, they must be referring to the finishing process described above. From around 1921, assembly did progress in Bordeaux, though, and in 1925 a new assembly plant was established in Asnières, outside Paris. See Loubet and Hatzfeld, 'Ford in France, 1916–1955: From an American Dream to a Failure', 323–25.
6. BFRC: Mira Wilkins papers, Møller.
7. BFRC: Mira Wilkins papers, Carlson.

8. Thalbitzer, *Ford Motor Company A/S gennem 25 Aar*, 22.
9. BFRC: Knudsen, report.
10. FMC: Minutes, vol. I, 25.06.1919. On request from Detroit "Dansk Monteringsfabrik" was changed to just "Monteringsfabrik" in 1921, and in 1926 the name was shortened to simply "Ford Motor Company A/S" (Ford Motor Company Ltd.).
11. BFRC: Mira Wilkins papers, Carlson.
12. BFRC: Agreements and Contracts subgroup, Knudsen.
13. FMC: Minutes, vol. I, 03.01.1920. BFRC: Mira Wilkins papers, Carlson.
14. FMC: Minutes, vol. I, 15.08.1919. BFRC: Mira Wilkins papers, Carlson.
15. FMC: Balance sheets, 1919–1922.
16. RA: Skafor 2709, Reports 30.01.1920 & 14.03.1923.
17. FMC: Minutes, vol. I, 03.01.1920. BFRC: Mira Wilkins papers, Beck. Thalbitzer, *Ford Motor Company A/S gennem 25 Aar*, 22.
18. Casey, *The Model T*, 70.
19. Casey, 62 & 72.
20. RA: Skafor 2907, Report 30.01.1920.
21. 'Besøg paa Ford's Automobilfabrik'. *Ingeniøren*, no. 38, 1920, 311–12. Scanpix 200161 & 200177.
22. 'Besøg paa Ford's Automobilfabrik'. *Ingeniøren*, no. 38, 1920, 311–12. Scanpix 200162, 200174, & 200179.
23. See Figure 10, p. 68 for an overview of available versions.
24. See pp. 51–52.
25. 'Besøg paa Ford's Automobilfabrik'. *Ingeniøren*, no. 38, 1920, 311–12.
26. This should not be confused with the later method of spray-painting using Pyroxylin, as described on p. 146f.
27. Arnold and Faurote, *Ford Methods and the Ford Shops*, 360–67.
28. Københavns Museum: Elf-div21566.
29. Københavns Museum: Elf-div21570, Elf-div21571, & Elf-div21567.
30. Casey, *The Model T*, 65; Arnold and Faurote, *Ford Methods and the Ford Shops*, 360.
31. Scanpix: 200161. Hyldtoft and Johansen, *Teknologiske forandringer i dansk industri 1896–1972*, 169.
32. BFRC: Mira Wilkins papers, Beck.
33. *Politiken*, 20.02.1920.
34. FMC: Abridged Balance Sheets, 1920 & 1923.
35. BFRC: Charles E. Sorensen records series, Sorensen, telegrams II, Copenhagen to Sorensen, 20.04.1922.
36. FMC: Minutes, vol. I, 10.09.1920.
37. BFRC: Charles E. Sorensen records series, Sorensen telegrams II, 21.02.1922–03.05.1922.
38. BFRC: Charles E. Sorensen records series, recapitulations.
39. Hounshell, *From the American System to Mass Production 1800–1932*, 226–27; Nye, *America's Assembly Line*, 47.
40. A large three-storey spinning mill had already been constructed in steel-reinforced concrete in 1908–1913, as part of the textile mill I.C. Modeweg & Søn, in Brede north of Copenhagen. Tønsberg, *Brede Klædefabrik. I.C. Modeweg & Søn A/S 1810-1956. Den danske klædeindustri i international belysning*, 61–62.
41. Thalbitzer, *Ford Motor Company A/S gennem 25 Aar*, 27. Skafor 8018, Report 25.01.25.
42. RA: Skafor 8018, Report 25.01.1925 with plan.
43. NM: Photo collection, DNT-70828, Thalbitzer, *Ford Motor Company A/S gennem 25 Aar*, 75.
44. NM: Photo collection, DNT-70804, DNT-70805, DNT-70815, & DNT-70827.
45. RA: Skafor 8018, Report 25.01.1925 with plan. According to press reports the assembly line was 100 meters long (*Politiken*, 16.11.1924) but measured from the plan it was around 80 meters.
46. Boggess, 'The Customer Can Have Any Color He Wants—So Long As It's Black', 29f.
47. NM: Photo collection DNT-70821
48. Johansen, *Om Trykluft*.
49. For more photos of bodies on conveyers in paint shops, see NM: Photo collection DNT-70822, DNT-70824, and DNT-70791.

50. Wilkins and Hill, *American Business Abroad*, 142–43; Nevins and Hill, *Ford: Expansion and Challenge 1915–1933*, 406.
51. Nieuwenhuis and Wells, 'Ford, Budd, and the History of Mass Production', 62–64; Casey, *The Model T*, 92.
52. Boggess, 'The Customer Can Have Any Color He Wants—So Long As It's Black', 38–39. The colours offered at other markets might have been slightly different. The "new" Model T should not be confused with the "English body" version, which had been available in grey since 1924.
53. *Ford Nyheder*, no. 3, 4, & 11, 1925.
54. *Ford Nyheder*, no. 3, 1925.
55. See note to the introduction of the "new" Model T on p. 28. Nieuwenhuis and Wells, 'Ford, Budd, and the History of Mass Production', 63.
56. FMC: Abridged Balance Sheets, 1925. Sørensen et al., 'Ford Denmark and the Scandinavian Market: From Regional Export Base to Periphery', 273.
57. 'Vor ny Fabrik i Sydhavnen' (Our new plant at the South Harbour), *Ford Nyheder*, no. 4, 1924; *Ford Nyt*, no. 1, 1959. Actual production figures in Figure 41.
58. 'Lord Mayor of Copenhagen Officially Opens New Ford Plant; Danish Premier Welcomes Company', *Ford News*, January 1925, 6. Similar phrases can be found in *Ford News*, September 1924, 5, and March 1926, 3.
59. Danish numbers calculated from Figure 41, English numbers from Wilkins and Hill, *American Business Abroad*, 436 appendix 3. In fact both England and Denmark were significantly surpassed in production figures by the Ford plant in Windsor, Canada. But that plant was just across the river from Detroit, and apparently not considered foreign by Ford in America, in the same sense as Manchester or Copenhagen.
60. Nye, *America's Assembly Line*, 68 & 91.
61. Note from manager Harrington to all employees in ABA: SSMF, correspondence, file 1060. The time for assembly is not stated, only the relative percentage. In the note, Harrington made a promise of reducing the work week from 48 to 44 hours, when the goal was reached. The 44-hour week was realised in late March 1920.
62. Total production of the year divided by average number of blue-collar workers throughout that year. Abridged Balance Sheets 1923 & 1925.
63. See p. 25..
64. *Clarté*, no. 10, 1926, 285.
65. ABA: VF, protocols of board meetings, 25.06. & protocols of general assemblies, 06.07.1926.
66. *Jærn og Metalarbejderen*, no. 11, 1927, 150.
67. ABA: SF, protocols of board meetings, 15.03.1927. ABA: VF, protocols of board meetings, 01.04.1927.
68. Thalbitzer, *Ford Motor Company A/S gennem 25 Aar*, 30.
69. Hounshell, *From the American System to Mass Production 1800–1932*, 283.
70. Wojcik and Frese-Madsen, *General Motors International A/S: 1923–1974*; Wolfson, *Danmarks industrielle Udvikling*, 431.
71. Bryan, *Henry's Lieutenants*, 153ff.
72. Wojcik and Frese-Madsen, *General Motors International A/S*, 36 & 42.
73. Nicolaisen, *Klip: Fra Citroëns historie i Danmark 1919–66*. Industriregistreringen, acc. 1427.
74. Based on figures in Sørensen et al., 'Ford Denmark and the Scandinavian Market', 280 table 3. This table shows export to different markets in different years, but is clearly not complete, as total sales 1919–1927 add up to only about half of the production. It does however provide grounds for a rough estimate. Unfortunately, Sørensen et al. make no reference to the original source material, and it has not been possible to locate the missing figures in the FMC archive. See also the discussion of production and sales figures in the Appendix on p. 330f.
75. *Politiken*, 26.01.1924.
76. See for instance advertisement in *Politiken*, 09.10.1923.
77. FMC: Deliveries, 1927.

78. BFRC: Mira Wilkins papers, Bülow; Sørensen et al., 'Ford Denmark and the Scandinavian Market', 269; *Danmarks ældste Forretninger*, 82.
79. BFRC: Mira Wilkins papers, Møller; Wilkins and Hill, *American Business Abroad*, 70.
80. BFRC: Mira Wilkins papers, Møller & Bülow.
81. BFRC: Agreements and Contracts subgroup, Knudsen.
82. BFRC: Mira Wilkins papers, Beck & Carlson.
83. BFRC: Nevins and Hill research, Roberge
84. Tolliday, 'The Rise of Ford in Britain', 13–14.
85. BFRC: Mira Wilkins papers, Beck & Møller.
86. Letter in the private archive of F. Bülow & Co., quoted in Wagner, 'Domesticeringen af Ford i Danmark: Den kulturelle tilegnelse af Ford og fordismen, 1920–1940', 29.
87. Wagner, 30.
88. BFRC: Charles E. Sorensen records series, Sorensen telegrams II, 23.06.19–21.06.20.
89. Kreuter, 'Die Ueberflutung Des Dänischen Automarktes Durch Ford'.
90. *Statistisk Aarbog*, 1922.
91. 6,000 is the average sales in 1920 and 1921. FMC: Balance Sheets, 1920 & 1921.
92. The study was conducted by Jørgen Burchardt and cited in Wagner, 'Domesticeringen af Ford i Danmark', 46–47.
93. Tolliday, 'The Rise of Ford in Britain', 18.
94. BFRC: Mira Wilkins papers, Beck.
95. The power of a car engine of this period was mainly determined by the number and volume of its cylinders. In England, cars were taxed according not to the full volume, but only the bore (diameter) of its engines. Ford's engines obtained their volume by a shorter stroke, but a larger bore compared to most English car engines. Consequently, Ford cars would be taxed considerably more than English cars with engines of roughly the same power. See Roberts, *Ford Model Y: Henry's Car for Europe*, 8–9.
96. Toft, Rasmussen, and Nielsen, *Hundrede års trafik: Trafikministeriet 1900–2000*, 14–20.
97. Møller, *Etaten og traditionerne: Dansk toldhistorie IV*, 227; Dam and Hansen, 'Oles nye autobil: Om registreringsafgiften i Danmark, før, nu og i fremtiden', 161.
98. BFRC: Mira Wilkins papers, Møller & Beck.
99. Examples in *Motor*, no 25, 12.08.1922. See also Wagner, 'Domesticeringen af Ford i Danmark', 37–39.
100. *Motor*, no. 26, 19.08. 1922.
101. Wilkins and Hill, *American Business Abroad*, 142–43; Nevins and Hill, *Ford: Expansion and Challenge 1915–1933*, 406. *Politiken*, 23.03.1924, 30.03.1924, & 04.05.1924. See also Figure 12.
102. *Ford Nyheder*, no. 3, 4, & 11, 1925.
103. Prices advertised in *Politiken*.
104. Despite its name, the Super Touring was Chevrolet's standard model. *Politiken*, 25.07.1924. A Citroën price list from November 1924 has kindly been made available from the private collection of Jens Møller Nicolaisen.
105. FMC: Balance sheets. To get the full number of units sold, 1529 tractors and 28 Lincoln cars should be added for 1923 and 531 and 7 respectively for 1916. Total sales figures for each year of the 1920s can be seen in Figure 41 in the appendix.
106. BFRC: Mira Wilkins papers, Falbe-Hansen; Knudsen, report.
107. BFRC: Agreements and Contracts subgroup, Knudsen; FMC: Minutes, vol. I, 25.06.1919.
108. FMC: Share Register.
109. FMC: Minutes, vol. I, 10.09.1920.
110. BFRC: Mira Wilkins papers, Carlson.
111. FMC: Minutes, vol. II, 31.03.1926.
112. BFRC: Mira Wilkins papers, Møller; *Ford Nyt*, June 1949.
113. Wilkins and Hill, *American Business Abroad*, 152–53.
114. Sørensen et al., 'Ford Denmark and the Scandinavian Market', 271.
115. FMC: Minutes, vol. I, 25.06.1919. For more details on F. Bülow's role as representative of Ford in Denmark, see p. 67.
116. FMC: Minutes, vol. 1, 15.08.1919.
117. FMC: Minutes, vol. 1, 10.09.1920.

118. See p. 69f.
119. FMC: Minutes, vol. I, 31.03.1921.
120. Bryan, *Henry's Lieutenants*, 155–56.
121. FMC: Minutes, vol. I, 31.03.1921.
122. The most obvious example during this period would be the decision to increase the company's share capital by DKK 29,500,000 to DKK 30,000,000, taken at a board meeting in Detroit in November 1923, with only Edsel B. Ford and Georg Carlson present. FMC: Minutes, vol. II, 05.11.1923.
123. Tolliday, 'Transplanting the American Model? US Automobile Companies and the Transfer of Technology and Management to Britain, France and Germany, 1928–1962', 81; Tolliday, 'The Origins of Ford of Europe: From Multidomestic to Transnational Corporation, 1903–1976', 158f.
124. FMC: Minutes, vol. I–III, 31.03.1921–27.03.1929.
125. BFRC: Nevins and Hill research, Sorensen to E.B. Ford.
126. FMC: Minutes, vol. II, 31.03.1924 & 01.08.1925. BFRC: Mira Wilkins papers, Carlson.
127. Bryan, *Henry's Lieutenants*, 148.
128. BFRC: Nevins and Hill research, Moekle.
129. Wilkins and Hill, *American Business Abroad*, 100.
130. BFRC: Nevins and Hill research, Moekle.
131. BFRC: Nevins and Hill research, Briggs.
132. BFRC: Mira Wilkins papers, Carlson. Wilkins and Hill, *American Business Abroad*, 107–08. Wilkins and Hill remark that while managers in England, France, and Spain were replaced, Harrington in Denmark remained as the only one. This is not entirely correct, as Harrington in fact left Copenhagen in late 1920. But of course, in his case it could be argued, that it was more of a promotion than a replacement.
133. Wilkins and Hill, 157.
134. BFRC: Nevins and Hill research, auditors to Detroit.
135. BFRC: Nevins and Hill research, Briggs.
136. Wilkins and Hill, *American Business Abroad*, 157.
137. BFRC: Edsel B. Ford office papers, EBF memoranda. See also p. 105..
138. FMC: Minutes, vol. II, 05.11.1923.
139. BFRC: Mira Wilkins papers, Møller.
140. The design and setting up of the production facilities at River Rouge were in fact just as much due to William Knudsen. But Knudsen was sidelined by Sorensen, as the latter took over *de facto* management of the Rouge. This was one of the reasons why Knudsen decided to leave Ford Motor Company. See Bryan, *Henry's Lieutenants*, 155 & 268–69.
141. BFRC: Charles E. Sorensen records series, Sorensen telegrams II & recapitulations. These sources are also used for the following.
142. Ford, *My Life and Work*, 151.
143. Mansa, 'Kraftmaskinanlæget paa Ford Motor Company's Fabrik i Sydhavnen: Foredrag holdt i Konstruktørforeningen den 24/3 1925'.
144. BFRC: Nevins and Hill research, Carlson re. expenses.
145. BFRC: Nevins and Hill research, Carlson re. expenses.
146. Wilkins and Hill, *American Business Abroad*, 139.
147. FMC: Minutes, vol. II, 31.03.1926.
148. BFRC: Mira Wilkins papers, Carlson.
149. Hounshell, *From the American System to Mass Production 1800–1932*, 283.
150. See p. 45 above.
151. Sørensen, 'Ford i Danmark 1919–1966: Danske holdninger og Fords betydning', 105. Sørensen also suggests that prime minister C. Th. Zahle was involved in the decision. That might well be, but the specific source cited by Sørensen does not substantiate this claim.
152. BFRC: Mira Wilkins papers, Falbe-Hansen; *Kraks Blaa Bog*.
153. FMC: Minutes, vol. I, 07.11.1921.
154. Ipsen, *Kgl. Dansk Automobil Klubs' Lommebog for Motorkørende 1925*, 150.
155. BFRC: Mira Wilkins papers, Møller.
156. FMC: Abridged Balance Sheets, 1919–1927.
157. FMC: Minutes, vol. I, 31.03.1921 & vol. II, 31.03.1923.
158. FMC: Minutes, vol. II, 05.11.1923 & 20.03.1924.

159. Johansen, *Industriens vækst og vilkår 1870–1973*, 190.
160. *Ford Nyheder,* no. 4, 1924.
161. See Table 2 on p. 95.
162. Ford, *Today and Tomorrow*, 260–61.
163. See p. 22.
164. Christensen, *Fabriksarbejdere og Funktionærer 1870–1972*, 184, table 3.5.
165. Note to all workers at Ford Motor Company A/S, March 1920, in ABA: SSMF, correspondence, file 1060. KB: *Overenskomst med Ford Motor Company,* 18.10.1922.
166. Ford, *My Life and Work*, 87.
167. For more on the workplace culture among skilled industrial workers, see Christensen, *Smedesvend og friherre: Maskinarbejde og arbejdskultur i København 1889–1914*, chapters 7 & 8.
168. Knudsen, *Dansk fagbevægelses historie frem til 1950: Fra arbejdets perspektiv*, 505.
169. Twice in 1934 it was discovered by members of the Metal Workers' Union that one of their colleagues was not a union member. In both cases, the person in question was soon "persuaded" to join the union. ABA: DM, protocols, 19.03.1934 & 21.08.1934.
170. As an example, the leading shop steward and chairman of the combined union club almost always belonged to one of these two unions.
171. These figures of course include members in all of the auto and bicycle industry, not only at Ford. ABA: DM, protocols 25.09.1919 & 20.07.1927. In 1972 the name of the association was changed from *Dansk Smede- og Maskinarbejderforbund* to *Dansk Metalarbejderforbund* (Danish Metalworkers' Association). Its archives are referenced by the latter name, even for the period before 1972.
172. The Upholsterers' Association was Scandinavian in scope until 1942–1943, when it was split into national associations.
173. ABA: DM, protocols 16.10.1924.
174. Christensen, *Septemberforliget 1899*, 66ff.
175. While its main features had been established during the first decade of the 20th century, it was not dubbed the Danish model of industrial relations by social scientists until some 80 years later. See for instance Due and Madsen, '20 år med den danske model'. For a critical approach to the concept, see Borchorst, Caraker, and Jørgensen, 'Den danske model i knibe—også for analytisk potentiale?'
176. See p. 230ff.
177. Letters to Lyngsie 02.02.1920 & 06.03.1920 in ABA: SSMF, correspondence, file 269/F.
178. Arnold and Faurote, *Ford Methods and the Ford Shops*, 372.
179. In 1925, 22 percent of all blue-collar industrial workers in Denmark were women. But women were mostly concentrated in certain trades, such as textile, and made up only five percent in the metal industries (*Erhvervstællingen,* 1925, table III, pp. 138–39). A special union for female industrial workers existed (KAD afd. 5), but there is no trace of this union being active at Ford.
180. Figure 14, p. 80.
181. ABA: SSMF, protocols, 07.10.1919; Letters to Lyngsie 02.02.1920 & 06.03.1920 in ABA: SSMF, correspondence, file 269/F.
182. ABA: SSMF, protocols, 03.02.1920, Letter to Lyngsie 02.02.1920 in SSMF, correspondence, file 269/F.
183. ABA: DM, protocols 28.01.1920; SSMF, protocols, 03.02.1920; SF, protocols of board meetings, 22.01.1920 & 04.02.1920; ABA: SSMF, letter to Ford Motor Company 12.02.1920 in correspondence, file 269/F.
184. Letter to Lyngsie 02.02.1920 in ABA: SSMF, correspondence, file 269/F.
185. ABA: SSMF, memorandum dated 23.02.1920 in correspondence, file 269/F.
186. Wage scheme in ABA: SSMF, correspondence, file 1060.
187. Letter to Brun 13.03.1920 in ABA: SSMF, correspondence, file 269/F; ABA: SF, protocols of board meetings, 03.03.1920, 10.03.1920, & 16.03.1920. The wage scheme is presented in more detail below.
188. BFRC: Edsel B. Ford office papers, EBF, memoranda.
189. Nevins and Hill, *Ford: Expansion and Challenge 1915–1933*, 325.
190. *Politiken*, 25.11.1919. It is likely that the paper had confused tailors with upholsterers.

191. BFRC: Agreements and Contracts subgroup, Knudsen. Average wages in *Statistisk Aarbog*, 1919.
192. Wage scheme in ABA: SSMF, correspondence, file 1060.
193. Wilkins and Hill, *American Business Abroad*, 53.
194. ABA: SSMF, correspondence, file 1060.
195. The Danish Krone was back to its original gold value again in late 1927, and consequently the actual exchange rate with the US dollar was, from that year and until the crisis in the beginning of the 1930s, equal to the par value used by Ford. Hansen, *Økonomisk vækst i Danmark: 1914–1970*, 2:25.
196. Danish wages in ABA: SSMF, correspondence, file 1060, 1920, and *Overenskomst med Ford Motor Company*, 18.10.1922. Exchange rates in *Statistisk Aarbog*, 1920, table 86 and 1923, table 91. Detroit wages in Nevins and Hill, *Ford: Expansion and Challenge 1915–1933*, 327 & 330.
197. Christensen, Hansen, and Kolstrup, *Arbejdernes Historie i Danmark 1800–2000*, 129–30.
198. ABA: SSMF, correspondence, file 1060; KB: *Overenskomst*, October 1922, *Overenskomst*, November 1926 & *Arbejdsregulativ*, April 1930.
199. ABA: SSMF, correspondence, file 1822.
200. These percentages are of course very rough approximations, possibly covering up substantial individual variations.
201. Nevins and Hill, *Ford: Expansion and Challenge 1915–1933*, 327.
202. Johansen, *Dansk økonomisk statistik 1814–1980*, 301.
203. Wage scheme in ABA: SSMF, correspondence, file 1060; KB: Arbejdsregulativ, April 1930.
204. *Arbejderbladet*, 07.09.1928.
205. Wage scheme in ABA: SSMF, correspondence, file 1060.
206. ABA: SSMF, protocols, 06.04.1920.
207. Nevins and Hill, *Ford: Expansion and Challenge 1915–1933*, 330.
208. *Ford Nyheder*, no. 2, September 1924.
209. *Arbejderbladet*, 09.03.1928.
210. Ford, *My Life and Work*, 262–63; Wilkins and Hill, *American Business Abroad*, 49.
211. Wilkins and Hill, *American Business Abroad*, 101.
212. Montgomery, *The Fall of the House of Labor: The Workplace, the State, and American Labor Activism, 1865–1925*, 424 & 438; Brody, 'Elements of Paradox in U.S. Labor History', 49.
213. ABA: DM, protocols 04.12.1920.
214. *Jærn og Metalarbejderen*, no. 4, 1928, 62.
215. KB: *Overenskomst med Ford Motor Company*, 18.10.1922.
216. 10 percent extra was paid for working night shifts in Detroit, but only for a short period, and it was removed around 1921 as part of the general pressure for cost reduction in the early 1920s. Nevins and Hill, *Ford: Expansion and Challenge 1915–1933*, 329.
217. For the Danish names of organisations and institutions referenced by their English names, see pp. 336–37 in the appendix.
218. Knudsen, *Arbejdskonflikternes historie i Danmark: Arbejdskampe Og Arbejderbevægelse 1870–1940*, 173ff.
219. See p. 117.
220. "Til alle arbejdere", etc., 31.12.1924, in ABA: SSMF, correspondence, file 1292.
221. BFRC: Mira Wilkins papers, Carlson part 2. It is possible though, that Carlson is confusing his reminiscence with the criticism he received from Detroit of the consumption of alcohol on the occasion of the factory opening in November 1924.
222. Christensen, *Smedesvend og friherre*, 82–83; Knudsen, *Dansk fagbevægelses historie frem til 1950*, 312–14 & 352. The concept of "parliamentarism at the workplace" was a reference to a parallel struggle going on in the political realm, to establish the principles of parliamentarism.
223. *Ekstra Bladet*, 27.02.1925.
224. Letters, transcripts of the minutes of the Board of arbitration and other documents in ABA: SSMF, correspondence, file 1292. *Den faste Voldgiftsrets Kendelser*, case no. 843, 1925.
225. Bryan, *Henry's Lieutenants*, 207–09.

226. ABA: SSMF, correspondence, file 1347. *Jærn og Metalarbejderen*, no. 4, 1928, 62.
227. ABA: DM, protocols 26.05.1926; Letter from unions, 15.06.1926, in ABA: SSMF, correspondence, file 1363.
228. *Jærn og Metalarbejderen*, no. 4, 1928. The critical tone of the article may have been influenced by the fact that it was written after Ford had announced that it would not renew its agreement with the unions.
229. ABA: DM, protocols, 04.12.1920, ABA: SSMF, protocols, 06.12.1920.
230. ABA: SSMF, protocols, 18.02.1925; *Clarté*, no. 10, 1926, 288.
231. ABA: SSMF, protocols, 09.06.1925 & 04.08.1925.
232. ABA: VF, protocols of board meetings, 25.06.1926.
233. Knudsen, *Dansk fagbevægelses historie frem til 1950*, 375.
234. Knudsen, 446f.
235. ABA: DM, protocols, 16.10.1924.
236. ABA: SSMF, protocols, 07.10.1924.
237. ABA: VF, protocols of general assemblies, 19.01.1926 & protocols of board meetings, 06.05.1926.
238. ABA: VF, protocols of board meetings, 06.05.1927. ABA: SSMF, protocols, 20.04.1927.
239. ABA: VF, protocols of general assemblies, 19.07.1927; ABA: SSMF, correspondence, file 1519.
240. ABA: SSMF, protocols, 24.04.1927.
241. ABA: SSMF, protocols, 03.05.1927.
242. ABA: SSMF, protocols, 19.04.1922.
243. *Jærn og Metalarbejderen*, no. 4, 1928, 62; ABA: SF, protocols of board meetings, 26.10.1920–28.11.1920; Letter to Lyngsie, 27.11.1926, in ABA: SSMF, correspondence, file 1467; KB: Småtryksafdelingen, *Overenskomst* 1926.
244. ABA: SSMF, protocols, 19.11.1927.
245. BFRC: Nevins and Hill research, notes from New York Times.
246. BFRC: Nevins and Hill research, postcard to Sorensen.
247. Bryan, *Henry's Lieutenants*, 272.
248. BFRC: Mira Wilkins papers, Møller.
249. BFRC: Nevins and Hill research, Møller on Labor. Unfortunately, the date and use of the note cannot be determined from its archival context, as it is part of the material which was compiled by Allan Nevins for his research during the 1950s, and never returned to its original location. But Møller states in his interview with Wilkins that he discussed the matter with both Charles Sorensen and Edsel Ford. It is not clear precisely how and when these talks took place, but according to other sources Møller was in Detroit in June 1927; see ABA: SSMF, protocols, 21.06.1927.
250. BFRC: Mira Wilkins papers, Møller.
251. ABA: SSMF, correspondence, file 1554.
252. Letter from Ford, 20.10.1927, in ABA: SSMF, correspondence, file 1554.
253. ABA: SSMF, protocols, 04.10.1927–18.07.1928. ABA: DM, protocols, 04.10.1927–29.02.1928. ABA: VF, protocols of board meetings, 07.10.1927–20.01.1928, ABA: SF, protocols of board meetings, 04.10.1927–08.08.1928.
254. ABA: SSMF, protocols, 22.07.1928.
255. ABA: DM, protocols, 01.11.1928.
256. ABA: SF, protocols of general assemblies, 17.10.1928.
257. ABA: DM, protocols, 01.11. 1928.
258. ABA: SSMF, protocols, 19.11.1927.
259. ABA: DM, protocols, 14.12.1928; ABA: SF, protocols of board meetings, 14.11.1928.
260. ABA: SF, protocols of board meetings, 14.11.1928–27.11.1928.
261. *Arbejderbladet*, 07.09.1928.
262. Gelsted, 'The Show Boat'. Translated by R.P. Keigwin. Original Danish title: 'Reklameskibet'.
263. 'Amerika i Kjøbenhavn', *Politiken*, 20.11.1919.
264. *Social-Demokraten*, 25.11.1919; *Politiken*, 25.11.1919.
265. *Ingeniøren*, no. 38, 1920, 311–12.
266. Casey, *The Model T*, 86.
267. *Motor*, 10.01.1920, 20.05.1922, & 15.03.1924.
268. Motzkus, *100 år i bilistens tjeneste: Historien om FDM*, 12–15 & 26; Engelstoft and Dahl, *Dansk Biografisk Leksikon*, 16:591–92.
269. *Politiken*, 27.09.1925.

270. *Politiken*, 05.04.1925.
271. See p. 70.
272. FMC: Balance sheets 1919–1927, relevant years.
273. FMC: Balance sheets 1919–1927.
274. *Politiken*, 08.09.1923.
275. The price of a Chevrolet Tourist Model was DKK 4,664 in January 1923, as compared to DKK 2,650 for a Ford T Touring. *Politiken*, 06.01.1923 & 14.01.1923.
276. Some of the GM ads might have been dealer ads, as they were signed by both Bülow and General Motors.
277. Judged from cursory reading of *Politiken* in this and earlier periods. Generally, modern marketing, partly inspired by the USA, was introduced in Denmark from around 1920 onwards. Kjær-Hansen and Olufsen, *Reklamen i det 20. århundredes Danmark*, 40–42.
278. Hawkins, *Certain Success*, 15.
279. Casey, *The Model T*, 74ff.
280. Casey, 82.
281. *Politiken*, 17.05.1925 & 09.12.1925; 09.12.1926.
282. Thomsen, *Da reklamen var ung*, 32 & 68. The poster for the 1924 Ford exhibition seen in Figure 18 was produced by Sylvester Hvid.
283. None of the ads that Ford Motor Company A/S published in *Politiken* in the 1920s are similar to American ads from the same time, published in Casey, *The Model T*, 76ff.
284. See for instance *Politiken*, 02.11.1925, 24.11.1925, 18.11.1925, 27.11.1925, & 09.12.1925, 21.02.1926, 20.04.1926, 05.09.1926, & 14.09.1926.
285. See for instance *Politiken*, 02.11.1925, 20.04.1926, 05.09.1926, & 14.09.1926. Furthermore, a full-size advert based on this pattern in *Politiken* 21.02.1926 makes reference to the South port factory and features a drawing of the plant.
286. *En Tur gennem Danmark med Ford.*
287. I am thankful to Thomas B. Møller of the local history archive at Museum Lolland-Falster for checking the directories of Nykøbing Falster on my request and confirming that no veterinarian by the name Bramsen is to be found..
288. *Motor*, no. 2, 12.01.1924; *Politiken*, 26.09.1924, 20.04.1925; 05.11.1926; *Ford Nyheder*, no. 5, May 1925 & no. 12, December 1926; Thalbitzer, *Ford Motor Company A/S gennem 25 Aar*, 74.
289. See p. 72.
290. *Politiken*, 06.01.1924 & 13.01.1924; *Motor*, no. 2, 12.01.1924.
291. Hounshell, *From the American System to Mass Production 1800–1932*, 283.
292. Thalbitzer, *Ford Motor Company A/S gennem 25 Aar*, 100.
293. *Ford Nyheder*, no. 6 & 7, 1926.
294. *Social-Demokraten*, 16.11.1924.
295. *Politiken*, 16.11.1924.
296. *Politiken*, 16.11.1924.
297. *Ford-Ejer Magasinet*, no. 4, December 1924.
298. *Politiken*, 01.10.1924. The ad was placed in a special section, published to celebrate the 40th anniversary of the newspaper. A number of business associates, including regular advertisers, had contributed with ads, of which Ford was the only larger car company represented. For later examples, see *Politiken*, 04.03.1934, 04.11.1934, & 19.01.1936.
299. *Ford Nyheder*, no. 3, 4, 5, & 6, 1925; *Ford Nyt*, no. 1, 1960.
300. See for example *Ford Nyheder*, no. 3, 1924.
301. *Ford Nyheder*, no. 1, 1925; Letter from Ford 03.12.1928 in ABA: SSMF, correspondence, file 1554.
302. *Ford Nyheder*, 1924, 1.
303. *Ford Nyheder*, 1924, no. 3, 1925, no. 2, 3, & 5, 1926, no. 6, 7, 11, & 12.
304. *Ford Nyheder*, no. 2 & 8 1924, no. 7 1925; *The Dearborn Independent* contained anti-Semitic content of a blatantly propagandist nature, see Eifert, 'Antisemit und Autokönig: Henry Fords Autobiographie und ihre deutsche Rezeption in den 1920er-Jahren', 213f.
305. One exception is the national-conservative writer H.J. Hansen, who made reference to Ford's publication *The International Jew* and to *The Dearborn Independent* in his anti-Semitic articles in the newspaper *Jyllands-Posten*. Thing, *Jyllands-posten, diktaturet,*

Krystalnatten og jøderne, 9. Parts of *The International Jew* were published in Danish in 1940 by a small publishing house of the far right, presumably in an unauthorized version: Ford, *Uddrag af Henry Fords Bog: 'The international Jew'* (Den internationale Jøde).
306. See for example the sarcastic comments on the "moral preaching" of Henry Ford by the editor in *Finanstidende*, 06.10.1926, followed by a comment in his defence by MSc in Economics Ove Lundbye, 20.10.1926. Also the chapter by MSc in Economics P.P. Sveistrup on Ford and the assembly line in Gammelgaard et al., *Industrien: Muligheder og Vilkaar*, 110ff.
307. Ford, *Mit Liv og mit Arbejde*.
308. Ford, *Idag og imorgen*; Ford, *Fremad—stadig fremad*.
309. *Protokol for den 20. Socialdemokratiske Partikongres i Vejle den 12.–15. Juni 1927*, 48–49. The original wording of the quotation is "An unemployed man is an out of-work customer"; Ford, *Today and Tomorrow*, 150.

1928–1940 · Time for Change
pp. 141–193

1. Thalbitzer, *Ford Motor Company A/S gennem 25 Aar*, 30.
2. Both photos in Thalbitzer, 78. The photos are not dated, but the cars featured are late 1930 models.
3. See pp. 29–30.
4. Nieuwenhuis and Wells, 'Ford, Budd, and the History of Mass Production', 63–65; Hounshell, *From the American System to Mass Production 1800–1932*, 274.
5. FMC: *Ford Salgshaandbog*, s. 55; Gelardi, *Automobilets Historie og dets Mænd*, 3:441–42.
6. Hyldtoft and Johansen, *Teknologiske forandringer i dansk industri 1896–1972*, 170.
7. The first record of electric welding stations is in an insurance report from 1943, when 36 were registered. As there would have been little use for new stations from 1940 onwards, they were probably all installed during the 1930s. RA: Skafor 8018, Report 07.06.1943.
8. Lundkvist, 'Elektrisk svejsning'.
9. Blaszczyk, *The Color Revolution*, 116.
10. Blaszczyk, 116.
11. See p. 76..
12. Blaszczyk, *The Color Revolution*, 119ff; Jakobsen, *Spray Painting Hazards: A Clinical and Experimental Hæmatological Study with Special Reference to Changes in the Differential Blood Cell Count*, 15ff; Wojcik and Frese-Madsen, *General Motors International A/S*.
13. Blaszczyk, *The Color Revolution*, 116 & 121; Nielsen, 'Lidt om automobillakering', 15.
14. See for instance ABA: VF, protocols of board meetings, 04.02 1927.
15. Boggess, 'The Customer Can Have Any Color He Wants—So Long As It's Black', 39.
16. Thalbitzer, *Ford Motor Company A/S gennem 25 Aar*, 30; *Politiken*, 18.02.1927; *Ford Nyt*, 1931, 2.
17. *Ford Nyt*, 1938, 2; Preisler, *Malerarbejde i Praksis*, 667.66-12.
18. Geertsen, *Vognmalerfaget i Kbh. indtil 1940 med særlig henblik på Vognmalernes Fagforening i København 1915–40*, 44 & 55.
19. Larsen, 'Har Sprøjteapparaterne deres berettigelse i Malerhaandværket?', 41. The auther was head of the painting section at the Danish Technological Institute.
20. Markussen, 'Danish Industry, 1920–1939: Technology, Rationalization and Modernization', 253; Jacobsen, *Velfærdens pris: Arbejderbeskyttelse og arbejdsmiljø gennem 150 år*, 256.
21. Jakobsen, *Spray Painting Hazards*.
22. Jakobsen, 'Om Ducolakkers indvirkning paa den menneskelige Organisme'; Jakobsen, 'Om Celluloselakkers indvirkning paa den menneskelige Organisme'; Lind, 'Om Sundhedsfarer ved sprøjtemaling, I'; Lind, 'Om Sundhedsfarer ved sprøjtemaling, II'.
23. ABA: VF, protocols of general assemblies, 26.10.1937, 25.10.1938, & 27.04.1939; protocols of board meetings, 06.08.1935, 10.09.1935, 09.07.1937, & 13.11.1937.
24. Jakobsen, *Spray Painting Hazards*, 84–85.
25. Jakobsen, 359ff.
26. The first dissertation in this area was published in 1937, on the possible toxic effect of fluorides in the chemical industry, followed by three more in the late 1930s, including the one by Jakobsen.

27. Jacobsen, *Velfærdens pris*, 242ff.
28. Refsgaard, 'Er sprøjtelakering sundhedsfarlig?'
29. The relative size of the "big three" automakers depends on which scale is used for measuring. Measured by value, General Motors had total assets of $1,098 million in 1928, while Ford's assets would amount to $742 million and those of Chrysler to $236 million. Nevins and Hill, *Ford: Expansion and Challenge 1915-1933*, 476.
30. *Politiken*, 09.02.1928. At launch, the model range also included a Roadster, a Coupe, and a Sports Coupe.
31. *Politiken*, 09.02.1928 & 22.06.1928.
32. These figures were total sales. But in 1930–1931 the vast majority of units sold were different versions of the Model A. In 1930 total sales were made up of 12,568 Model A passenger cars and vans, 7,104 Model A trucks, 15 Lincoln passenger cars, and 347 tractors. FMC: Deliveries 1927–1946.
33. *Politiken*, 01.06.1932, 26.02.1933, & 02.06.1933.
34. FMC: Minutes, vol. IV, 13.09.1933. For more about the marketing activities, see p. 181f.
35. Thalbitzer, *Ford Motor Company A/S gennem 25 Aar*, 42. FMC: Deliveries 1927–1946.
36. Lund, *Kongelig køreglæde: Med benzin og blåt blod i årerne*, 64ff. *Ford Nyt*, no. 2, 1939.
37. FMC: Deliveries, 1927–1946.
38. Wilkins and Hill, *American Business Abroad*, 186 & 199.
39. Roberts, *Ford Model Y*, 54; Thalbitzer, *Ford Motor Company A/S gennem 25 Aar*, 41.
40. *Politiken*, 04.10.1933.
41. Tolliday, 'The Origins of Ford of Europe: From Multidomestic to Transnational Corporation, 1903-1976', 163; Roberts, *Ford Model Y*, 141.
42. Tolliday, 'The Origins of Ford of Europe', 164; Roberts, *Ford Model Y*, 194. Citing the same source as Tolliday, Roberts gives the surprising number of 3,898 units sold from Helsinki. However, this includes 3,740 units allegedly sold in 1935, compared to less than 100 for the other years. Therefore I assume this to be a misreading from the sources, and the number given by Tolliday to be correct.
43. FMC: Deliveries, 1927–1946.
44. Roberts, *Ford Model Y*, 150ff; Tolliday, 'The Origins of Ford of Europe', 162. German quotes in English: "in steel an iron by the labour of skilled German workers", "the car for everyone" and "popular type".
45. Oswald, *Deutsche Autos 1920-1945: Alle deutschen Personenwagen der damaligen Zeit*, 112ff.
46. See p. 73.
47. Wilkins and Hill, *American Business Abroad*, 155.
48. Wilkins and Hill, 187–89.
49. Wilkins and Hill, 193ff.
50. Wilkins and Hill, 305.
51. Wilkins and Hill, 193–96 & 358.
52. BFRC: Mira Wilkins papers, Beck.
53. FMC: Minutes 1926–1932, 10.05.1929.
54. Wilkins and Hill, *American Business Abroad*, 193–97.
55. FMC: Reorganisation. *Politiken*, 14.05.1929; Sørensen et al., 'Ford Denmark and the Scandinavian Market', 282–83.
56. 12 million DKK nominal worth of shares were owned by Ford of England, 10 million by Ford Motor Company A/S, and 8 million by outside investors.
57. FMC: Minutes, vol. IV, 27.03.1934.
58. FMC: Minutes, 1926–1932, 27.03.1929 & 10.05.1929.
59. BFRC: Mira Wilkins papers, Falbe-Hansen.
60. Wilkins and Hill, *American Business Abroad*, 295. At least three visits by Sorensen are recorded in the minutes of board meetings between 1929 and 1940.
61. FMC: Minutes, vol. III, 10.05.1929, vol. IV, 09.10.1935 & 27.03.1936.
62. Between 1929 and early 1938, Perry was present at 18 out of 30 board meetings. From early 1938 until the occupation in April 1940, he took part in only one out of ten.
63. FMC: Minutes, vol. IV, 12.08 1936.
64. As revealed by telegrams and other items of communication in his archive.

65. FMC: Minutes, vol. IV, 07.12.1933 & 28.12.1933; KB: Regnskab, 1934.
66. Wilkins and Hill, *American Business Abroad*, 246.
67. Tolliday, 'The Origins of Ford of Europe', 160–66; Wilkins and Hill, *American Business Abroad*, 295.
68. Wilkins and Hill, *American Business Abroad*, 296.
69. BFRC: Mira Wilkins papers, Falbe-Hansen.
70. BFRC: Mira Wilkins papers, Møller.
71. FMC: Minutes, 1926–1932, 27.03.1930; KB: Regnskab, 1929.
72. Toft, Rasmussen, and Nielsen, *Hundrede års trafik*, 22.
73. See Figure 43 in the Appendix for details.
74. Technically, the dividend was 15 percent, with an added bonus of 5 percent.
75. Wilkins and Hill, *American Business Abroad*, 252.
76. Tolliday, 'The Origins of Ford of Europe', 170.
77. Wojcik and Frese-Madsen, *General Motors International A/S: 1923-1974*, 42f.; Industriregistreringen, acc. 2047.
78. Industriregistreringen, acc. 1422.
79. Industriregistreringen, acc. 1426; *Samling af Anmeldelser til Handelsregistrene*, 1934, no. 9; *Kraks Blaa Bog*, 1950, 1467–1468.
80. *Erhvervstællingen,* 1925, table II, pp. 120–21 & 1935, table I, pp. 110–11.
81. Thomsen, *Industri, stat og samfund 1870-1939*, 211; Hansen, *Økonomisk vækst i Danmark: 1914-1970*, 2:41ff.
82. Thomsen, *Industri, stat og samfund 1870-1939*, 296 & 300.
83. Hansen, *Økonomisk vækst i Danmark: 1914-1970*, 2:50.
84. BFRC: Mira Wilkins papers, Møller; FMC: Minutes, vol. IV, 12.09.1932.
85. FMC: Minutes, vol. III, 31.07.1930.
86. 'Møller, H.C.', *Kraks Blaa Bog*, 1947.
87. Hounshell, *From the American System to Mass Production 1800-1932*, 283.
88. BFRC: Mira Wilkins papers, Møller.
89. *Statistisk Aarbog*, 1934.
90. Christensen, Hansen, and Kolstrup, *Arbejdernes historie i Danmark 1800-2000*, 167–69.
91. Christensen, *Fabriksarbejdere og funktionærer 1870-1972*, 249–52.
92. *Jern- og Metalarbejderen*, no. 5, 1930, 79–80; BFRC: Charles E. Sorensen records series, Perry Report.
93. ABA: DM, protocols, 18.12.1929.
94. Letter, 05.08.1932 in ABA: SSMF, correspondence, file 1822.
95. ABA: DM, protocols, 24.08.1932; Letter, 17.10.1932 in ABA: SSMF, correspondence, file 1822.
96. Letter, 16.01.1933 in ABA: SSMF, correspondence, file 1895.
97. Report (no date but must be from *ultimo* March 1935 according to content) in ABA: SSMF, correspondence, file 1895; *Arbejderbladet*, 04.04.1935; ABA: DM, protocols, 12.04.1935.
98. ABA: VF, protocols of general assemblies, 27.04.1938.
99. ABA: SSMF, correspondence, file 1709.
100. Specialised Workmens' Union would become part of the Metalworkers' Association in 1957.
101. ABA: SSMF, correspondence, file 2423.
102. Transcript of ruling by the court, 12.10.1931, in ABA: SSMF, correspondence, file 1709.
103. Based on samples from randomly selected years in FMC: Balance sheets.
104. ABA: SSMF, correspondence, file 1822.
105. This does not take into account the negative effects on employment caused by the lack of parts for assembly during and immediately after WWII, as discussed in the following chapters.
106. ABA: DM, protocols, 26.03.1935.
107. ABA: DM, protocols, 15.12.1932, 25.04.1935, 06.06.1939, & 07.09.1939.
108. ABA: SSMF, correspondence, file 1822 & protocol 06.10.1931; ABA: DM, protocols, 10.12.1931.
109. ABA: SSMF, correspondence, file 2217. DM, 14.07.1936.
110. Andersen, *Fra erhvervsråd til økonomisk tænketank*, 2.

111. ABA: DM, protocols, 18.07.1935, 04.02.1936, 22.04.1936, 20.10 1936, 30.08.1938, & 11.10.1938; ABA: SSMF, protocols, 07.02.1939.

112. ABA: DM, protocols, 20.10.1936.

113. ABA: DM, protocols, 04.05.1932, 11.05.1932, 01.11.1932, & 07.11.1932

114. Knudsen, 'Kampen om samlebåndet: Rationalisering og arbejderbevægelse i Danmark i 1920'erne', 126.

115. ABA: DM, protocols, 20.10.1932; KB: *Love for Fællesklubben paa Ford Motor Co., vedtaget på generalforsamlingen i november 1932.*

116. ABA: DM, protocols, 24.07.1928 & 07.05.1930.

117. ABA: DM. 26.03.1935 & 31.03.1936.

118. BFRC: Mira Wilkins papers, Møller.

119. Wilkins and Hill, *American Business Abroad*, 292–93; Tolliday, 'The Diffusion and Transformation of Fordism: Britain and Japan Compared', 67.

120. Kimes, *The Cars That Henry Ford Built*, 80; Watkins, *The 100 Greatest Advertisements 1852-1958: Who Wrote Them and What They Did*, 98–99.

121. *Politiken*, 23.01.1928.

122. No sources have been located in the FMC archive revealing the precise origin of any of Ford's advertisements.

123. *Ford Nyt*, no. 6, 1931.

124. None of the ads that Ford Motor Company A/S published in *Politiken* in the 1930s is similar to European ads from the same time published in Bonin, 'The Ford Brand's Image: Its Evolution from the 1930s to the 1980s'.

125. Hawkins, *Certain Success*, 317.

126. For a rare example, see *Politiken*, 02.06.1933.

127. Andersen and Sørensen, 'Fra Madison Avenue til København: Amerikaniseringen af reklamebranchen i 1920'erne', 60–61.

128. FMC: Minutes, vol. IV, 13.09.1933.

129. For an example, see *Politiken*, 16.12.1938.

130. The new name was just a shorter form of the original one, both meaning "Ford news".

131. *Ford Nyt*, 1931, 1.

132. *Ford Nyt*, 1933, 1. About Jonals Co., see Meyer, *Jonals Co. og det moderne fotografis gennembrud i Danmark*.

133. Andersen and Sørensen, 'Fra Madison Avenue til København'. "Frantz Harlang" in *Dansk Biografisk Leksikon*, vol. 6.

134. RA: Harlang & Toksvig, Hovedbog for tryksager, 1935–1936; *Ford Nyt*, 1938, 3.

135. *Ford Nyt*, no. 7 & 9–10, 1931.

136. *Ford Nyt*, no. 8, 1931 & no. 10, 1932; Thalbitzer, *Ford Motor Company A/S gennem 25 Aar*, 101; *Politiken*, 06.07.1931.

137. Thalbitzer, *Ford Motor Company A/S gennem 25 Aar*, 100.

138. Thalbitzer, *Ford Motor Company A/S gennem 25 Aar*, 102–03.

139. FMC: Minutes, vol. IV, 13.09.1933.

140. Thalbitzer, *Ford Motor Company A/S gennem 25 Aar*, 38 & 90 (photo). *Ford Nyt*, no. 9–10, 1934. BFRC: Charles E. Sorensen records series, annual General Manager's meeting, 1934.

141. FMC: Minutes, vol. III, 30.01.1931 & 15.09.1931.

142. For several examples, see Thalbitzer, *Ford Motor Company A/S gennem 25 Aar*, 91–98.

143. Thalbitzer, 91 (photo). Sørensen, 'Aarhus Motor Compagni A/S: Den største Ford-forretning i Europa', 8–14.

144. FMC: Minutes, vol. III, 31.01.1931.

145. Ford, *My Life and Work*, 188ff.

146. BFRC: Hauge, report.

147. Thomsen, *Industri, stat og samfund 1870-1939*, 299.

148. BFRC: Hauge, report.

149. FMC: Minutes, vol. IV, 11.07.1934.

150. FMC: Minutes, vol. III, 31.03.1932.

151. FMC: Minutes, vol. IV, 11.07.1934 & 27.03.1935.

152. See p. 96 above.

153. FMC: Minutes, vol. III, 18.05.1931, & 15.09.1931, vol. IV, 10.05.1936.

154. FMC: Minutes, vol. V, 20.07.1937.

155. Estape-Triay, 'Ford in Spain: The First Stage (1920-1954)', 430ff.

156. BFRC: Mira Wilkins papers, Beck; FMC: Minutes, vol. V, 21.12.1939, 19.02.1940, & 27.03.1940.

157. FMC: Minutes, vol. V, 27.03.1940.
158. FMC: Minutes, vol. V, 20.9.1939 & 21.12.1939.

1940–1945 · Interregnum
pp. 195–211

1. Christensen et al., *Danmark besat: Krig og hverdag 1940-45*, 125ff.
2. BFRC: Mira Wilkins papers, Beck.
3. FMC: Production.
4. FMC: Memorandum, 1944.
5. FMC: Memorandum, 1944.
6. FMC: Memorandum, 1944.
7. FMC: Memorandum, 1944. For more on the sabotage, see p. 210.
8. FMC: Memorandum, 1944.
9. See Figure 42 in the Appendix.
10. FMC: Minutes, vol. V, 27.03.1940; Christensen et al., *Danmark besat*, 71.
11. FMC: Production 1940–1944, balance sheets 1940–1944.
12. Petrick, *Die Okkupationspolitik des Deutschen Faschismus in Dänemark und Norwegen (1940-1945)*, 21.
13. Zgórniak, *Europa am Abgrund-1938*, 39f.
14. Christensen et al., *Danmark besat*, 128.
15. Christensen et al., 289.; Birgit Nüchel Thomsen, *Værnemagerne: Danmarks bidrag til den tyske krigsøkonomi under den tyske besættelse—i europæisk perspektiv*, 39.
16. FMC: Memorandum, 1944.
17. RA: Industrirådets arkiv, no. 89, file X.2798/A.9388, 05.09.1944 & 20.10.1945.
18. FMC: Minutes, vol. V, 09.04.1940.
19. Tolliday, 'The Origins of Ford of Europe', 166–67.
20. FMC: Memo, 1944.
21. Perry was re-elected as member of the board at each of the 5 general meetings held during the period of occupation, and as chairman at the following board meetings. FMC: Minutes, vol. V, 26.03.1941, 24.03.1942, 25.03.1943, & 17.03.1944, vol. VI, 21.03.1945.
22. Until the USA declared war on Germany in December 1941, it was in principle still possible to communicate with Dearborn. Such communication took place on a few occasions but seems to have been patchy.
23. Quoted from Christensen et al., *Danmark besat*, 197–98.
24. BFRC: Mira Wilkins papers, Beck.
25. BFRC: Mira Wilkins papers, Beck.
26. FMC: Minutes V, 16.09.1941 & 24.03.1942.
27. FMC: Minutes V, 17.06.1943.
28. Christensen et al., *Danmark besat*, 273.
29. Christensen et al., 274.
30. FMC: Balance sheets 1941; ABA: SSMF, correspondence, file 2767. The pay rate for work other than car assembly was stipulated as DKK 2.00 per hour, but with price-compensation and the contribution reserved for vacation, it reached DKK 2.58 on average during 1941.
31. FMC: Balance sheets 1939 & 1944; *Statistisk Aarbog*, 1940 & 1945.
32. ABA: SSMF, correspondence, file 2854.
33. ABA: SSMF, correspondence, file 2993.
34. ABA: DM, protocols, 25.05.1943.
35. Christensen et al., *Danmark besat*, 496ff.
36. RLS: Axel Sjølander, box 11.
37. Thalbitzer, *Ford Motor Company A/S gennem 25 Aar*.
38. Jensen, 'Ford for Mig!'
39. Information kindly provided to the author by Dr. Karola Fings, NS-Dokumentationszentrum der Stadt Köln.
40. FMC: Memorandum, 1944; Balance Sheets, 1945.
41. Sørensen et al., 'Ford Denmark and the Scandinavian Market', 290. Unfortunately Sørensen et al. does not offer any further reference to the source and nature of these rumours.
42. The application was handled by the Industrial Council; see RA: Industrirådets arkiv, no. 89, file X.2798/A.9388, 25.08.1943, 24.02.1944, 03.03.1944, & 20.03.1945. Unfortunately the application contains no exact information about the purpose and nature of the boats.
43. I am thankful to Mr. Karl Scheuch, editor of *Die Schnellboot-Seite* (http://s-boot.net/) who helped me, through personal communication, in identifying the boat type. See also https://de.wikipedia.org/wiki/Sprengboot_Linse. The boats built in Copenhagen share some distinguishing features with the

Linse-type, such as the overall form and the long outboard propeller shaft. The flange that can be seen around the bow may be for fixing the rail that activates the detonator. If the boats built in Copenhagen were *Sprengboote*, they must have been an improved version, since the hull was made from sheet metal, not wood as in the original type.

44. Kjeldbæk, *Sabotageorganisationen BOPA 1942–1945*, 124–25; Hansen, *Daglige Beretninger om Begivenheder under den Tyske Besættelse*, 325–26.

45. Hansen, *Daglige Beretninger om Begivenheder under den Tyske Besættelse*, 429.

46. According to the resistance database of the National Museum, all three were attached to the resistance movement. As mentioned below, in June 1945 they all received a donation from FMC, allegedly for carrying out the sabotage without damaging the rest of factory. FMC: Minutes, vol. VI, 14.06.1945; NM: Frihedsmuseets arkiv, Torben Fischer-Madsen, 07B-854.

47. Hansen, *Daglige Beretninger om Begivenheder under den Tyske Besættelse*, 703–04; RA: Industrirådets arkiv, no. 89, file X.2798/A.9388, 20.03.1945. The first account does not state the boats as being produced by Ford and the second does not give a date for the episode, but it is clear from the content that they must be about the same incident.

48. FMC: Minutes, vol. VI, 24.10.1944; NM: Modstandsdatabasen.

49. NM: Frihedsmuseets arkiv, Otto Carlé, 08A-13977-3; Kjeldbæk, *Sabotageorganisationen BOPA 1942–1945*, 124–25; Hansen, *Daglige Beretninger om Begivenheder under den Tyske Besættelse*, 325–26.

50. FMC: Minutes, vol. VI, 24.10.1944 & 14.06.1945; NM: Frihedsmuseets arkiv, Torben Fischer-Madsen, 07B-854.

51. Christensen et al., *Danmark besat*, 683. Thomsen, *Værnemagerne*, 77.

52. Thomsen, *Værnemagerne*, 154.

1945–1958 · New Expectations
pp. 213–255

1. Quoted from Sørensen et al., 'Ford Denmark and the Scandinavian Market', 292.

2. No exact numbers for production have been located for 1946–1947. But according to FMC: Beretning og Regnskab, 1946, production was "about half of pre-war production". Discussions in the Cooperation Committee, referenced in ABA: Vognmalers Klub, 09.07.1946–04.10.1948, reveal that production must have been very low, probably just a few hundred in 1947. For production figures for 1948 onwards, see Figure 41 in the Appendix.

3. RA: Skafor 8018, Reports 07.06.1943 & 12.08.1960.

4. *Ford Nyt*, July 1950.

5. ABA: VK, 23.04.1953, 09.11.1953, 16.05.1956, 02.10.1957, 23.10.1957, & 22.04.1958.

6. FMC: Copenhagen Summary.

7. FMC: Copenhagen Summary. The report has no date and no recipient stated but judging from the content it must be from late 1954 and directed at Ford's European management.

8. FMC: Copenhagen Summary.

9. FMC: Copenhagen Summary.

10. FMC: Minutes, vol. VII, 16.01.1956.

11. FMC: Minutes, vol. VII, 04.12. 1956.

12. The road was the current Sluseholmen.

13. ABA: SSMF, protocols, 05.03.1952; VF, protocols of board meetings, 16.06.1952.

14. Asher, 'The 1949 Ford Speedup Strike and the Post War Social Compact, 1946–1961', 137.

15. ABA: DM, protocols, 19.10.1955; VK, 15.10.1958. Workers' reactions to time studies are treated in more detail on p. 242f.

16. FMC: Deliveries; ABA: VK, 15.09.1947; *Ford Nyt*, July 1950.

17. BFRC: Mira Wilkins papers, Beck.

18. FMC: Minutes VI, 19.02.1946.

19. BFRC: Mira Wilkins papers, Beck.; BFRC: Mira Wilkins papers, Møller; Sørensen et al., 'Ford Denmark and the Scandinavian Market', 294.

20. On the origin of the Directorate for Product Supply, see p. 200.

21. *Politiken,* 02.10.1949. *Avisårbogen,* 30.01.1951.
22. The dollar premium was calculated as a percentage of the net price of the car, but when locally assembled the labour cost etc. could be deducted.
23. ABA: VK, 15.09.1947.
24. Photos and notes in OBL: Private collection; FMC: Beretning og Regnskab, 1948 & 1949.
25. FMC: Copenhagen Summary.
26. *Ford Nyt,* July 1950.
27. BFRC: Mira Wilkins papers, Beck.
28. Based on number of registered cars per year in *Statistisk Aarbog.*
29. FMC: Copenhagen Summary. Here and in the following, market share is understood as the relative share of the total number of cars sold that year. It should be taken into account that Opel was a subsidiary of General Motors, which had an additional market share of nine percent with their GM and Vauxhall brands.
30. FMC: Copenhagen Summary.
31. *Statistisk Årsbok för Sverige,* 1950 & 1959.
32. For yearly numbers, see Figure 41 in the Appendix.
33. *Ford Nyt,* July 1950.
34. Damkier, *Fra bilernes lømmelalder: 50'er biler,* 81 & 113.
35. The only exception being the 20M, launched in 1964, which was essentially a 17M with a V6 engine.
36. FMC: Financial Statements and Operation Reports, 1953 & 1958.
37. Tolliday, 'The Origins of Ford of Europe', 181; Wilkins and Hill, *American Business Abroad,* 365.
38. FMC: Copenhagen Summary.
39. *Ford Nyt,* November 1949; ABA: VK, 01.11.1955; FMC: Copenhagen Summary.
40. FMC: Beretning og Regnskab, 1953.
41. FMC: Financial Statements and Operation Reports, 1953 & 1958.
42. Damkier, *Fra bilernes lømmelalder: 50'er biler,* 98–101.
43. FMC: Financial Statements and Operation Reports, 1958.
44. FMC: Deliveries, 1927–1946.
45. Wilkins and Hill, *American Business Abroad,* 370.
46. Wilkins and Hill, 338 & 359.
47. Wilkins and Hill, 358–59.
48. Wilkins and Hill, 362.
49. *Ford Nyt,* April 1948. Apart from the four-page illustrated report, Henry II's speech at the dinner party was printed as a supplement.
50. Tolliday, 'The Origins of Ford of Europe', 174.
51. Wilkins and Hill, *American Business Abroad,* 370.
52. Wilkins and Hill, 371–72.
53. Wilkins and Hill, 376 & 379.
54. Wilkins and Hill, 377.
55. Wilkins and Hill, 365–66.
56. Tolliday, 'The Origins of Ford of Europe', 170. Tolliday refers to Denmark, Belgium, and the Netherlands as "small sales branches". But in fact all three had assembly plants. And measured by capital invested, Denmark was 62 percent the size of Ford in Germany and 74 percent of France.
57. FMC: Minutes VI, 16.06.1947 & 30.03.1948.
58. FMC: Minutes VI, 15.12.1949 & 16.03.1950.
59. FMC: Minutes VI, 31.07.1945.
60. FMC: Minutes VI, 06.03.1948, 27.04.1949, & 23.11.1950.
61. FMC: Minutes VII, 03.12.1954.
62. FMC: Minutes VI, 16.12.1948.
63. BFRC: Mira Wilkins papers, Beck; FMC: Minutes VI, 23.11.1950; Wilkins and Hill, *American Business Abroad,* 372. Møller himself does not touch upon his retirement in his interview with Wilkins.
64. BFRC: Mira Wilkins papers, Beck.
65. *Ford Nyt,* June & November 1949.
66. *Ford Nyt,* June 1952. FMC: Minutes VII: 03.03.1952.
67. *Ford Nyt,* November 1949.
68. FMC: Minutes VI, 16.06.1947 & 12.11.1947.
69. FMC: Minutes VI, 29.04.1950 & 07.06.1950.
70. FMC: Minutes VII, 24.06.1955 & 13.07.1955.
71. BFRC: Mira Wilkins papers, Beck.
72. FMC: Minutes VII, 16.01.1956.

73. E.g. FMC: Minutes VII, 03.12.1954.
74. FMC: Minutes VII, 09.04.1953 & Minutes 09.01.1964.
75. FMC: Minutes VII, 24.06.1955.
76. FMC: Minutes VI, 27.04.1949.
77. Bryan, *Henry's Lieutenants*, 33.
78. Nevins and Hill, *Ford. Decline and Rebirth, 1933–1962*, 302ff.
79. *Statistiske Meddelelser*, 4. rk., 126 bd., 3.hf, 1946.
80. Knudsen, *Dansk fagbevægelses historie frem til 1950*, 638–39.
81. According to Sjølander's own recollection, he was elected leading shop steward in 1941. But his predecessor was still signing letters in this capacity until December 1942. The first letter signed by Sjølander is from January 1943 (ABA: SSMF, correspondence, file 2993). Sjølander left his personal papers to a municipal archive. He is therefore the only blue-collar worker at Ford Motor Company A/S whose personal and political experiences can be documented in some detail.
82. Letters dated 26.12.1957 & Christmas 1957 in RLS: Axel Sjølander, box 12.
83. ABA: DM, protocols, 26.09.1945.
84. Letters dated 26.12.1957 & Christmas 1957 in RLS: Axel Sjølander, box 12.
85. ABA: SSMF, correspondence, file 4583.
86. Wilkins and Hill, *American Business Abroad*, 404–05.
87. ABA: SSMF, correspondence, file 4943 & 5083.
88. For examples, see ABA: SSMF, correspondence, files 4583, 4943, 5040, 5083, 5315, 5619, 5922, 6073, and 7020 plus unnumbered files, dated 01.03.1965 & 01.03.1966.
89. "Overenskomst" in Danish.
90. ABA: SSMF, correspondence, file 4583.
91. Dalgaard, *Ved demokratiets grænse: Demokratisering af arbejdslivet i Danmark 1919–1994*, 99ff.
92. Cf. Dalgaard, 132. Original in *Arbejdsgiveren*, 12, 1947.
93. Dalgaard, 128.
94. ABA: VK, 09.07.1946.
95. Unfortunately, no material relating to the committee can be located in the archive of the FMC. The main source for the workings of the committee is the protocol of the Coach Painters' Club, which contains detailed reports from its meetings during the first ten years of its existence.
96. ABA: VK, 09.07.1946.
97. ABA: VK, 09.07.1946.
98. ABA: VK, 09.07.1946.
99. ABA: VK, 24.01.1947.
100. ABA: VK, 25.03.1948 & 04.10.1948.
101. ABA: VK, 17.12.1947 & 04.10.1948.
102. ABA: VK, 25.03.1948.
103. ABA: VK, 17.12.1947 & 25.03.1948.
104. *Ford Nyt*, April 1948.
105. The letter and its content are only known indirectly from Henry Ford II's answer to Sjølander.
106. Letter from Henry Ford II, 1948 in RLS: Axel Sjølander, box 18.
107. Knudsen, *Amerikaniseringen af den danske fagbevægelse: Marshallhjælp, kold krig og transatlantiske forbindelser, 1945–1956*, 54–55.
108. Letter to Godfredsen, 1949, in RLS: Axel Sjølander, box 10.
109. *Land og Folk*, 12.01.1948. Letter dated Christmas 1957 and letter to Hans Rasmussen, 1966, in RLS: Axel Sjølander, box 12.
110. From 1954 to 1958 he was shop steward for the metal workers, and from then until 1961 he was again leading shop steward. Letter dated July 1963 in RLS: Axel Sjølander, box 12.
111. ABA: VK, 24.10.1946.
112. Letter dated Christmas 1957 in RLS: Axel Sjølander, box 12.
113. Letter dated Christmas 1957 in RLS: Axel Sjølander, box 12. Knudsen, *Dansk fagbevægelses historie frem til 1950*, 638.
114. Dalgaard, *Ved demokratiets grænse*, 123.
115. See for instance ABA: VK, 30.04.1947 & 17.12.1947, and 25.03.1948.
116. ABA: VK, 25.03.1948.
117. See for instance ABA: VK, 29.04.1954.
118. ABA: VK, 29.04.1957.
119. ABA: SSMF, protocols, 03.04.1952; DM, protocols, 11.05.1954.
120. ABA: SSMF, protocols, 05.03.1952; VF, protocols of board meetings, 16.06.1952.
121. See p. 32.

122. ABA: VF, protocols of board meetings, 15.01.1957; ABA: VK, 15.10.1958.
123. See p. 304.
124. According to ABA: DM, protocols, 19.10.1955, Detroit was sending standard assembly times to Copenhagen, but unfortunately, nothing is known about how these times were calculated, or if they differed from the standards used at the American plants. In theory, it would be possible to compare labour productivity on an aggregate level between Ford's American plants and Copenhagen, but this would not be meaningful, since the productive activities carried out in Copenhagen were only a subset of the total production of the American plants. To make a precise comparison it would be necessary to locate sources detailing the time spent assembling comparable units. The character of the source material kept at the Danish FMC archive makes it highly unlikely that such comparable numbers could be found.
125. Besides the two shop stewards from Ford, union representatives from General Motors, Nordisk Diesel Auto, DOMI, Bohnstedt Petersen, and Skandinavisk Motor Co. were invited. Jørgen Paldam of the Economic Council of the Labour Movement (Arbejderbevægelsens Erhvervsråd) also took an active part in the discussions at the meeting. ABA: SSMF, correspondence, file 5697.
126. *Amerika er anderledes: Med den danske fagforeningsdelegation til U.S.A.*
127. Knudsen, *Amerikaniseringen af den danske fagbevægelse*, 110 & 143. For details about the *Work Study Training Programme* see *Danske industriarbejdere i U.S.A.: Beretning fra 42 danske arbejderes ophold i U.S.A. i 1952–53*. The purpose and outcome of these trips will be discussed further on p. 304f.
128. ABA: VK, 23.04.1953, 28.10.1954, & 16.04.1955. The American Ford representative was referred to as Mr. Williams; his position in Ford is unknown.
129. ABA: DM, protocols, 20.06.1950 & 21.08.1950.
130. ABA: SSMF, correspondence, file 5697.
131. ABA: DM, protocols, 27.09.1955 & 15.11.1955.
132. Both numbers based on the collection of *Dansk Veteranbil Klub.* (Danish Vintage Car Club). See http://www.dvk-database.dk/bro_forside.htm. Brochures from Ford have been registered under two headings: Ford Europe and Ford USA. Despite this being the most complete repository of its kind, numbers may not be complete.
133. The brochures of the post-war period have been thoroughly presented in Bang, *Ford, forbrug og fortællinger om det lykkelige liv.*
134. *Ford Nyt*, June 1955.
135. ABA: VK, 30.04.1947, 15.09.1947, 17.12.1947, 25.03.1948, & 04.10.1948.
136. *Kraks Blaa Bog*, 1949.
137. According to Peter Sørensen, H.C. Møller was a man whose words carried weight and who had a reputation of being good at negotiating with the authorities. Unfortunately Sørensen does not provide any sources for his evaluation of Møller, but based on a general knowledge of Møller's activities it does not seem unjustified. Sørensen, 'Ford i Danmark 1919–1966', 115.
138. FMC: Minutes, 26.09.1952.
139. FMC: Minutes, 14.01.1954 & 03.12.1954.
140. FMC: Minutes, 20.06.1957. According to the minutes, a meeting had been held with the minister of finance. This is most likely an error since the political negotiations regarding import were handled by the minister of trade.
141. *Vejtransporten i Tekst og Tal,* 1959, 21.
142. Quoted from Bang, '*Ford, forbrug og fortællinger om det lykkelige liv*, 12. The article was actually a reference to criticism against "bad taste" in car design, voiced by a contemporary American observer.
143. Bang, 13f.
144. See p. 221.
145. The story was told to the author by Ben Larsen through personal communication. Ben Larsen is the son of Orla Larsen, who was the sales manager of Ford Motor Company A/S in this period. Ben Larsen was also employed by the company himself for a couple of years around 1960.
146. *Politiken*, 13.02.1958.
147. Bang, '*Ford, forbrug og fortællinger om det lykkelige liv*, 47–50.

148. *Ford Nyt,* April 1948 & August 1952.
149. *Ford Nyt,* April 1948. See also p. 223.
150. *Ford Nyt,* no. 1, 1956.
151. *Ford Nyt,* no. 2, 1958.
152. First article in *Berlingske Tidende,* 11.12.1949, last 29.12.1949. During the first week of Eriksen's visit, the paper carried at least one interview or article per day.
153. *Berlingske Tidende,* 15.12.1949.
154. Letter to Godfredsen, 1949, in RLS: Axel Sjølander, box 10.

1958–1966 · Expansion and Decline
pp. 257–279

1. *Politiken*, 23.01.1959.
2. Plan in RA: Skafor 8018, 31.01.1958.
3. RA: Skafor 8018, 31.01.1958. Quite surprisingly, considering its magnitude, there is no reference to it at all in any of the few previous written accounts of the history of Ford in Copenhagen.
4. *Ford Nyt*, no. 1, 1959.
5. FMC: Minutes, vol. VII, 25.03.1958; *Ford Nyt*, no. 1, 1959.
6. ABA: VK, 22.04.1958.
7. ABA: VK, 22.04.1958; FMC: Minutes, vol. VIII, 16.11.1959; RA: Skafor 8018, 06.12.1962.
8. FMC: Minutes, vol. VIII, 16.11.1959; RA: Skafor 8018, 12.08.1960.
9. RA: Skafor 8018, 12.08.1960.
10. FMC: Minutes, vol. VIII, 16.11.1959 & 09.08.1960. In November 1959, the board decided to invest roughly DKK 1 million. In August 1960, an investment of DKK 1.2 million was approved. Unfortunately, the minutes of the last meeting are not very specific, meaning that the latter amount could either be a confirmation and adjustment of the previous decision, or an additional investment.
11. Out of the total investments in 1959–1960, only DKK 415,000 was specifically designated for raising the production capacity, but some of the other investments probably contributed to this too. For comparison, the profit before tax was DKK 2.3 million in 1960. FMC: Beretning og regnskab, 1961.
12. *Ford Nyt*, no. 1, 1960.
13. *Ford Nyt*, no. 1, 1963.
14. See Figure 41 in the Appendix.
15. Tolliday, 'The Origins of Ford of Europe', 184ff.
16. Sørensen et al., 'Ford Denmark and the Scandinavian Market', 297.
17. *Statistisk Årbog*
18. 1953 numbers from FMC: Copenhagen Summary; 1964 numbers from Tolliday, 'The Origins of Ford of Europe', 185. Unfortunately, no comparable numbers have been found in the FMC archive for the 1960s. The numbers quoted from Tolliday refers to American sources. Unfortunately, these include only British- and German-made cars, but the market share of American Fords was almost negligible. For 1962 it can be calculated at 0.4 percent in Denmark from other sources (FMC: Financial Statements and Operation Reports, 1962 & *Vejtransporten i tal og tekst*, 8:15). It was probably not much higher in the other Nordic countries. For some reason, the absolute numbers given by Tolliday are clearly too high by a factor 1,000, which has been corrected here. All percentage figures have been rounded to the nearest integer.
19. Tolliday, 'The Origins of Ford of Europe', 185. Precisely how many of the cars sold in Sweden were assembled in Copenhagen is not known.
20. FMC: Minutes VIII, 09.08.1960 & 27.03.1961; *Ford Nyt*, no. 2, 1960.
21. For sales numbers during the early 1960s, see Figure 41 in the Appendix.
22. *Ford Nyt,* no. 1, 1960.
23. Tolliday, 'The Origins of Ford of Europe', 185. All percentage figures have been rounded to the nearest integer.
24. Tolliday, 'The Origins of Ford of Europe', 184.
25. FMC: Financial Statements and Operation Reports, 1962; Damkier, *På rette vej: 60'er biler*, 36ff & 91ff. While front-wheel drive had been offered by some competitors for a long time, most notably by Citroën since the 1930s, it was still only on the verge of becoming widespread.
26. Tolliday, 'The Rise of Ford in Britain', 33ff.

27. FMC: Financial Statements and Operation Reports, 1962. 1962 is the last year for which data on the sales numbers of different models have been found.
28. FMC: Financial Statements and Operation Reports, 1958–1962.
29. Bang, *Ford, forbrug og fortællinger om det lykkelige liv'*, 12f.
30. FMC: Minutes VIII, 09.08.1960 & 27.03.1961; *Ford Nyt*, no. 2, 1960.
31. FMC: Minutes VIII, 16.11.1959. No reason is given for Beck's retirement in the minutes, nor does he state one himself in his interview with Wilkins, which took place shortly after.
32. FMC: Minutes VIII, 04.071962.
33. FMC: Minutes VIII, 04.09.1961.
34. FMC: Minutes VIII, 28.04.1959.
35. FMC: Minutes VIII, 28.04.1959 & 06.12.1961; Grosbois, 'Ford in Belgium', 206.
36. Minutes IX, 26.11.1965.
37. *Statistisk Årbog.*
38. See Figure 43 in the Appendix.
39. FMC: Beretning og regnskab, 1959–1960.
40. Telegram, 09.03.1962; attached to FMC: Financial Statements and Operation Reports, 1961.
41. FMC: Minutes VIII, 27.04.1961.
42. Memorandum, 26.03.1962; Letters, 26.03.1962 & 04.04.1962; attached to FMC: Financial Statements and Operation Reports, 1961.
43. *Børsen,* 01.05.1962.
44. Sørensen et al., 'Ford Denmark and the Scandinavian Market', 296.
45. Sørensen et al., 296–97; FMC: Minutes IX, 09.01.1964.
46. Sørensen et al., 297.
47. Sørensen et al., 298–99.
48. Sørensen et al., 298–99.
49. Sørensen et al., 297–99; RA: Skafor 2709, Reports 29.07.1966 & 19.09.1980.
50. Sørensen et al., 299.
51. Politically advertised as *Helhedsløsningen* (The comprehensive solution).
52. ABA: SSMF, protocols, 18.10.1963 & 17.04.1964.
53. Based on a 45-hour workweek. Computed from average hourly wages, incl. piece rate and overtime, but excl. holiday bonus in all industries in Copenhagen, 1965. *Statistisk Årbog,* 1967, table 244.
54. ABA: SSMF, protocols, 05.09.1962, 19.09.1962, & 06.02.1963.
55. ABA: SSMF, correspondence, 'Sagen Blomgren', unnumbered. Neither union sources nor a cursory overview of the archives of the Working Environment Authorities have revealed other major incidents in this period. RA: The Working Environment Authorities.
56. *Politiken*, 15.07.1966.
57. ABA: SSMF, correspondence, 'Ford Motor produktionsomlægning' (Unnumbered file); SSMF, protocols, 16.02.1966; SF, Protocols of board meetings, 21.03.1966.
58. *Politiken,* 26.06.1959.
59. FMC: Beretning, 1959; *Politiken,* 26.06.1959.
60. *Politiken,* 26.06.1959.
61. *Ford Nyt*, no. 1, 1961. The two neon lights in Copenhagen were placed at the corner of Åboulevard and Rosenørns Allé and at Svanemøllebro respectively.
62. *Ford Nyt,* no. 1, 1960.
63. *Politiken*, 25.01.1966; ABA: SSMF, correspondence, 'Ford Motor produktionsomlægning' (Unnumbered file).
64. RA: Skafor 2709, Report 19.09.1980.

The Transformation of Fordism
pp. 281–321

1. Examples of previous use are Shiomi and Wada, *Fordism Transformed* and Tolliday, 'The Diffusion and Transformation of Fordism'.
2. Boyer, 'Hybridization and Models of Production', 32.
3. Tolliday, 'The Diffusion and Transformation of Fordism', 64.
4. Boyer, 'Hybridization and Models of Production', 38.
5. See pp. 42, 125f.

6. Knudsen, *Amerikaniseringen af den danske fagbevægelse*, 103ff.
7. Schröter, *Americanization of the European Economy: A Compact Survey of American Economic Influence in Europe since the 1880s*, 64; Tarbensen, 'Den amerikanske kapital: Spørgsmålet om amerikanske investeringer i Danmark i 1950'erne', 234–35; Pedersen, 'Amerikanske ting og tankers betydning for dansk erhvervsledelse', 326.
8. Boyer, 'Hybridization and Models of Production', 38.
9. See p. 33.
10. Iversen, *Amerikanske Tilstande: En Rapport til unge Nordboer*, 9.
11. A similar picture is painted by Peder Hedebol in his vivid report from Washington, where he took part in the first plenary conference of the International Labour Organization, October–November 1919: *Social-Demokraten*, 27.12.1919.
12. The aforementioned Sven Trier was in the USA as a representative of the Danish Parliament, not officially as a social democrat.
13. Based on a systematic reading of the party magazine *Socialisten* and the leading union journal *Jærn- og Metalarbejderen* 1919–1939, and a cursory reading of the daily newspaper *Social-Demokraten* during the same period.
14. *Jærn og Metalarbejderen*, no. 11, 1927, 150.
15. See for example Hedebol, 'Bagdørs-Socialisme i U.S.A.' The title translates to "Back-door socialism in the USA".
16. Based on his published speeches as well as manuscripts in ABA: Thorvald Stauning archives.
17. *Ford-Ejer Magasinet*, no. 4, December 1924.
18. *Protokol for den 20. Socialdemokratiske Partikongres i Vejle den 12.-15. Juni 1927*, 49–50.
19. *Protokol for den 20. Socialdemokratiske Partikongres i Vejle den 12.-15. Juni 1927*, 49–50.
20. As referenced in *Jern- og Metalarbejderen*, no. 5, 1930, 79–80. Apparently Perry repeated his remarks in his report to the general assembly of the Danish Ford company, see BFRC: Perry, report, and *Politiken*, 28.03.1930.
21. *Jern- og Metalarbejderen*, no. 5, 1930, 78.
22. *Jern- og Metalarbejderen*, no. 10, 1932, 211–13.
23. *Social-Demokraten*, 06-07.02.1929.
24. *Social-Demokraten*, 06-07.02.1929.
25. See p. 26.
26. Christensen, *Fabriksarbejdere og Funktionærer 1870–1972*, 208–09; Christensen, Hansen, and Kolstrup, *Arbejdernes Historie i Danmark 1800–2000*, 215–18.
27. See pp. 234–35.
28. *Amerika er anderledes*
29. Knudsen, *Amerikaniseringen af den danske fagbevægelse*, 110 & 143. For details about the *Work Study Training Programme* see *Danske industriarbejdere i U.S.A.*
30. Knudsen, *Amerikaniseringen af den danske fagbevægelse*, 107–08.
31. *Politiken*, 10.11.1949.
32. *Amerika er anderledes*, 21.
33. *Amerika er anderledes*, 53–54.
34. It was not just the critical remarks in the report about the lack of social security, but also what ECA saw as "an exaggerated concern [...] for the negro issue", which made the Americans back out in the first place. In the end, a limited English edition was actually printed by the United States Information and Education Program, but for use abroad, not in the USA. Knudsen, *Amerikaniseringen af den danske fagbevægelse*, 126–28.
35. Ford, *Today and Tomorrow*, 260–61.
36. Christensen, *Septemberforliget 1899*, 66ff.
37. Gramsci, *Selections from the Prison Notebooks of Antonio Gramsci*, 285.
38. Ford, *Today and Tomorrow*, 252.
39. The first known use of the verb "to Americanise" in Danish is in an article in the newspaper *Berlingske Politiske og Avertissementstidende*, 05.07.1833.
40. Nolan, *The Transatlantic Century*, 5.
41. Elteren, *Americanism and Americanization*, 102.
42. Gramsci, *Selections from the Prison Notebooks of Antonio Gramsci*, 285–56.
43. Gramsci, 317–18.
44. 46 percent, including mining, to be precise. Hobsbawm, *The Age of Empire: 1875–1914*, 51.

45. Schröter, *Americanization of the European Economy*, 23.
46. Boje, *Danmark og multinationationale virksomheder før* 1950, 64, 76ff, & 140ff.
47. Schröter, *Americanization of the European Economy*, 20–21.
48. Schröter, 45.
49. Quoted from Nye, *America's Assembly Line*, 127.
50. Rupert, *Producing Hegemony*, 56–57.
51. Rupert, esp. 80 & 92ff; Nolan, *The Transatlantic Century*, 193ff.
52. Schröter, *Americanization of the European Economy*, 25 & 73–75.
53. Schröter, 6; Elteren, *Americanism and Americanization*, 115; Nolan, *The Transatlantic Century*, 5.
54. Christensen, 'Den moderne arbejderklasse: Bidrag til en skabelsesberetning', 66ff.
55. A search of Google Scholar will reveal at least 45,000 books or articles that refer to the terms "Post-Fordist" or "Post-Fordism".
56. For an introduction to various criticisms of Post-Fordism, see Jessop, 'Fordism and Post-Fordism'.
57. Clarke, 'The Crisis of Fordism or the Crisis of Social-Democracy?', 259.

Appendix
pp. 323–337

1. Bonin, Lung, and Tolliday, *Ford, 1903–2003: The European History*.
2. Tolliday and Zeitlin, *Between Fordism and Flexibility: The Automobile Industry and Its Workers—Past, Present and Future*; Tolliday, 'The Diffusion and Transformation of Fordism'; Tolliday, 'Transplanting the American Model?'.
3. Freyssenet, 'Developing Analytical Tools to Identify the "Fordian Model" in Europe'.
4. A search for memoirs has been undertaken in the Workers' and Journeymen's Memoirs of the National Museum (NIHA), the Library and Archive of the Workers Museum (ABA), the Copenhagen City Archive, and the joint database of Danish municipal archives (arkiv.dk).
5. "Beretning og regnskab" in Danish.
6. BFRC should not be confused with Ford Motor Company Archives, which is the corporate archive of Ford in Dearborn. Since most material from the latter regarding the period before 1964 has been transferred to BFRC, it has not been consulted for the purpose of this book.

References

Source material, photographs, and film

Collections of unpublished source material used, including photographs and films, are listed in the order of the archives, museums, and libraries to which they belong. Unpublished material is referenced in the notes with an abbreviation of the holding institution, followed by the name of the collection (and sub-collection if relevant) and, if needed, details for precise identification, such as a date or an item number.

In some cases, most notably that of the archive of Ford Motor Company A/S, the material is not ordered and numbered, and may be identified by description only.

ABA: Arbejdermuseets Bibliotek og Arkiv (Library and Archive of the Workers Museum), Copenhagen

DM: Dansk Metalarbejderforbund Afdeling 14, Automekanikernes Fagforening (Metalworkers' Association, Branch 14, Union of Automechanics), archive no. 2442.
Correspondence etc. 1960–1966, box 1
Protocols of general assemblies and board meetings 1919–1959, box 2–4.

LO (Danish Confederation of Trade Unions), archive no. 1500.
Den Internationale Faglige Central (IFTU), box 555–619

SF: Sadelmagernes Fagforening af 1874 (Union of Upholsterers), archive no. 569.
Protocols of board meetings 1919–1966, box 3–5.
Protocols of general assemblies 1919–1966, box 6–7.

SSMF: Støberi, Special og Maskinfabrikarbejdernes Forbund (Union of Workmen in the Metal Industries), archive no. 1770.
Correspondence (in relation to employers) 1919–1966, box 60–61.
Protocols of general assemblies and board meetings 1919–1966, box 4–12.

Thorvald Stauning arkiv (Archive of Thorvald Stauning)

VF: Vognmalernes fagforening, København (Coach Painters' Union, Copenhagen), archive no. 1448. Protocols of general assemblies 1919–1954, box 1.
Protocols of board meetings 1926–1966, box 2–3.

VK: Vognmalernes klub, Ford: (Local union club of Coach Painters, Ford), archive no. 1449: Protocols of meetings 1946–1966, box 1.

BFRC: Benson Ford Research Center, The Henry Ford, Dearborn, Michigan

Agreements and Contracts subgroup, Office of the Secretary (FMC) records, acc. 95:
Knudsen, report (Report dealing with establishment of foreign Branches [...], as submitted by W.S. Knudsen, 1. Oct. 1919), folder 21.

Brubaker records subgroup, FMC Financial records collection, acc. 128:
Brubaker statement (Statement showing number of clerks reduced, Europe, 26.02.1928), box 2.

Charles E. Sorensen records series, Superintendents Office (FMC) records subgroup, FMC Manufacturing records collection, acc. 38:
Annual General Manager's meeting, Denmark, box 21.

Recapitulations (Two recapitulations of telegrams between Detroit and Copenhagen regarding building of South Port plant, for the period 05.10.1922–14.07.1923), box 48.
Hauge, report (Report on Interview on 07.01.1932, with Mr. C.N. Hauge, Minister of Commerce and Industry in Denmark), box 8.
Perry, report (Report of Directors presented at the second ordinary general meeting), box 2.
Sorensen telegrams I (Various telegrams between Sorensen and Bülow, Copenhagen and others, 14.12.1918–21.06.1920), box 132.
Sorensen telegrams II (Various telegrams between Sorensen and Ford Motor Company A/S regarding plans for new factory, 1922), box 133.

Edsel B. Ford office papers, General correspondence, acc. 6:
EBF, memoranda (Memoranda conference 1920), box 2, folder H.

Ford Motor Company Incorporation records series, Incorporation records subgroup, Office of the Secretary (Ford Motor Company) records, acc. 85.
Minutes of Meetings of Board of Directors, box 1.

Henry Ford, The Engineering Laboratory Office records subgroup, Business and Personal Correspondence series, acc. 284.
Bülow to Liebold (Letter concerning aid to Germany, 04.03.1920), box 13.

Mira Wilkins papers, acc. 880:
Beck to Wilkins (Interview with Mr. Arthur Beck, 1960), box 5.
Carlson to Wilkins (Interview with Mr. George Carson, Copenhagen 1960, part 1 & 2), box 5.
Denmark, minutes (Transcribed minutes from board meetings and general assemblies of Ford
Motor Company A/S, 1919–1930), box 5.
Falbe-Hansen to Wilkins (Interview with Mr. Falbe-Hansen, 1960), box 5.
Møller to Wilkins (Conversation with H.C. Møller, Copenhagen 1960), box 5.

Nevins and Hill research, Original Documents and Notes series, Internal Research subgroup, Archives (FMC) records, acc. 572 (Documents compiled from other parts of the archive by Nevins and Hill for their books, and never returned to their original location)
Auditors to Detroit (Unsigned report from auditors to Detroit, 07.01.1927), box 16.
Briggs (Reminiscences of L.E. Briggs), box 16.
Carlson re. expenses (Letters from Detroit and Carlson's answer regarding expenses, 21.03.1925–02.06.1925), box 16.
Moekle (Reminiscences of H.E. Moekle), box 16.
Møller on Labor (Notes on the Labor Situation, no date), box 30
Notes from article in New York Times, 22.08.1926 (Regarding Ford's resistance t o Work Councils in Germany), box 16.
Postcard to Sorensen from Italy, box 20.
Roberge (Report to C. Sorensen, 18.11.1921), box 16.
Sorensen to E.B. Ford (Telegram, 17.12.1921), box 16.

FMC: Ford Motor Company A/S, historical archives, Ballerup

Balance Sheets, 1919–1927, 1929–1934, & 1935–1949.
Beretning og regnskab (Annual reports), 1946–1955, 1959–1962, & 1964–1965.
Copenhagen Summary, 1950–1954.
Deliveries, 1927–1946.
Financial Statements and Operation Reports, 1949–1962.
Ford Salgshaandbog (Ford Sales Manual), 1930.
Memorandum, H.C. Møller, December 1944.
Minutes of Board and General Meetings (English translations), volume I–IX, 1919–1966.
Production, 1920-
Photo collection, marketing, and PR.
Reorganisation (File containing correspondence etc. regarding the issue of shares in 1929)
Share Register, 1919–1929

KB: Det Kongelige Bibliotek
(The Royal Library, national library of Denmark), Copenhagen
Småtryksafdelingen (Small print dept.)
Arbejdsregulativ, April 1930
Beretning og regnskab (Annual reports), 1929–1930, 1934, 1937–1943, 1945, 1961, & 1966.
Overenskomst med Ford Motor Company, 18.10.1922.
Overenskomst med Ford Motor Company, 25.11.1926.
Images collection

KM: Københavns Museum
(Museum of Copenhagen)
Photo collection

NA: US National Archives
Film collection
Around the World with Ford, part III. FC-FC-4264. https://catalog.archives.gov/id/93393
Danish Ford Rodeo. FC-FC-1511. https://catalog.archives.gov/id/91838

NM: Nationalmuseet (National Museum of Denmark), Copenhagen
Frihedsmuseets arkiv (Archive of the Museum of Danish Resistance)
Industriregistreringen (National register of Industrial Heritage), http://industri.natmus.dk
Modstandsdatabasen (Database of the Resistance Movement), http://modstand.natmus.dk/
Photo collection of the dept. of Modern History and World Cultures, partly available online at http://samlinger.natmus.dk

OEL: Orla E. Larsen
Private collection of notes, clippings, and photographs by former sales manager Orla E. Larsen, in the custody of his son, Ben Larsen.

RA: Rigsarkivet (The Danish National Archives), Viborg and Copenhagen
Arbejdstilsynet (Working Environment Authority), Kreds København / Frederiksberg (Copenhagen and Frederiksberg branch)
Cases relating to Ford, 101 183a/4214
Dansk Forening for Skadesforsikring, SKAFOR, inspektionsberetninger (Danish Insurance Association, reports on risk evaluation)
Skafor 2709 (Report on Heimdalsgade 28)
Skafor 8018 (Various reports on Frederikskaj 2 & Sluseholmen 1–3)
Harlang & Toksvig, archive no. 05585
Hovedbog for tryksager, 1935–1936
Kontrakter, 1934–1979
Industrirådets arkiv, Ekstraordinære industrileverancer, journalsager (Industrial Council, Extraordinary industrial deliverances, cases), archive no. 06308
No. 88: Flyvemateriel—Ford A 7305
No. 89: Ford A 7400—Forenede

RLS: Rødovre lokalhistoriske samling
(Rødovre municipal archive), Rødovre
Axel Sjølander, personal archive no. A77, box 1–18.

Scanpix: Ritzau Scanpix photo agency,
Copenhagen
Photo collection

Newspapers, periodicals, and handbooks

Articles in newspapers etc. with no author stated are referenced in the notes by the name and date of the publication. Articles by a known author can be found in the list of books and articles.

Arbejderbladet. Newspaper, published twice a week by the Danish Communist Party.
Clarté. Non-partisan socialist journal.
Dansk Biografisk Leksikon. Danish biographical encyclopaedia. 3rd ed., Copenhagen, 1979f.
Den Faste Voldgiftsrets Kendelser. Rulings by the Permanent Board of Arbitration. Ed. by E. Steincke, published by G.E.C. Gad.
Ekstra Bladet. Daily newspaper, tabloid.

Erhvervstællingen. Statistics of Industry, Commerce and Transport, published infrequently by the Department of Statistics (*Det Statistiske Departement*).
Fagtidsskrift for Malere. Monthly members' journal, published by the Painters' Association in Denmark.
Ford News. Magazine published by Ford Motor Company in the United States 1920–1942.
Finanstidende. Weekly financial magazine.
Ford Nyheder. Magazine published monthly or bi-monthly by Ford Motor Company A/S 1924–1931. Originally aimed at employees of the company, later also dealers etc. Continued as *Ford Nyt*.
Ford Nyt. Magazine published by Ford Motor Company A/S 1931–1964 at varying intervals: originally monthly but later typically twice a year. Aimed at dealers and the general public. Continuation of *Ford Nyheder*.
Ford-Ejer Magasinet. Independent magazine for Ford owners and distributors, 1924–1927.
Ingeniøren. Weekly journal published by the Danish Society of Engineers.
Jærn- og Metalarbejderen, from 1930: *Jern- og Metalarbejderen*. Monthly journal for members of the Danish Metalworkers' Association a.o. Published by the Cooperating Committee of Unions in Metal Industries (*CO Metal*).
Kraks Blaa Bog. Yearly biography of public figures.
Motor. Monthly magazine published by the Federation of Danish Motorists, FDM.
Politiken. Daily newspaper, politically social-liberal.
Samling af Anmeldelser til Handelsregistrene. Notifications to the Register of Commerce, published by the Ministry for Trade and Industry.
Social-Demokraten. Daily newspaper published by the social-democratic labour movement.
Socialisten. Journal on social democratic politics and theory. Originally published by the Social-Democratic Debate Societies, later by the Workers Education Association (*Arbejdernes Oplysnings Forbund*) and the Social Democratic Party.
Statistiske Meddelelser, Statistical announcements, published by the Department of Statistics / Statistics Denmark (*Det Statistiske Departement / Danmarks Statistik*).
Statistisk Årbog. Yearbook of Statistics, published by the Department of Statistics / Statistics Denmark (*Det Statistiske Departement / Danmarks Statistik*).
Statistisk Årsbok för Sverige. Yearbook of Statistics for Sweden, published by the Central Bureau of Statistics (*Statistiska Centralbyrån*), Stockholm.
Tidsskrift for Ingeniør- og Bygningsvæsen. Journal on building construction and technology, published by the Association of Building Professionals (*Konstruktørforeningen*).
Vejtransporten i Tal og Tekst. Statistics on motor vehicles and transportation, published yearly from 1959 by employer and trade organisations related to the car business (*Motorsagens Oplysningsråd*).

Books and articles

Amerika er anderledes: Med den danske fagforeningsdelegation til U.S.A. København: Fremad, 1950.
Andersen, Lars, ed. *Fra erhvervsråd til økonomisk tænketank*. København: Arbejderbevægelsens Erhvervsråd, 2011.
Andersen, Morten, and Nils Arne Sørensen. 'Fra Madison Avenue til København: Amerikaniseringen af reklamebranchen i 1920'erne'. In *Postordrecowboys og andre fortællinger om danskernes møde med Amerika*, edited by Nils Arne Sørensen, 540:57–70. University of Southern Danmark Studies in History and Social Sciences. Odense: Syddansk Universitetsforlag, 2017.
Arnold, Horace Lucien, and Fay Leone Faurote. *Ford Methods and the Ford Shops*. 1919. Reprint, Leipzig: Elibron Classics, 2005.
Asher, Robert. 'The 1949 Ford Speedup Strike and the Post War Social Compact, 1946-1961'. In *Autowork*, edited by Robert Asher and Ronald Edsforth, 127–54. Albany: State University of New York Press, 1995.

Asher, Robert, and Ronald Edsforth. 'A Half Century of Struggle: Auto Workers Fighting for Justice'. In *Autowork*, 1–37. SUNY Series in American Labor History. Albany: State University of New York Press, 1995.
Bang, Tobias. *Ford, forbrug og fortællinger om det lykkelige liv*, 2008. http://static.sdu.dk/mediafiles/Files/Om_SDU/Institutter/Ihks/Projekter/Amerikansk paa dansk/Artikler/Ford forbrug og fortllinger.pdf.
Blaszczyk, Regina Lee. *The Color Revolution*. Cambridge, Mass.: MIT Press, 2012.
Boggess, Trent E. 'The Customer Can Have Any Color He Wants - So Long As It's Black: A Study of the Materials and Methods Used to Paint Model T Fords During the Black Era'. *Vintage Ford* 32, no. 6, 1997, 26–41.
Boje, Per. *Danmark og multinationationale virksomheder før 1950*. Odense University Studies in History & Social Sciences, Vol. 229. Odense: Odense Universitetsforlag, 2000.
Bonin, Hubert. 'The Ford Brand's Image: Its Evolution from the 1930s to the 1980s'. In *Ford, 1903-2003: The European History*, edited by Hubert Bonin, Yannick Lung, and Steven Tolliday, 1:443–588. Paris: P.L.A.G.E., 2003.
Borchorst, Anette, Emmett Caraker, and Henning Jørgensen. 'Den danske model i knibe — også for analytisk potentiale?' *Tidsskrift for arbejdsliv* 14, no. 2, 01.06.2012, 82–104.
Boyer, Robert. 'Hybridization and Models of Production: Geography, History and Theory'. In *Between Imitation and Innovation: The Transfer and Hybridization of Productive Models in the International Automobile Industry*, edited by Robert Boyer, Elsie Charron, Ulrich Jürgens, and Steven Tolliday, 23–56. Oxford: Oxford University Press, 1998.
— *The Regulation School: A Critical Introduction*. New York: Columbia University Press, 1990.
Boyer, Robert, and Michel Freyssenet. 'A New Approach of Productive Models. The World That Changed the Machine'. *Industrielle Beziehungen* 07, no. 04, 2000, 385–412.
— *The Productive Models: The Conditions of Profitability*. Edited by Michel Freyssenet and Robert Boyer. London: Palgrave Macmillan, 2002.
Brody, David. 'Elements of Paradox in U.S. Labor History'. *Monthly Labor Review* 110, no. 8, 1987, 48–50.
Bryan, Ford R. *Henry's Lieutenants*. Great Lakes Books. Detroit: Wayne State University Press, 1993.
Casey, Robert. *The Model T: A Centennial History*. Baltimore: The Johns Hopkins University Press, 2008.
Christensen, Claus Bundgård, Joachim Lund, Niels Wium Olesen, and Jakob Sørensen. *Danmark besat: Krig og hverdag 1940-45*. 4th ed. København: Informations Forlag, 2015.
Christensen, Jørgen P. *Fabriksarbejdere og funktionærer 1870-1972*. Dansk industri efter 1870, bd. 6. Odense: Odense Universitetsforlag, 2002.
Christensen, Lars Kjølhede. 'Den moderne arbejderklasse: Bidrag til en skabelsesberetning'. *Arbejderhistorie*, no. 3/1, 2009: 55–74.
— *Septemberforliget 1899*. 100 danmarkshistorier. Aarhus: Aarhus Universitetsforlag, 2020.
— *Smedesvend og friherre: Maskinarbejde og arbejdskultur i København 1889-1914*. SFAH's Skriftserie Nr. 36. København: SFAH / Center f. Arbejderkulturstudier, Københavns Universitet, 1995.
Christensen, Lars Kjølhede, Anette Eklund Hansen, and Søren Kolstrup. *Arbejdernes historie i Danmark 1800-2000*. SFAHs Skriftserie. København: Selskabet til Forskning i Arbejderbevægelsens Historie, 2007.
Clarke, Simon. 'The Crisis of Fordism or the Crisis of Social-Democracy?' In *Henry Ford: Critical Evaluations in Business and Management*, edited by John C. Wood and Michael C. Wood, 2:252–76. London: Routledge, 2003.
Coopey, Richard, and Alan McKinlay. 'Power without Knowledge? Foucault and Fordism, c.1900–50'. *Labor History* 51, no. 1, February 2010, 107–25.

Dalgaard, Niels. *Ved demokratiets grænse: Demokratisering af arbejdslivet i Danmark 1919-1994*. København: Selskabet til Forskning i Arbejderbevægelsens Historie, 1995.
Dam, Henrik, and Søren Friis Hansen. 'Oles nye autobil: Om registreringsafgiften i Danmark, før, nu og i fremtiden'. In *Festskrift til Ole Bjørn*, 145–86. København: Jurist- og Økonomforbundets Forlag, 2004.
Damkier, Mogens H. *Fra bilernes lømmelalder: 50'er biler*. København: Gyldendal, 1993.
—. *På rette vej: 60'er biler*. København: Gyldendal, 1995.
Danske industriarbejdere i U.S.A.: Beretning fra 42 danske arbejderes ophold i U.S.A. i 1952–53. Teknisk bistand under Marshallplanen. Udenrigsministeriet / Høst & Søn, 1954.
Due, Jesper, and Jørgen Steen Madsen. '20 år med den danske model'. *Tidsskrift for arbejdsliv* 15, no. 1, 01.03.2013, 94–103.
Edsforth, Ronald, and Robert Asher. 'The Speedup: The Focal Point of Workers' Grievances, 1919-1941'. In *Autowork*, 65–98. Albany: State University of New York Press, 1995.
Eifert, Christiane. 'Antisemit und Autokönig: Henry Fords Autobiographie und Ihre deutsche Rezeption in den 1920er-Jahren'. *Zeithistorische Forschungen/Studies in Contemporary History* 2009, no. 6, 2009, 209–29.
Elteren, Mel. *Americanism and Americanization: A Critical History of Domestic and Global Influence*. Jefferson: McFarland & Company, 2006.
En Tur gennem Danmark med Ford. København: Ford Motor Company A/S, 1924.
Engelstoft, Povl, and Svend Dahl, eds. *Dansk Biografisk Leksikon*. København: H. Schultz Forlag, 1932-1944.
Estape-Triay, Salvador. 'Ford in Spain: The First Stage (1920-1954)'. In *Ford, 1903-2003: The European History*, edited by Hubert Bonin, Yannick Lung, and Steven Tolliday, 2:427–38. Paris: P.L.A.G.E., 2003.
Ford, Henry. *Fremad - stadig fremad*. Kbh, 1932.
— *Idag og imorgen*. København: V. Pios Boghandel, 1926.
— *Mit Liv og mit Arbejde*. København: V. Pios Boghandel, 1923.
— *My Life and Work: In Collaboration with Samuel Crowther*. Garden City, N.Y.: Doubleday, Page & company, 1922.
— *Today and Tomorrow: In Collaboration with Samuel Crowther*. London: William Heinemann, 1926.
— *Uddrag af Henry Ford's Bog: 'The international Jew' (Den internationale Jøde)*. Charlottenlund: Den Ny Tids Forlag, 1940.
Freyssenet, Michel. 'Developing Analytical Tools to Identify the "Fordian Model" in Europe'. In *Ford, 1903-2003: The European History*, edited by Hubert Bonin, Yannick Lung, and Steven Tolliday, 1:45–60. Paris: P.L.A.G.E., 2003.
Gambino, Ferruccio. 'A Critique of the Fordism of the Regulation School'. *The Commoner*, no. 12, 2007, 39–62.
Gammelgaard, Hjalmar, Oluf Bertolt, Erik Schou, P.P. Sveistrup, and Knud Korst. *Industrien: Muligheder og Vilkaar*. København: Martins Forlag, 1926.
Geertsen, Henning. *Vognmalerfaget i Kbh. i ndtil 1940 med særligt henblik på Vognmalernes Fagforening i København 1915-40*. Københavns Universitet, 1984.
Gelardi, Th., ed. *Automobilets Historie og dets Mænd*. Vol. 3. København: Alfred Jørgensens Forlag, 1938.
Gelsted, Otto. 'The Show Boat'. In *Contemporary Danish Poetry: An Anthology*, edited by Line Jensen, translated by R.P. Keigwin, 31:28–30. The Library of Scandinavian Literature. Copenhagen: Gyldendal, 1977.
Gramsci, Antonio. *Selections from the Prison Notebooks of Antonio Gramsci*. Edited by Quintin Hoare and Geoffrey N. Smith. 1929. Reprint, New York: International Publishers, 1971.
Grosbois, Thierry. 'Ford in Belgium'. In *Ford, 1903-2003: The European History*, edited by Hubert Bonin, Yannick Lung, and Steven Tolliday, 2:197–232. Paris: P.L.A.G.E., 2003.
Hansen, Søren, ed. *Daglige Beretninger om Begivenheder under den Tyske Besættelse*. København: Bianco Luno, 1946.
Hansen, Svend Aage. *Økonomisk vækst i Danmark: 1914-1970*. Vol. 2. København: Akademisk forlag, 1974.

Hardach, Gerd, Dieter Karras, and Ben Fine. *A Short History of Socialist Economic Thought*. London: Edward Arnold, 1978.

Hawkins, Norval A. *Certain Success*. 1920. Reprint, Auckland: The Floating Press, 2009.

Hedebol, Frederik. 'Bagdørs-Socialisme i U.S.A.' *Socialisten*, no. 2 , 1936, 61–65.

Hobsbawm, E.J. *The Age Of Empire: 1875-1914*. London: Weidenfeld and Nicolson, 1987.

Hobsbawm, Eric. *How to Change the World: Reflections on Marx and Marxism*. Yale University Press, 2011.

Hounshell, David A. *From the American System to Mass Production 1800-1932: The Development of Manufacturing Technology in the United States*. Studies in Industry and Society, 4. Baltimore: Johns Hopkins University Press, 1984.

Hughes, Thomas P. *American Genesis: A Century of Invention and Technological Enthusiasm, 1870-1970*. Chicago: The University of Chicago Press, 2004.

Hyldtoft, Ole, and Hans Chr. Johansen. *Teknologiske forandringer i dansk industri 1896-1972*. Dansk industri efter 1870. Syddansk Universitetsforlag, 2005.

Ipsen, E. J., ed. *Kgl. Dansk Automobil Klubs' Lommebog for Motorkørende 1925*. København: Auto's Forlag, 1925.

Iversen, Herbert. *Amerikanske Tilstande: En Rapport til unge Nordboer*. København: H. Aschehoug & Co., 1920.

Jacobsen, Kurt. *Velfærdens pris: Arbejderbeskyttelse og arbejdsmiljø gennem 150 år*. København: Gads Forlag, 2011.

Jakobsen, Jakob. 'Om Celluloselakkers indvirkning paa den menneskelige Organisme'. *Fagtidende for Malere*, no. 3, 1937), 1–3.

— 'Om Ducolakkers indvirkning paa den menneskelige Organisme'. *Fagtidende for Malere*, no. 4, 1934, 20–21.

— *Spray Painting Hazards: A Clinical and Experimental Hæmatological Study with Special Reference to Changes in the Differential Blood Cell Count*. København / London: Munksgaard / Oxford University Press, 1939.

Jensen, Johannes V. *Ford Nyt*, 12, 1944, 12–14.

Jessop, Bob. 'Fordism and Post-Fordism: A Critical Reformulation'. In *Pathways to Regionalism and Industrial Development*, edited by Allen J. Scott and Michael Storper, 43–65. London: Routledge, 2005.

Johansen, H C. *Dansk økonomisk statistik 1814-1980*. Edited by H. P. Clausen, Svend Ellehøj, and Søren Mørch. Danmarks historie, bd. 9. København: Gyldendal, 1985.

Johansen, Hans Chr. *Industriens vækst og vilkår 1870-1973*. Dansk industri efter 1870, bd. 1. Viborg: Odense Universitetsforlag, 1988.

Johansen, J. F. 'Om Trykluft'. *Ingeniøren*, no. 30, 1926, 359–64.

Kimes, Beverly Rae. *The Cars That Henry Ford Built*. Automobile Heritage Publishing & Co, 2005.

Kjær-Hansen, Max, and Peter Olufsen. *Reklamen i det 20. århundredes Danmark*. København: Nyt Nordisk Forlag, 1974.

Kjeldbæk, Esben. *Sabotageorganisationen BOPA 1942-1945*. København: Frihedsmuseets Venners Forlag, 1997.

Knudsen, Dino. *Amerikaniseringen af den danske fagbevægelse: Marshallhjælp, kold krig og transatlantiske forbindelser, 1945-1956*. København: Museum Tusculanum, 2012.

Knudsen, Knud. *Arbejdskonflikternes historie i Danmark: Arbejdskampe og arbejderbevægelse 1870-1940*. SFAH Skriftserie nr. 41. København: Selskabet til Forskning i Arbejderbevægelsens Historie, 1999.

— *Dansk fagbevægelses historie frem til 1950: Fra arbejdets perspektiv*. SFAH's Skriftserie. København: SFAH, 2011.

– 'Kampen om samlebåndet: Rationalisering og arbejderbevægelse i Danmark i 1920'erne'. *Den Jyske Historiker*, no. 35–36, 1986.

Kocka, Jürgen. 'Organisierter Kapitalismus oder Staatsmonopolistischer Kapitalismus? Begriffliche Vorbemerkungen'. In *Organisierter Kapitalismus: Voraussetzungen Und Anfänge*, edited by Heinrich August Winkler, 19–35. Kritische Studien Zur Geschichtswissenschaft. Göttingen: Vandenhoeck & Ruprecht, 1974.

Kreuter, C. 'Die Ueberflutung Des Dänischen Automarktes Durch Ford'. *Der Motorwagen*, 31.03.1923.

Larsen, Sven. 'Har Sprøjteapparaterne deres berettigelse i Malerhaandværket?' *Fagtidende for Malere*, no. 8, 1934, 39–41.
Lind, Gerhard. 'Om Sundhedsfarer ved sprøjtemaling, I'. *Fagtidende for Malere*, no. 2, 1939, 21–24.
— 'Om Sundhedsfarer ved sprøjtemaling, II'. *Fagtidende for Malere*, no. 3, 1939, 38–40.
Link, Stefan. 'Rethinking the Ford-Nazi Connection'. *Bulletin of the GHI*, 49, Fall 2011, 135–50.
Loubet, Jean-Louis, and Nicolas Hatzfeld. 'Ford in France, 1916-1955: From an American Dream to a Failure'. In *Ford, 1903-2003: The European History*, edited by Hubert Bonin, Yannick Lung, and Steven Tolliday, 2:323–83. Paris: P.L.A.G.E., 2003.
Lund, Martin, f. 1963. *Kongelig køreglæde: Med benzin og blåt blod i årerne*. Frederiksværk: Nautilus, 2009.
Lundkvist, O. E. 'Elektrisk svejsning'. *Ingeniøren*, 1925.
Maier, Charles S. *In Search of Stability: Explorations in Historical Political Economy*. Cambridge Studies in Modern Political Economies. Cambridge: Cambridge University Press, 1987.
Mansa, H H. 'Kraftmaskinanlæget paa Ford Motor Company's Fabrik i Sydhavnen: Foredrag holdt i Konstruktørforeningen den 24/3 1925'. *Tidsskrift for Ingeniør og Bygningsvæsen*, no. 10, 1925.
Markussen, Ole. 'Danish Industry, 1920-1939: Technology, Rationalization and Modernization'. *Scandinavian Journal of History* 13, no. 3, 1988.
Meyer, Mette Kia Krabbe. *Jonals Co. og det moderne fotografis gennembrud i Danmark*. Holte: Gl. Holtegaard, 2000.
Møller, Anders Monrad. *Etaten og traditionerne: Dansk toldhistorie IV*. København: Toldhistorisk Selskab, 1990.
Montgomery, David. *The Fall of the House of Labor: The Workplace, the State, and American Labor Activism, 1865-1925*. Cambridge: Cambridge University Press, 1987.
— *Workers' Control in America: Studies in the History of Work, Technology, and Labor Struggles*. Binghamton, N.Y.: Cambridge University Press, 1981.
Motzkus, Frank C. *100 år i bilistens tjeneste: Historien om FDM*. FDM, 2009.
Nevins, Allan, and Frank Ernest Hill. *Ford: Decline and Rebirth, 1933-1962*. New York: Charles Scribner's Sons, 1954.
— *Ford: Expansion and Challenge 1915-1933*. New York: Charles Scribner's Sons, 1957.
Nicolaisen, Jens Møller. *Klip: Fra Citroëns historie i Danmark 1919-66*. København: Citroën Danmark, 2003.
Nielsen, Vilhelm. 'Lidt om automobillakering'. *Fagtidende for Malere*, no. 1, 1937, 15–16.
Nieuwenhuis, Paul, and Peter Wells. 'Ford, Budd, and the History of Mass Production'. In *The Model T Reconsidered: Proceedings from the World of the Model T Conference*, edited by Judith E. Endelman, 61–68. Dearborn, MI: The Henry Ford, 2008.
Nolan, Mary. 'Productivism and Technocracy in Historical Perspective'. In *Technology and Democracy: Obstacles to Democratization - Productivism and Technocracy: Proceedings from Workshop 3*, edited by Sissel Myklebust. TMV Skriftserie Nr. 28. Oslo: Centre for Technology and Culture, 1997.
— *The Transatlantic Century: Europe and America, 1890-2010*. Cambridge: Cambridge University Press, 2012.
— *Visions of Modernity: American Business and the Modernization of Germany*. New York: Oxford University Press, 1994.
Nye, David E. *America's Assembly Line*. Cambridge, Mass.: MIT Press, 2013.
Oswald, Werner. *Deutsche Autos 1920-1945: Alle deutschen Personenwagen der damaligen Zeit*. Stuttgart: Motorbuch Verlag, 1990.
Pedersen, Jan. 'Amerikanske ting og tankers betydning for dansk erhvervsledelse'. In *Det amerikanske forbillede? Dansk erhvervsliv og USA, ca. 1920-1970*, edited by Nils Arne Sørensen, 305–29. Odense: Syddansk Universitetsforlag, 2011.

Petrick, Fritz. *Die Okkupationspolitik des Deutschen Faschismus in Dänemark und Norwegen (1940-1945)*. Berlin: Hüthig Verlagsgemeinschaft, 1992.
Pizzolato, Nicola. *Challenging Global Capitalism: Labor Migration, Radical Struggle, and Urban Change in Detroit and Turin*. Palgrave Macmillan Transnational History Series. Palgrave Macmillan, 2013.
Preisler, Bahne, ed. *Malerarbejde i Praksis*. København: Georg Andersens Forlag, 1948.
Protokol for den 20. Socialdemokratiske Partikongres i Vejle den 12.-15. Juni 1927. København: Fremad, 1927.
Raff, Daniel M. G., and Lawrence H. Summers. 'Did Henry Ford Pay Efficiency Wages?' *Journal of Labor Economics* 5, no. 4, 1987, 657–86.
Raushenbush, Carl. *Fordism*. New York: League for Industrial Democracy, 1937.
Refsgaard, M. 'Er sprøjtelakering sundhedsfarlig?' *Fagtidende for Malere*, no. 4, 1937, 1–2.
Roberts, Sam. *Ford Model Y: Henry's Car for Europe*. Dorchester: Veloce Publishing, 2001.
Rupert, Mark. *Producing Hegemony: The Politics of Mass Production and American Global Power*. Cambridge Studies in International Relations: 38. Cambridge: Cambridge University Press, 1995.
Schröter, Harm G. *Americanization of the European Economy: A Compact Survey of American Economic Influence in Europe since the 1880s*. Dordrecht: Springer, 2005.
Shiomi, Haruhito, and Kazuo Wada, eds. *Fordism Transformed: The Development of Production Methods in the Automobile Industry*. Fuji Conference Series 1. New York: Oxford University Press, 1995.
Sørensen, Gert. *Gramsci og den moderne verden*. København: Museum Tusculanum, 1993.
Sørensen, Peter. 'Aarhus Motor Compagni A/S: Den største Ford-forretning i Europa'. *Århus Stifts Årbøger* 89, 2006, 7–30.
— 'Ford i Danmark 1919-1966: Danske holdninger og Fords betydning'. In *Udenlandske investeringer: Hvorfra og hvorfor*, edited by Peter Sørensen and Kasper Szöke Skovgaard, 103–36. Århus: Academia, 2009.
Sørensen, Peter, Jesper Strandskov, Kurt Pedersen, and Per Boje. 'Ford Denmark and the Scandinavian Market: From Regional Export Base to Periphery'. In *Ford, 1903-2003: The European History*, edited by Hubert Bonin, Yannick Lung, and Steven Tolliday, 2:267–319. Paris: P.L.A.G.E., 2003.
Tarbensen, Kenn. 'Den amerikanske kapital: Spørgsmålet om amerikanske investeringer i Danmark i 1950'erne'. In *Det amerikanske forbillede? Dansk erhvervsliv og USA, ca. 1920-1970*, edited by Nils Arne Sørensen, 195–237. Odense: Syddansk Universitetsforlag, 2011.
Thalbitzer, Carl. *Ford Motor Company A/S gennem 25 Aar*. København, 1944.
Thing, Morten. *Jyllands-Posten, diktaturet, Krystalnatten og jøderne*. Skriftserie Fra Roskilde Universitetsbibliotek 56. Roskilde: Roskilde Universitetsbibliotek, 2013.
Thomsen, Allan Mylius. *Da reklamen var ung*. Frederiksberg: Sylvester-Hvid & Partners A/S, 1999.
Thomsen, Birgit Nüchel. *Værnemagerne: Danmarks bidrag til den tyske krigsøkonomi under den tyske besættelse – i europæisk perspektiv*. Selfpublished e-book, 2014. http://værnemagerne.dk.
Thomsen, Niels. *Industri, stat og samfund 1870-1939*. Dansk industri efter 1870, bd. 3. Odense: Odense universitetsforlag, 1991.
Toft, Erik, Hanne Rasmussen, and Hans-Carl Nielsen, eds. *Hundrede års trafik: Trafikministeriet 1900-2000*. København: Trafikministeriet, 2000.
Tolliday, Steven. 'The Diffusion and Transformation of Fordism: Britain and Japan Compared'. In *Between Imitation and Innovation: The Transfer and Hybridization of Productive Models in the International Automobile Industry*, edited by Robert Boyer, Elsie Charron, Ulrich Jürgens, and Steven Tolliday, 57–95. Oxford: Oxford University Press, 1998.
— 'The Origins of Ford of Europe: From Multidomestic to Transnational Corporation, 1903-1976'. In *Ford, 1903-2003: The European History*, edited by Hubert Bonin, Yannick Lung, and Steven Tolliday, 1:153–241. Paris: P.L.A.G.E., 2003.

— 'The Rise of Ford in Britain: From Sales Agency to Market Leader, 1904-1980'. In *Ford, 1903-2003: The European History*, edited by Hubert Bonin, Yannick Lung, and Steven Tolliday, 2:7–57. Paris: P.L.A.G.E., 2003.

— 'Transplanting the American Model? US Automobile Companies and the Transfer of Technology and Management to Britain, France and Germany, 1928-1962'. In *Americanization and Its Limits: Reworking US Technology and Management in Post-War Europe and Japan*, edited by Jonathan Zeitlin and Gary Herrigel, 76–119. New York: Oxford University Press, 2000.

Tønsberg, Jeppe. *Brede Klædefabrik. I.C. Modeweg & Søn A/S 1810-1956. Den danske klædeindustri i international belysning*. Århus: Erhvervsarkivets Forskningsfond, 2004.

Vejtransporten i tal og tekst. Vol. 8. København: Sammenslutningen af Automobil-Fabrikanter og Importører, 1966.

Wagner, Michael F. 'Domesticeringen af Ford i Danmark: Den kulturelle tilegnelse af Ford og fordismen, 1920-1940'. In *Det amerikanske forbillede? Dansk erhvervsliv og USA, ca. 1920-1970*, edited by Nils Arne Sørensen, 19–49. Odense: Syddansk Universitetsforlag, 2011.

Watkins, Julian. *The 100 Greatest Advertisements 1852-1958: Who Wrote Them and What They Did*. Reprint. Mineola, N.Y.: Dover Publications, 1993.

Wilkins, Mira, and Frank Ernest Hill. *American Business Abroad: Ford on Six Continents*. 2. 1964. Reprint, New York: Cambridge University Press, 2011.

Wojcik, Henrik, and Bent Frese-Madsen. *General Motors International A/S: 1923-1974*. København: Books on Demand, 2011.

Wolfson, Eugen, ed. *Danmarks industrielle Udvikling*. København: Gjellerup, 1943.

Zgórniak, Marian. *Europa am Abgrund-1938*. Münster: LIT Verlag, 2002.

Index